THE ECHOES THAT REMAIN

A history of the
New Zealand Field Engineers
during the Great War
at Gallipoli, France and the Hampshire town of
Christchurch

First published in 2013 by Natula Publications
Natula Ltd. www.natula.co.uk

ISBN 9781897887967

Front Cover Illustration:
New Zealand Engineers having completed a deep dugout as part of their
training on St Catherine's Hill at Christchurch. Note the overhead layers that
are designed to absorb the impact of bombardments.

*Photo courtesy of Alexander Turnbull Library, Wellington, New Zealand and
Royal NZ RSA Collection. Reference number: 1/2-013869-G.*

Contents

Introduction

It had been the same weather all week long: wet, the sky overcast and a chilly wind that swept across Salisbury Plain. This Tuesday morning promised a continuation of the same, and despite it being early summer in England, the sun had no warmth. It was the 22nd of June 1916.

Soldiers across various military training camps on the Plain knew by now that their corrugated iron huts would be damp by the afternoon and they would spend another evening around the two iron fire stoves installed in each barrack hut, trying to get their clothes dry. It had become an art of judgement and co-ordination; knowing just when an item was dry enough to remove, and quickly filling the vacated space with damp trousers, socks, shirts or other items of clothing in need of drying before the spot could be claimed by someone else.

There were numerous military camps dotted around the Plain. These contained the Australian Imperial Force (AIF), the New Zealand Expeditionary Force (NZEF), the Canadian Expeditionary Force (CEF) and British Army recruits. They were predominately infantry training camps, although the Artillery had ranges at Lark Hill; there were hospitals and army store depots at Codford and the Royal Flying Corp had aerodromes around Netherhampton, where aviators were trained.

The NZEF and AIF had first fought during the Gallipoli campaign in 1915, returning to Egypt at its conclusion and had then retrained for fighting in France. In March 1916, it was decided by both the Australian and the New Zealand Governments that for reasons of war economy, all base establishments and training depots in Egypt should be moved to England.

The lack of readily available transport ships resulted in these NZEF establishments not arriving in England until late May 1916. The Infantry went to Sling Camp on Salisbury Plain, occupying the camp originally built by the NZEF British Section in 1914. The N.Z. No.1 Field Hospital took over the military hospital at Brockenhurst, which had previously been occupied by the Lahore and Meerut Divisions Indian Army. The

7

Army Service Corps found a home at Codford on Salisbury Plain, while the Artillery found a welcome at Ewshot. They left behind in Egypt a much reduced logistical support for the N.Z. Mounted Brigade. These were horse-mounted troopers, part of the Anzac Mounted Division, serving in Sinai and Palestine, fighting the Turks.

The June weather had not deterred the New Zealand instructors from putting their trainees through the various marching drills, and the 'Piccadillies' which were essentially close-marching reviews. Once these parade ground rituals had ended, a long route march in full battle equipment awaited the men. Such route marches would thread their way along the muddy, hilly-backed roads of Salisbury Plain, past the thatched cottages that lined the villages of Winterbourne Stoke, Shrewton, Chitterne and Tilshead, past the pre-historic Stonehenge stone structures and then back to camp.

Off to one side of the parade ground that morning and away from the Piccadillies, another company comprising ninety-seven men began to form up. The men were suntanned. They wore a mixture of topical Imperial Army uniforms faded by the desert sun, New Zealand militia khaki jackets and trousers and recently issued British Army clothing. Further variety was added by home knitted woollen vests and colourful pullovers. Some were huddled in their greatcoats feeling the shock of the inclement northern weather. The heavy, blanket-woven military greatcoats were the only items of clothing that gave this company any semblance of a common uniform. The company comprised the merged 10th and 11th Reinforcements of the NZEF Field Engineers.

The 10th had begun its training in Egypt after arriving there in early March 1916 and was immediately used to bring the newly formed 3rd Field Engineers to full strength as they readied for France as part of the N.Z. Division's deployment to the Western Front. Those not selected from the 10th remained in Egypt for training, undoubtedly feeling somewhat disappointed. They eventually embarked for England where, with no Engineers' depot, they were sent to Sling Camp, to join the infantry for training.

The 11th had only arrived at the Australian Engineering camp at Tel-el-Kebir in Egypt in mid-May. Tel-el-Kebir was described as being "a very dirty little place with a few dirty shops"[1], a canal and lots of flies. After a week there they boarded H.M. Troopship Nile for passage to England and joined their fellow Engineers who had been at Sling Camp for less than three weeks.

For the 11th Reinforcements, their time at Sling was the longest period in any one camp since they had left New Zealand nearly three months before. After the 45°C heat of Tel-el-Kebir and the cramped conditions aboard the troopships en route to England, Sling Camp was an oasis with its social facilities, fresh food, and mail from home which had finally caught up with them. It all helped to make the cold English weather tolerable.

Without any engineering training, stores or instructors amongst the various camps on Salisbury Plain, the Engineers passed their days undertaking route marches, field craft, and parade ground drills, until a training depot could be arranged. They were often used as Town Police in nearby Amesbury, frequented by those soldiers granted an evening leave pass. At Sling rumours had begun to circulate that they were to undergo their training at the Royal Engineers Depot at Christchurch Barracks in Hampshire, part of the Southern School of Instruction in Engineering.

The rumour mill proved to be correct. On the morning of the 22nd of June 1916 with their base kits and meagre military equipment all packed, and the inspection of their barrack huts completed, they moved out onto the parade ground. Once again they were classed as 'troops in transit'. Joining them were approximately fifty Tunnellers and Signallers, who would also be trained at Christchurch. Those Engineers from Canterbury province in New Zealand were naturally interested to see if there was any similarity with their own home city of Christchurch in the South Island of New Zealand. Others wondered about the nature of the training they would receive, while some had spoken with the ladies who staffed Sling Camp's YMCA and had learnt that the holiday resort of Bournemouth was located nearby. They had even found the town of

Christchurch in a map book of the British Isles.

In command of the enlarged company was twenty-three year old Second Lieutenant Francis Corkhill, an engineer from Otahuhu near Auckland, who came from a family of sawmill workers. His experience in military command was limited to the 11th Reinforcements during their three months aboard troopships. Throughout the past twelve days at Sling Camp, he had taken responsibility for all the Engineers.

With formations such as the Engineers, divides would have existed between those who were qualified Engineers, draughtsman, tradesmen and those who had never completed an apprenticeship. All now served as Sappers or junior NCOs and the usual civilian hierarchies took some time to soften. The instructors at Sling Camp provided the regimen needed to mould the men into one company, and to leave their civilian prejudices behind.

A tradition at Sling Camp was that the band would play-in new reinforcements and play-out those leaving. So with the encouragement of the band, the company marched down to the railway head to board the waiting steam train. Their trip was uneventful, apart from the change of platform and train at Southampton station. The civilians sharing the train carriages undoubtedly wondered who these oddly-attired troops were. Although obviously colonials, they could not be Australians, as they wore wide brimmed, felt hats, rather than the well-known 'slouch' hats associated with the Australian troops. Stencilled in faded black on some of the military bags piled in the overhead luggage nets were the capital letters "NZEF". The fern leaf hat badges, with "NZ" prominently in the middle, confirmed that these men were from New Zealand and therefore Anzacs, who had fought on the Gallipoli Peninsula the previous year. Tales of the Anzacs' exploits and self-sacrifice had filled every local newspaper during 1915 and they had won many admirers.

At 3pm on the 22nd of June 1916, the New Zealanders arrived at the Christchurch Depot. Altogether there were around one hundred and fifty Engineers, Tunnellers and Signallers. They were marched into camp, undoubtedly marvelling at the more permanent brick barrack buildings, the closeness of farms, civilian houses and shops. Around five hundred Australian Engineers had arrived an hour earlier[2]. On the parade ground they were welcomed by the British Commanding Officer, Lieutenant-Colonel Keen, Royal Engineers. The military requirement for discipline was stressed, as was the normal practice for British officers when addressing colonial troops. They were shown to their new quarters – rows upon rows of white canvas bell tents at the westerly end of the Christchurch Barracks, bordered at the rear by the River Stour. The accommodations were pleasant enough, (though lacking sufficient latrines, washing and dining facilities), and Christchurch was acknowledged to be warmer than Salisbury Plain.

After being assigned to their tents, they stowed their kit and precious blankets, organized their tent lines and filled mattresses with straw from the stable area. Following their evening meal, some visited the camp facilities and began conversations with British Royal Engineers already undergoing training. The New Zealanders would begin their course on the Monday, so they took the opportunity to find out what they could expect from the British instructors. Many would have written a quick letter to their families in New Zealand telling them where they were and assuring them all was well. Buoyed by the good news that they had been granted local weekend leave, many were intent upon visiting Bournemouth, where they heard there were plenty of young, single women.

As they settled down for the night in their new camp, they were all keenly aware that they were now one step closer to fighting in France. It was a great adventure - a chance to see Europe, to visit relatives, and to help protect the Empire from its enemies. The men of the NZEF had travelled half-way around the world to fight in a European war. Along with their Australian comrades-in-arms they would go on to display aggressive fighting ability and to be considered amongst the best divisions in France.

The New Zealanders would eventually suffer a 58% casualty rate throughout the entire war and the highest percentages of wounded and killed per national population. Their presence in England has all but been forgotten. Only glimpses exist in faded photographs and curled newspaper clippings.

Chapter One: A holiday by the sea

The year was 1907 and for the past thirty-five years Europe had enjoyed relative peace. The European conflicts within recent memory had been the Franco-Prussian War of 1870-1871, won by Prussia and the German states to which it was allied. Prior to the end of this conflict the German states had unified under King Wilhelm I of Prussia forming the new nation of Germany.

The next major conflict that occurred was the Russo-Turkish War of 1877-1878, fuelled by the Serbian and Montenegrin conflict with the Ottoman Empire. The Russians defeated the Turks and advanced toward Constantinople, at which point Britain threatened war on Russia. This was avoided after negotiations returned to Russia territories it had ceded at the end of the Crimean War, which re-established its access to the Black Sea. The various European nations settled down and contented themselves vying for territories in North Africa and China.

In June 1888, Kaiser Wilhelm II, Queen Victoria's grandson, had succeeded to the throne as the German Emperor and King of Prussia. His desire was to push Germany into international prominence, or a "place in the sun" as he called it, and he adopted an aggressive approach in the pursuit of this aim, principally striving to make Germany a major sea power, to rival Britain's Royal Navy.

He soon made his intentions felt in South Africa after the abortive Jameson Raid incident of 1896, where six hundred Irregular English militiamen from the British Cape Colony crossed into the Transvaal, intending to provoke an uprising of English workers against the Boer Government there. It failed with all the raiders either being killed or taken prisoner. The Kaiser seized the opportunity to strengthen Boer-German relations and sent the famous Kruger telegram[3]. In it he congratulated the Boers on repelling the invaders without having to ask for help from a "friendly power". The telegram was as ill-conceived as the raid. The 'Jameson affair' should have remained merely a colonial sideshow, but it escalated into an international incident aimed at embarrassing Britain. Jameson and his men were soon seen as heroes by the British Press and in no time at all anti-German sentiment was openly expressed by an outraged British public. Any hopes that the Kaiser may have held towards allying Germany with the Transvaal vanished when the second Boer War in South Africa began in 1899, eventually concluding in a British victory by 1902, with the Boer Republics becoming part of the British Empire.

The next five years saw a significant change in world politics, starting with France making an agreement with Italy that they would not interfere as France expanded her interests into Morocco, the last of the independent North African states. In 1904, France extended this agreement to Britain, at which point Germany felt that instead of an 'open door' policy towards North Africa, France had deliberately excluded it from pursuing any interests in North Africa.

With Europe's gaze towards North Africa, Germany had continued to strengthen its relationship with the Ottoman Empire. In 1903 a German consortium had begun extending the Berlin to Baghdad Railway through Anatolia and Mesopotamia, eventually reaching the port of Basra in the Persian Gulf. Upon its completion, it would give Germany a commercial land route east and provide easier access to the oil and raw materials of her African colonies, at that time being: German South West Africa (now Namibia), German South East Africa (now part of Tanzania), Togo and Cameroon.

These efforts by Germany to strengthen her political ties with the Ottoman Empire were considered by Russia to be a direct challenge to her own commercial interests in Persia, and risked shifting the balance of power throughout that region. This shift happened unexpectedly when Russia was defeated by Japan in the Russo-Japanese War of 1904-1905, after being besieged in their Pacific port of Port Arthur and suffering several military defeats to the Japanese Army in Manchuria.

Amidst these Russian set-backs and emboldened by Germany's international ascendancy, the Kaiser chose this time to arrive at the Moroccan port of Tangiers in person in March 1905 directly challenging

French influence there. In a speech to the Sultan and his council, the Kaiser offered German support for Moroccan independence and the assistance to maintain it. This provocation sparked diplomatic protests and military posturing from France and resulted in the 1906 Algeciras Conference. The conference was hosted by Spain and was attended by all the leading powers: Britain, Russia, Italy, Spain and America, who's President Theodore Roosevelt, mediated in the dispute. The eventual outcome was that France's interests were upheld, effectively isolating Germany along with its support for Moroccan independence. Although Germany's relationship with Turkey strengthened through its pro-Islamic policy with Morocco, it did not out-weigh the humiliation felt by Germany at the Conference.

Possibly spurred on by the growing threat Germany now posed, Britain and Russia signed an agreement in August 1907, resolving their disputed interests in Persia, Afghanistan and Tibet which had lingered since the Russo-Turkish War of 1877. Their Accord formalised their zones of influence and in so doing, they effectively capped Germany's expansion into the region. Germany was now limited to the Ottoman controlled areas and neutral regions.

This new Anglo-Russian accord would also bind France, through virtue of its earlier agreements made with both nations[4]. Britain, France and Russia now formed what was to become known as the Triple Entente, although reputedly Britain possessed no knowledge of the terms contained within the early Franco-Russian treaty, to which it was now bound.

Europe was now awash with tension as nations attempted to deny or control access into regions they regarded as being within their political or commercial spheres of influence. To enforce their policies the French relied on their highly regarded Army, while the British depended upon the Royal Navy and the English Channel for protection.

In October 1907 the Second Peace Conference took place at The Hague. All of those states attending agreed to seek peaceful means and mediation before resorting to force of arms in settling any international disputes. Consensus was also reached on important matters such as the banning of poison or poisonous weapons, the treatment of prisoners of war, and the conduct of naval warfare. Despite diplomatic urging, the vital talks on armament limitation were abandoned. Mistrust had been steadily built up between the major powers for several years, so consent on this matter was beyond the reach of the diplomats. The "arms race" which the conference had tried to avert, ultimately quickened with Germany assigning the question of limitation of armaments to beyond the remit of practical politics[5].

The following month[6], against this backdrop of international unease, Kaiser Wilhelm II and his Empress[7] arrived at Portsmouth for a State visit to Britain. The intention of the visit was to enhance Anglo-German relations. Their first engagement was at Windsor Castle, where the Kaiser's uncle, King Edward VII and Queen Alexandra held a banquet in their honour.

The King, in proposing an after dinner toast to his illustrious guests' health, assured them of their welcome. He said their visits to Britain were always a sincere pleasure for the Royal Family, as well as to the nation. He concluded by saying that not only did he fervently hope for the prosperity and happiness of Germany, but also for the maintenance of peace.

In his reply, the Kaiser touched upon the close relationship existing between their two families. Alluding to matters at hand, he intimated that it was his earnest hope that such an accord may be reflected in the relationship between their two countries; thereby ensuring the peace of the world, the "maintenance of which was his very own constant endeavour, as he knew it to be also that of the King"[8].

In reality, both men disliked one another[9] with an "entente contempt" existing between them.

English literature had contributed to the fuelling of mistrust of the Kaiser and Germany. It began innoxiously enough in 1871, with the publication of the "Battle of Dorking"[10] , in which a Germanic speaking army invades and occupies England. This book's publication followed soon after the formation of the German Empire that same year. From 1906, with European disputes reaching boiling point, this genre of literature became popular. Publications such as the "The Invasion of 1910" and "Spies of the Kaiser"[11] fermented a German military threat. The stories of German spies stealing British naval secrets or mapping coastal defences in readiness for "the day" when Germany would invade England, lead to questions being asked[12] in the House of Commons of the Minister of War in 1908, as to the presence of German spies in the coastal areas of Norfolk, Suffolk, Essex and elsewhere.

At the end of the week, with their official duties concluding, the Empress returned to Germany and the Kaiser decided to stay in England to take a short 'rest and cure' holiday. This also meant he could remain far removed from the on-going domestic turmoil concerning the accusations of homosexuality amongst the Kaiser's cabinet and entourage in the Harden-Eulenburg affair.

On the 18th of November, the Kaiser travelled to Highcliffe Castle, a large country manor on the Hampshire coast. Here he stayed as the guest of Colonel Stuart-Wortley.[13]To make the Kaiser's holiday as pleasant as possible; the King suggested that his favourite chef, Rosa Lewis from London, cooked at Highcliffe.

Rosa's first task was to prepare a meal for ninety people on the first night at Highcliffe. Unaware that the Kaiser had a disability, his left arm being withered as a result of an injury sustained at birth, she chose quail as a suitable dish for the time of year. Although he was fond of game, the Kaiser did not like to eat anything containing small bones and often a servant helped him to cut his food. The quail served that night, although enjoyable, would therefore have caused some initial awkwardness for the staff.

Another problem facing the cook was that the nearby towns, like Christchurch, were small agricultural towns. Soon Rosa Lewis was travelling to London to buy essential ingredients for her menus, with the early morning train stopping at Hilton Admiral delayed, while kitchen staff unloaded the necessary foodstuffs ordered from London.

The sea breeze and walks at Highcliffe delighted the Kaiser. The day always commenced with affairs of state, but afterwards there was no fixed itinerary. A brisk walk, a spot of lunch, and the weather determined the rest of each day's activities. Some of the destinations included the seaside town of Bournemouth, the ruins of Corfe Castle as well as visits to one of the Kaiser's many acquaintances in the area. He was often asked to plant trees to commemorate his visit at the various nearby country estates, such as Kingston Lacy. He lunched with the Earl of Pembroke at Wilton House, near Salisbury, and even managed to visit Lord Montague at Beaulieu.

A keen sportsman, the Kaiser twice visited Lord Arlington at his country home at Crichel[14], reputed for its fine game shooting. International politics were never too far away and during a dinner one evening at Crichel, the guest seated beside the Kaiser was Mrs Alice Keppel, King Edward's mistress. Another guest was the Austrian Ambassador, Count Mensdorff, a second cousin of the King, who recognising the seating arrangements for what they were, wondered at just what sort of report Mrs Keppel would eventually send back to the King at Sandringham. Regardless of such intrigue, Mrs Keppel did send the Kaiser a photograph of her recent portrait. It showed her with a plunging neckline, flicking at her pearls.[15]

Earl Malmesbury[16] of Heron Court, near the local town of Christchurch, had asked if the Kaiser would agree to be the godfather to his newly born son, William Harris[17]. The Kaiser obliged and made several visits to Heron Court, often cheered by the people he passed by in the Christchurch countryside. One afternoon when leaving Heron Court, children from the local Holdenhurst School gathered at the estate gates and as he drove out of the long drive they gave three hearty cheers. Graciously the Kaiser halted, bowed to the children, and then continued on his way back to Highcliffe.[18]

Wherever he toured, crowds often turned out especially to cheer him. Providing this information to the public was undertaken by the local newspaper, *The Daily Echo,* in conjunction with the Post Office telex operators based at Highcliffe Castle. They were there especially for the duration of the Kaiser's visit to allow telegraphic communications on German affairs of state. Once known, a telex operator would detail the Kaiser's travel intentions for that day and the newspaper would print these onto broadsheets, which the newspaper boys distributed and posted around the towns. Undoubtedly the cheering crowds that turned out in their hundreds, and the warmth shown to the Kaiser by the local people, surprised him, particularly when compared to comments in the press and possible muted greetings he received in parts of Germany. It undoubtedly lifted his mood as the weeks passed and he realised that it was he the people wanted to see. He returned this warmth on one occasion when the band of the Royal Yacht *Hohenzollern* held a concert at the Globe Hotel in Highcliffe. It was a rare musical treat for the people of Christchurch and proved to be very popular. The mayor, Mr Newlyn, wrote to the Kaiser expressing the Borough's gratitude. The performance raised a substantial sum of money which was used to provide a second Christchurch cot in the Boscombe Hospital.[19]

The weather during the second week of his stay had been wet and stormy. On the 30th of November around two hundred children gathered at the local Hinton Village School. They were going to entertain the Kaiser with a tea party. At around three o'clock they were marched in orderly fashion into the school building, where final preparations and rehearsals took place. Seated, they then waited in relative silence with their nervous teachers and other civic guests.

Outside, the crowd had swollen to around a thousand people[20], parents and on-lookers all intent on greeting the Kaiser on that autumnal afternoon. At a quarter past five, with the sun beginning to set, his motorcade arrived from Crichel and as he alighted he was greeted by a large cheer. The cheer was renewed several times as he walked into the school playground and on each occasion he acknowledged it by raising his motoring cap.

Two tiny girls, Ina Barrett and Winnie Young, aged eight and seven, both dressed in white and wearing sashes in the German colours of red, white and black, handed the Kaiser two beautifully decorated baskets of flowers, consisting of chrysanthemums in tints of yellow and bronze. The handles of the baskets were tied with silk streamers in red, white and black. There was a further presentation by the Vicar's daughter on behalf of the German ladies in the neighbourhood. The sudden pop and burst of the magnesium flashlight during the official photographs startled the two small girls and the Kaiser, presumably in a jovial mood, laughed at their momentary alarm.[21]

The centre piece in the school hall was a huge iced cake decorated with British and German flags. The Kaiser was handed a knife with which to cut the cake. Limited to the use of only one hand and confronted by the thick icing, he found the task awkward. In order to cut the cake, he took the knife in his good hand and resorted to hacking at the third tier of the cake. Having successfully removed a large piece for himself, he handed the knife back to the ladies. The cake was then sliced and distributed along the tables of delighted children. It was not every day that one had a tea party with royalty.

The following day, Sunday the 1st of December, was Advent Sunday and the Kaiser, accompanied by Baron von Reischach, Prince Furstenberg, Count P.W. Metternich (the German Ambassador), Count Eulenburg, Admiral Mueller and others, attended divine service at the Priory Church, Christchurch.

The flag of St George, as opposed to the Imperial German standard, floated on the church tower giving no announcement of his pending arrival at the Priory Church – but news quickly spread and people flocked to the Priory in great numbers. It was soon crowded, regardless of its capacity to seat six hundred or more people comfortably. For many of that large congregation attending the service, it would have been a rare and unique opportunity to be so close to royalty or a head of state.

The Service was sung to plain chant, it being the desire of the Kaiser that the service should be of the plain, simple kind, to which he was accustomed in the Lutheran Church.[22] During the service the hymn "Now thank we all our God" was sung, supposedly with some gusto, as it happened to be the hymn sung by the Prussian Army after the battle of Leuthen[23], the anniversary of which was soon to be commemorated.[24] The coincidence was not lost on the Kaiser who later remarked favourably on its choice.

The Reverend E.D. Benisen led the service and the sermon was preached by Reverend T.H. Bush, taking his text from John XIV 18 – "I will not leave you comfortless; I will come to you." During the sermon, the Reverend Bush spoke of uncertainty and the need for guidance in life; in particular of how the problems of life become more complicated every year. He referred to the need for a wisdom and power greater than man's. One wonders if Wilhelm reflected on these words, especially with his immediate domestic problems and in consideration of how a strong Germany would react to being squeezed both politically and commercially by France, Britain and Russia.

The Reverend Bush continued: "As we turn then, once more to face the uncertainties of the future, we will look up to Him … for the solution of the problems of today, believing that if the world is to be transformed it must be, not by a great social upheaval from below, but by the spirit and power from above… and creating a new order of moral forces, ideals and hopes."[25]

The new moral forces were already taking shape across Europe. In the Advent sermon the Reverend's words resonated with the hope that conflict could be avoided. Later the Kaiser would sign two copies of Reverend Bush's sermon for the Church-wardens.

At the conclusion of the service, the congregation was asked to remain seated until the royal party had left the Priory Church, and on his way out the Kaiser signed the visitor's book[26]. His visit to the Priory Church passed into local history, even though a stained glass window in the Priory shows it occurring in 1901 - six years earlier than it did.

Kaiser Wilhelm's visit ended two weeks later when on the 14th of December 1907 he departed from Hinton Admiral Station bound for Lewes.

Before leaving, he made several awards to some local townspeople: Superintendent Mayes, Hampshire Police Force, in recognition of the service of the police, was awarded the 4th Class Order of the Crown; Sergeants Deacon and Lowes were awarded the Medal of the Red Eagle, and all the constables who had undertaken duties during the visit were awarded medals of the Crown. Mr McArdie and Mr A.F. Skinner were presented with the 4th Class Order of the Red Eagle and Mr E.W. Wedlake, assistant surveyor at the Post Office – was conferred the 4th Class Order of the Royal Crown for the special postal staff that were on duty and who allowed many thousands of words to be despatched by telegraph.[27]

On the surface the Anglo-German relationship had warmed. The local Priory School diary contained no reference to the Kaiser's visit. It showed more interest in the preparation for the forthcoming Christmas holidays and an outbreak of ringworm amongst the children.

This was also the year in which Baden-Powell founded the Boy Scouts and they held their first Scout Camp on Brownsea Island over that summer. In September New Zealand had become a self-governing Dominion within the British Empire. Marconi had achieved fully reliable transatlantic communication. In October, under the direction of the American Samuel Franklin Cody[28], the first powered airship flight[29] in Britain occurred. Rudyard Kipling accepted the Nobel Prize for Literature. The suffragette newspaper "Votes for Women" was launched and it was the first year women were allowed to stand as candidates for local councils. In December Miss Reina Lawrence was elected onto the Hampstead Borough Council after winning a by-election with a majority of three hundred and nineteen votes, declaring her political interests to be: housing, swimming baths and infant mortality. It was the year that the silent movies "Ben Hur" and "20,000 Leagues Under the Sea" were released, and that in which the short magazine Lee-Enfield Mk III with the eighteen inch bayonet, had been officially introduced into British Military Service.

International controversy was never too far behind the Kaiser. Later in December 1908 the *Daily Telegraph* printed an account of discussions allegedly held between the Kaiser and Colonel Stuart-Wortley during his stay at Highcliffe Castle in 1907.

In the interview, the Kaiser declared his staunch friendship towards England, which he felt to be amply demonstrated by his refusal to meet the Boer delegation as they sought European allies; and had rebutted Russian and French military overtures in December 1899 for Germany to join with them to humiliate a weak England, following its three military defeats in six days during the opening stages of the Boer War. He also argued that Germany's political action in Morocco in 1905 was not contrary to these peaceful intentions.

The Kaiser had intended that such a frank declaration of friendship would help to paint a more favourable image of him - but it backfired. Firstly with his own German people who, by his own admission, were generally not friendly towards England. Then, he alienated the English after the press seized upon his unfortunate reference to the English as "mad, mad, mad as March hares" over the apparent suspicion that with one hand he offered friendship, while in his other he held a dagger.

Later the Foreign Secretary of the time, Sir Edward Grey, would opine that "the German Emperor is ageing me; he is like a battleship with steam up and screws going, but with no rudder, and he will run into something some day and cause a catastrophe"[30].

King Edward VII died on the 6th of May 1910. Nine crowned heads of Europe attended his funeral. They were: the kings of England, Norway, Spain, Portugal, Belgium, Sweden and Denmark, the Tsar of Bulgaria and Kaiser Wilhelm II. A host of minor royalty and foreign ambassadors were also there. Theodore Roosevelt attended on behalf of America.

The "Uncle of Europe" was dead and his son, George V became King. During his reign he would grapple with the spiralling Irish crisis particularly the Third Home Rule Bill and the mutiny at the Curragh, the militancy of the Suffragette Movement and the greatest armed conflict of that era which became known as "The Great War".

His Imperial Majesty Kaiser Wilhelm II (the fourth adult from the left, standing at the back of the room with his right hand in his coat pocket) and school children from the Hinton Village School at Highcliffe, Hampshire. The multi-layered, flag decorated cake in the centre of the room, has most of the children's interest.

Photo courtesy of Mr Ian Stevenson

Chapter Two: The Pacific region and rising tensions in Europe

Kaiser Wilhelm's "place in the sun" for the German people in world affairs would extend beyond the constrained boundaries of Europe and North Africa. He desired a large chunk of the international cake and began securing territories in Central Africa and the Pacific region. By the 1880's all the major European naval powers possessed some political or economic sway amongst the Pacific territories, except Germany. New Guinea would change all of that. The Netherlands already administered the western half of New Guinea. The British colony of Queensland, Australia, administered the south-eastern part from 1883. This left an opportunity for one other European power, and Germany seized upon it. In November 1884 Germany laid claim to the then unsettled north-eastern part of New Guinea, naming it Kaiser-Wilhelmsland. Along with a string of volcanic islands off the north east coast, named the Bismarck Archipelago, the German Protectorate of German New Guinea was founded. In 1885 the German protectorate was extended to include the northern Solomon Islands and by 1899 Germany's territorial holdings in the region had steadily increased through the purchase of the economically unimportant Mariana and Caroline Islands from Spain, who had just ended its disastrous war with America over Cuba. By 1906 the Marshall Islands were added.

Samoa was a source of tension amongst the international community throughout the 1890's as it was an important refuelling site for the coal-fired shipping from America, Germany, France and Britain. France laid no claim to Samoa, but the other three nations did and each sent warships at the height of the tensions to enforce their interests. In April 1899, to avoid a major international incident, the Treaty of Berlin placed the eastern group of islands under the formal control of America and the western islands, being the greater landmass, were granted to Germany. Britain gave up all claims in return for Fiji and some Melanesian territories.

New Zealand had always assumed that its remoteness, along with the Royal Navy's continued superiority on the seas, would ensure its protection. With Germany having established trading footholds in the

Pacific, and Japan's shock victory over Russia, by 1905 the balance of naval power in the Pacific region was becoming less certain. It must have been with some relief therefore, that in 1906 the British launched their new class of battleship – the Dreadnoughts. Possessing big 12 inch guns and steam turbine propulsion, this class of battleship helped to ensure that Britannia would rule the waves for the time being at least. It did not take long though, until every major nation adapted the Dreadnought design and began to build their own "all-big-gun" battleships. Even Brazil, Argentina and Chile entered into their own regional arms-race and had Dreadnoughts laid down for them at British shipyards.

Realising its dependency on the Royal Navy, the Dominion of New Zealand offered to pay for two battleships, only one of which, *HMS New Zealand* a King Edward VII class battleship, was eventually built. She was laid down in June 1910 and completed by November 1912 at a cost of £1,783,190.[31] Naval ships had become the gambling chips in a worldwide game of poker.

During this period, military tension in Europe had continued to grow. In 1908 Austria-Hungary annexed Bosnia and Herzegovina against the objection of Russia; in 1911 France and Germany disagreed again over France's interventions in Morocco and in 1912 Italy and Turkey fought a year long war for the control of Turkey's North African territories. Turkey was defeated and forced to hand over Libya, Rhodes and the Dodecanese Islands to the Italians. The ease with which Turkish forces were defeated soon encouraged the small Balkan League states[32], with backing from Russia, to lay historical claims to the Turkish controlled territories of Macedonia and Albania. This ignited the First Balkan War of 1912 to 1913 which concluded with the collapse of the Turkish forces in that area. The peace treaty was signed in London in May 1913 and the Ottoman Empire boundaries were again redrawn as all European territories were ceded.

With the Balkans now alight, it took less than a month before the Second Balkan War erupted. This was ostensibly regarding Bulgaria's territorial claims over the Macedonian region, complicated by Serbia being forced to relinquish territory in the newly independent state of Albania. Greece and Serbia were pitted against their former ally Bulgaria. The fighting soon drew in Romania against Bulgaria, while the Ottomans were quick to take advantage of the overall situation by re-occupying territory they had been forced to cede to Bulgaria in the earlier war. The fighting soon reached a stalemate by July 1913, when Bulgaria asked for an armistice. Eventually Macedonia was divided diplomatically between Greece and Serbia. Romania also gained some territory from Bulgaria and Ottoman Turkey and despite Russia's unease, retained all of its gains.

With military hostility still simmering, the violence that had characterised the region restricted itself to occasional bouts of civil unrest and isolated revolutionary acts. Any hope that calm would return to the Balkans was dashed when on the 28th of June 1914, Franz Ferdinand, Archduke of Austria, and his wife Sophie were assassinated in Sarajevo by a young Serbian nationalist Gavrilo Princip. Matters subsequently took their own course. Austria-Hungry quickly blamed Serbia and after several anxious weeks and hapless diplomacy, war was declared between them on the 28th of July. The following day the opening shots of what would soon escalate into being the "The Great War" were fired by Austrian artillery as it bombarded Belgrade.

Events moved briskly. Having pledged support to Austria-Hungary, Germany issued an ultimatum to Russia on the 31st of July for it to cease the mobilization of its military and naval forces, citing such action as a direct threat against Germany. The challenge was ignored, and on the 1st August, Germany declared war on Russia. On the 2nd of August Germany occupied Luxemburg and on the same day made a request to neutral Belgium for the German Army to be allowed unhindered passage through their territory as it marched towards France. Belgium refused. On the 3rd of August Germany declared war on France and the next day, ignoring Belgium's prior refusal, they crossed the frontier, thereby violating Belgium's neutrality. This act provided Britain with the justification it sought to declare war on Germany on Tuesday the 4th of August 1914 – an act that constitutionally drew the entire British Empire into a state of War[33].

Chapter Three: The turmoil of war

In Bournemouth, a local newspaper, *"The Guardian"* observed that the war clouds had affected the number of holiday makers visiting the town over the August bank holiday weekend. Grasping for some positives amidst the turmoil, it lamely predicted that with a war in Europe, the English who would usually have holidayed abroad, would rather choose British seaside towns such as Bournemouth, thereby benefiting the local economy. Such attitudes reflected the sense of overwhelm experienced by ordinary people as they struggled to accept the reality of events. Britain had not been engaged in a major European war since Waterloo – ninety-nine years earlier.

Although the possibility of war had been written about, forecast, and speculated upon, adequate sentiments eluded the newspapers when trying to encapsulate the situation. Six European nations were at war, an unbelievable scale for any conflict which consigned the Crimean War (1854-1856) to a dispute on a tiny Black Sea peninsula, and the Boer War to being a distant colonial conflict[34]. In their neatly inked, typecast newspaper columns, the words most commonly used were, 'absurd' and 'incredible'.

"The Guardian" did comment that Britain's entry into the war was the 'right thing to do', particularly with Belgium's neutrality having been violated. The newspaper observed that the people of Britain, living on an island, had little concept of what it meant to merely have a row of boundary posts marking where one country ended and another, possibly hostile nation, began.[35] It voiced a national sense of confusion as the whirlpool of war pulled more countries into the conflict at such speed, and people could not understand why Austria, which was considered a friendly country, would wish to help Germany to attack France.

Britain's actions were not beyond reproach in this first week of the war. Even though Turkey had not entered the war, Churchill instructed the Royal Navy to take command of two Turkish battleships being built in England, one completed and one approaching completion. They had already been given Turkish names and their Turkish crews had arrived in England to sail them back. The money to pay for them had been raised in Turkey through public subscription in the towns and villages up and down that country. Turkey was outraged at Britain's action. Within the week they began to mobilise although the immediate purpose for doing so was not clear. Two Chilean destroyers still under construction in Britain were likewise confiscated for Royal Navy service.

Britain rapidly moved toward a war footing. In Bournemouth, mobilisation for the war began to create regional turmoil. It was harvest time and the calling up of the local Reservists, along with the military commandeering farm horses, severely reduced the farmers' ability to bring in the harvest. Several local Germans were arrested on suspicion of espionage, increasing the sense of confusion. Accustomed to shortages from the various union strikes in the past, people quickly realised that a European war could bring on similar hardships, though for a longer period. 'Panic buying' began, initially of foreign goods but soon spreading to all foodstuffs; and rapidly became so rampant that the price of provisions soared. Within the first week of the war, sugar prices doubled, cereal prices increased by a half a penny per pound, while flour was difficult to buy, as the millers had limited their supply solely to bakers. Bread rose by 33%[36] in one week, while the price of cereals, peas, bacon, tinned meats, butter, cheese and fresh meat also increased.

This buying behaviour was criticised for creating unnecessary pressure on the open market. At one stage the daily demand for goods equalled that of a pre-war week! The situation was unsustainable.

Governmental assurances were given that there was sufficient wheat to supply the whole of Britain for about four months[37] and although the Russian and Continental food supplies had stopped, they would soon be replaced by market produce from the New World – America, Canada, Australia and New Zealand. Comfortingly, it was reported that the harvest being gathered was the best for years and as such guaranteed ample food supplies for months ahead. The public were also told that both vegetables and fruit were in plentiful supply.[38]

The British public were further assured by the Government that there was no serious menace on the sea to disrupt merchant shipping, thanks to the Royal Navy, which would continue to act as a shield for Britain and the Empire in this hour of trial[39].

To further ease general anxiety, the public were advised that any comparison with the hardships resulting from the recent General Strike was ridiculous. Officials declared that food prices would not be permitted to rise beyond what was enforceable by law - a warning to would-be profiteers. It was even pointed out that some goods were being sold below market value,[40] though no-one really believed that. Sound common sense was called for.

This appeal was ignored by a portion of the Bournemouth town's shopkeepers, who reacted to the melee by closing their shops during part of the day, or regulating the number of customers permitted to enter their store, thereby creating queues. They withdrew credit facilities, refused payment by cheque and conducted business on a cash-only basis. This, and a 'run' on cash, quickly exhausted the local banks' reserves, forcing them eventually to close for three days. Being a holiday resort, the closure of the banks in Bournemouth created some anxious moments for holidaymakers trying to settle hotel bills. It also created problems for those people dependent on cashing their wage cheques so as to access their money. Cash was in such short supply in Bournemouth that when a tradesman placed a bag full of cash on the bank's counter for depositing the clerk exclaimed "What, cash, that's a novelty!"[41]

The local grocers at an emergency meeting on Wednesday the 5th of August passed a resolution to the effect that they had confidence in the Government and would take all necessary steps to secure the nation's food supply during the ensuing conflict. The banks then reopened on Saturday the 8th of August making that first week of the war the first ever four day bank holiday week. Matters began to settle down and in an effort to ease the cash crisis the Government printed more paper money, recalled gold sovereigns and issued for the first time £1 and 10 shilling paper notes.

The following week heralded a totally different challenge, with the introduction of austerity measures. The town mayor of Bournemouth was forced to ask people not to withhold their custom from the shopkeepers during the war as such practice would lead to business failure and unemployment. The mayor reiterated the Chancellor of the Exchequer's concern that if the public hoarded money; trade would give out, depleting the economies of the towns. To avoid such distress, the resumption of normal business was recommended.[42] The agricultural report for the South of England advised that although the harvest was not as bountiful as expected, it could yet equal that of 1913 if sufficiently good weather throughout the remainder of August allowed for it to be brought in.[43]

Under the Defence of the Realm Act 1914, the south coast was officially a prohibited area to all "enemy aliens". These people were required to register with the police and were issued special permits from the Restriction Officer if they were to remain living in prohibited areas. They were not allowed to drive motor vehicles without permission from the police, presumably to prevent possible acts of sabotage, as suggested in the vogue fictional literature of the time. Legal prosecution followed any breaches of the Act and in one Bournemouth court case a 72 year old German lady holidaying in the area was arrested for not registering as an enemy alien. She spoke no English and the registration forms were not in German. As she was not considered dangerous, she was released, and ordered not to return to the Bournemouth area for the duration of the war. In another, an English woman who was married to a German subject was arrested for not registering – she left for Manchester to live with her sister.[44]

Importation of goods from Germany was prohibited by Royal Proclamation and a local merchant, W. Price and Sons Ltd, advertised that due to the actions of the Germans in provoking the war, it was selling all German pianos in stock at enormously reduced prices.

Motor vans and lorries used by local businesses were soon requisitioned by the military and people were also urged to sell their horses to the military. The annual town fireworks display which raised funds for the local hospitals was abandoned and rumours began to circulate that wire entanglements were to be erected along Bournemouth's beaches. Presumably during all of this, those who had been presented with medals by the Kaiser during his stay in 1907 must have felt extremely awkward. In all probability to avoid any pro-German stigma, they would have either privately or publicly destroyed their medals. Rosa Lewis, the King's cook at Highcliffe Castle during his visit there returned her medal directly to the Kaiser.

British tourists returning from holidays in France or Germany described their ordeals in trying to reach England as news of war reached them. The French train on which one particular group was travelling was commandeered by the French military, and having waited for another train, they finally reached Paris after a 48 hour journey and 30 hours without a meal! In Paris they found that the milk supply had been stopped as it was allegedly poisoned. Ironically the largest milk depot in Paris was owned by a German firm. Another party of four ladies were searched when departing Germany, before being allowed to continue their journey. The Germans then began blowing up the railway line behind their train as it rumbled out of the station.[45]

The local Territorial Companies of the 7th Hampshire, who were at their annual camp at Bulford, on Salisbury Plain when war was declared, moved to Portsmouth for defence duty, and the Royal Horse Artillery contingents left from Christchurch station for Aldershot and Ireland amongst cheering crowds. Some of the local business owners, whose employees served with either the Territorial or Army Reserves and had been called up, agreed to make up the difference between Army pay and their regular pay, as well keeping their jobs open for them.

In Swindon, Frederick Blundson, a veteran of the Boer War and a Reservist with the Wiltshire Regiment was preparing to report to his Regiment, where he would serve alongside his five brothers and two brothers-in-law. At home he left his wife Theresa to look after their five young children. Although anxious, she knew it would not be for long as everyone was saying that the war would all be over by Christmas.

This belief in a short war emanated from several sources. Firstly, Germany did not have the economic base to sustain a long and costly war; the German Army had not fought in any major conflict since 1871; and its Navy was new and untested. Experts opined in numerous articles that with the advanced weaponry available no war could possibly last more than a matter of weeks; at the most months. This all contributed towards the British Army and Royal Navy confidence that they could defeat Germany in a sharp decisive scrap. As one officer observed, victory had been plotted down to the last range-finder[46] and now was the moment for it all to happen. Such an attitude ignored certain realities: it had taken Britain nearly three years to subdue fifty thousand Boers; that there were seventy million Germans; and even with Britain and France fighting together, this would be a totally different proposition given the advances in artillery, machine guns and aircraft.

Regardless, the "brief affair" view held ascendancy for several months and showed itself in matters such as the forthcoming America's Cup yacht race. This event between the New York Club and the Royal Ulster Yacht Club was postponed for a month on the basis that if war extended the event would be held the following year in 1915. In reality, it would not be raced again until 1920[47].

At Tidworth Barracks, on the morning of the 16th of August, the abrupt sound of reveille at 2:30am announced to Captain Arthur Osburn, a doctor with the 4th Royal Irish Dragoon Guards and a Boer War veteran, that he was off to war again. Over the next week his regiment advanced steadily through France. It was pleasant enough; the weather was hot and dry and the French public warmly welcomed the British troops as they passed through the various villages and towns. The only major incident was the death on the 17th of August of Sir James Grierson, the commander of II Corps from a heart attack while travelling in the train taking him to the front. He was a leading authority on the German Army and had even published books on the subject. He was a rival to General Sir Douglas Haig, and he remains one of the great 'might-have-beens' of the war.

On the 22nd of August the Royal Irish Dragoon Guards arrived in the

Mons area. They were the first British Army regiment to engage with the Germans. The British Infantry had also arrived. Amongst them Private Fredrick Blundson, undoubtedly tired and foot weary from marching with his 80lbs of equipment in the hot August weather, dug in with his regiment; the 1st Wiltshires. It would not be long before he and his comrades would hear the fierce cracking sound of Germany infantry rifle fire and then see the German Taube aircraft flying overhead, dropping smoke signals to mark targets for the artillery. This was nothing like the Boer War, and the sound of rifle fire kept getting steadily nearer.

The Battle of Mons was underway and the intensity of the fighting was proven by the official British casualties, which reported fifty-four officers and one hundred and seventy-nine men killed, one hundred and thirty officers and nine hundred and forty-one men wounded and staggering one hundred and eighty-one officers and eight thousand, eight hundred and fifty-five[48] men missing amidst the confusion of the fighting. Mons was the worst upset that the British Army had received since Lord Cornwallis had surrendered to the American revolutionaries at York Town in 1781. The long hoped-for short scrap with the German Army had resulted in the British being bewildered and scattered by the German advance.

A disorganised British Army soon retreated from Mons and over the next week continued to fall back towards Paris and the Marne River. Their discarded equipment marked their route and was a testament to poor leadership and the utter confusion which reigned. Eventually they managed to regroup and were reinforced by four fresh brigades from England. Six months later the first Victoria Cross of the war would be awarded at Buckingham Palace to Captain F.O. Grenfell for saving the guns of the 119th Battery, Royal Field Artillery during the retreat.

August passed quickly, with the Russians launching attacks on the Germans in East Prussia and the Austro-Hungarians in Galicia, Poland. In the west, the French routed the Germans in Alsace and occupied the towns of Altkirch and Malhausen, while in Belgium the Germans were in Liege where atrocities were emerging of young Belgian girls being raped and civilians being buried alive by German Calvary. The propaganda war had begun, although there were rumours in some Belgian quarters that they had at first actually welcomed the German invasion, fearing France's European ambitions more than German aggression[49].

Despite the military set-backs, in Britain the "Rush to the Colours"[50] continued. Patriotic posters declaring "Fight for King and Country", or "England expects every man to do his Duty" were stirring the public conscience. Then there was the iconic poster in every public place, of Kitchener pointing and declaring: "Your Country Needs You". Unlike many of the optimists, Lord Kitchener believed the war would last at least three years, and he was ridiculed by some for holding this view.

Most recruitment centres were soon awash with enthusiastic men, all wanting to get to France and stop the Germans. The Bournemouth and Christchurch areas responded overwhelmingly to this call to arms. In that first September of the war an average of 20 men a day enrolled in either the local Territorial or the Regular Army battalions.

By early October, the 43rd (Wessex) Division[51], which included the locally raised Territorial 1/7th Hants Battalion, were under orders to proceed to India to relieve Regular Army battalions being deployed back to France and Belgium. In a farewell address to the Hampshire Brigade, the Bishop, the Reverend Dr Talbot predicted their deployment would be 'the greatest adventure of their lives'. The 1/7th Hants would land in Karachi November 1914 and remained in India for most of the war, being transferred to various Indian Divisions until January 1918 when the battalion moved to Aden.

Other locally raised units were the 1/5th Hants Howitzers Royal Field Artillery, recruited on the Isle of Wight. They would serve at Kut in Mesopotamia, eventually surrendering to the Turks along with the rest of the 6th (Indian) Division. Their sister unit 1/6th Hants (1st Reserve) Royal Field Artillery would serve the entire war in India. While the 1/8th (Isle of Wight Rifles, Princess Beatrice's) Battalion would land at Suvla Bay, Gallipoli, as part of the 54th Division on the 9th of August 1915 and continue on to fight in Sinai and Palestine from 1916 as part of the Egyptian Expeditionary Force.

The local response was so remarkable, that the War Office granted permission to the local battalion commander, Colonel Hobart, to raise another Infantry battalion from Bournemouth, New Forest and Southampton for the Regular Army - the 2/7th Hants, part of the 45th(2nd Wessex) Division. They sailed for India on the 13th of December, 1914 and would serve initially in India and later in Mesopotamia, arriving at Basra in September 1917. They would become a line of communication battalion.

As active recruitment steadily robbed the area of many of its young men and agricultural workers, the first Belgian and French refugees began to arrive in Bournemouth, and Red Cross trains began to arrive weekly with wounded British and Belgian soldiers. The wounded were distributed amongst the hospitals across the Bournemouth, Boscombe and Christchurch area. The putrefying smell of gangrenous wounds, the sight of thickly dressed battle wounds, mangled or severed limbs and the vacant stares of the more seriously wounded, made the war seem suddenly very near, not merely "over there" or described in patriotic terms on pages of newspapers.

The first recorded war death in the Bournemouth area was that of Private William Stevens, of 1st Wiltshire Regiment, aged twenty-three. He died in a local hospital from wounds sustained at Mons. Later Belgian Sub-Lieutenant Lucien Dome, 2nd Regiment of Carabineers aged twenty-nine, died on the 6th of November from wounds sustained at Keyem in Belgium. He was buried in the Boscombe War Cemetery.

With the overwhelming number of wounded regularly arriving, it did not take long before the local hospitals' resources were exhausted. Appeals were made to the public for additional supplies of pillows, bath and hand towels, soap, matches, writing materials, vegetables, jam, glass dishes or bowls for fruit, and most urgently, cigarettes. Individual donations provided short term assistance, though with each hospital making regular appeals, it was realised that properly organised fund raising events, such as fetes and musical entertainment were needed. The call was taken up by church groups and various societies. They were also a welcomed distraction from the ever present wartime restrictions. The local newspapers assisted by advertising the events and then reporting what happened and how much money was raised.

To relieve the pressure on the local hospitals, Lady Malmesbury opened her home at Heron Court, near Christchurch, as a Convalescence Hospital in November, 1914. The Heron Court Auxiliary Hospital, as it became known, originally accommodated twenty patients coming from the Boscombe Military Hospital. In 1916, a new ward, (effectively a corrugated tin hut with open fires), was opened to cope with the increasing number of patients. It was staffed by Sister Hughes, a trained nurse, eight Volunteer Aid Detachment helpers (known as VADs) and Dr. Shell, the Medical Officer.

With prices continually rising and unemployment growing, a boost to the local economy occurred when in October 1914 it was announced that due to the shortage of barracks for the large number of troops coming to the area for training, between 12,000 and 18,000 troops would be billeted throughout the Bournemouth conurbation. The procedure was that two to three men would be allocated to a house. The only grounds for a householder refusing to billet soldiers were if there was no male in residence[52]. The seaside resort was rapidly becoming a distinct shade of khaki.

Across the battlefields of Europe the pace of the war had not slackened and the casualties from the fighting had highlighted a shortage of medical personnel to attend to them. A local party of eight trained nurses and three doctors[53] left from Bournemouth for St Malo in France to provide medical assistance at a hospital being established by the resident English community. Another contingent of nurses and orderlies left for the Red Cross Hospital at Rouen, in the British sector of the fighting, aboard Lord Brassey's personal yacht, 'Sunbeam'[54]. Evidently they were urgently needed or the delays being encountered with cross-channel military shipping necessitated this approach, but it also displayed the supportive attitude prevailing at this time.

Chapter Four: New Zealand mobilises

Meanwhile, twelve thousand miles away in New Zealand it was winter when war was declared. The Governor General, Lord Liverpool, addressed a crowd gathered around the steps of the Parliament building in Wellington with the words: "Fellow subjects. War has broken out with Germany". It came as a surprise. Its causes were not fully understood, yet it was believed to be the right thing to do and "the enemy" was now clearly the "Hun". New Zealand was a self-confident nation and believed that once the British Army entered the fray then the German war machine would be easily overthrown. Volunteers were immediately sought after.

The only overseas war in which New Zealand had ever been involved was the South African War (1899 – 1902), where it had sent 6500 "mounted rifles" in ten contingents[55], so naturally the question of national and imperial defence became a major political discussion point as other foreign powers gained influence in the Pacific. The 1909 Defence Act created a territorial force recruited from Compulsory Military Training[56]. It was designed to create an adequate national defence force, based around the major provinces of Auckland, Wellington, Canterbury and Otago.

Each district was to provide a quarter of the total national military force which was designated as:

> 1 Brigade of Mounted Rifles, comprising 3 Regiments
> 1 Brigade of Infantry, consisting of 4 Battalions
> 1 Brigade of Field Artillery and Ammunition Column
> 1 Company Field Engineers, 1 Mounted Company Field
> Engineers and 1 Divisional Signals Company
> 1 Mounted and One Field Ambulance, 1 Company Mounted
> Supply Company, 1 Army Service Corps Company and Costal
> Defence Troops.

Mounted and Infantry territorial companies formed across the country, adopting local regional names such as the Otago Hussars, Heretaunga Mounted Rifles, the Ruahines, the Taranaki Rifles. They contributed to the make-up of the new defence force whose role it was to oppose small scale naval raids and more importantly, to allow for rapid mobilisation in case of war. Boys aged fifteen to eighteen were to serve in the cadet corps, and for those between eighteen and twenty-five, service in the Territorial Army was compulsory[57].

This structure was reviewed and refined by Lord Kitchener, Imperial Commander in Chief, when he visited New Zealand in February 1910 and resulted in a British officer, General Alexander Godley, being appointed the following year to command and re-organise this rapidly expanding military force. The New Zealand public's attitude was that in the event of a war, it would send contingents of fully equipped and trained troops, exactly as it had done during the South African War.

With patriotic songs, such as Rule Britannia, being enthusiastically sung in the agricultural towns and cities across New Zealand, volunteers were keen to enlist before the battalions filled up. Preference was given to Territorials and men with previous war experience, aged between twenty-five and thirty-five years[58]. The country's drill halls were soon full of eager bodies like the young Cecil Malthus and his friends from the Nelson Territorial units. There was no question at all about staying at home. Like so many others, the prospect of seeing active service was a thrill[59] and brothers, friends and relations all joined up together.

John and Leonard Keating from Wingatui both joined the Otago Infantry Battalion and were issued with consecutive Army numbers 8/58 and 8/59. James Wareham a 20 year old Insurance clerk at National Mutual Life Assurance Company, who had served with the Karori Cadets in Wellington, volunteered on 19th August and was placed with the Mounted Brigade's Army Service Corps section as a driver. He would serve in the Main Body under Captain Norman Hamilton of the ASC, who was the enlisting officer that day and obviously had a vested interest in where recruits were posted.

The reasons for volunteering varied. There was the romantic notion of adventure and living those enticing stories from boyhood, of the flag waving parades and coming home to civil receptions for the local heroes. For others it was a way out of a mundane job, a chance to travel, to see England and to visit relatives. All considered it their duty to protect the Empire to which they were proud to belong, and besides, it would be a short war – everyone said so. Whatever their reasons, about 94% of the early volunteers were single men[60].

John A Lee wrote "…the people were cheering. You could understand it – a long period of what was comparative prosperity…no great happening for a long time…everyone rushed to enlist."[61] Lee would also enlist, and would be awarded a Disguised Conduct Medal but at the price of losing part of his arm at Messines[62] in 1917.

The Australian view was similar to that of New Zealand. They realised that the "old country" was embroiled in a struggle in which she may actually cease to exist as a great nation. Their trade and security was dependant on the Royal Navy. They disliked Germany's military policy, especially as it was now on their doorstep in New Guinea and Samoa.

On the 5th of August 1914, New Zealand offered the British Government its Expeditionary Force. This was accepted and on the 7th of August a request was received from London for New Zealand troops to seize the German wireless station at Apia, German Samoa. The Samoa (NZ) Expeditionary Force or "Advance Party" of 1,413 all ranks was immediately mobilised[63] from existing military units. Accompanied by three aging cruisers and warships from the Australian Squadron they captured German Samoa on the 29th of August, becoming the first Allied troops of the war to successfully occupy German territory.

Australian troops later captured Kaiser-Wilhelmsland and the nearby islands in early September, whilst the Japanese, who through their 1902 Alliance agreement with Great Britain had declared war on Germany on the 13th of August, seized all the remaining Germany territories in the Pacific and China by November 1914.

The public read about their fellow New Zealanders volunteering in "the old country" to serve in British Army units. William Balcombe-Brown studying at Oxford University and Eric Goodfellow studying medicine at Edinburgh, both from Wellington, received commissions in the Royal Field Artillery; Lieutenant C. Campbell served with 22nd Manchester Battalion; Lieutenant Laing with the East Surreys; Lieutenant White joined the 9th Royal Scots; while G.S. Bogle and J.E. Anderson had just received commissions in the Royal Engineers. Major J.K. Cochrane, of the Leinster Regiment, had held until recently the post of Director of Military Operations in New Zealand, and upon his return to England he was appointed to the General Staff of the 12th Division of Kitchener's New Army. Major-General J.M. Babington, who had been the military Commandant in New Zealand from 1902-07 was given command of the 23rd Division. The Hon. J.D. Boyle joined the Royal Flying Corps, and Major G.S. Richardson of the N.Z. Staff Corps joined the newly created Naval Division, along with the Lieutenant Bernard Freyberg who had just arrived in England after fighting in the Mexican Civil War for General Villa.

Other young New Zealanders at universities near London had chosen to join King Edward's Horse in favour of their university's Officer Training Company. Soon 'the Horse' had reached its full strength and had a long waiting list. This led to Captain Norton Griffiths's 'Irregular Horse' becoming a popular alternative. An infantry reserve company, called 'the British Section', was raised by Captain Lampen, NZSC, from New Zealanders living in England. New Zealand doctors in England volunteered for the Royal Army Medical Corps (RAMC), New Zealand nurses joined the Queen Alexandra's Reserve[64], the Red Cross or the St John's Ambulance. Most medical personnel were quickly sent to France and Belgium, where they would serve throughout the war with the British Army.

Amid this heady excitement, the *Wellington Evening Post* reported the more sobering news of the first New Zealander to be wounded in the war. Corporal M. Ryan had served in the Otago Hussars and had left for England with the intention of joining a cavalry unit, but considered to be too tall, he was advised to join a line regiment instead. He was serving in

France with the 1st King's Liverpool Regiment at Maubeuge, near the Belgian border, where the 6th Brigade (commanded by General Davies – another New Zealander) acted as the rearguard covering the British Expeditionary Force as it withdrew from Mons. He was hit in the leg by an artillery shrapnel round bursting fifty feet above the ground. Another countryman, Lieutenant H.J.I. Walker, from Auckland, who was serving with the Warwickshire Regiment, was reported as 'missing' and it was hoped that his name would appear later as a prisoner of war[65].

In New Zealand, the newspapers quickly replaced the joy of the New Zealand Expeditionary Force's (NZEF) successful capture of German Samoa with reports of the large scale fighting across Europe, and particularly in the northern sector of France and Belgium where the British Army seemed to have become bogged down. In time, many of those place names: Ypres, Messines, Choisy, Amiens, Longueval, Ploegstreet Wood and St Quentin, would become familiar to all New Zealanders.

The military set-backs and the retreat from Mons of the British Army, in no way paused the preparations of the NZEF as it mustered for war. Enlistment and training continued apace as a much larger contingent – termed the 'Main Body' – was readied to sail for England, where it would undergo training before being sent onto France. Due to the sheer numbers volunteering, strict medical standards applied across all four major recruiting districts, although there was awareness that their quota for men had to be filled as soon as possible.

The minimum height was 5'4", 111 lbs weight; chest measurement of 34" or better, good eyesight and preferably good teeth, (which often provided grounds for medical rejection). Men with false teeth were accepted. Once passed 'fit' and interviewed by an officer, the men were attested for active service and kitted out. They were instructed where and when to report next, which was often the local drill hall, parks such as Tahuna, Dunedin or even racecourses such as Awapuni near Palmerston North, before marching into established camps such as Trentham or Featherson as embarkation approached. Many needed to settle their business affairs and they would form later reinforcement drafts. No one wanted to fail their Army medical, but many did. A year later, with the ever-increasing demand for reinforcements, those rejected in 1914 would be just what the recruiters were looking for.

By the 28th of August, the 'Main Body', also jokingly termed, 'Bill Massey's Tourists', after the Prime Minister of the time, was ready to sail for England. The expeditionary force totalled 8,574 men, with 3,818 horses. Its structure differed from that foreseen in 1910 and despatched during the South African War. It comprised:

> Headquarters with three sections from the Signals Company, Army Pay and Base Depot
>
> 1 Mounted Brigade comprising: 3 Mounted Regiments; 1 Field Troop of Engineers, 1 Mounted Army Service Corps Troop; and 1 independent Regiment being the Otago Mounted Rifles;
>
> 1 Brigade of Infantry, comprising 4 battalions;
>
> 1 Brigade Field Artillery with an Ammunition Column;
>
> 1 Signal Troop New Zealand Engineers:
>
> 1 Mounted Brigade Field Ambulance; 1 Field Ambulance with Dental Surgeons and a Veterinary detail.

The departure from Wellington was delayed as the New Zealand Government was reluctant for it to sail without an adequate naval escort. HMS *Psyche* and HMS *Philomel* were the only escort ships available to accompany the convoy, and with the whereabouts of the powerful German East Asia Squadron[66] unknown, the threat was considered too great.

This was borne out by two separate incidents: on the 16th of September the German cruisers *Scharnhorst* and *Gneisenau* had lain off Apia in German Samoa without incident, watched by the recently arrived New Zealand garrison. Presumably they did not want to shell German territory, though on the 30th of September they had no such qualms when they bombarded the town of Papeete (in French Tahiti).

The fear of German naval action did not entirely stop shipping crossing the Pacific. Sappers Harold Dick and Alex Angus serving with the Samoa Advance Force as Railway Engineers applied for and were granted discharges while still in Samoa. They left Samoa on the 26th of September and upon arriving back in New Zealand they joined the Engineer Troop of the Mounted Brigade that were about to leave as part of the Main Body.

The British Admiralty eventually agreed to send a more powerful escort from their China Station given the German threat, and on the 16th of October the convoy of ten N.Z. troop transport ships finally left Wellington harbour bound for Hobart and then Albany, escorted by *HMS Philomel, HMS Pyramus, HMS Minotaur* and the Japanese battle cruiser *H.I.J.M.S. Ibuki*. The Imperial Japanese Navy continued to play a major role throughout the Great War, regularly using the port at Singapore.

At Albany, on the west coast of Australia, the New Zealand convoy joined the 28 Australian transport ships carrying the Australian Imperial Force (AIF). The route to Europe was originally agreed to be via the Cape of Good Hope as a revolt had broken out amongst the Dutch in South Africa and the New Zealand and Australian troops would be useful reinforcements for General Botha.

It was calculated that coaling stops and fuel consumption were likely to present major problems if the convoy were to take that route, however, by the end of October Botha had calmed the unrest. With the need for military assistance removed, the Suez Canal route was adopted.

News reached them that on the 28th of October a German light cruiser, the *Emden* had suddenly appeared in the port of Penang in the Straits Settlements and commenced to sink a Russian cruiser and a French destroyer. Two British warships were now hunting her in the Indian Ocean. The massive convoy left Australian waters on the 1st of November, accompanied by two additional escorts, the cruisers HMAS *Sydney* and HMAS *Melbourne,* concerns remaining as to the whereabouts of the German Squadron in the Pacific.

Once the convoy had set sail, it was announced that on the 29th of October two Turkish warships, the former German battle-cruiser *Goeben* and the light-cruiser *Breslau*, both manned by German crews, had bombarded the Russian Black Sea ports of Odessa, Sebastopol and Novorossiysk. Germany had given Turkey the ships to replace the two ships confiscated by Britain back in August. The Russians declared war on Turkey on the 2nd of November, followed by separate declarations from both France and Britain. Turkey's entry into the war meant that the conflict was no longer limited to European battlefields. The Middle East was now drawn in and the main shipping route through the Suez Canal was threatened by the Turkish garrisons in the Sinai and Palestine. Every major nation, apart from America, was now involved in the burgeoning conflict.

The troop convoy sailed as tactically as possible despite the smoke plumes emitted by all the coal burning warships and transports. On the morning of the 9th of November, an SOS signal was received from the Cocos Islands that a strange warship has been sighted. *HMAS Sydney* immediately left the convoy and in the naval action that followed, it engaged, out-gunned and beached the German cruiser *SMS Emden*.

After the excitement of the naval action and with future threats removed, the anticipated crossing of the equator gave rise to a degree of onboard frivolity. The routine coal stop at the port of Columbia in Ceylon (now Sri Lanka) provided a change of scenery for the troops. At Ceylon, the convoy bid farewell to the *Ibuki* who left to join the South Japanese Squadron, while a contingent from the Ceylon Rifles Regiment, bound for Egypt joined the troop convoy. They were later attached to the Wellington Infantry Regiment as a fifth company for Gallipoli and eventually served as the guard for Lieutenant General Birdwood and the ANZAC Headquarters at Anzac Cove.

Training continued onboard ship, with lectures undertaken by the company officers, as well as parades and drill on deck.

At their next coaling stop at Aden, the Australians and New Zealanders mixed with British soldiers bound for India. From them they first heard of the staggering losses inflicted upon British battalions fighting on the Western Front, particularly the near annihilation of some battalions. The convoy finally left Aden on the 26th of November and escorted by *HMS Hampshire* it set a course for the final leg of the journey, through the Suez Canal and on to England. There, Colonel E. S Heard, a British Army officer who had served in New Zealand, had already arrived to take charge of a department at the War Office, specially formed to direct the Overseas Contingents once they arrived in England. He would later be appointed Chief Staff Officer for the Canadian troops.

By now the troops were familiar with their on-board routines and were aware that they would be undertaking further training before facing the Germans. The extent of British losses would have been the subject of considerable conversation and analysis amongst the soldiers. Whether they understood that over 60% of casualties resulted from artillery action, with the machine gun accounting for perhaps another 30% in those early clashes on the Western Front, is unclear. If they did, their training did not reflect the acquisition of such knowledge.

With Turkey now allied with Germany, Churchill and the War Cabinet looked for a way to get the Royal Navy into the war. The Dardanelle Straits, linking the Aegean Sea to the Sea of Marmara and thence to the Black Sea, were controlled by Turkey and had been closed off and mined. Churchill began to consider a plan to force open the Straits, thereby providing a direct supply route to Russia and at the same time knocking Turkey out of the war. For a reckless Churchill, it was worth the gamble.

Chapter Five: A fine lot of fellows

The sudden influx of new recruits across Britain resulted in many regiments quickly reaching their allocated capacity, so waiting lists were created until the War Office announced their intentions for additional regiments. In the meantime, those regiments overwhelmed by the number of volunteers were faced with a more immediate problem of just where to house all of these recruits. Barrack buildings were in dire shortage, as were messing facilities, uniforms, equipment, and instructors. This situation became more acute once the Regular and Reserve regiments became fully mobilised and readied for embarkation to France, with other Reservist battalions undertaking guard duty for important locations such as ports, bridges and railway junctions against would-be saboteurs.

There were numerous New Zealanders living in England at this time, either attending universities or engaged in commerce and industry. Many of these men had previously enlisted with British Territorial or Reservist battalions such as the Fusiliers or King Edward's Horse, as part of their university or professional associations. Those men had mustered at their regiments' drill halls in August and avoided the queues outside the recruitment depots.

At the New Zealand High Commission in London, most of the military staff officers had been seconded to British Army regiments. Only Captain Francis Lampen remained as the sole New Zealand military representative. He was continually inundated with requests from New Zealanders in England wishing to 'do their bit', or New Zealand militia reservists looking to be assigned to a regiment. Some applicants were placed with regiments, such as the Artillery, Medical Corps and Royal Engineers where they received Commissions. With the remainder, Lampen had the notion of raising a company of Infantry. Sir Thomas McKenzie, the New Zealand High Commissioner at the time, readily agreed with the concept and authorised its formation in August 1914. This would be a company of reinforcements once the Dominion's Expeditionary Force[67] arrived in England.

The company soon attracted men with varied military experience, social backgrounds and geographies. A number of the men had fought in the South African War and one had even fought in the Spanish-American War. Some lived in England; some were on business there, while others had come to England specifically to enlist.

Robert Wright from Belfast had served in the Boer War and lived in New Zealand for a number of years. Frank Burton had served for nine years with the Grenadier Guards, had settled in New Zealand for six years and in Norfolk Island for eight years before making his home in the Scilly Isles.

Among those born in New Zealand were: two well known rugby players, Lancelot Todd who played for Wigan and Ellis Wrigley, a farmer from Auckland living in Hampshire; university students John Hamon Massey from Invercargill, Alan Wallace and Frederick Maunsell both from Auckland; James Lucena from Hawera; Cedric Salmon, a qualified engineer from Hawera; Francis Fear a cheese maker from Wellington; and Norman Kwongtsu Lowe a civil engineer from Dunedin.

There were also volunteers of German parentage - Fredrik Reichardt, a sailor from Wanganui and Otto Friedlander, a mining engineer from Ashburton; as well as men from Canada. Robert Armfeldt was from British Columbia and Albert Osment, a carpenter, was from Ontario. Alexander Abbey was from Russia. Amongst the Australians who enlisted there were Angus McKenzie from Tasmania; James Holland, a Brisbane farmer and Edward Ruddock a medical student at Edinburgh University.

The contingent was called 'The British Section' and for several weeks they received training in military drill on Wandsworth Common, South London until a suitable training area was found for them. Being part of the NZEF, they received the N.Z. Government pay scale of five shillings a day for a private soldier serving overseas, plus lodgings; as opposed to the standard British Army pay for private soldiers of one shilling a day plus allowances. During their weeks on Wandsworth Common the

German threat to Paris had been alleviated, the French and British Armies had rallied and the Allies had advanced northwards from Aisne to Messines.

After protracted diplomatic involvement, part of the military area around Salisbury Plain was eventually made available to the Dominion troops from Canada, Australia and New Zealand who would soon be arriving in England to undergo military training. The New Zealand camp was to be next to the existing Bulford Camp, so the British Section entrained in early autumn for Bulford. The new huts in which they were to be housed had not yet been started by civilian sub-contractors, so tents sufficed in the interim while the camp was erected. They were not alone in their predicament, as also camped amongst the villages and valleys of the Plain was an influx of 24,000 volunteers for the new Kitchener's Army, making the entire area one long tapestry of tented military camps.

At Bulford throughout that late September the weather was warm and dry, although the nights gradually began to get colder. After suffering frosty mornings and wet weather under canvas for two weeks the British Section patience ended and they took possession of their half-finished corrugated iron huts. Rapidly organising fatigue parties, they completed and occupied around a dozen huts by the end of September. Crucially, each hut had two stoves installed for heating.

The dry weather abruptly ended in the middle of October and an exceptionally wet period brought over an inch of rain in five days. During this period, the first Canadian and Newfoundland troops arrived at Plymouth and proceeded to Salisbury Plain occupying the West Downs and Pond Farm areas. A similar situation existed for them with their barracks and camp facilities not ready, so tents were provided.

The military days at Bulford comprised company drill, field work, signalling, infantry training and musketry on the ranges. The field work consisted of route marches along muddy and increasingly overused roads. The intensity of these marches rose and by November the British Section could march twelve miles a day carrying the standard British Infantry equipment load of around 70lbs.

Rain and high winds dominated the area of Salisbury Plain throughout October and November. Not only was it extremely wet, it was also getting colder and regular flooding became a feature. Training for the tens of thousands of Canadians and Kitchener's Army soldiers, who were all still under canvas, became almost non-existent.

There were no sleeping cots in the tents which would have helped keep the sleeping men off the wet ground. So as the ground became increasingly water logged, sleeping on the ground became impossible. Added to the problem was an insufficient supply of dry straw or hay for the men's mattresses, as it was also needed for the horses. Blankets soon became damp and then thoroughly wet through.

Exhausted men tried vainly to dry rain soaked uniforms and blankets, and keep themselves clean and warm, despite the mud, the cold and the persistent damp that permeated every tent and every blanket. Rations for the battalion cookhouses and fuel for the cookers soon depleted as supply wagons and vehicles could not get through the mud.

Hot food and even a hot cup of tea became luxuries. The area near the railway station was renamed 'Codford in the Mud'[68] by the British soldiers whose tented camps were soon reduced to tiny islands surrounded by a sea of knee deep mud. Discipline became an issue and the medical authorities were increasingly anxious about the risk of pneumonia in such conditions.

Colonel H.G. Chauvel, the Australian representative at the War Office in London, concluded that a similar plight awaited the Australian and New Zealand contingents once they arrived in England. Additionally, with an estimated 180,000 men[69] now camped on Salisbury Plain in November, the overcrowding would not bode well for a high standard of training. He took his concerns to the Australian High Commissioner, who in turn sought to avert the problem by discussing the matter directly with Lord Kitchener. At the time the Australian and New Zealand contingents were nearing Egypt. It was quickly agreed that the men from the South Pacific would disembark in Egypt and undertake training there before joining the British Army on the Western Front.

With hindsight it was a wise decision, as by February 1915 nearly 24 inches of rain had fallen across the entire Salisbury Plain training area. It must have been totally miserable for the Canadians and British soldiers there.

Chauvel would eventually command the 1st Australian Light Horse Brigade in Gallipoli, as part of the New Zealand & Australian Division, and in 1916 take command of the Anzac Mounted Division during the Sinai campaign, where he won several battles. He progressed to command the Desert Mounted Corps as a Lieutenant General during the fighting in Palestine in 1917.

Steaming steadily northwards through the Red Sea towards the Suez Canal, the Australian and New Zealand convoy received an urgent signal that they were to disembark in Egypt, at Alexandria. They were further informed that 'due to unforeseen circumstances'[70] the troops would undergo four months of intensive training in camps around Cairo, proceeding to 'The Front' from there. They would also be used to help protect the Suez Canal from possible Turkish attack. On 3rd December, after six weeks at sea, the convoy finally docked at Alexandria. Lieutenant-General Sir John Maxwell commanded the Forces in Egypt, and the Australians and New Zealanders now formed part of his command.

In the early hours of the 4th of December, the first trainload of New Zealanders reached their new home, the desolate camp at Zeitoun in the northern outskirts of Cairo. The area that denoted their new camp was kindly described by the men as being 'very rough'.

In preparation for their arrival, a contractor had begun to lay water pipes to the camp areas, though given the time this was still not finished. Maxwell was unaware that neither the Australians nor New Zealanders had bought any tents with them. Tents for 8,500 men were initially provided and the remainder would arrive from England two weeks later[71]. Until then, they had to cope as best they could. Those men without tents slept under the stars with their blankets or constructed some form of water-proof shelters. With such basic conditions confronting the men their bushman skill in building temporary shelters become invaluable, particularly having to cope with the bitterly cold Egyptian winter nights. Sanitation was a different matter entirely.

Over the next week the troops, their horses and equipment continued to be unloaded at the Port of Alexandria and entrained to Zeitoun. With the number of troops increasing daily, the NZEF started to organise hospitals for the sick, to provide sanitation, arrange rationing and build cook houses and messing facilities. Ordnance had to be unloaded, equipment issued and supplies procured. All this activity contributed towards making the camp comfortable and to the maintenance of military order. Zeitoun quickly became a canvas town, with dust and dirt getting into everything. With no sleeping cots in their tents the troops had to make do with only a blanket between them and the ground. There were no trees, no grass, no distractions; just featureless desert in a biblical landscape.

As the camp improved, so did the military training and by mid-December the Infantry battalions paraded each morning in full marching order and began their daily trek across the desert sands to their training area. It was important that after such a long sea voyage, in cramped conditions, that they regained the physical conditioning they had achieved prior to their departure from New Zealand.

Despite the disappointment in their surroundings, the NZEF's time at Zeitoun was a major point in its history. It provided the first opportunity for that force to train together as a single military formation. As the training commenced, most men realised that the idea of them visiting their relatives in England was a long way off, as was the dwindling prospect of a short war.

Chapter Six: Attacks on the British mainland

The British mainland was never immune from enemy attacks and by the end of 1914 the threat of invasion, fuelled partially by popular spy fiction and more recent audacious German coastal raids in the North-East, made invasion a real possibility in the minds of the British public and His Majesty's Government.

By August 1914 the Germans had begun laying sea mines in the shipping channels and along the British coast intending to harass the free movement of all naval and merchant vessels. The light cruiser "HMS Amphion" was an early victim in the North Sea to a sea mine and "HMS Audacious" also sank after hitting a mine off the coast of Northern Ireland in October 1914. Submarine warfare had also commenced with a number of Royal Navy cruisers and light cruisers being torpedoed in various parts of the North Sea during the first three months of the war.

The first naval engagement between the Royal Navy and the German Imperial Navy occurred on the 3rd of November 1914 when a German Naval squadron appeared off Great Yarmouth. Unmolested they began sea mine laying operations along the harbour channel. For their temerity, they were eventually engaged by British destroyers. The Germans retired after damaging three British patrol trawlers and having fired at the town where their shells exploded on the beach area in front of the town. No civilian casualties were reported. Later that day a British submarine leaving the harbour struck one of the sea mines. It sank with a loss of twenty-four naval personnel killed or wounded. Amidst these events and mounting concern, there was an unshaken faith amongst the public that the Royal Navy would protect the coastal areas of Britain.

By mid December, brisk Christmas shopping was underway as the public busied itself buying all those special treats and gifts that it could send to relatives and loved ones who were fighting in France or serving elsewhere in the Empire. The postal service was soon inundated with modest parcels that had been posted early in the hope that they would reach the addressee in time for Christmas. These festive preparations were a welcomed distraction from the uncertainty caused by war, although this was brutally disrupted in the early morning of the 15th-16th of December 1914 when several German battle cruisers launched a surprise naval raid along the Yorkshire coast. They successfully evaded the pursuing British Fleet and shelled Scarborough, Whitby and Hartlepool, reportedly killing 101 civilians and injuring another 200[72], as well as causing damage in the towns. When the Royal Navy eventually closed in, the German ships withdrew using a bank of North Sea mist to hinder any determined pursuit.

The outrage caused by these events provided useful propaganda for the military recruiters and soon recruitment posters proclaimed "Remember Scarborough". The greater menace lay not in the damage caused, but in the adverse effect on public morale. Who would protect their shores if the Royal Navy could not? Attitudes swayed from anger to helplessness.

Emotions aside, the Government began to believe that a German invasion was a real threat, although it conveniently overlooked the practicality that any sustained invasion would need access to channel ports for logistical support, none of which were held by the Germans.

The Royal Navy argued that it could protect the British coastline against large troop landings. It was the smaller scale naval raids which frustrated the Royal Navy as their ships could never decisively close with and engage with the enemy.

The other dilemma facing the Royal Navy was the detection of German submarines. These vessels favoured the stealth tactic of approaching shipping and coastal areas submerged and then surfacing to torpedo their victims or else bombard any opportunistic coastal targets, usually harbour buildings and railway lines, using their deck cannon.

The British Army had their own worries as the land defence against an invasion would normally be the responsibility of the Regular Army Infantry divisions, but these were already fully committed to the fighting in France. The task was instead passed to the partially trained and poorly equipped local Territorial battalions and Army Training establishments located along coastal areas. The BEF in France had first call on all trained manpower, weapons, munitions, aircraft, guns and other essential supplies, so home defence relied upon troops of a lesser fighting calibre armed with obsolete equipment. Invasion drills were conducted to boost public morale, but lacked any semblance of a military plan.

At Bulford Camp, an air of anticipation prevailed as the British Section was unexpectedly granted embarkation leave. Many took the opportunity to go home and celebrate an early Christmas with their families, relatives and friends. Then on the 12th of December, 1914 they marched out of Bulford Camp and embarked that night at 7pm from Southampton Dock on board the Troop Ship 'Dunera'. The wet, bleak and miserable night would not have dampened the excitement amongst the men, finally going off to war. Some thought they were bound for France, so obviously their destination had not been widely divulged.

A grateful Canadian Expeditionary Force soon took over the huts vacated by the British Section and they wasted no time in lending carpenters, bricklayers and unskilled labour to the civilian contractors to complete the construction of 'Sling Camp' as the weather worsened.

As the Australians were also in Egypt, the 2nd and 3rd Canadian Infantry brigades, along with their Engineers, occupied the Australian huts being constructed at Larkhill. Despite this unexpected increase of barrack huts, by Christmas 1914 there were still 11,000 Canadian troops under canvas[73] at West Downs.

The British Section's shipmates for their voyage to Egypt were the 2/7th Hampshires, a Territorial battalion bound for India and set to replace a Regular battalion that would be sent to France. The Hampshires' hygiene and eating habits were of constant amazement to the British Section. One particular feat was that of eating food off their knife. This caused surprise amongst the New Zealanders especially when no-one actually cut their mouth. The convoy's route took it past Gibraltar and Malta. It was a long trip and the men passed the time putting on concerts, reading, some training, and boxing matches. No alcohol was allowed aboard military transports, so apart from smoking, gambling soon became their other vice. The favourite card games were Faro and Crown, although a roulette wheel was also rigged up. On Sunday there was a Church Parade onboard ship.

The convoy dropped anchor at the port of Alexandria on the 24th of December 1914 where the British Section disembarked. Remaining onboard the ships were the lads from Hampshire, busy preparing for their Christmas celebrations. This was the closest that any of them got to Egypt. All they could do was to gaze in some wonderment at that foreign shoreline with all its different sights and smells and watch the ships being loaded and unloaded by a swarm of Egyptian boats in an incredibly busy harbour. Ironically, the NZEF would be back in England before the 2/7th Hampshire Regiment. By that evening the British Section had entrained for the 133 mile, eight hour trip to Helmeih near Cairo.

In late December, a group of sixty men reached England from the Federated Malay States. All had the intention of enlisting in the British Army. One was Roland Garret, who had served in the Wanganui Highland Volunteer Rifles and the Federated Malay States Volunteer Rifles. Upon learning that the NZEF were in Egypt and that the British Section had already left, Garret joined King Edward's Horse, until he could enlist in the NZEF.

Also, arriving in England via 'Bibby' Line[74] from Ceylon was Private Hugh McLoughlin of the Otago Infantry Regiment. McLoughlin had enjoyed too good a time ashore in Colombo during the NZEF convoy's brief stay in mid November. Consequently he had failed to return onboard his troopship before curfew and had been left behind. He joined the "stay behind party" from the British Section at Bulford, who were finalising administrative matters. In January he accompanied them to Egypt with a number of recently joined New Zealand volunteers. Upon re-joining the NZEF in Egypt at the end of January 1915, McLoughlin was charged with misconduct, as opposed to the more severe charge of desertion. He was found guilty and served four months in a military prison in Egypt before being discharged from the NZEF.

Chapter Seven: Creation of the New Zealand & Australian Division

After their arrival in Egypt, it was decided that the NZEF and AIF, would be formed into a single Corps, to be named the "Australian and New Zealand Army Corps", abbreviated to A. & N.Z.A.C [75] for military purposes. Major-General W.R Birdwood, a British Regular officer then serving with the Indian Army, was appointed to command it, although at the time of its formation he was still in India. He and his staff sailed from Bombay on the 12th of December and arrived in Cairo on the 21st of December.

The new Corps comprised three divisions: the 1st Australian Division; a Mounted Division; and a composite 'New Zealand and Australian Division' (NZ&A Division), under the command of the New Zealand commander General Sir Alexander John Godley. The newly formed NZ&A Division consisted of two infantry brigades: the New Zealand Infantry Brigade, commanded by Lt-Colonel F.E Johnston and the 4th Australian Infantry brigade, commanded by Colonel J. Monash; and two mounted brigades: 1st Australian Light Horse, commanded by Colonel H.G Chauvel and N.Z. Mounted Rifles, commanded by Brigadier-General A.H Russell, as well as artillery.[76] Godley was considered by Carlyon[77] as a 'robotic soldier, made for drill and peacetime soldiering and someone who fostered the attitude that all citizen-soldiers were amateurs'. Unfortunately, Godley was all the New Zealand military had in the way of a possible Divisional Commander at that time.

Godley's new Division was woefully lacking in essential skills. Its Stationary Medical Hospital was only staffed for the two original NZEF brigades, not a full Division. Its Army Service Corps lacked sufficient clerks, drivers, store men and the like, to staff the larger organisation and there were no Engineers[78].

When the NZEF Advance Party embarked for Samoa back in August 1914, it had taken with it two full sections of Engineers: 60 officers and men, as well as the N.Z. Railway Company, consisting of 258 officers and men , leaving a mere handful of trained Engineers in New Zealand. This resulted in none being available for attachment to the Main Body apart from a NZ Engineers Signal Troop of thirty-seven men under the command of Lieutenant E.J. Hulbert and a composite Territorial Mounted Field Engineer Troop of three officers and eighty men, attached to the N.Z. Mounted Brigade, under the command of Captain Shera. Shera had commanded No.3 Auckland Co. of N.Z. Field Engineers and had served in the Boer War as a lieutenant, where he had gained the King's Medal with two clasps.

When the NZEF eventually sailed from New Zealand there were no engineering stores and only a few tools, although the Mounted Engineers brought along their pontoons and the Mounted Brigade ASC Troop had wagons.

This absence of Field Engineers for the N.Z. Infantry Brigade is surprising, particularly at a time when British military thought favoured one Field Engineer Company per Infantry Brigade[79]. Given this ratio and the additional Australian brigade now being part of his command, Godley was woefully short of men and equipment for two Field Engineering Companies to support the Infantry Brigades and another engineering troop for the Mounted Brigade. The absence of such a vital battlefield asset was not ideal, although it would soon be partially resolved in a purely military way.

The British Section eventually arrived at Pont de Koubbeh station, a few miles outside Cairo, at 11:30pm Christmas Eve. As the tired men disembarked into the cold, mid winter Egyptian night, they began to unload their equipment and stores partially assisted by the dim station lighting. A number of staff officers came onto the platform so the men were fallen in for a hasty inspection. All went well until they were ordered to 'Fix Bayonets!' which they struggled to find amongst all the other equipment they were carrying. They then heard what Sapper Beamish described as a scream of 'Lampen take them away!' and looking over he saw for the first time General Godley sitting in his staff car with his 22 year old Guards Captain adjutant. Then to Beamish's surprise they drove away, without a word of welcome or any other address.[80]

Zeitoun camp did offer them a warm welcome from friends and family who had gathered to greet them. There was also a hot meal and they heard their first camp rumour - it involved them.

On parade the following morning, Christmas Day, Godley abruptly informed the British Section that they would be disbanded. The men would be allocated between an Engineer Field Company and the Army Service Corps. This confirmed the rumours of the night before. Godley advised them that they could choose either the Engineers or ASC, but he gave them a third option, which was being discharged and sent back to New Zealand. No one wanted that especially those who came from England, Ireland, Canada and Australia[81]. By 28th of December the dispersal of the British Section was well underway, as was a growing resentment towards Godley.

Confronted with a doubling in the administrative burden following the formation of the NZ&A Division, the ASC troops of the Mounted Brigade came under Divisional command. The ASC sought out men who were skilled in driving motorised transport and could repair mechanical engines. Also considered highly desirable was anyone familiar with dockyards or railway operations. The Port of Alexandria, with its railway system, was the NZEF lifeline for reinforcements, moving their sick and injured to hospitals, along with supply lines for munitions, foods, equipment, clothing, mail and all other military goods. The British Section possessed men suitably qualified for these duties.

The Field Engineers meanwhile, tended to attract many of the civil engineers, as well as carpenters, bricklayers, drivers, farmers, university students, teachers, draughtsman, artists, and accountants who had avoided joining the N.Z. Divisional Train. Leslie Shaw, the sixteen year old company bugler, also found a place with them. Interestingly, the electrical and marine engineers were divided roughly equally between the ASC and the Field Engineers.

Lieutenant Fitzherbert, Privates Patrick Holmes, Percy Thomas and James Mossman all joined Infantry or Mounted Rifle Regiments. Norman Clark and John Whitney joined the N.Z. Artillery as drivers. Lieutenant

Fredrick Hellaby was assigned staff duties. Captain Lampen was transferred to the N.Z. Divisional Train, N.Z. Army Service Corps – satirically referred to as "Ally Slopers Cavalry" after the *Judy* magazine cartoon character at the time.

In January 1915 a cablegram was sent to New Zealand asking for a second Field Company to be raised and the New Zealand newspapers immediately began to advertise this new company in an effort to attract recruits. It would take several months to recruit, train and fully equip the 2nd Field Company. This would be commanded by Major Barclay, a Boer War veteran, recently returned from Samoa. The 2nd Field Company was the first fully equipped field company to leave New Zealand, arriving in Egypt at the end of May 1915.

Chapter Eight: Formation of the 1st Field Company, New Zealand Engineers

Lieutenant-Colonel G.R. Pridham, Royal Engineers (R.E.), was appointed Commander Royal Engineers for the NZ&A Division. The responsibility to form and command the N.Z. Engineers 1st Field Company was given to Captain S.A. Ferguson R.E., and Captain McNeil R.E., was appointed as the chief instructor. All three men were British Royal Engineer officers then serving with the Army of Occupation in Egypt.

The 1st Field Company consisted originally of one hundred and twenty men, all from the British Section, divided into two sections, commanded by Captain Simson and Lieutenant Skelsey. The company was short of about one hundred men, so volunteers were sought amongst the Infantry battalions. The request resulted in only thirteen Main Body men coming forward, one was Bruce Joll who resigned his commission as a 2nd Lieutenant with the Wellington Mounted Rifles to serve as a Sapper with the Field Company.

When the N.Z. Infantry Brigade was hurriedly mobilised on the 25th of January to the Canal to oppose an expected Turkish attack, the N.Z. Field Engineers were not sufficiently trained or equipped to support them. It was therefore no surprise that the Australian Engineers saw action instead. The New Zealanders remained behind in Zeitoun to continue with equipping, training and organisation. The desert climate and the cold January winds conspired to increase their discomfort and frustration. There was so much dust and sand in the air that it sometimes resembled a heavy fog.

The No. 1 Field Company finally came up to its full strength of around two hundred officers and men in February when the 2nd Reinforcement arrived in Egypt from New Zealand. Fifty-nine tradesmen were reassigned from the Infantry to serve as Field Engineers.

This would have been a 'patchwork' command for Captain Ferguson. The majority of the men had been trained as infantry. In their ranks were qualified and highly experienced civil, marine and mining engineers as well as skilled tradesmen. Many of the original British Section formed the No.1 (British) Section; they knew their New Zealand officers and NCOs and had established a common bond throughout their time training together in England. The other three sections were cobbled together with the remaining British Section, Main Body volunteers, 2nd Reinforcement and commanded by newly appointed officers.

The New Zealanders had their own militia standards and bridled at the "spit and polish" British Army approach overseen by the British Royal Engineer officers who were unfamiliar with colonial troops. Into this cauldron was added disgruntled ex-infantry men, the desert heat, Egyptian flies, a sub-standard camp, side effects from their recent inoculations, their resentment of Godley and an exasperating lack of equipment. The entire situation would have created a general desire to be somewhere else, and preferably not with the Field Engineers.

Organisation and training became immediate priorities before a cohesive, military formation could be placed into the field.

The discipline, previously more relaxed, became stricter. Sapper Felix Thetford soon received three days punishment for not taking proper care of his rifle. Maurice Newbould and Alan Wallace were more fortunate after being arrested in Cairo by the military pickets for being drunk and disorderly. Captain Ferguson dismissed the behaviour with a caution, and a week later[82] Newbould was promoted to 2nd Lieutenant and Wallace to Sergeant.

The 1st Field Company now consisted of four sections, with No.1 (or B) Section commanded by Captain Simson, the South African War veteran; No.2 Section commanded by Lieutenant Skelsey; No.3 Section commanded by the newly promoted 2nd Lieutenant S.W Paine recently transferred from the Mounted Field Troop; and No.4 Section commanded by 2nd Lieutenant Maurice Newbould having received a field commission. Lieutenant Fred Waite, who had arrived with the Mounted Field Troop was appointed company adjutant. Later, 2nd Lieutenant the Honourable R.P Butler R.E joined the company in the

Headquarters section.

The new Field Company was expected to be able to function wherever the N.Z. Infantry Brigade operated, while the Engineers in the Mounted Field Troop, under the command of Captain Shera, filled the similar role for the Mounted Brigade.

Time, like the Engineers' equipment, was in short supply, and the pace of training did not slacken as each man grappled with the skills and knowledge that under normal peacetime conditions a Royal Engineer had six months to learn. As the organisational problems were being addressed, the training aspects focused on the small matters of obtaining engineering supplies and equipment such as wire, posts, timber, tools, pontoons, wagons, horses, harnesses and numerous other items. They managed to have some of their war materials made in the various government workshops throughout Cairo, while other items were purchased from local shops, including a number of bicycles.

Training programmes were devised and areas suitable for instruction and conducting exercises were allocated. The Field Engineers learnt how to create entrenchments, how to differentiate types of wiring, the use of explosives, mining, road-building, pontooning, the construction of fortifications, the transportation of equipment by wagon and other essential field skills. They were taught field geometry, how to use a map and compass and how trench systems connected and interlinked. In the desert environment they became expert in the use of sandbags to sure up the entrenchments that they dug in the soft sand. They soon dreaded the hot khamsin desert winds, which could obliterate days of trench work under clouds of drifting sands.

Bomb making and the means of throwing these became a keen subject. The Engineers experimented with devices of varying explosive potential and narrowly missed being injured in the process. In their opinion, some of their home-made bombs were fearsome contraptions.

The officers were also busy moulding the skills and effectiveness of their sections. They practiced various engineering techniques, familiarised themselves with British Army equipment and methods, as well as attending courses designated as essential for their rank. During this time, Godley insisted on full Brigade manoeuvres and later NZ&A Divisional exercises. Pridham undoubtedly evaluated the benefit of the Field Engineers involvement in these exercises against the pressing demands of his training cycle considering the competency displayed by the various sections, the criticality of instruction in which they were engaged and the on-going commitments they already had around the building of the Divisional camp at Zeitoun.

A memorable moment during one of these exercises occurred when the Field Engineers of 1st (British) Section were tasked with preparing a defensive position and receiving attacking infantry. By way of note, it is interesting that the Brigade considered the Field Engineers capable of this task, once normally considered the realm of the infantry. The digging of the positions had been particularly hard, with rocky ground preventing any practical excavations beyond a depth of three feet. Plain wire had been instructed to be used for the exercise, but the Engineers managed to intermingle barbed wire with the other defensive entanglements. Additionally they added trip wires, tin cans attached to the wire for early warning, dummy mines and flares.

During the night the rattle of the tin cans announced the arrival of an "enemy" patrol. Some of the "enemy" became entangled in the barbed wire; their uniforms ripped and torn from their efforts to try and free themselves. They were rapidly taken prisoner by the Engineers. Soon a frontal attack was mounted by the "enemy" onto the position which failed when they could not get through the wire. A second attack was mounted and the Engineers added to the "enemies" annoyance by firing their blank rounds into the attackers. When the attacking infantry did not "die" the Engineers began throwing stones at them. The "enemy" were eventually forced to manually haul the wire away in order to capture the position, though for the exercise purposes, most of them were already "dead"[83]. For the ex-Infantryman amongst the Engineers, it would have been considered a good night's work and for days afterwards the subject of soldierly banter with the infantry.

During these exercises, few lessons from the fighting in France were included. As a result, the stopping power of the machine gun and the destructive effect of concentrated artillery bombardments were conveniently disregarded in Godley's manoeuvres. This lack of imagination reduced the exercises to a style similar to Boer War training[84]. In most instances the Field Engineer sections merely followed the Infantry and Mounted columns through the desert, then dug in, fortified the positions, and moved on again. Other than route marching, the exercises introduced few newly acquired skills.

As the weather became warmer, training was restricted to early mornings and evenings to avoid the heat of the day. The afternoon route marches were also curtailed. When not training, the Engineers were granted leave to go to Cairo or they could relax in the Zeitoun camp, perhaps catching up with their friends and relatives in other regiments. The men occupied their weekend afternoons with concerts, boxing matches, tennis and rugby games; even polo was played.

The camp conditions gradually improved as bath and shower tents, cook houses, and mess halls were erected. Although these added to the overall comfort, disease was inevitable and there were numerous outbreaks of influenza resulting in troops being hospitalised and unable to train. One early victim to disease was Sapper Eugene Bonsor who died on the 28th of February 1915 in the N.Z. Hospital in Cairo. He was eighteen years old and had been a British Section volunteer from Surrey, in England. Many diseases were carried by flies but the Anzac soldier's habit of not being too fussy about where and what they ate when off duty also frequently accounted for illness. Many soldiers were hospitalised as a result of outbreaks of dysentery. In June 1915 meningitis was brought into Zeitoun by reinforcements arriving from the over crowded conditions at Trentham Camp in New Zealand.

On the night of the 10th of April, 1915 the NZ&A Division less the Mounted Brigade, left Zeitoun. This time the entire 1st Field Company went with them, only leaving several drivers behind to care for the horses.

As they mounted their lumber wagons or climbed aboard their assigned train carriages bound for the port of Alexandria, they would have known that they had succeeded in preparing for war in twelve weeks, with minimal equipment, in difficult training conditions, and with a great deal of improvisation. Now they joined the NZ&A Division going to war. There were still valuable skills to be acquired, but for now grit, intelligence, and sheer luck would be the currencies needed to fill any gaps.

Chapter Nine: An original undertaking - Gallipoli

The rugged Turkish peninsula of Gallipoli lying between the Aegean Sea and the Dardanelle Straits was known to the British from past encounters. The Dardanelle Straits, or the "Narrows" as they were also known, had been forced in 1807 by a British Fleet commanded by Sir John Duckworth. He had managed to enter the Sea of Marmara, but had paid dearly when getting out, due to the effectiveness of the cannon fire from the Turkish fort defences along the coastal straits. Later in 1854 during the Crimean War, Britain, France and Turkey were allied against Russia and the Gallipoli area was used by both the Navy and military for encampments and provision purposes. The people, climate, topography and military advantages of the area had been familiar then to both France and Britain, but by 1915 most of this knowledge had lapsed.

Now the ally and the opponent had changed places: Turkey was the adversary and Russia the friend. At the start of the war Russia possessed limited industrial capacity to efficiently supply its vast armed forces opposing the German Army in the east. It quickly fell on France and Britain to help to equip the Russian military in exchange for much needed grain. As long as Russia remained a plausible threat along the Eastern Front, they would deny Germany any opportunity of transferring troops to the fighting on the Western Front. With matters so finely balanced there, it was believed that the arrival of fresh troops from the Eastern Front would tip the advantage in Germany's favour. It was therefore of vital strategic importance that the German Ninth Army was kept fully engaged in the east, fighting the Russians.

With few supply routes to Russia at the Allies' disposal, it was eventually decided in January 1915 to approve plans put forward by Winston Churchill, First Lord of the Admiralty for a naval attack on the Dardanelles. By forcing the narrow strait of the Dardanelles and sailing to Constantinople, the fleet could force Turkey, who was considered a weak enemy, to surrender thereby "knocking them out of the war" and opening up a sea route to supply Russia.

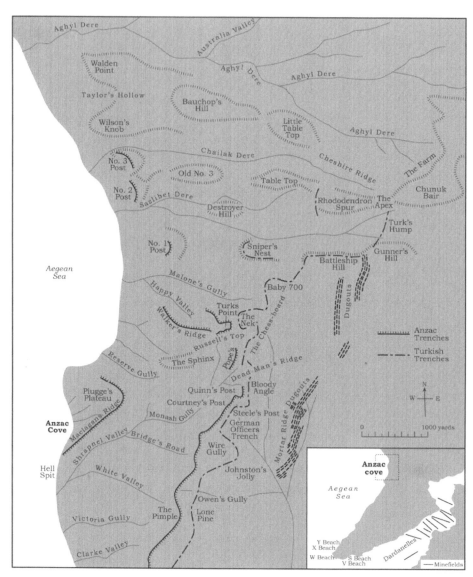

Anzac and Turkish positions during the Gallipoli Campaign. The terrain was comprised of deep gullies and razor back ridges, which made offensive actions difficult.

Drawing by Jenny Kynaston.

Churchill knew that the Royal Navy had a large number of obsolete, pre-Dreadnought class battleships, which although of no use against the German High Seas Fleet in the North Sea, could be useful in another theatre. The initial plan was that the attack on the Dardanelles would be made by the Royal Navy with a token force of Army or Royal Marines required for routine occupation tasks after the Strait had been captured.

The Gallipoli campaign, as it would become known, began on the 19th of February 1915 with a strong Anglo-French fleet bombarding the forts along the Aegean coast which protected the Narrows. This was followed up with shore landings by parties of Royal Marines, who confirmed damage to the outer forts. Strong south-westerly gales and low visibility suspended further operations and the Marines were withdrawn. Further attempts to break through into the Sea of Marmara occurred on the 25th of February and the 1st of March, but the only real effect of these efforts was to make the Turks fully aware of the vulnerability of their coastal defences.[85]

It became apparent through these failures that ground forces would be needed to eliminate the Turkish mobile artillery hindering the minesweepers from clearing a safe path through the minefields for the larger ships. Consequently, on the 12th of March 1915 Lord Kitchener appointed General Sir Ian Hamilton to command the Mediterranean Expeditionary Force. The MEF would "secure command of the Dardanelles" and the Royal Navy was tasked with "landing the Army and supporting it till its position is secure, after which the Navy will attack the fortifications at the Narrows, assisted by the Army."[86]

Hamilton expressed his thoughts when he left England to take up his new command by writing: "When I set out for the Dardanelles on Friday the 13th of March 1915 to command an unknown Army against an unknown enemy in an unknown country that was an original undertaking."[87]

The "unknown Army" under Hamilton's command comprised the Australian 1st Division and the New Zealand and Australian Division; the Regular British 29th Division; the British 10th Division from

Kitchener's New Army; the Royal Naval Division (RND) and the French Oriental Expeditionary Corps (including four Senegalese battalions).

The New Zealanders would not have been totally unknown to Hamilton. He had visited that country in May 1914 in his role as the Inspector General of Overseas Forces, and a lasting memory for him was that on the day he arrived at Invercargill, the one millionth New Zealander was born.[88]

On 18th March, sixteen battleships launched an audacious naval attack. The objectives were the same: to force the Narrows and bombard all the forts along its length; sweep a path through the known minefield; enter the Sea of Marmara and engage and destroy the two German capital ships[89] outside Constantinople. The Army, under Hamilton, would then be landed and advance along both sides of the Narrows to secure the forts. The Anzac Corps would be landed near Ari Burnu, advance across the Peninsula and link up with the British and French forces. The goal was to occupy Constantinople[90].

On paper it was straightforward; unfortunately during the naval action the fleet was severely damaged by sea mines recently laid *parallel* to the shore rather than across the bay and by the Turkish shore-based artillery. It withdrew. Three battleships had been sunk (HMS *Ocean* and HMS *Irresistible* and the French *Bouvet*), while the battle cruiser HMS *Inflexible* and the French battleships *Suffren* and *Gaulois* were badly damaged. Not since Trafalgar had the Royal Navy suffered such losses in a single engagement.

Although Churchill and others urged Vice-Admiral de Robeck to attack again, he decided that no further attempts would be made until the Army had been securely landed.

It was later reported that de Robeck was too distraught by the losses to conduct another action. Unbeknown to him, ammunition for the Turkish large guns had almost been expended and another attempt would not be as vigorously defended. One more roll of the dice and de Robeck had a good chance of forcing the Narrows. Further action was not ordered and the naval campaign, through silent consensus, ended. The only other naval action took place on the 17th of April when the submarine E15 attempted to force the new minefield and was taken off course by the strong current and beached, where upon the Turkish shore batteries disabled it. The surviving crew were taken prisoner and Royal Navy vessels torpedoed E15 in position shortly afterwards to prevent the Turks from salvaging her.

Looking towards Ari Burnu from the eastern end of Walker's Ridge. The razor like ridgeline on the left is "The Sphinx" and behind that is Anzac Cove.

Chapter Ten: Dig in and stick it out – the Anzac landings

The N.Z. Field Engineers were assigned to a captured German cargo boat, the "Goslar" which had been left idle in the harbour at Alexandria for eight months. It was dirty, covered in coal dust below decks and swarming with brown and black beetles. They shared it with the N.Z. Field Ambulance and Army Service Corps.

After loading their horses, wagons and other equipment, the men settled into their sleeping quarters, which for the Engineers were on the deck directly below the horses' stalls. The urine and water from the stalls unfortunately dripped through into the men's quarters and with dysentery already rife, the "Goslar" was declared unsanitary, taken back alongside the quay, unloaded and thoroughly cleaned. By the 17th of April the Field Ambulance, Army Service Corps and Engineers had re-loaded all their equipment, including a supply of the explosive gun-cotton.

Those with dysentery were "cured" thanks to liberal spoonfuls of Castor Oil and the "Goslar" began steaming north along with numerous other vessels. Their next stop would be the sheltered port of Mudros, on the island of Lemnos near the Dardanelle Straits.

The 21st of April was the original date for the Gallipoli landings, but due to rough seas and high winds they were delayed. The 23rd of April dawned bright, so it was decided that the landings would be executed on the 25th of April. Final preparations were made.

Early on the morning of the 25th of April the convoy upped anchors and left the harbour.

Finally they were steaming towards the Dardanelles and the Gallipoli peninsula. There they would knock the Turks out of the war as their Generals had ordered. They knew that the Turks considered the peninsula to be impregnable, and were ready for a tough time during the initial landings. The troops were warned to conserve their water and not to waste ammunition as they advanced inland. They were told that the eyes of the world were upon them, and with the help of God and the Navy they would overwhelm the Turkish positions on the peninsula and help to bring the war one step closer to ending.

On the 25th of April 1915 troops landed on the Gallipoli peninsula around Cape Helles, Gaba Tepe and what was to be later called Anzac, - the cove where the Australian and New Zealand Army Corps first landed.

By mid-day on the 25th of April, the Engineers were lined up along the decks of the "Goslar" watching the infantry of the Anzac Corps disembark from their boats and onto the beach regardless of the Turkish artillery and rifle fire. No one was aware that they were being landed at the wrong place; they were a mile further north of Z Beach than planned. The valleys, ridges and terrain at Anzac Cove cannot be adequately described; they have to been seen and explored. The terrain is rugged, consisting of sheers cliff faces, deep valleys and a tangled collection of high ridge lines interconnecting at various points. It is broodingly isolated and dangerous. Terrain that on a map appears to be flat, is in fact punctured by two or three deep valleys. The gradients are steep, and under fire it would have been lung pumping, leg burning work.

The Engineers carried 45lbs of equipment, fifty rounds of ammunition and they had their water bottles filled with tea. They did not carry blankets, only their waterproof sheets. By 4pm, after transferring to the destroyer HMS *Foxhound* they climbed aboard barges and began rowing with no great skill towards the beach.

Reaching the gravelly shore, one of the Engineers' boats ran up alongside another full of the wounded. Urged by an excited Corporal Abbey to smartly disembark from their beached vessel, Sapper Farrer jumped onto the boat filled with wounded soldiers, intending to make a short jump into shallow water. In his haste, he tripped on one of that boat's rowlocks and fell head first into three feet of water; soaking him, his clothing and equipment[91].

Incoming bursts of shrapnel provided further encouragement to move quickly off the pebble beach and up to the safety and shelter of the cliffs. They reached there as a dislocated group, and during a brief respite, subconsciously captured their intense personal memories of the moment. They had a panoramic view of the hectic activity on the beach below them; the rows of dead and wounded, disorganised piles of supplies, men disembarking in increasingly rough waves, shouted commands, aerial shrapnel bursting and the continual shifting of khaki shadows on a chaotic, war strewn beach.

Some time passed before their officers located them. With fresh instructions, they fixed bayonets in readiness for combat and carrying their picks and shovels, moved eastwards, through Reserve Gulley and onto the high ground of Plugge's Plateau. It was early evening when they began digging fire trenches as a support line, overlooking the low ground towards The Sphinx to their left and Monash Gully to their right. Ahead, and further to the east, were the features later named 'Quinn's Post' and 'Courtney's Post'. The expectation among the Anzac commanders was that there would be a heavy Turkish counter attack by dawn. A line of trenches to support the dispersed Anzac line was therefore vital if it was to hold. There was also a rumour that the troops may be evacuated.

The trench line they dug was positioned forward of a single Australian howitzer gun that had gone into action, firing on the Turkish positions. In fact, it was the only artillery piece landed and engaging the Turks at that time along the whole of the Anzac line. Soon the Turkish artillery began to lob shells in its direction, much to the Engineers' unrest. Sergeant Otto Friedlander was wounded in the neck, Captain McNeil in the leg and Sapper Sunderland was evacuated after sustaining a gunshot wound to the head.

Later that evening, the 21st Indian Mountain Battery joined the action. To get into position, their gun laden mules had to jump across the trenches being dug by the Engineers. Captain Simson was active, directing and encouraging his men under enemy artillery fire for the first time.

Unlike the soft sands of Egypt, the ground was hard and stony which made for slow progress. Still, by late evening, spurred on by the artillery shelling and stray bullets – they had dug part of the trench down to the correct depth. They remained in that position for what became a wet night, surrounded by the constant noise of machine gun and rifle fire. When not on sentry look-out, they continued to dig and fortify the position, ensuring that it was capable of whatever task lay ahead.

Birdwood, Bridges and Godley had considered withdrawing their forces, but Hamilton informed them that it would take two days to re-embark the divisions already ashore at Anzac. Hamilton issued one of his rare orders of the campaign, telling his commanders to dig in and stick it out.

In the early hours of the morning, Corporal Saunders gathered up some men to dig gun emplacements. They walked up and down the beach area for several hours looking for, but not finding, any guns. At 6am they were back digging in their trench on Plugge's Plateau and being shelled by shrapnel.

Lieutenant Newbould took a party along a gully to dig for water, but the Turkish shelling and shrapnel prevented any real work from being carried out. The men spent most of the time sitting under a bank near the beach until it was safe to return. With the heavy fighting and the inability to locate water in Anzac Cove, re-supplies began to be landed from the naval ships.

Also finally being landed in the late morning, were the two New Zealand howitzers that Corporal Saunders and his party had been seeking during the night. It appears that the artillery was either waiting for daylight before they landed the guns, or until the decision to stay or evacuate was made by the Anzac commanders.

When news of the landing eventually reached Britain, the *Christchurch Times*[92] reported that:
"The disembarkment of the Army began before sunrise ...six different beaches were used, and the whole operation was covered by the fleet. The landing was immediately successful on five beaches, although opposed with vigour by a strongly entrenched enemy in successive lines, protected by barbed wire

entanglements, in some places fifty yards wide and supported by artillery. ..During the afternoon of Sunday, strong counter-attacks by the enemy began, and hard fighting took place."

Hamilton had met his 'unknown' enemy in their 'unknown' country, and his 'unknown' Anzac troops had performed extremely well, despite being in the wrong place, without water and taking more casualties than anticipated.

On the evening of the 26th of April, most of the field engineer sections were detailed to Walker's Ridge where they began to widen the existing track to allow artillery to be pulled up the hill. It rained, and the men were soon wet and cold. Other Engineers were assigned beach jobs, helping to establish their supply dump at "Hell's Spit", the southern extremity of Anzac Cove. Here, their stores of explosives, sandbags, any timber that was available, coils of wire, various tools, boxes of nails and other supplies were kept.

Lieutenant Newbould led No.4 section forward to the firing line at Walker's Ridge in an attempt to erect wire entanglements. This venture was short lived when the Turks counter-attacked and drove them back.

The Anzacs were fighting furiously for elbow room in their advanced positions around Quinn's Post, Courtney's Post, Walker's Ridge[93] and Pope's Hill and were suffering heavy losses as a result. With little time to prepare proper firing positions they were susceptible to the Turkish snipers, enfilading machine gun fire and heavy bombing. The stretcher bearers soon found themselves carrying the wounded men down and ammunition back up. With a sorry lack of stretchers and the sheer number of casualties, makeshift stretchers were constructed from rifles, puttees or waterproof sheets.

The precarious nature of the skirmishing had kept the infantry occupied and prevented them from establishing proper defensive trenches. From their hastily dug pits and natural folds in the ground, the Anzacs barely held on at the susceptible points of Quinn's Post and Walker's Ridge. Without battlefield instructions from Godley and Bridges, the men still held the belief that the Turks would be soon outflanked and would withdraw from the ridges, whereupon the Anzacs could begin their advance towards the Narrows. There seemed to be no doubt about this, so it made perfect sense to them to remain engaged in the scattered fighting rather than digging deep trenches that would not be needed. No-one bothered to tell them, even if perchance they knew, that the original battle plan was in tatters and they risked being swept off those narrow ridges at any time.

Inevitably, on the 27th of April, all the available N.Z. Field Engineers were sent forward into the more vulnerable positions to help to construct proper, more secure defensive lines, in accordance with Hamilton's "Dig, dig, dig until you are safe" message given to his Anzac commanders in the early hours of the 26th of April.

Dead men and dead mules littered the mile and a half of Shrapnel Gully that the Engineers tramped along from their dump at Hell's Spit to get up to the firing line of Quinn's Post, Courtney's Post and Walker's Ridge. The Anzacs had no time to bury the dead, nor would any attempt be made for several more days. The bodies were merely piled on top of one another in the gully and covered with groundsheets, blankets or whatever was available. It did not prevent the flies from feeding on the corpses, or lessen the sickening smell, but it did add some decency to the events of war.

As they climbed upwards through the muddy gullies, they continually stopped to allow the stumbling and slipping stretcher bearers to pass by with their wounded cargo and shout some words of encouragement. The gullies were the natural drainage for the rainwater and had been churned into mud by the constant traffic. Later the Engineers would construct steps from the empty wooden supply boxes making the job of the stretcher bearers easier, especially at night.

Half of the Engineers were assigned to work at Quinn's Post, while the other half worked at Walker's Ridge. At all other firing positions, like Steele's Post and the "Nek", the infantry dug in as best they could, though hindered by a shortage of picks and shovels. In all of these positions there were no support or communications trenches, just a single ragged line of shallow scraps and fighting hollows across or close to the ridgelines. It would take weeks of hard work before a recognisable military position emerged.

The Engineers moved forward with only their rifles and tools, running in certain places to avoid the snipers. Once in the position, they began to deepen and connect the shallow scrapings that the infantry had been using. These were barely deep enough for a man to lie down in. Their next task was to widen the tracks leading up from the gullies. This helped make the evacuation of the wounded easier and lessened the difficulties for the re-supplies arriving by donkey or fatigue parties, particularly at night in the wet weather.

The Turk and German commanders soon reasoned which gullies were used as supply routes to the firing line, so ordered their artillery to target those areas at intervals, both day and night. This made all movement risky. The most popular route was from Hell's Spit up the long valley leading to the forward positions and this was so regularly shelled that it became known as 'Shrapnel Valley'. Further along, the valley joined the more sheltered 'Monash Gully' which linked to the front line firing positions of Courtney's Post, Quinn's Post and Pope's Hill.

In an attempt to prevent the Anzacs improving their positions around Walkers Ridge, the Turks launched a determined daytime attack on the 27th of April. The ferocity of it panicked some of the battle fatigued Infantry and Engineers on Walker's, who reacted by retreating down the ridge. Other men working in the gullies assessed the danger and quickly rallied by grabbing the nearest rifle and joining the Infantry on the top of the hill, who were by then under accurate and heavy Turkish fire.

The Engineers, under the command of Corporal C. W Saunders, soon reoccupied a section of vacated trench line and began to engage the attacking Turkish troops with accurate rifle fire. As the fighting intensified, Lieutenant McColl of the Wellington Battalion came down from the hilltop looking for more men. More Engineers moved forward and reinforced the frontline positions; their willingness to join the battle became vital in those dire moments. Sapper Farrer volunteered to move to the left and tell the Australian troops there to stop firing at the Wellington position. When he eventually found the Australians, they were all wounded and sheltering from Turkish fire. It was more than likely that the Turks, hidden in the folds of the ground and the tall brushwood, were the source of the disruptive fire onto McColl's open position. Having established what was happening, Farrer slipped away through the bushes only to be stopped by another New Zealand officer who thought he was running away – the whole situation was confusing.

After the Turkish attack had petered out, occasional rifle and sniper fire recommenced. As they were no longer needed in the firing line, the Engineers gradually filtered back to their task of deepening, widening and straightening the trench system around Walker's Ridge.

Below the crest at Courtney's Post, eighteen year old Sapper Francis Pearson died of gun shot wounds and was buried with twenty-nine other unidentified Anzac soldiers found in the same area – a single cross marking their common resting place. Pearson, who had joined the Engineers in Egypt as part of the 2nd Reinforcements from the Otago Infantry Battalion, was the first fatality suffered by the Engineers at Gallipoli.

For his command and reactions under fire during the engagement, Corporal Saunders was awarded the Distinguished Conduct Medal. It was the first decoration to be won by the N.Z. Engineers on Gallipoli, but not the last.

The gallantry of the Australian and New Zealand troops at Sari Bair was given a special mention. They were reported to have " *pushed on with the utmost boldness after landing on Sunday, had been engaged almost constantly with the enemy, who made strong and repeated counter attacks, which were invariably repulsed… Early on Tuesday morning a fresh Turkish division was launched against Sari Mair, preceded by heavy artillery fire. A hot engagement followed. The enemy came on boldly time after time, but the Australians and New Zealand troops defeated every attempt, and by three o'clock in the afternoon had resumed the offensive."*[94]

Across the entire firing line, the task of the Engineers was made perilous by Turkish rifle fire from the neighbouring hills. It was an assortment of rapid fire and explosive sniper rounds coming from any direction, including the rear of the position. In reply, the Allied battleships would send over the occasional shell which would pass close overhead aiming for the Turkish lines.

The inadequately deep trenches left the men exposed to injury from all the incoming fire. The initial work was undertaken by one man lying on his stomach low to the ground, scraping out the dirt and passing it back, to be used to fill sandbags or disposed of down the gullies. If it was thrown up onto the top edges of the trench, it indicated where the Engineers were working and provided a target for the Turks. Once deep enough, the Engineers could crouch in the space, and once widened, two men could work together. The work continued into the dark of night, without any lights so as not to reveal their location to snipers, bombs or Turkish trench mortars. Finally, in the early hours of the morning, the tired and thirsty Engineers connected the trenches to the trackway coming up from the gully below.

The Engineers returned to their dugouts behind the ridge line in Shrapnel Gulley to sleep covered by the greatcoats which had belonged to dead infantryman. Later the Engineers would relocate their base further down the ridge, to another gulley about a quarter of a mile away from Quinn's Post. There they created larger, sandbagged and corrugated iron dugouts for themselves which afforded some protection from Turkish shrapnel.

Some cheerful news reached the men on Gallipoli at this time, as the Royal Navy had also been busy. The commander and crew of the British Submarine E14 penetrated the minefield in the Narrows and entered the Sea of Marmara on the 27th of April. There they sunk two Turkish gunboats and a large military transport, full of troops. Upon their return on the 18th of May, a Victoria Cross was awarded to Lt-Commander Edward Boyle R.N, a Distinguished Service Cross to Lieutenant Edward Stanley R.N, and the Distinguished Service Medal to each crew member.

The next morning, the 28th of April, the Engineers were back on Walker's and Quinn's, continuing to work on the trenches, as bullets continually hit the parapets or sang overhead. Occasionally the cry would go up, "Everyman in the firing line!" and they would take their rifles and sit in the trenches ready for a Turkish attack. Being an Engineer on Gallipoli was anything but dull. They soon realised they were only deployed to areas where the fighting was the hardest, the firing the heaviest and the positions the most vulnerable.

Onboard the "Goslar", the horses of the Field Company, ASC and Field Ambulance were still being cared for by their drivers, as the horses were not required on land given the state of the campaign. They would remain aboard ship for the next four weeks until eventually the order came to return all horses to Egypt. With many of the Field Company's drivers already employed onshore at Anzac as Engineers, a small party of drivers were selected to accompany the horses back to Egypt and care for them there until they were needed; amongst those selected were Drivers Palmer and Tester.

As the entrenchment progressed, the Engineers were rotated in small groups to the beach area for some respite and to return with extra supplies. This meant running the gauntlet of Turkish snipers. Carrying timber struts for the various emplacements was the worst job, as it took two men to carry these, and meant running uphill over broken ground so as to avoid being shot. They soon learnt it was easier to leave the timbers and other awkward stores in a central location and collect them at night.

Private John Simpson Kirkpatrick, the donkey handler immortalised along with his donkey "Murphy", for evacuating the wounded down the steep gullies, gave the Engineers some useful advice. He told them that the snipers had eight rounds in their rifle magazines before they had to reload. So the secret was to count until all eight rounds had been fired; then run like hell, hoping you had counted correctly.

Quinn's Post was the most dangerous of all the tenuous positions during those early days after the landings and rapidly gained such strategic significance across the Anzac line that it could not be lost to the Turks.

The distance between the Turkish lines and Australian infantry was about twenty yards at the centre. It was prone to the threat of bombs, of which the Turks had many and the Anzacs none. There was also a real risk of a surprise attack across such a narrow front.

With five yards of foothold to work in, with no trenches and a limited field of fire available to the infantry, it was a wonder that it was held. The Engineers deepened the existing rifle pits and connected them to make a serviceable firing line. Then they began sapping forward to just over the crest of the ridge at Quinn's using "T-Head" trenches. Over the next fortnight the series of these trenches were gradually connected to provide better observation and field-of-fire along the narrow ridge. The Turks were only thirty yards away whilst this work was being undertaken and the Engineers relied on the Australian infantry to provide some warning of danger and protective rifle fire. It was extremely hazardous.

As the Engineers sapped forward, bombs were tossed by the Turks to where they saw dirt being thrown up. No aggressive Australian sniping was apparent at that time on Quinn's. The Engineers became adept at catching the Turkish "cricket-ball" variety bombs and either throwing them back or pulling out the burning fuses. Sapper Warburton, from Palmerston North, tried to return one bomb that had landed in the trench where he was digging. It exploded as he threw it, severely wounding him in the head and injuring his fellow engineer working alongside him. They were rapidly evacuated off the ridge, but Warburton died of his wounds. The remaining six Engineers in his work party continued sapping forward, accepting the obvious dangers. Apart from the fear of the bombs, Driver Sullivan described it as, 'not the most encouraging sensation' to hear rifle fire passing overhead from the Turks in front and the Australian infantry shooting to the rear of them[95].

A small observation post, which became invaluable to the trench system at Quinn's, was constructed by Corporal C.W. Salmon. He was under constant enemy fire throughout the entire construction and would be awarded a Distinguished Conduct Medal for his actions.

Looking towards Russell's Top from Quinn's Post. The middle ridge is "Pope's", to the right is "Deadman's Ridge", the "Chessboard" and on the skyline "The Nek".

New Zealand Engineers, presumably at Quinn's Post, using a homemade catapult. The soldier near the parapet is using a periscope to sight the shot; while his mate in the trench holds a cigarette ready to light the bomb's fuse, then release the springs to catapult the bomb towards the Turkish trenches.

Photo courtesy of Alexander Turnbull Library, Wellington, New Zealand and Royal NZ RSA Collection. Reference number: PAColl-4173-1.

On the 28th of April, Lieutenant Skelsey, who commanded the Engineers at Quinn's, was asked to protect the post with wire entanglements. That night, in heavy rain, he crawled out in front of Quinn's Post to consider the ground from the Turkish perspective. He weighed up how best to anchor the wire in place, as hammering or thudding would only attract Turkish fire. He concluded that the only way to put out wire was to fling it from the trenches and let it lie there, on the basis that this would provide some early warning of Turkish troops approaching. This was done, but the Turks merely crawled out and pulled the unsecured wire towards their own trenches to reinforce their position. The Turks were just as fearful of surprise attack as were the Australians.

After completing the main firing positions, communications trenches were dug back from the main firing lines and tracks constructed. Particularly steep gradients were reinforced with salvaged timbers or ammunition boxes used to aid the construction of all-weather steps. The tracks provided better footing for men coming down, and assisted in the mile long climb up the steep gully, which rose to a height of 500 feet near Quinn's. This track became the main arterial route for the sick and wounded being evacuated, and the re-supply of food, water, ammunition, artillery shells and all other supplies carried up by men and mules.

With defensive work well underway and the prospect of staying longer than intended along the coastal strip and beaches, the Anzac commanders decided to deal with the troublesome and accurate Turkish fire aimed at the barges as they neared the beach. They deduced that artillery observers had uninterrupted observation of the entire Anzac Cove beach area from just two sites; one across the bay at the northern Nibrunesi Point, the other just south of Anzac Cove on the well-defended promontory at Gebe Tepe. It was vital that these threats were removed.

On the 30th of April, the Royal Navy landed a small party at Nibrunesi Point but the observers had escaped. In response, at dawn on the 2nd of May, a party of fifty New Zealanders from the Westland Company, commanded by Captain Cribb and accompanied by Captain Fred Waite who commanded the two Engineers from the 1st Field Company, made a surprise raid. The sleeping Turks were either killed or captured and then the Engineers set about blowing up several huts with guncotton and destroying the telephone wires. The following night the Australians' raid at Gebe Tepe was frustrated by wire entanglements and a well-placed machine gun. Eventually that raiding party retired, leaving the position intact and in Turkish hands for the rest of the Anzac campaign.

Upon his return from the successful raid at Nibrunesi Point, Captain Waite was again in action on the evening of the 2nd of May. With three N.Z. Engineer officers already wounded, he led two parties of Engineers released from the work at Walker's and Quinn's, one commanded by Sergeant Alan Wallace, the other by Sergeant Alexander Abbey. Each party comprised around twenty Engineers and their role was to support the attack planned that evening by the 4th Australian Infantry Brigade. If the advance was successful, they were to assist with the building of roads for artillery and all other essential tasks, such as entrenching and wiring[96].

The 4th Brigade, along with the Canterbury and Otago Infantry Battalions, were to capture the ridge named 'Bloody Angle', which would enable the Anzac line to be straightened along the high ground and include the feature known as 'Baby 700'. The capture of this ground would prevent the Turks from being able to fire into the back of Quinn's Post and other nearby positions. It was also expected to improve communications and support between the various Anzac positions on the ridges, currently achieved by moving back down, along and then up the low gullies. This co-orientated attack was to be launched across the narrow ridge in front of Pope's Hill and Quinn's Post. The Turks held the high ground from 'The Nek' to 'The Chessboard'.

The attack began just before sunset and at 7pm six warships in the bay bombarded the Turkish trenches for thirty minutes, after which, according to the plan, three separate and co-ordinated assaults from Courtney's, Quinn's and Pope's were to commence. On the left of the assault line, the Otago Battalion arrived late at their start point having been delayed by rough country and sheer cliffs. In spite of this, the

Canterbury Battalion attacked while the 16th and 13th Australian Battalions took their attack in across the narrow ridge near Quinn's, possibly hoping the darkening evening would provide some cover or advantage. The Australians were swept with effective Turkish machine gun fire during their advance, yet took the ridge and began digging in.

At about midnight, a party of eighteen Engineers moved forward in an attempt to help them with the digging and remove any wire entanglements. The Turkish line was less than 50 yards away. Standing up to dig, the Engineers were silhouetted on the ridge by the star-filled night and they immediately began to take casualties while trying to deepen the shallow infantry trenches. Sid Crawford received a severe gunshot wound that fractured his right arm and Bert Hunt was shot in the thigh. Robert Wright was hit in the shoulder by a bullet ricocheting off a pick, whilst other rounds hit his water bottle and blew his rifle out of his hand. Thrown off balance, he stumbled backwards and trod on another soldier's face. He apologised and then realised the man was dead[97]. All the Engineers involved in that action, apart from three, were either killed or wounded.

Amidst what was later described as the heaviest of fire, Wallace, along with Sappers Scrimshaw, Clifton and Carlyon, commenced recovering the wounded before first light. Carlyon was particularly remembered for his daredevil feats; standing on the parapets, exposed to Turkish fire yet handing the wounded down to the safe hands in the trenches or the gullies where aid posts had been established. Wallace, Scrimshaw and Carlyon were all recommended for honours, but only Scrimshaw received a Distinguished Conduct Medal for the 'Bloody Angle' action.

By early morning the situation was recognised as hopeless. The remaining party of Engineers under the command of Abbey was instructed to recover wounded infantry lying in a gully between Pope's and Quinn's. Despite the obvious dangers and the constant Turkish small arms fire, the party spent several hours cutting a passable track up an old watercourse and into the gully and creating traverses and buttresses.

Two battalions of the Royal Naval Division[98] originally intended to support the disastrous night assault, assisted in the work and were extremely useful with the digging and the shaping of buttresses, or hooking in the sides, along the length of the track for the ease of evacuating the stretcher cases. While the Navy finished their work, the Engineers had already begun to collect the wounded Australians and New Zealanders lying on the open ground, in depressions or behind bushes. Most had lain in the open ground and were delirious and thirsty. The available medics and the Engineers were kept busy for several hours bandaging wounds and arranging to have the wounded evacuated down the track.

Inaction was never an option during those early days on Gallipoli and by mid-morning on the 3rd of May, the two battalions from the Royal Naval Division were ordered by Godley to continue the attack and capture the high ground around 'Bloody Angle'. As they reached the ridge they became visible to the Turkish machine gunners on the flanking ridge line and were cut to ribbons. The ground remained littered with dead Navy Division lads for days afterwards and the area was christened 'Dead Man's Ridge' by the Anzacs.

With no chance of holding the ground captured at 'Bloody Angle', the Australians and New Zealanders slowly withdrew leaving behind the half completed communications trenches and many of their dead. One was Private Robert Chapman of the Otago Infantry Battalion. He would be posted as 'missing' from this action until a Court of Enquiry in February 1916 would eventually declare him as "believed dead". He has no known grave.

A strong Turkish counter-attack occurred on the morning of the 5th of May and all the ground fought over for the past three days was retaken by the Turks. They occupied the trenches, eventually incorporating the newly dug Anzac trenches into their defensive trench system known as 'The Chessboard'. The Anzac dead would have been rolled into the nearby gullies and left unburied by the Turks.

Of the twenty Field Engineers in Sergeant Wallace's section that had supported the Australian 4th Brigade for the duration of these attacks, only five remained[99]. Those wounded and evacuated were: Sergeant William Abbott, Lance-Corporals Martin O'Brien and Acland Thomas; Sappers Fred Cameron, Robert Collins, Sydney Crawford, Bert Hunt, Geoffrey Otterson, John Ramsey, James Logan, Arthur Howell, Thomas Bradley, Lestock Reid who had been shot in the left arm, and Ernest Sunderland. Sapper Edward Reid was posted 'missing in action' and at a later Court of Enquiry in February 1916 he was officially listed as 'believed dead', being killed on the night of the 2nd of May. His body would have been amongst those left on 'Bloody Angle' and disposed of by the Turks. William Abbot died of his wounds aboard the hospital ship on the 4th of May; Bert Hunt died of his wounds six weeks later while at the 15th General Hospital in Alexandria. Sappers Robert Wright and Albert Thompson remained on Gallipoli as walking wounded, although by now many of their close friends were either dead or evacuated.

Sapper Lestock Reid recovered from his chest wounds; he was later commissioned as a 2nd Lieutenant and served with the N.Z. Pioneer Battalion in France. In May 1916 he was killed by machine gun fire just over a year after being wounded at 'Bloody Angle'.

For the action at 'Bloody Angle', Captain Fred Waite would be awarded the DSO for his decisive leadership and personal gallantry during the 2nd of May attacks and Abbey would receive the DCM for his initiative and good work in evacuating the wounded.

The entire episode was viewed as being badly planned and extremely wasteful.

The next day the surviving Engineers returned to their labours at Quinn's and Walker's; and on the 5th of May they received their first rum ration. From then on, every Wednesday night a rum ration was issued to the Engineers.

Despite their mounting casualties, the 1st Field Company continued connecting trenches, digging saps, constructing firing loopholes and linking up communications trenches. Gullies and pathways had to be properly graded and vital work began building the bomb-proof shelters in the gully directly behind Quinn's. These shelters would eventually be properly roofed to provide a safer area from bombs, shade from the sun and allow space for men in the reserve or supporting the firing line to rest as best they could. Overhead cover became important protection, and necessary to limit the casualties caused by Turkish hand-thrown bombs.

On one occasion while sapping forward at Quinn's the Engineers encountered the Turks digging their own sap towards them, so a short bombing war erupted. It was not unusual either when digging these saps in other areas that they would come across bodies of Anzacs, Ceylon Planters or Turks left undistributed since those distant April weeks of fighting. As a rule, they would stop whatever they were doing and properly bury the remains. This was for two reasons, one partially out of respect while the other was more practical, in that they did not want to unearth the remains later, and in a worst state of decay.

Firing loopholes were constructed using metal plates that allowed a rifleman to fire without exposing himself; and more machine gun positions were dug to better defend the overall area and disburse the inevitable Turkish assaults. A number of the B (British) Section men had trained on machine guns in England and they understood the science behind the apparatus. This knowledge allowed them to ensure the maximum ground was "beaten" by effective, enfilading fire.

Given the constant demands being made on the Engineers and to better deploy this dwindling resource, their work methods changed. They began to supervise infantry work parties for the larger construction works. The infantry began to undertake much of the manual labour such as sapping, carrying timber, sandbags, wire and other stores from Hell Spit to wherever needed at Anzac. These were called "boss jobs". All work close to the firing line was now undertaken at night to limit casualties. As the days blurred into weeks, the biggest challenge became staying awake, as exhaustion and battle fatigue crept up on each man. Once sickness and dysentery became widespread, each section of Engineers worked a four hour shift before being relieved by another section.

It took over a month to make Quinn's Post secure, although it was still disorganised and would remain largely so until Colonel Malone took over as Post Commander in July. The men serving there found it very stressful and rarely slept until relieved. The Engineers described it as a "jumpy" place with the constant bombing, sniping and the most dominant smell being that of unburied bodies. For Sapper John Woodhall, the Turkish bombs continued to unnerve him. His condition was not helped when he saw how a bomb had torn to shreds an old greatcoat used by the men in the trench to blanket an explosion[100].

New Zealand Engineers digging for water in Monash Gulley.

Photo courtesy of Alexander Turnbull Library, Wellington, New Zealand and Royal NZ RSA Collection. Reference number: PAColl-0-308-20.

Mining operations at Quinn's Post.

Photo courtesy of Alexander Turnbull Library, Wellington, New Zealand and *Royal NZ RSA Collection.* *Reference number:* 1/2-168806-F.

Chapter Eleven: Dominating the enemy

In conjunction with everything else happening at the time, a great achievement was in bomb manufacturing. It was recognised early in the campaign that the ample supply of German made bombs possessed by the Turks resulted in them also having the upper hand in the trench bombing war, especially at the Anzac's vulnerable point of Quinn's Post.

The situation was remedied during the first week when the Australian and New Zealand Engineers began manufacturing crude "homemade" bombs at Hell's Spit. These were manufactured from jam tins, cigarette tins and just about anything that could contain explosives. Soon they were producing around 300[101] grenades a day. For the New Zealand Engineers, those mad training days spent in the deserts of Egypt experimenting with the making of bombs and perfecting how to launch their lethal inventions, paid dividends. This know-how reduced the need for experimentation and gave the entire process a credibility that was immediately evident in the lethal effect that these devices had on the Turkish trenches and defenders.

Each container was packed with metal objects with the explosive element, gun cotton being wrapped in cloth and inserted into the container. The final product would have been plugged, fuse inserted and finally strips of barbed wire, or telephone wire used to bind it all together.

The availability of cloth was improved by a supply of unstitched shirt back and front panels which were landed as part of the beach supplies. Having no obvious use as items of clothing in that incomplete state, the Army Service Corps donated all the bales of shirt panels to the bomb makers.

There was nothing artistic about the end products. They were functional, clumsy slabs of explosives with random aerodynamic qualities. They were quickly packed off to the infantry on the firing lines where the Engineers initially provided instructions as to the fuse time and preferred method of flinging, lobbing or throwing.

Some 'bombs' were made to order depending on their intended target. On one occasion, Sapper Wright constructed a special bomb to destroy a Turkish listening post near a section of trench at Quinn's. The estimated explosive impact meant the 'bomb' being wrapped in a sandbag and secured with barbed wire.

After a few practice swings to get used to the weight, adjustment for the constriction in the trench and the angle of the throw necessary for direction and distance, the bomb fuse was lit and the whole contraption lobbed directly into the Turkish trench with devastating effect. After the dust had cleared, the position no longer existed. Such events demonstrated the technical ability of the bomb manufacturers, and the growing expertise amongst the men to hit the selected target.

The brave feats and dash at Gallipoli were overshadowed in Britain and elsewhere by the grim news that the Germans had launched a new offensive in Belgium on the 22nd of April near the town of Ypres (2nd Battle of Ypres). This had been preceded for the first time by the release an estimated 5,700 cylinders of chlorine gas in this one attack. The effects of this new weapon initially forced the French troops to fall back. The front line was later restored by the sheer determination and bravery of the Canadian troops who advanced under machine gun fire and retook the lost ground in fierce fighting.

On the 7th of May the Cunard liner RMS Lusitania, en route to America, was torpedoed and sunk off the coast of Ireland by a German submarine, killing 1,959 people including 159 American civilians. This single event provoked massive anti-German sentiment around the world, especially in America.

Later in May another account was received from the Ypres sector reporting a huge 40 foot high chemical gas cloud, caused by gas shells bombarding a five mile-long sector of the frontline for four and a half hours. The events of May made the war incomprehensible to a majority of the general public.

With so much happening close to English shores, and the delays caused by the heavy censoring of military reports from Gallipoli by Sir Ian Hamilton's staff officers, the public did not hear about the landing on Gallipoli until early May. Some initial stories had circulated among journalists in Alexandria, although these were mainly the by-product of speculative bar talk rather than actual accounts by any of the official war correspondents on Gallipoli.

"Rumours" that had become newspaper reports always overstated the progress and barely mentioned the casualties. Eventually, even the delays imposed by Hamilton could not stop the flow of news from war correspondents in Gallipoli. What captured the most attention was the shockingly long casualty lists. The accounts of traditional warfare with daring bayonet charges managed to engross the newspaper readers.

They admired the grit and determination being shown by the men of Gallipoli, as different from the reports of the scientific war of gas and mass artillery bombardments raging on the Western Front, with all of its unimaginable horrors. The public's interest in the Gallipoli campaign soon grew.

With the Engineers making steady progress with the defence and other needs at Anzac, the meticulous and skilled task of map making was also given to them. As the ANZAC Corps had been landed in the wrong place, reliable maps of the immediate area in which they were fighting were urgently needed.

The original maps issued by the military for the Gallipoli campaign were tourist maps or old naval maps showing vast blank and featureless areas along the coastal strips and further inland. Either due to lack of need or importance in the past, the area had never been fully surveyed and mapped. Corporal Cecil Mathius, a scout with the Canterbury Battalion, commented that the old maps showed the area to be good sheep grazing country. It was anything but, with its razor backed ridges and labyrinthine deep gullies in which Infantry companies became disorientated, confused and lost during assaults. Where ridges and slopes should logically join, they instead crumbled into deep gullies.

Expanses that seemed to represent high ground along a ridge were often dominated by an even higher feature, usually hiding Turkish troops.

The lack of detailed maps is partially explained by the fact that the plan at the outset was to move rapidly inland to the plains of Achi Baba. It was never envisaged that several weeks after the landing the men would still be fighting on the coastal cliffs.

For the military commanders to effectively "see" the battlefield and plan co-ordinated assaults; properly scaled and referenced maps were essential.

Although not skilled map makers, there were two well known illustrators and artists, Sapper Moore-Jones and Private Lovell-Smith, who were attached to the N.Z. Engineers. They are generally credited with the drawing of the landscape around Anzac Cove, to provide some visual context for commanders. They managed this by observing the landscape from ships, walking the ground and in Lovell-Smith's case, several hundred feet up in the air, in a captured balloon.

The new maps allowed the artillery to direct accurate fire onto Turkish positions and assisted in the planning of future operations. Moore-Jones would later paint, from memory, the fondly remembered Simpson[102] and his donkey, Murphy.

It is not clear why the naval aerial photographs taken at this time over the Turkish positions were never shared with the military commanders – they would have afforded valuable military intelligence to the Anzac planners.

As the New Zealanders continued with the work atop the Anzac ridges, the 2nd Australian Field Company helped in the NZ&A Division sector by building a series of five foot high barriers of sandbags at intervals along Monash Valley. This restricted the Turk's view of the area and provided some cover from Turkish fire, for the men as they moved to and from Quinn's and Pope's.

On the 5th of May the Engineers under the command of the Hon. Lieutenant R.P Butler R.E, a trained engineer assigned from the N.Z. Engineers Headquarters section, began counter-mining activities by digging three tunnels. Their entrances were on the rear slopes of Quinn's Post. There was a growing concern that the Turks had already commenced mining in an attempt to blow the Anzacs off the ridges at Quinn's and Courtney.

The diggers were commanded by Sergeant Abbey – a mining engineer in Russia before the war, along with several ex-coal and gold miners drawn from both the New Zealand Field Engineers and the Australian Infantry. Armed with entrenching tools they progressed slowly as they adapted their techniques for the terrain, the need for silence, and awareness of their proximity to the enemy. By the 8th of May they had advanced the tunnels sufficiently to enable "listeners" to try and detect sounds of Turkish underground activity. Nothing was heard. General Godley visited the position and determined that a reconnaissance raid should be made of the Turkish trenches opposite Quinn's to confirm if enemy mining was underway[103].

Raiding had become the new offensive tactic after the disastrous set-backs of the week before at 'Bloody Angle'. Given their heavy casualties and the lack of reinforcements available, the commanders had decided that for now, no further large scale attacks would be ordered. Instead, raiding would be encouraged and if a raid was successful, the ground captured would extend the Anzac position. The foray from Quinn's Post would test the new doctrine.

The raid was planned for the night of the 9th of May and was to be made by the Australian 15th Battalion, supported by the survivors of the depleted 13th and 16th Battalions who had assaulted days earlier at 'Bloody Angle'. The N.Z. Engineers would be in support to ensure that the infantry were properly entrenched and to destroy any detected mining works. The assault consisted of three parties of about forty men. If in the opinion of the officer leading any one of the assault parties, a captured Turkish trench could be held and used as a new front line, then one of three designated digging parties would move forward. Their immediate task was to change the firing parapet to face the Turks and then sandbagging it to make it defensible. Then they would begin digging a new communications trench and connect this to the Quinn's trench line – effectively making a trench for reinforcements to use.

Sandbags were to be carried by the digging parties, along with picks and shovels, but no rifles. The digging parties of between twenty to thirty men were from the 13th and 16th Battalions and were directed by N.Z. Engineers attached to each party.

The action began well enough. The Turkish trenches were taken and no mining works were discovered in the captured area. One assault group had managed to move 200 yards through the Turkish line before the Turks counter-attacked in large numbers, inflicting severe casualties on the Australians. Unaware of this and taking advantage of the early success, the digging parties had already began to move forwards to fortify, sandbag and connect the captured Turkish positions. They were immediately caught in heavy rifle fire and sustained casualties. Many lay hugging the earth as bullets ripped overhead and set the scrub around them on fire. To stand up was certain death. It was like reliving the events of the week before. The right and left parties soon organised the digging of their separate communications trenches back towards Quinn's, while the centre party made their way back as best they could. The right flank trench was completed before first light, but progress on the left flank was slower and by daylight the job was still incomplete. With the new trenches being overlooked by the opposing ridges, the Australians had no option but to withdraw, as in the dawn light the Turks could better choose their targets and it was not long before the assault parties came under intense machine-gun fire from the Turkish positions on 'Baby 700'.

Many more men were killed or wounded attempting to get back to their own lines or assisting in recovering the wounded. Several seriously wounded men had to be abandoned in the Turkish trenches[104].

Amongst the Engineers, Sappers Fred Burton, Lawrence Allen, George Shearwood and John Keating were killed. Captain Donald Simson was severely wounded in the head and neck and the intrepid Captain Fred Waite received minor wounds. Amongst the wounded who were evacuated were Corporals Kilbride and Cyril Salmon; Sappers Thomas Drysdale, Percy Gibbs, and Walter Naylor. Naylor later died aboard a hospital ship bound for Malta with his wounded friends Salmon and Drysdale close by.

Earlier that same day, Sergeant Alan Wallace, who was a Rhodes Scholar studying at Oxford University in England before the war, was shot while talking with Major Quinn in a trench at Quinn's Post. The trenches were obviously not deep enough to provide sufficient protection against snipers. Adding sandbags for extra height along the parapet merely gave the Turkish machine gunners fresh targets to shoot at. The only solution was to dig deeper trenches, but the deeper they became; the harder it was for men to climb out during an assault. A shallow trench allowed men to "jump the bags" quickly and pace in any attack was a huge advantage in reaching the Turkish positions. The depth of the Anzac trenches at this stage of the campaign gives a clear indication that they still saw this as an offensive campaign that could be won, not defensive trench warfare. By July though, those trenches would be deeper.

This view of the campaign no longer concerned Alan Wallace. He was evacuated from Gallipoli but died aboard the hospital ship on the 10th May and was buried at sea the same day. He never received his Distinguished Conduct Medal for 'Bloody Ridge', as he was killed before the recommendation for the award was made; although he was later mentioned in despatches by Sir Ian Hamilton for his courage and leadership.

By the 15th of May, Australian "listeners" from the mining operations at Quinn's Post could hear the faint knocking of muffled picks coming steadily nearer. The Turks had advanced their mining activities closer to Quinn's. It was recognised that if the Turks detonated a sizable mine under Quinn's, it would easily destroy the Anzac trenches along the ridge. More mine tunnels were started to locate and destroy the Turkish tunnels before a practical problem arose.

The Engineers and diggers were experienced miners; who in usual circumstances would never have someone digging towards them. Judging the distance of the on-coming, often muffled, noise and then calculating the amount of guncotton needed to close an enemy tunnel, was largely a hit and miss affair with only a little science applied. A *camouflet*[105] charge of 32lbs of guncotton[106] was fired near one suspected Turkish tunnel. It transpired that this was too far away, so the *camouflet* had no impact. Due to the urgency of the situation, caution was thrown to the wind and the next charge was dramatically increased. The 100lbs charge of ammonal[107] effectively closed a Turkish tunnel with the added effect of shaking the Australian fire trenches and creating a small crater in no man's land, as the Turkish tunnel collapsed.

During the first eight days of counter mining, the diggers located and blew up five Turkish galleries, at a cost of three of their own men killed. The Hon Lieutenant Butler received several wounds while attempting to take measurements of the distance and direction of the various tunnels from an exposed position on the parapet at Quinn's. He was fortunate not to be killed. Ignoring his wounds he remained at his post directing the mining operations and the only allowance he made was to have his wounded arm placed in a sling.

During the early hours of the morning of the 29th of May, the Turks eventually succeeded in detonating two mines in front of Quinn's. One blew a substantial gap in the No. 3 subsection through which a determined group of Turks quickly advanced. The other exploded halfway between the two opposing trench lines. A fierce and bloody hand-to-hand struggle ensued to recapture the broken trenches, during which Major Quinn was killed. Eventually all the Turks withdrew or were killed, while the small band of Turkish survivors at No. 3 subsection were persuaded to surrender.

During this action Lieutenant Butler was hit in the head by shrapnel. He continued to command while his Engineers tried to clear up and repair the trench system in daylight. It was a difficult task, as dead men, timbers and dirt all had to be shifted. The operation was impeded by the narrow working conditions and the near-by Turks who continually tossed or rolled bombs down the ridge into the damaged section of trench. The removal of bodies, body parts and debris was slow work.

Eventually safe access could only be made through one small tunnel. The space was only sufficient for one man to work in. Sentries gave warnings when Turkish bombs were being thrown. A shouted alarm gave the sapper precious time to dive back into the safety of the tunnel. It was time-consuming, hard, nerve-wracking work, but enough progress was made so that by nightfall the Engineers could begin to reconstruct the trench. Australian Infantry work parties moved in to help and took over the grim task of removing and burying the dead bodies of their friends.

At this time Lieutenant Butler was removed from Quinn's when it was pointed out to him that he was in danger of losing his arm to septic poisoning. He was evacuated from Gallipoli the following day to a hospital in Egypt. As well as being mentioned in despatches, he was awarded a well-earned Military Cross for his determination and leadership.

The Turks did not stand idly by after their mines had detonated. They took full advantage of the confusion and quickly occupied both craters in no man's land, which they soon fortified. The next day the Australian Light Horse attacked both craters to drive the Turks out. They managed to gain the smaller of the two craters, taking many casualties before facing the threat of being driven off. Although barely able to defend themselves, the officer-in-charge refused to abandon the crater or the wounded to the mercy of the Turks. It was hurriedly decided to dig a tunnel to connect the crater to Quinn's.

Working furiously, the N.Z. Engineers completed the tunnel in four hours. The wounded were evacuated, while the Engineers continued to tidy up the loose dirt in and around the crater, as well as preparing fighting positions as best they could. They increased the depth of the crater and erected overhead bomb shelters. During all this time they were a mere nine feet from a Turkish fire trench. The Turks speculatively dropped some bombs into the crater, killing an Australian sergeant[108]. Eventually with their work completed, the Engineers retired, leaving the position in the capable hands of the battle hardened Australian troops.

It would remain a forward listening post throughout the campaign Although it was heavily roofed with sandbags, being positioned so close to the Turkish lines, was a stressful ordeal for the men manning it. The roof was frequently blown in, inflicting heavy causalities and there were continual repairs. Cecil Malthus serving in the N.Z. Canterbury Battalion remembers the sheer strain brought on by the level of heightened awareness when occupying that position. He mentions that it always showed in the wild, staring eyes of the men when they were being relieved[109].

The Turkish blockhouse built in the larger crater remained a nuisance for some time. It was also too close to Quinn's for artillery fire to effectively destroy it.

On the night of the 1st of June, two N.Z. Engineers, Lance-Corporal Fear, (who had just recovered from a bout of gastro-enteritis), and Sapper Hodges, slipped over the parapets at Quinn's in the dark of night and silently crawled towards the extreme left hand edge of the blockhouse. They carried 12lbs of guncotton in haversacks, with time fuses. It took them almost an hour to cover the 40 feet of ground, during which time the Australians created diversions that distracted the Turks' machine gun and rifle fire away from where the two Engineers approached. Upon reaching the blockhouse they carefully placed their explosives, lit the fuses inside the haversacks to conceal the flame and beat a hasty retreat.

Their return leg was covered in a considerably quicker time, and no sooner had they crawled back into the trenches at Quinn's than the guncotton exploded with a tremendous 'boom'. The blockhouse was reduced to nothing more than smoke, tumbled earth, broken beams and Turkish dead. Two weeks later they both received Distinguished Conduct Medals for their gallantry.

Chapter Twelve: The Anzac caldron

Some respite came for the exhausted Field Engineers when the N.Z. Mounted Brigade arrived on Anzac on the 12th of May. With them they brought their Mounted Field Troop of Engineers. They quickly moved up onto Walker's Ridge and on the 13th of May the Mounted Field Troop took over all engineering work there, freeing up the depleted 1st Field Company sections. The immediate task for the Mounted Field Troop was to build a road up to Russell Top. A 'road' constituted a graded trackway with a solid surface, wide enough for wagons and artillery pieces to be moved along it. It also provided easier passage for troops and supplies, especially at night and in wet conditions.

With the high casualty rate sustained, the 1st Field Company had dwindled below that of an effective command. Reinforcements were sought from troops already on Gallipoli and these mainly came from the drivers of the Mounted Field Troop and infantry volunteers, such as Privates William Manley and George Harris, both from the Otago Infantry Battalion and Private George Scales from the Wellington Infantry Battalion, among others.

Following the 'Bloody Angle' action, the Engineers became friendly with the young Marines of the Royal Naval Division, mainly the Deal Battalion who had relieved the Australians along parts of the firing line. These lads called themselves C.I.Vs or "Churchill's Innocent Victims", as it was Winston Churchill's idea to form a Naval Division using the surplus naval volunteers not required for the ships at sea.

Although they were not enthusiastic about their new role as infantry on Gallipoli, their determined assault at 'Bloody Angle' and the leadership demonstrated by their officers had earned the respect of the Anzacs. There were some notable humorous moments, one in particular involving a Naval Division officer the Engineers soon christened "Skyline Bill". He would often shout up at them as they undertook their work along the nearby ridges: "Get down off the skyline will you! Are you in the pay of the Turkish Army?"[110] The Engineers, obviously more familiar with the dangers on Gallipoli, politely ignored him.

The construction and improvements made by the Engineers and their working parties were borne out on 18th/19th of May, when 42,000 Turks launched a major attack across the Anzac lines then held by 10,000 troops. The resultant carnage left over 7,000 Turkish casualties, of which an estimated 2,000 were killed, while the Anzacs suffered 160 killed and 468 wounded.

The Turkish losses were so great that a truce was called on the 24th of May to allow the Turkish dead to be buried. Mr Asquith, the British Prime Minister at the time, commented that "just as the Canadians had recently won for themselves an everlasting name in France during their defence of their trenches during the first German gas attack at Ypres, so too on that far off peninsula of Gallipoli, the Australians and New Zealanders had shown themselves worthy of their colonial comrades"[111].

Although the number of Anzacs killed was minor in relation to the Turks dead, twenty-one year old Sapper Thomas Farrer knew three of those killed that day. All were serving with the Auckland Mounted Rifles – one was his comrade from his days in England with the British Section on Salisbury Plain, Private James Mossman, one was a friend from Egypt, Private Wastel Brisco and the other was his older brother, Sergeant Christopher Farrer. After hearing the news of his brother's death, he tried to find the vicar who conducted the burials to establish where his brother's resting place was. It took most of the day, but he eventually found his brother's hastily dug grave in the gulley next to a semi-circular firing line that protected the left of Walker's Ridge. He had been buried with Brisco. They had been in the same tent together in Egypt and now they shared a common grave on Gallipoli. The nearby fire trenches were occupied by the Australian Light Horse who had buried his brother. He could only gaze at the rough grave while crouching low in the safety of the fire trench. Undoubtedly it was a solemn moment, a snatched prayer and then a thought as to how he was going to write to their mother and break the tragic news of her eldest son's death.

The same day that Farrer's brother was killed, No.3 section was undertaking trench repair work on Pope's Hill, when a sniper shot 2nd Lieutenant Sydney Paine while he was reconnoitring a section of trench. Ignoring the threat posed by the sniper, Sapper Carlyon ran out and reached Paine, hoisted him onto his back and carried him to the safety of a deeper trench, but Paine was already dead.

For this action Carlyon was reputedly recommended for a Victoria Cross, but he was never awarded that nor the Distinguished Conduct Medal for his gallantry at 'Bloody Ridge' as he was killed on the evening of the 1st of June while having his evening tea. Shrapnel rounds started to burst over the Engineers' rest position behind Quinn's and a jagged piece of metal lodged in his throat[112]. He rapidly bled to death. Of the fifty-odd Engineers sheltering in their dugouts at the time, he was the only one injured. His death affected many of his younger comrades, who considered him a true hero. He was later mentioned in despatches by Sir Ian Hamilton.

Sergeant Henry Clark, from the Signals Troop, with more seniority than the other Engineer NCOs, was awarded a battlefield commission on the 20th of May and took over 2nd Lieutenant Paine's command of No. 3 section. It was a brief command, as 2nd Lieutenant Clarke was wounded and evacuated the following week.

Sapper Murdock Mackenzie was also killed at Quinn's on the 19th of May. It was a peculiar event as a Turkish round hit the blade of his shovel as he threw dirt from a trench. The round then ricocheted down the shovel handle and hit him in the head, killing him immediately[113].

By way of note there were only two gallantry decorations available to non-commissioned ranks at the start of the Great War: the Victoria Cross and the Distinguished Conduct Medal. If neither award was granted, an act of bravery could still be recognised by one of two other means: 'Mentioned in Despatches' or a 'Certificate of Gallantry'. The Despatch was a report of military operations published in the *London Gazette*. If a subordinate officer or a soldier performed a noteworthy action that was included in the report, he is said to have been "mentioned in despatches". The soldier would receive a certificate and be entitled to wear a bronze oak leaf on the campaign or war service ribbon of the medal issued to them for that particular campaign.

The Certificate of Gallantry was just that, and Field Marshall Haig had signed several for actions on the Western Front earlier in the war. It was not until the 25th of March 1916 that the Military Medal was struck as a third Gallantry award. It was to be awarded to non-commissioned ranks for acts of bravery that were insufficient to merit an award of the Distinguished Conduct Medal or the Victoria Cross. For those men who were already recipients of a Certificate of Gallantry, they could exchange it for a Military Medal if they so desired.

The presence of Turkish snipers continued to plague the Engineers as they moved up to or back from the firing line, often carrying heavy stores for the work being undertaken. At daybreak on the 26th of May, Turkish snipers were watching the gullies at the back of the Quinn's Post. This area happened to be the location of the Engineers' dugouts. As the early morning light brightened at about 4am, some of the Engineers formed up, gathered tools and stores, and then began to move up the gulley for their shift at Quinn's. Suddenly several shots were fired by the waiting snipers. Five Engineers were shot in quick succession. Sappers Thomas Cooke and Thomas Ridgley died from gunshot wounds. The three remaining wounded were hastily carried down from the position on stretchers to the medical tent on the beach. One of the casualties had a bullet lodged in his spine which had paralysed his legs. After this encounter, the Engineers moved their dugouts further away from Quinn's and closer to the beach. Better a longer walk, than being the target of a sudden sniper's bullet fired in the still of the early morning.

Their innocent training days in Egypt seemed long ago and Gallipoli was hardening the men emotionally. On Pope's Hill after building a concealed machine gun post, Sappers Jamieson and Farrer were given the task of starting a tunnel as an alternative route back into the main trench system, from the gun position. They had dug for about five yards when they unearthed, from below, a dead Turk buried during the 24th of May armistice. The smell was terrible and after supporting the body with pick axe handles and sacking soaked in disinfectant, they continued working. Some time later on, one of the Turk's legs slipped through the sacking, so it was just left to dangle. Many men working in the area remembered the rotting Turk and generally ignored him.

Winston Churchill paid the price for the failure of the Dardanelles campaign. He was dismissed as First Lord of the Admiralty in May when Asquith formed a National Government with the Unionists. Churchill was given a minor government post. He resigned from the Government in November and rejoined the Army in France as a Lieutenant Colonel commanding the 6th Royal Scots Fusiliers.

By June, Gallipoli had reached a standoff in static trench warfare, just as had occurred on the Western Front. If there was a plan, it was hard to discern. Each man was only aware of what was happening in his part of the firing line. In his tiny world all meaningful experiences were bordered by the deep gullies on both side of his trench.

The change in tactics had little effect on the Engineers who maintained their efforts to repair, deepen, connect and improve the trench systems. They continued to set out wire entanglements, lay tracks and dig new communication saps. Just as importantly with the heat of summer approaching, they found and dug wells for drinking water.

With the opposing trenches so close in some parts of the firing line, wire entanglements were in demand as an early warning device and to slow any Turkish assault. The Engineers considered any attempt to slip over the parapets to complete such a task to be suicide, so they prodded the wire out in front of the trenches with wooden spars[114].

Sandbagging was another important daily task. The Turks would add to the misery by using machine gun fire or bombs to destroy the sandbags along the parapets. The Engineers would then have the unenviable job of trying to repair these gaps, while under constant harassment. Sandbags were the only other commodity in greater demand than water.

Food was a constant talking point and for the most part the Engineers' daily diet consisted of a tin of bully beef, six army biscuits and a ration of three Dixie pans of water. These were supplemented when available by one piece of bacon, cheese, tea, sugar and jam. Potatoes, onions and some bread were occasionally added to their diet. All were consumed only after the flies were removed. The men were resourceful and kept the bacon fat, re-using it to cook chips when they had potatoes. It was also used to lubricate their rifle firing bolts and barrels.

At the end of May, seven weeks after leaving Zeitoun, they received their first fresh meat ration – it was savoured. The other moment of enjoyment was receiving mail and newspapers.

To cook they needed firewood, as field kitchens were not available and would have been impractical because of their shift patterns and the widely scattered troops. Finding firewood created its own challenge as did washing and shaving, particularly when they were constantly on the front line; although the men did wash in the sea when they could get down to it. Most had lost their packs on the first day, so shaving had to wait until razors could be acquired. As the campaign continued, the state of the men's clothing became a concern, and the Signallers' discarded telephone wire was widely prized as a replacement for rotting bootlaces.

With the persistent fighting in a confined area, Gallipoli was becoming a vast graveyard. The flies that fed on the dead bodies, latrines and other refuse became a plague, contaminating everything. In addition to the flies, there were also maggots, lice, snakes, scorpions, centipedes and tarantula spiders for the men to contend with.

The problem of disease became as deadly as the Turks as the men at Anzac became prone to sickness. Typhoid, enteric fever and dysentery prevailed, with serious treatment in a main hospital being essential to recovery. Deaths from these ailments were not uncommon. Dysentery was particularly rife amongst those who had already suffered a bout during their months in Egypt. If detected and treated early enough dysentery could be remedied. It required that the man received proper food and adequate rest, which would normally suppose a stay in a hospital at Mudros. Daily, dozens of men would be sent away on the hospital ships to Mudros or wherever the chaotic RAMC clearing system determined.

Many men who received prompt medical treatment returned to the fighting at Gallipoli after several weeks away. If left to linger, they often spent months in a general hospital; slowly recovering from the ravages of the disease.

One advantage of a stay at Mudros was that once passed fit, the men would try to draw some pay and then go into the local town. There they would buy some luxury items such as: cocoa, sugar, tinned foodstuffs and maybe even some eggs. These were taken back to the peninsula to be shared amongst their mates. Such efforts helped morale and added some variety to an increasingly monotonous diet.

When an Engineer became sick, particularly with dysentery, they would have to parade in front of the Medical Officer who doled out big teaspoons of castor oil. Alternatively, they could ask their section sergeant for "the day off" and remain resting in their dugout. The logic may have been that it was better to have a fit man back on duty after a few days, than a sick one who would be a liability to his mates. With the shortage of available Engineers, becoming ill did not automatically qualify a man for evacuation to Mudros. Only after several days of protracted debility was that even considered.

On one occasion, 2nd Lieutenant Saunders had to intervene on behalf of Sergeant Abbey who was suffering with chronic dysentery. The Medical Officer would not evacuate him. In the end Lieutenant Colonel Pridham was approached and he permitted Abbey to be evacuated. Abbey spent several months in a hospital in England recovering. Once restored to near full health he was granted an Imperial Army Commission in the Royal Engineers in November 1916, at which time his service with the NZEF ended.

Such a high rate of sickness reduced the numbers of fit fighting soldiers available to serve on the firing line, which added to the mounting concerns of the Anzac commanders.

After six weeks on the peninsula, the 1st Field Company had lost around 60% of their numbers[115] to enemy action, pleurisy, diarrhoea, typhoid, enteric fever, septic wounds and shingles. During this time they had earned a DSO, six DCMs, an MC and nine 'mentioned in despatches'. In a letter to his parents, Driver Sullivan observed that the opportunities to win medals were few, but it was up to the individual to make the most of any opportunity as it arose[116].

Chapter Thirteen: From turmoil to legend

The need for reinforcements was urgent and on the 3rd June, the 2nd Field Company, under the command of Major Barclay, arrived at Anzac after a short stay in Egypt. The 2nd had been trained at the Trentham camp in New Zealand and were the only fully equipped Field Company to leave New Zealand.

On arriving, Barclay learned that the Australian Engineers had already relieved the 1st Field Company the day before. Lieutenant Skelsey had remained at Quinn's to help with the handover but his luck ran out when a Turkish bomb wounded him in the eye and foot. He was evacuated back to Egypt while the remnants of the 1st Field Engineers were given three days rest by rotation down at the beach area. They were paid 10 shillings each and advised by General Godley that "Soft soap is cheap", or in military speak "clean yourselves up!" There was an Australian YMCA hut on the beach where the men could buy soap and razors as well as a quartermaster's store where they could be issued replacement clothing.

Given their proximity to the beach, the men bathed in the sea as often as they could muster the energy, between sleeping and meals. The joke that went around Gallipoli was that the lice had succeeded where the Turks had failed – they had driven the Anzacs into the sea!

One of Sapper Farrer's many letters to his mother back in Oxford was published in the *Christchurch Times* in England about this rest period[117]. In it he told her that they were having a good time, not too much work or shrapnel. He made light of the effectiveness of the Turkish artillery, but noted the deadly skills that the Turks had with their rifles. He told her that he had bacon and chips for breakfast that morning and managed to read a newspaper in bed while he waited for the rain to ease. It was all rather idyllic and reassuring to a worried mother who had just lost her eldest son three weeks earlier at Gallipoli.

Back in Cairo, the condition of the Engineers' horses had deteriorated due to lack of exercise and care. If the much discussed 'big advance' was to happen, these animals needed to be in peak condition. The remaining Engineers' drivers were withdrawn to Cairo to exercise and care for their horses. Of the original twenty-two drivers who had come ashore on the 26th of April and chose to serve as sappers, only fourteen remained.

During the rest period, Sergeant Saunders was commissioned in the field to 2nd Lieutenant, in place of the invalided Captain Simson. Sergeant C.W Salmon was also commissioned to 2nd Lieutenant replacing the wounded Lieutenant Skelsey. The latter was promoted to Captain and transferred to the 2nd Field Company to replace Captain Antoine Beekman who had been invalided back to New Zealand shortly after the 2nd Field Company's arrival in Egypt. Skelsey joined the 2nd Field Company once he was discharged from hospital.

Captain Beckman became a Field Engineer instructor at Trentham camp upon his return to New Zealand. He was unfortunately killed in June 1916 in a bomb-throwing accident. Evidently, he held onto the bomb for too long after lighting the 15 second fuse. It exploded immediately after he had thrown it. The Governor General and Lady Liverpool had been watching the bomb throwing demonstration at the time of the accident.

Having another full strength company available gave Lieutenant Colonel Pridham the opportunity to reorganise his Field and Mounted Engineers across the NZ&A Sector. His perpetual problem was Quinn's, so he allocated three sections from the 2nd Field Company and one section from the 1st Field Company to cope with the relentless demand there. The combining of the two companies meant that the veterans of the 1st Field Company could provide some practical instruction to the inexperienced and as yet untried 2nd Field Company. The Engineers of the Field Troop carried on as before at 'Russell Top', supporting the Mounted Brigade who had been engaged at the end of May in capturing and holding the 'Old No 3 Post'. Eventually the squadrons retired after several days of constant fighting with the Turks who were determined to recapture the position.

Courtney's Post and Pope's Hill were each assigned one section from the

1st Field Company, along with fifty miners, while the remaining section of the 2nd Field Company was assigned roads and wells in Monash Gully. They also improved the road from Howitzer Gully, so that a 4.5 Howitzer could be brought up onto Plugge's Plateau, thereby providing better fire support for the front line trenches and defensive posts.

The 2nd Field Company was soon in action on the night of the 4th of June, when they supported the Canterbury Battalion in a raid on the Turkish trench opposite Quinn's. As had become standard operating procedure, if the captured ground from a raid could be held, it would be strengthened and incorporated into Quinn's defences. The infantry soon captured the Turkish trenches and called the Engineers forward. As this was their first engagement, the Engineers were naturally very nervous and aware of the threat of enfilading machine gun fire from the Turkish positions around 'German Officer Trench'. They quickly covered the exposed ground while carrying sandbags, planks of wood and galvanised iron that were essential to strengthen the captured area against counter-attack. Once in the enemy trench, they changed the firing parapet, built trench blocks with the sandbags, repaired damaged areas and then started constructing overhead shelters. As they orientated themselves to their new surroundings, souvenir hunting most likely took place as well.

The Turks' counter-attack was fierce. After prolonged and confused fighting during the 5th of June, the Canterbury infantry withdrew from the captured trenches, ordering the Engineers back with them to Quinn's. In their haste, the Engineers left intact the trenches and bomb-proof shelters which the Turks quickly occupied. When he heard the news, General Godley was furious at the Engineers. A follow-up raid was ordered to destroy the saps and bring back as many engineering materials as possible. This was carried out by the Auckland Battalion two days later.

Given the stalemate at Anzac, it was decided that for the time being the Engineers would continue to strengthen the existing defences at Quinn's. This work would fully occupy the four engineering sections until July. The improvements were directed by Colonel Malone of the Wellington

Battalion, now the Post Commander. Entrenchments were strengthened using sandbags filled with gravel from the beach, which infantry work parties carried up the gullies to the position.

Tunnels, steel loop holes for snipers, better terracing and overhead cover was extended to the support lines. Room was made for sleeping spaces and these were roofed over to make them both sun and shrapnel proof. Chicken wire was erected in front line trench sections as a screen to stop Turkish bombs being tossed or rolled down into the trenches. The bombs were effectively held by the wire and then exploded on the parapet above. Quinn's became considerably safer for the troops, with Malone later referring to it as almost an armchair[118] posting.

After a few weeks of exposure to the fighting at Quinn's, the 2nd Field Company reflected on the pointless training in trench warfare they had received at Trentham camp. There, the trenches had been neatly dug, landscaped with carefully arranged river stones and then the soil precisely raked off prior to their Sunday visitors arriving. It was all a far cry from the realities on Gallipoli. It was generally agreed that their time at Trentham would have been better spent blowing up the trenches every week and then reconstructing them[119].

Mine warfare across Anzac increased and more shafts and tunnels were dug. By the 8th of June, with experienced coal and gold miners conscripted from the infantry, there were one hundred and sixty miners working beneath Quinn's. In September, Captain P. Keenan arrived on Gallipoli with the 5th Engineer Reinforcements. He assisted with the mining, having trained the Engineers at Trentham in this phase of war, including the firing of *camouflet* charges.

The remaining sections from the 1st Field Company were given the two main tasks; one was to build a deep water pier to facilitate the landing of supplies and troops. The other was to supervise the numerous construction works essential for a busy waterfront area.

The construction of the pier was necessary as the cliffs restricted the possible landing areas. There were only two narrow beaches at Anzac

Cove, both around 200 yards wide, where everything arrived. Small jetties had been erected by the Australian Engineers to help evacuate the wounded. As the campaign dragged on so did the demand for more troops, munitions, food, water, tools, guns, wagons, medical supplies, engineering stores, animals and a myriad of other essential items.

Given the available beach space, a deep water pier was the obvious solution as it would allow the trawlers and large lighters to unload their cargoes in a quick and efficient manner. The building project began well and as the pier extended into the deeper water a pile driver was needed.

A "West African Expert"[120], possibly Sapper Joseph Corbett, realised that they needed a blacksmith and a heavy metallic tool, preferably with a sharp point at one end. As resourceful as ever, an unexploded Turkish 9.5 inch shell was produced. This device, once properly fitted and the shell proven to be a dud, was extremely efficient in creating the hole on the seabed and then driving in the wooden piles. It was still dangerous work for the Engineers, not because of the risk from the dud artillery shell, but from the live rounds of Turkish shrapnel being fired at the beach area and also bullets being fired from Turkish machine gunners in the direction of the beach.

Once the Turks realised that a pier was being built, high explosive shell fire became more regular, and overhead German Taube aircraft attempted to bomb the pier. When the beach came under direct fire, all work would cease until the shelling stopped. Despite such interruptions, the pier was in use by mid July. Sergeant Foote and Corporal Atkinson later received Military Medals for their efforts in building the pier under these hazardous conditions.

As the pier progressed, the Engineers constructed dirt roads along the cliffs to allow more exit points from the beach area. A system of electric lighting was rigged up so that waterfront activities could continue during the night. With sea water often seeping into and contaminating the fresh water barges, it was decided to construct water reservoirs at various points along the shore at Anzac Cove. This was achieved by laying over a mile of water pipes and installing a pumping system. One reservoir was in Shrapnel Valley. The other, a large man made dirt reservoir over 100 feet long, had been dug 40 feet into the side of the hill just above NZ&A Divisional Headquarters. The water pipes were laid in a trench a foot wide and a foot deep. The drinking water was pumped from the barges into these distributed storage tanks and the infantry work parties collected their water ration from these points. Armed sentries were stationed at all the water points to prevent unauthorised use of such a vital commodity.

As a morale booster at the end of June, Sapper Farrer managed to obtain permission from Captain McNeill, who commanded his Field Engineer's section, to go to the nearby island of Lemnos for a Field Company "shopping" expedition at the main town and port of Mudros. Captain Waite, the adjutant, agreed to this and Farrer returned two days later with 100 cans of Swiss milk, tins of candied peel, cocoa, sugar, tinned green beans and other goods that he managed to buy. Altogether he had six sacks and several boxes of "shopping" for his comrades.

On the return trip to Gallipoli, Farrer met an Australian chaplain who had also been to Mudros on a similar errand. His supplies were possibly bound for the YMCA hut on the beach. Also on board, accompanying a number of staff officers was his friend Sapper Trezise, the professional singer from the British Section days in England. They were returning from Egypt where Colonel Lobimer, the CRE of the Anzac Corps, had bought water ships with pumps. After delays in disembarking due to Turkish artillery fire, Farrer managed to get himself and his stores ashore that night with assistance from the NZASC. He was met by Captain Edwards from the NZE Signal Company and some of his Signallers as they had heard a rumour that supplies were arriving for the N.Z. Engineers and they hoped they were for them. Regardless, they helped to deliver the "shopping" to the Field Engineers' dugouts just before a thunderstorm soaked everyone.

The Engineers' Store at Hell's Spit had become a factory, making trench periscopes, trench mortars, moveable wire entanglements and just about anything else that was needed.

The trench mortars were copied from the Japanese mortar already in use at the time in the trenches. As no springs were available, the Engineers instead used a double fuse method. The first fuse allowed the mortar to propel the bomb skywards and the other fuse cut specifically for the time required, detonated the bomb. With limited parts available, the design was crude and the device temperamental, but remained effective for its intended role. One unfortunate accident occurred though on the 2nd of August with one of the homemade trench mortar. Sergeant Robert Nairn, an Engineer with the 2nd Field Company, was in an observation position at Quinn's, using the mortar in an attempt to destroy bomb-proof covering over the Turkish trench. Although the bomb detonation fuse burnt well, the mortar propulsion fuse failed to ignite. Nairn tried to extract the bomb's detonator fuse, but the 6lbs of guncotton in the bomb exploded, blowing off his hand and forearm. He died soon afterwards.

Where the trench mortar required careful handling, the innovation shown in the creation of the wire entanglements was a more precise and practical solution to an immediate problem. The construction was basically two crossed pieces of wood with barbed wire fixed loosely around the protruding arms. When erected on the firing line, wire could be strung between the individual crosses to connect several of these structures together making an effective fence. Alternatively, the structures could be wired and then stacked on top of one another for height. In this manner, the length, height and direction of a wire obstacle could be quickly constructed based upon the terrain, and the need to stop or neutralise a threat.

Placing wire entanglements in front of the trenches at night always incurred casualties, so the design took this into account and could be placed using wooden prods. Special attention was given to securing these structures as silently as possible, all the while working close to Turkish positions. It was important that the wire structures remained fastened where intended, as the Turks displayed a willingness to crawl out and reposition the wire entanglements to their own advantage.

On the night of the 22nd-23rd of July, Corporal Philip Pearce of the Field Troop was mentioned in Army Orders for gallantry when setting wire entanglements thirty yards from the Turkish line at Russell's Top. He was wounded twice and later received a Military Medal for his courage.

A similar event happened on the night of the 1st of October when a working party from the 2nd Field Company attempted to place wire entanglements between the Apex and a Turkish blockhouse seventy yards away. Although working as silently as possible, they were detected and fired upon. The Engineers retreated back to their trenches, but Lance Corporal Matthew Charles had been hit and was left lying on the open slope. A bright moon had risen, illuminating any movement across the ground. Regardless of the obvious danger, Lance Corporal William Riddell slipped out, fastened a rope to Charles, while ignoring the Turkish rifle fire pattering all around him. Once back in the trench with the rope, the Engineers pulled Charles back in. He was dead. Riddell was later awarded the Military Medal for his initiative and courage.

By the 24th of July the Allied casualties at Gallipoli were 544 officers killed and 7,543 other ranks killed, with the wounded amounting to 1,257 officers and 25,557 other ranks. Those missing were just as numerous totalling 135 officers and 7,401 other ranks.

Back in England, the readers of the local Bournemouth newspaper, *The Guardian*, were delighted with the encouraging headline news that the Coal Strike was over. This joy was short-lived as the newspaper proceeded to list the heavy losses suffered by the local 2nd Hampshire Battalion at Gallipoli. It made for grim reading and reflected the uncompromising fighting that had taken place amid those distant gullies and ridges. The most sobering evidence was the numerous columns of those categorised as "Missing in Action". The 'missing' exceeded those known to have been killed. Gallipoli ceased to be some far off peninsula as the Crimean War had been. Its blood soaked dirt held the mortal remains of their Hampshire lads. A soldier's photograph on a mantelpiece was all that remained, along with his family's cherished memories.

The attrition of experienced Engineers continued throughout this time.

Lieutenant Maurice Newbould of No. 4 Section was evacuated with enteric fever. Captain Hulbert from the Signal Troop took over command of No. 4 section from Newbould. Hulbert was viewed by the men as "a man with a grievance"[121] and prone to criticising them. He was evacuated as sick from Gallipoli a few weeks later and returned to New Zealand as medically unfit[122]. Newbould returned in August, only to be wounded shortly afterwards, suffering a loss of memory and temporary paralysis in his right arm and leg.

Others injured during this time were Sapper Felix Thetford who after being shot in the hand in May, was caught in heavy shelling in early July and suffered a compound leg fracture. He had his left leg amputated in hospital at Alexandria. Sapper Thomas Simmonds received a gunshot wound to the thigh at the end of July; he was evacuated to Gibraltar where his left leg was amputated. Lieutenant Saunders was evacuated from Gallipoli with sunstroke and enteric fever in August and repatriated back to New Zealand in December 1915. He later returned to active service in France and was eventually assigned to essential munitions work in England. He was mentioned in despatches by Sir Ian Hamilton in August, 1915.

The British public's imagination had been gripped by the brave and daring feats reported from Gallipoli. To them, Gallipoli was characterised by fierce hand-to-hand fighting, and ultimately the achievements of personal prowess, sinew and muscle. The Turks were admired for their bravery in battle and their courage in defending their homeland whilst the British Territorials were highly thought of for facing withering fire without flinching and the Anzacs were respected for their indomitability.

Gallipoli was exposing weaknesses with Kitchener's New Army battalions as they struggled to adapt to the conditions. The New Zealanders pitied them as young and inexperienced troops, even at times ignorant and bewildered. Whilst under less taxing conditions they may have been brave enough, but in the rough, wild surroundings of Gallipoli, they seemed immature and liable to panic[123]. Even the experienced Lieutenant Colonel Richardson of the Royal Naval Division at Cape Helles, did not think very much of "K's new army".[124] In his view they had inexperienced officers, did not maintain their defensive positions and trenches properly, neglected sniping and showed no organisational initiative at all.

The Anzacs were seen as good sportsman, quick witted, informal and having a sense of humour. Their skills in sniping and bombing were widely acclaimed in the British press columns. Their devil-may-care feats were often recounted. In one report popularising their sniping and counter-sniping abilities, it was explained that both the Turks and Anzacs fashioned homemade periscopes. These were constructed using mirrors or shiny tin to see over the top of the sandbags into no-mans-land. Should a Turkish periscope be sighted, an Anzac sniper would quickly fire at it to render it useless. Often the Turks would put sham tin periscopes up, just to draw a shot.

The Christchurch Times reported an article written by Captain Bean of the Australian Press on Gallipoli. He explained what happen when the Turks put up a Christian cross made from shiny tin:
"Every rifle was silent. Nobody fired at that sign. The Australian is certainly not what you would certainly call a religious man … not so far as the observance of his religion goes. But the moment that sign appeared the shooting stopped… two men that scarcely ever missed drew a line on that object, and in two shots they cut the stick away from the tin."[125]

Bombing was another pass-time, and on the 23rd of July the *Guardian's* special correspondent wrote of being in the front trenches at Quinn's Post enjoying a pleasant Aegean sunset, where even the snipers had been lulled into a hush. Suddenly there was a hoarse cry and a big brown sack crashed into the Australian's trench. Instinctively the men snatched their weapons and crouched down waiting for the expectant explosion. Then somebody opened the bag and found walnuts inside. The gift was returned with tobacco, which the Turks seem to resent, for it was hailed with a chorus of derision. One bare-chested Australian expressed the opinion that the Turks were getting too "uppish" of late, and that a bomb would be more appropriate. So within twenty minutes more than thirty yards of enemy trenches had been burned out completely by a furious fusillade of homemade bombs that rained from Quinn's Post.[126]

Even the New Zealand Maori soldiers' pastime of fishing with improvised bombs was mentioned by the newspapers. Their method was simple: to explode one bomb in the sea and then dive in to recover the stunned fish.

Such stirring stories of war were more exotic, daring and understandable than the trench warfare of the Western Front.

By the end of July the improvements made at Quinn's Post, coupled with the aggressive counter-mining were having the desired effect on the Turks. A Turkish deserter told of the fear they had of the Anzac's mining activities and that volunteers were often sought, to occupy the trenches opposite Quinn's. The position was considered to be so hazardous that all volunteers were promised promotion to corporal[127]. In addition, the aggressive Anzac sniping had forced the Turks to abandon their loopholes, and the bombing parties organised by Colonel Malone threw around two hundred bombs a day to maintain an offensive presence.

The positions at Pope's Hill, Courtney's Post and Russell Top were also undergoing defensive re-work and counter-mining activity. Russell Top had become a rabbit warren of tunnels as the Mounted Field Troop denied the Turks of any possible advantage there.

The Anzac commanders planned a major offensive to begin on the 3rd of August, with their objectives being to seize the high ground of Aghyl Dere and the Chailak Deres. From there they would be able to see across the peninsula to the Narrows. For the offensive, the Engineers were tasked with supporting the attacking columns and specifically to breach any obstacles such as wire entanglements. They were then to consolidate all captured positions, build roads as required and locate wells for drinking water.

The Mounted Field Troop supported the Right Covering Force which contained elements of the N.Z. Mounted Brigade, while the 1st and 2nd

Field Engineer Companies supported the Right and the Left Assaulting Columns respectively. The Left Covering Force was mainly a British affair and supported by 72nd Field Company of the Royal Engineers.

One of the first tasks was to widen the "Big Sap" communication trench to around five feet to speed up the movement of men and supplies to the Deres that would be the focus of the main assault. The original purpose of the "Big Sap" until then had been merely to connect the beach to the northern No. 1 and No. 2 Posts, although it had proven to be useful as a series of support trenches during the May assault to take "Old No. 3 Post" from the Turks. Now it was to become a major communication route.

The work to widen it was undertaken by the N.Z. Native Contingent[128], who had arrived on Gallipoli from Malta in early July, Australian infantry from the 4th Brigade, Australian Light Horse work parties from Walkers Ridge and work parties from N.Z. Mounted Rifles[129]. Where the "Big Sap" was subject to enfilading fire its direction was altered, overhead protection was built at intervals, and recesses were dug into the sides to allow soldiers to stand aside and let the transport mules pass by. Over time, munitions, foodstuffs and other supplies moved along it all to be stockpiled at a predetermined location for the big assault.

The assault was launched on time and over the next few days the fighting was as fierce as it had ever been. The Mounted Field Troop, assisted by the N.Z. Native Contingent, managed to clear the dense wire entanglements that lay all along Chailak Dere. These obstacles blocked the advance and were covered by Turkish machine guns and accurate rifle fire. Evading the effective Turkish defensive fire as best they could, the Mounted Engineers attached grappling irons to the wire so the Maoris, positioned in the gullies below, could pull on the ropes until the wire came away.

Sapper K. W. Watson was awarded the Distinguished Conduct Medal, for conspicuous bravery on the night of 6th -7th of August at Chailak Dere. He assisted in the demolition of the wire entanglements under concentrated Turkish fire. Although wounded himself, he refused help.

Later he rescued a wounded officer, braving enemy fire in the process[130].

Captain L. M. Shera received the Military Cross for his leadership during the August offensive and was further mentioned in despatches by Sir Ian Hamilton.

The 1st Field Company relieved the Mounted Field Troop and spent the rest of that night clearing all further wire obstacles. They constructed a trackway to allow mule trains to bring up much needed supplies of food, water and munitions to the infantry. Possibly relying on the wire entanglements for complete protection, the Turks had constructed trenches that were only two feet deep. Given the exposed ground that had been captured, these trenches were unusable so the Engineers busied themselves making them deeper, digging gun pits and generally consolidating the entire area with captured Turkish wire and other obstacles.

Several sections of the 2nd Field Company were tasked with digging wells in the nearby gullies for much needed water. It was dangerous work and in one instance, an observer saw a Turkish sniper open fire on three Engineers digging a well. One was killed immediately, one ran for cover behind a knoll and the third jumped into the partially dug well hole and pulled a piece of corrugated iron over him, a purely instinctive reaction given the circumstances. The Turkish sniper reportedly put several rounds through the corrugated iron[131]. There was no further comment if the engineer in the well hole survived or not.

Despite their casualties, the New Zealand Infantry eventually captured the high ground at both Chunuk Bair and the Apex. Mention should be made of the Victoria Cross won by Corporal Cyril Bassett of the N.Z. Divisional Signallers, who laid telephone lines to the forward positions on Chunuk Bair and then continually repaired them under heavy fire. Long afterwards all he would say about the intense fighting and the circumstances of his award was that his mates only got wooden crosses.

After incurring over seven hundred casualties in the fighting and losing their commanding officer, Colonel Malone, along with most of his

Headquarters group killed by "friendly" artillery shells, the remnants of the Wellington Battalion at Chunuk Bair were relieved on the evening of the 9th of August by the 6th Loyal North Lancashires, a recently arrived "K" New Army battalion. Two companies of the 5th Wiltshires, also a "K" battalion, were placed in reserve to support the 6th Lancashires now occupying the main position on the ridge. The New Zealand machine gunners remained in place at the 'Apex'.

In the early hours of the 10th of August, spurred on by bugle calls and religious cries, the Turks counter-attacked. The sudden assault caught the New Army soldiers utterly unprepared; most were asleep and when roused many were without their rifles as these had been neatly stacked out of reach. Using their bayonets, this avalanche of determined Turks quickly got in amongst the bewildered English troops and drove them off Chunuk Bair and down the ridge. The New Zealand machine gunners opened fire from the 'Apex' and this helped to slow down the wild Turkish charge. The New Zealand machine gunners were then ordered to target three to four hundred New Army troops running towards the Turks with their hands up[132]. This controversial action may have been due to the New Army troops restricting the machine gunner's line of fire onto the Turks and thereby causing a slower rate of fire than that required to stop the Turk's headlong bayonet charge.

The situation along the ridge top became desperate and the fierce rifle fire was soon coming in from all directions. Many Engineers joined the infantry on the firing line, while others, under the instructions of Captain Skelsey, continued consolidating the trenches still held at the 'Apex' and 'Rhododendron Spur'.[133] Sapper Wilfred Kennedy serving in the 2nd Field Company had suffered from severe dysentery all that week, but not wanting to leave his mates during the August assault, he had not reported sick. That morning he found himself close to the ridge, busy digging a reserve trench for the Ghurkhas. Kennedy was lying in the shallow trench and commented on what a good time he was going to have when he got back to Auckland. He then pivoted on his elbow to speak to someone behind him and a Turkish bullet struck him in the head[134]. He died quickly.

The Turkish assault was soon stopped and the pockets of Turks in amongst the Anzac and British positions were dealt with. The heights at Chunuk Bair were never retaken by the Anzacs and during the remainder of August the Engineers consolidating trenches, especially around Hill 60 as the fighting intensified along that part of the Anzac front line. Five Engineers from the Mounted Field Troop were reported as missing during the scattered fighting; they were all finally confirmed as killed in action on the 27th and 28th of August. They were: Lance-Corporals W. Findlay and J.W. Gibbs; Sappers M.A. Strong, E.B. Edwards and J.R. Tonkins. The Engineers continued to dig wells for water as demand intensified along with the summer heat. During a search for water in Monash Gully the Engineers sunk a thirty foot well shaft and found traces of gold. Most decided to return after the war to validate their find.

Corporal Cecil Malthus of the Canterbury Battalion had been on Gallipoli since the initial landings on the 25th of April. In mid July he had been evacuated to Mudros with dysentery. After convalescing for less than four weeks he returned to Anzac Cove on the 8th of August and found nearly all his old friends gone. Some had been killed the day before while taking 'Rhododendron Spur', while others were either sick or wounded. He was a total stranger to the wide eyed replacements who had just been allocated to his Battalion an hour earlier. The "old hands" he managed to find showed signs of heavy strain[135] from the recent fighting. He later reflected on this particular period of the Gallipoli campaign while on the Somme preparing for the Battle of Flers-Courcelette in September 1916. In France he viewed the risks of death or damage as fairly calculable. For every chance of being killed there were two of getting through unharmed, and four, possibly five, of being wounded[136]. Contrasting risks at the Somme with the fighting on Gallipoli that August, he reckoned that the risk of death, disease or damage was a certainty.

Despite the ferocity of the fighting and the hardships being faced every day, the men never lost their humanity. Trooper Stuart Tennant, serving with the Wellington Mounted Rifles, was badly wounded in mid August after being shot in the head. While the stretcher bearers were carrying him along the communications trench, Sergeant Percival Taylor noticed that Tennant's wristwatch had fallen into the sand as the strap had broken. Taylor put the watch in his pocket intending to send it on to him later. Taylor was himself wounded later that night. While recovering in England he heard of Tennant's death. After enquiries, he forwarded the wristwatch to the man's mother. In her reply, acknowledging the arrival of the wristwatch, she expressed her joy and thanks to God for that reminder of her son.

Along with the news columns describing details of the August fighting, the public read with interest the newspaper dispatches sent by Mr Ellis Ashmead-Bartlett, a reporter at Anzac. He lightened his readers' war gloom by describing the marvellous spirit amongst the New Zealand and Australian soldiers. Their lean, athletic physiques after four months of bitter fighting on Gallipoli amazed him. In his view, no European nation had men comparable with the Anzacs; not even the hand-picked Prussian Guard.

Ashmead-Bartlett commented on the way the colonials sauntered around, without the need for officers or NCOs to march them anywhere and tell them what to do. He observed that they tended to operate in small groups, had their own rules which they disciplined themselves and always had an unofficial leader in their midst. They were not an army, but a community he thought. He found their matter-of-fact approach refreshing. He painted a vivid picture of one group at the beach tasked with carrying stores and water back up to their firing line; the group sat about for awhile; some smoked their pipes and then one man slowly stood up and said: "Well boys, its got to be done; so the quicker we get it over the better"[137]. This attitude, born in the hardship of the fighting, was sustaining each of them through those grim months. In a dispatch for *The Guardian,* their correspondent at Gallipoli explained to his readers that the position called ANZAC was coined from the initial letters of the "Australian and New Zealand Army Corps". He went on to mention an observation made by a captured Turkish officer, who informed him that "Anzak"[138] was also a Turkish word – meaning "only just".[139] Doubtless, given the bewildering execution of the campaign to date, the irony would not have been lost on anyone.

At the start of September, the arrival of the 2nd Australian Division allowed the NZ&A Division to be withdrawn from Anzac for a deserved rest on the nearby island of Lemnos. This hand-over was conducted gradually, with the new Australian battalions rotated into the line to replace the depleted NZ&A battalions, who promptly left for the beach and a transport ship to Lemnos. The 1st Field Company and the Mounted Field Troop were also withdrawn from Anzac.

Arriving during this time were fifty-seven reinforcement Engineers who were allocated to the dwindling 2nd Field Company, in which only seventy-five healthy Engineers remained from the original two hundred and twenty men who had arrived at Anzac three months earlier. Among those evacuated was Major Barclay, who had succumbed to enteric fever. The 2nd Field Company was not withdrawn; instead it was attached to the 3rd Australian Light Horse. The company set about improving the defensive position at 'Rhododendron Spur' and the 'Apex'. New trenches were built, roads improved, machine gun and observation posts were created, shelters dug and existing trenches repaired. The trenches they constructed, especially those at 'Rhododendron Spur', were praised by the infantry because they were deep.

By mid September[140] the N.Z. Engineers had sustained the following casualties:

Killed or Died of Wounds	1 Officer	27 Men
Wounded	6 Officers	123 Men
Missing		5 Men

Once all of the companies of Engineers were back at Anzac, they were primarily tasked with road construction and the repair of water pipes damaged by artillery. A further fifty Engineer reinforcements arrived at Anzac and were distributed across the two Field Companies. These occasional drafts never provided enough men to keep pace with the casualty rate and the Engineers continued to be under-manned. It is estimated that by October, the Anzac Engineers had dug about sixteen miles of trenches throughout the entire Anzac sector.

The routine of trench maintenance continued unabated and as the weather began to turn cooler the wetter weather resulted in flooding along the gullies and brought with it a major risk of disease. By this time, Anzac was one massive graveyard and the water tended to collect in the gullies where men had been buried. This water then ran off into the natural wells, risking contamination. Being able to guarantee an ample supply of clean drinking water for the troops became an acute problem. The autumn storms began, preventing the Royal Navy from being able to land any supplies, including the fresh water barges. The delay in supplies created uncertainty, which led to rationing.

At Sulva Bay, the storms impacted in a different way, causing flash flooding. The water cascaded down the gullies and into the nearest run-offs – usually being the Allied trenches. The rushing water drowned several men of the 29th Division who held those low lying trench systems. Improving the drainage along the roads and in the gullies quickly became a high priority. The wet weather was followed by very low temperatures and severe frosts, resulting in sections of the vital water pipes bursting and having to be re-laid. Conscious of the impending winter, the Engineers began mining and tunnelling to construct suitably deep dugouts to enable the infantry to continue to fight in winter conditions.

The senior commanders were not ignorant of the situation, particularly the dependency upon the Royal Navy for re-supplying the peninsula. To the Turks and their German advisors it was obvious that the Allied campaign had stalled and they were now hemmed in along the coastal strips, unable to break out.

After months of bitter and sometimes desperate hand-to-hand fighting at Lone Pine and Chunuk Bair, severe losses had been inflicted on both sides with no advantage gained. Despite all their best efforts the Allied forces continued to hold precarious footholds on the Gallipoli peninsula. It was far from the stroll through green countryside and pleasant villages expected by the men when they had first landed back in April.

Chapter Fourteen: Leaving no monuments, only the dead

In October, Hamilton had been replaced by General Sir Charles Monro, who arrived on the peninsula on the 27th of October. He had been instructed by the British Government to advise whether the campaign should continue.

After talking with his commanders and seeing the situation for himself, he recommended evacuation. His assessment and reasoning was quite telling. *"..We merely hold the fringe of the shore and are confronted by Turks in very formidable entrenchments, with all the advantages of position and power of observation."*[141]

He went on to point out that as the flanks of the Turkish positions could not be attacked, frontal assaults were the only option. This approach would result in limited success as there was insufficient room on the beaches to assemble the divisions needed to sustain such attacks and the artillery to support them, if familiar Western Front tactics were to be used. The naval gunfire employed throughout the campaign had merely supplemented the limited artillery. The trajectory of naval fire, although effective against the Turkish forts, had been largely ineffective in destroying enemy trench systems.

Munro realised that the winter weather would present a major challenge for the Royal Navy attempting to land essential supplies on the peninsula in support of a winter campaign. Although the Suvla Bay assaults in August had been predicated on securing a winter beaching area, this was now dismissed as an unworkable strategy. Finally, Munro highlighted the large number of soldiers being evacuated daily having succumbed to sickness. A force could not be maintained during the winter months with this high rate of depletion.

In the absence of any suitable rearguard areas for training and resting the troops, he believed that the Corps and Divisional commanders did not command sufficient advantage to maintain a reliable fighting machine. With the exception of the New Zealand and Australian Army Corps,[142] the troops were not equal to a sustained effort.[143]

Churchill would later comment on Munro's decision: "He came, he saw, he capitulated".

In mid November, Lord Kitchener visited Anzac Cove. As he disembarked from the picket-boat on the North Pier he was afforded a "soldier's welcome", being greeted by cheers from those gathered who suddenly recognised him. The word soon spread and the cheers continued as he toured the trenches. He told the men: "His Majesty the King has asked me to tell you how splendidly he thinks you have done. You have done excellently well. Better, even than I thought you would."[144]

His inspection of the position took two hours[145], including the 'Nek' where the Light Horse had charged on the 7th of August. He stopped at the small canteen operated in those tough conditions by the Sydney YMCA for the benefit of the troops. The rumour mill reported that during his rapid inspection of the positions he simply exclaimed "Good God!"[146] Kitchener supported Munro's assessment. In his view it was an awful place and he saw no way of breaking the deadlock that had been reached.

The senior commanders had also grasped another important fact. Germany had successfully invaded Serbia earlier in October, enabling them to secure the 200 miles of railway in the north of that country. A railway line from Berlin to Constantinople via Vienna now existed over which war supplies could freely move eastwards and into Turkey. This enabled Germany to supply Turkey with modern artillery guns, high explosive shells and other essential military equipment. The fortified Allied positions at Gallipoli were thus assessed as untenable against such modern heavy artillery. This consideration alone made the evacuation a necessary measure.[147]

By the end of November, the troops experienced the effects of the first winter snows along the Gallipoli terrain, as tarpaulin roofs on shelters collapsed due to the weight of snow and men began suffering from frost bite. Preparations had been underway for several weeks preparing dug-outs and shelters to help cope with winter weather and after the first blizzard the ordinance stores issued extra clothing to the troops more suitable for colder weather.

Rumours of an order to evacuate Anzac and Suvla Bay began to circulate and were soon corroborated. In preparing for evacuation, silence and minimal movement were ordered. Such restraint was essential to replicate the effect of thinning the line and to lull the Turks into believing that this low level of activity was the Anzacs new trench practice. If the Turks accepted it, then it would make the withdrawal of troops easier, otherwise any suspicion could be disastrous. Nevertheless, after a few days of this new tactic, the cautious Turks sent patrols to investigate. These patrols were greeted with sudden, concentrated fire which had the effect of satisfying their curiosity. The patrols ceased.

Beginning on the 13th of December, the evacuation continued for the next seven days. Gradually fewer and fewer troops occupied the frontline positions. Tensions ran high, sleep was almost impossible and the bogus trench routines continued with the knowledge that if the Turks suspected anything a major offensive would be launched. Machine guns were therefore continuously manned and bombs remained close by.

While the Allies evacuated silently, the Turks were busy with their own surprise. Batteries of newly arrived Austrian howitzers were being deployed at Gallipoli. When they were first used, this modern weapon quickly caused devastation to an Australian post at 'Lone Pine', and then 'Rhododendron Spur' which was shelled on the 19th of December[148].

Sapper Borthwick Haliburton, one of the remaining originals who had landed at Anzac on that distant April day, became the last New Zealand engineer to be killed on Gallipoli. He was working at Hill 60 at the time of his death and his friends buried him in the frozen ground between Tipperary Sap and Evan's Well on the 11th of December 1915.

The N.Z. Engineers finally evacuated Gallipoli in the early hours of the 20th of December 1915 after assisting the Australian Engineers with a final job, the demolition of anything left behind. This included all stores, a Hotchkiss gun and a 5-inch howitzer not considered worth removing. The final act occurred in the early hours of the 20th of December as the "diehards" anxiously left the forward positions at 'Lone Pine', the 'Apex' and Chunuk Dere and made their way through the dark to the beach for embarkation. The men at the 'Apex' and 'Hill 60' reported that the Turks were busy putting out wire in anticipation of a big attack.

Shortly afterwards, a timed fuse detonated a mine at the 'Nek' and around 3am all remaining stores on the shore line were set alight as the flotilla of motor barges and trawlers carrying the last party of troops, finally left Anzac. Once aboard the warships, they were treated to hot cocoa and pea soup before being landed at Lemnos with their comrades.

On the morning of the 20th of December, the Turkish artillery could fire all it wished without anyone caring. The evacuation had been completed the night before, leaving Anzac silent and occupied only by the dead.

On the 8th of January 1916, the last of the Allied troops left Cape Helles and the peninsula. The entire evacuation was so skilfully prepared and executed that there were no losses, which in itself was remarkable considering the high casualty rate which had been anticipated[149]. As if to validate the decision, a storm on the 10th of January wrecked the piers used so effectively for re-supply.

The official communiqué stated:
"Without the Turks being aware of the movement a great army has been withdrawn from one of the areas occupied on the Gallipoli Peninsula, although in closest contact with the enemy. By this contraction of front, operations at other points of the line will be more effectively carried out."[150]

The adventure had come to a close. Christmas passed with the Anzac troops either onboard transport ships returning to Egypt, or remaining on Lemnos Island. Christmas dinner consisted of the interminable bully beef and biscuits with the addition of the rare treats of rice and prunes[151].

An Australian was quoted as saying that he was glad not to be at home when the news was received that the Dardanelles had been evacuated[152]. Too many friends were left behind in some type of grave and he felt that the public would not understand why the campaign had been abandoned. Others thought that the British commanders had neglected the lessons taken from the Japanese landing and capture of the Lioatung Peninsula from the Russians in 1904. There, surprise and superior forces at decisive points, both often lacking during the Gallipoli campaign, prevailed.

Throughout the eight month campaign, 8,556 New Zealanders had been landed on Gallipoli; 2,721 had been killed and 4,752 wounded – a total of 7,473[153]. They had been awarded one Victoria Cross (won by Corporal C.T.G Bassett on Chunuk Bair), twenty-one Companions of the Distinguished Service Orders, twenty-five Military Crosses, fifty-nine Distinguished Conduct Medals and two hundred and sixteen Mentioned in Despatches.[154] Total Allied casualties for the Gallipoli campaign were officially given as 209,604 killed, wounded and missing.

Gallipoli, like all significant moments in the emergence of young nations, still retains a special place in the histories of Australia and New Zealand. It is commemorated each year on the 25th of April.

After the war, Anzac Day dinners were held, and the toast of "The glorious memory of those who fell at the Dardanelles", was honoured with a silence. Nowadays those battlefields on the Gallipoli peninsula are again occupied on Anzac Day by young Australians and New Zealanders. Many are backpackers who walk along Lone Pine and Chunuk Bair listening to their guide's version of history. Many feats from that bygone generation are forgotten, the only testament to them ever being there, are the marks in the ridges and the graveyards, many with headstones bearing a simple inscription which says "Known only Unto God".

Chapter Fifteen: I suppose you just had to be there

The grit, intelligence and sheer luck needed by the N.Z. Field Engineers to get through a campaign as harsh as Gallipoli was amply demonstrated during their time on the peninsula. It was a complete baptism to warfare for everyone, including the Mounted Field Troop.

One Australian officer wrote of the pluck and endurance he witnessed by the 1st Field Company. He believed that due to their energy and hard work they enabled the Anzacs to take and hold onto many of the most dangerous positions in those early days. He praised how they were always about, performing some dangerous task in an exposed position along the parapets. Most memorable for him was the splendid work undertaken in trench work, pier building, water divining, bomb proofing, pumping and also their mining operations[155].

The Engineers learnt important lessons from Gallipoli and they would carry these with them into their next theatre of war – the Western Front, among them the need for high morale and being able to stay healthy.

They understood that training in infantry field craft was important, particularly as they inevitably found themselves on the firing line with the infantry, and additionally, the need to co-ordinate their activities with the infantry, particularly during assaults where haste was vital.

The ability to strengthen defences in a captured stretch of trench before the enemy could counter-attack was critical and had to be properly organised during the advanced planning stages with the infantry. Men and materials had to arrive at the right time and in a pre-arranged order to ensure a captured trench could be consolidated in minimal time. The sequence of tasks started with sandbags to create trench blocks and to add extra trench height for protection.

These had to be carried over either pre-filled or be hastily filled while under enemy fire and then stacked along the new parapet during those early critical minutes. Then men with picks and shovels began to reverse the firing parapet of the captured trench and using the loose dirt in the trench they could fill extra sandbags and add them along the parapet. Further bags and dirt could be piled onto this elevated parapet later.

Once the firing line was established, work then began on gun positions, trench repairs, digging new communications trenches to evacuate the wounded and bring reinforcements forward; and finally the construction of protective overhead cover. Congestion in the new trenches was always a problem and often provided a concentrated target for the enemy, so it was up to the officers and NCOs to ensure they controlled the trench area.

Officers needed to let NCOs make decisions on the engineering works near the firing line. This was more than likely developed as an informal practice after several engineering officers had been killed or wounded during the fighting in May.

They always needed to be prepared to destroy a defensive position if the assault should fail, and not retire, as 2nd Field Company had done on the 4th-5th of June, leaving serviceable bomb-proof shelters and materials behind for the enemy to occupy. Carrying an explosive such as guncotton in an assault, for just this purpose, was invaluable.

Skill and experience were highly valued battlefield commodities, especially when it came to improvising with what was available, as was demonstrated with the efforts to find water, dig wells, make home-made bombs and trench mortars. On Gallipoli the men soon learned that "fit for purpose" sufficed, regardless of how crudely something was manufactured or constructed.

One observation was made in New Zealand in early 1916, by the Public Works Department. The Department openly criticised the NZEF for its wastage of engineering skills. It pointed out that of the thirty-two qualified civil and electrical Engineers who had volunteered from the Department since 1915, only nine had been commissioned and all of these served as officers within the NZ Engineer Tunnel Company. The remainder of the qualified Engineers served as sappers in the various

Field Companies. This opinion was supported by the Institute of Engineers who pointed out that in the British Army, qualified Engineers were commissioned into the Royal Engineers, whereas the practice within the NZEF was the opposite, favouring non-Engineers for commissions and then to have qualified Engineers serve as sappers, thereby never fully exploiting their skills and experience.

Gallipoli showed that being a field engineer required more than the technical skills based on construction and destruction. A field engineer needed courage to fight with the infantry on the firing line, to cope with incredible hardship and to maintain high morale. If a man possessed a particular skill it was soon identified and put to full use. But only those who lived or died through those desperate months could truly judge whether every man's skills and experience had been fully exploited.

Chapter Sixteen: Britain's Home Defence and the war in the air

As the transport ships carrying the Anzacs sailed away from Gallipoli waters to Egypt, the newspapers in England reported that the War Budget showed estimated revenue of £305 million and a deficit of £1,285 million. The kit allowance for British Territorial soldiers was increased from 2 pence to 2½ pence a day effective 1st of January 1916 and Income Tax increased by 40% to pay for it all.

When news of the evacuation reached Egypt the prestige of the British Empire fell amongst the Egyptians. British and French residents in Cairo were jostled off footpaths and even spat upon. As the animosity grew, armed military patrols began guarding important buildings and bridges. One Sunday, hundreds of rioters assembled in the Place Saladin and the Australian Light Horse were assembled and charged through the mob, reformed and charged again. No further riots were reported and calm descended upon the city[156].

The failure of the Gallipoli campaign and the stalemate on the Western Front were not the only problems facing His Majesty's Government. The British public realised that this would not be a short war. Any argument to the contrary was dispelled by May 1915 when Lord Kitchener appealed for more men. To encourage enlistment, Kitchener had raised the recruitment age for those joining the Regular Army to forty years of age, while the standard height requirement was lowered to five foot two inches for infantry, including Territorials. It was estimated at the time that Britain would need three million men to win the war. Six months later this number was revised upwards to four million men. In January 1916, the first of two Military Services Acts was passed which effectively meant conscription. Those exempt were: conscientious objectors, those medically unfit and those already in essential war work. All others who were eligible were expected to report for duty.

In an attempt to address the chaotic situation of home defence, the command of the British Home Forces was given to Field Marshall Viscount Sir John French in December 1915, following his removal as commander-in-chief of the BEF, now commanded by Sir Douglas Haig. Considered mainly a ceremonial role, Commander of the British Home Forces encompassed the burgeoning problem of air defence, which from early 1915 had begun to absorb more resources, when the German airships increased their attacks on naval ports and towns along the south-east of England.

Airships were a relatively recent innovation, having been pioneered in the early 1900's in Britain by the American, Samuel Cody. After his successful powered airship flight in 1907, his company developed aircraft for the Royal Navy. In October 1908 these contracts were cancelled when the War Office's Committee of Imperial Defence decided aircraft were not an essential part of modern warfare. This was still the era where Calvary provided rapid movement and observation on the battlefield and the Royal Navy had little use for land based airships. Besides which, the Hague Convention of 1899 had prohibited the dropping of bombs from balloons and so by interpretation limited any useful military contribution the aircraft could make; or so the War Office convinced themselves.

This decision was rapidly reversed in 1910 in response to the pace which both Germany and France had developed the role of aircraft in battlefield observation[157] and spotting for the artillery. By late 1911 the Italians had gone one step further by pioneering aerial bombing against the Turks during their Libyan campaign. They dismissed protests that they had violated The Hague Convention by simply arguing that winged aircraft were not airships or balloons, and were therefore exempt from the Hague Convention.

German airships were recognised as a threat early in the war, when they bombed the British and Belgian forces at the port of Antwerp on the 26th of August 1914. Airship raids over England became common place from February 1915 with docks and factories employed in war production being the targets. Soon London, parts of Essex, Ipswich, Bury St Edmunds, Dover, Sheerness and Maldon were amongst the towns and cities bombed by Zeppelin and Schütte-Lanz airships.

These airships would pass high over the towns, their engine noise clearly audible. They would then drop incendiary or high explosive bombs intending to destroy military installations. The problem was that bombing was still an inaccurate science, so when the bombs missed their intended target, the surrounding area was impacted. If this was not woods or fields, then they risked landing amongst urban buildings, houses and shops. These often inflicted civilian casualties, damaged road surfaces and burst gas and water pipes. Invariably this caused wide spread panic and afterwards an anti-government resentment. The Germans hoped that the outraged public would eventually force the British Government to the negotiating table.

It was therefore critical that effective counter measures were put in place; unfortunately the British struggled to mount anything like a co-ordinated response to this new type of air threat. Part of the problem lay in that the aircraft used for defence were not under a single, central command.

The Admiralty had its aircraft attempting to intercept the German airships and bombers before they reached the British coastline, their aim being to prevent damage to the port areas. Whereas, the Army's aircraft would only engage the Germans once they crossed the coast and were overland. Communication between the two services was poor and by the time enemy aircraft had crossed the coast, the slow, outdated RFC Army aircraft sent to do battle and defeat them lacked the much needed ability to reach the cruising heights of the German airships and bombers, let alone keep pace with them.

Artillery was soon deployed to oppose the air threat, although this could not be elevated sufficiently to fire at the overhead airships, nor could they adequately detect where they were in the night sky. Being unable to effectively see and engage the enemy reduced the artillery as a deterrent. Finally, there was no air to ground communication and blackout procedures in streets and houses were not enforced, so towns and cities were unintentionally lit up for the German aircrews. It was all very haphazard and certainly helped the Germans achieve their early air successes over England in 1915.

With Paris also being bombed, retaliatory aircraft raids were conducted by the Allies over German territory. In June 1915, twenty-three allied aircraft raided Karlsruhe, in Baden near the French-German border. It had a population of 160,000 people with an estimated garrison of 4,000 soldiers. The intended targets of the air raid were the castle, arms factory and railway station[158] though twenty-nine civilians were killed and more were wounded. Karlsruhe would be targeted again in 1916 and amongst the casualties were children attending a circus.

Improvements to the Home Defence would eventually enable the British gun crews to light up German airships by searchlights and then engaged them with anti-aircraft guns. Military night air patrols armed with new incendiary ammunition for their machine guns would wreak havoc on the airships.

These bullets were loaded into the gun's magazines in a pre-arranged sequence. First to be chambered were the tracer bullets partially developed by Flight Lieutenant F.A. Brock. These would light the trajectory of the bullets and allow the pilot to make necessary flight corrections. After a number of tracer rounds, the next rounds to be chambered in the load sequence were explosive bullets devised by a New Zealand engineer John Pomeroy. This alternating sequence of tracer and then explosive bullets was highly effective. The sparkle of the tracer rounds allowed the pilot to bring the gunfire onto the airship and then the incendiary bullets would tear into the balloon fabric and rapidly ignite the gases inside with devastating effect, as the airships suddenly turned into an aerial fireball. If the rounds missed, a fresh magazine could be loaded into the guns and another pass made with the same firing pattern: tracers followed by incendiaries.

Being both incendiary and soft nosed the bullet was against the agreed rule of war[159], therefore it was restricted for use only against raiders over Britain. The first "downing" of an airship was over London in September, 1916 when a Schütte-Lanz airship was destroyed, much to the joy of the watching public. The young pilot responsible, Second Lieutenant Leefe-Robinson, won the Victoria Cross for his determination and skill.

With the ever present menace from air raids, light restrictions and black-outs were imposed under the Lights (England and Wales) Order. This mandated that all inside lights had to be reduced and shaded by shutters, dark blinds or curtains. No light could be visible from any direction and no part of the pavement, road, building or other object could be distinctly illuminated.

Vehicles could only be lit up half an hour after sunset. Any vehicle using the roadway, including handcarts and horse drawn wagons, had to have red lights to the rear after dark. To help with public adherence, the local newspapers published weekly timetables showing the time from when blackout precautions had to be in place by. These were to the minute; for example on 26th of February 1917 the blackout had to be effective from 6:13pm.

Bright lights from buildings and vehicles were restricted in prohibited areas, such as Northumberland, Durham, and East Ridings of Yorkshire as well as the coast areas of Hampshire, so while Bournemouth and Christchurch had enforced black-outs, the Dorset coastal town of Poole just a mile away had no such restrictions. It was a beacon in the surrounding darkness. This changed in winter 1916 when the regulations extended across the county boundary and was applied to Dorset, and so Poole was also blacked out.

Unaware that German airships did not have the range to get as far Bournemouth, the local Christchurch police still enforced the Order, and breaches were prosecuted with the offender being fined. Mrs Jane Burt in Mudeford was fined 5 shillings for light shining out of one of her windows and Captain Stanley Thompson, Royal Naval Division pleaded guilty to using headlights and not obscuring an electric lamp on a motor car. He was fined 10 shillings. A New Zealand Medical Officer returning to Brockenhurst from the Royal Engineers Training Depot in Christchurch was also fined for showing a bright light on his motor car.

During the Great War, an estimated 280 tons of German bombs were dropped on English cities, killing around 1,413 people and injuring another 3,408[160].

Chapter Seventeen: Formation of the New Zealand Division

The 1st and 2nd Australian Divisions along with the New Zealand and Australian (NZ&A) Division returned piecemeal throughout December and January to Egypt. This time their camp was at Moascar on the Suez Canal near the town of Ismailia, which the men thought was more pleasant than Cairo. The New Zealand Patriotic Societies had sent Christmas billies[161] full of treats to the NZEF and these were distributed throughout January and February as troops were also arriving back from hospitals.

Now that the Gallipoli campaign was finished, military order and routine had to be re-established amongst the exhausted soldiers, many of whom had for months not worn a complete uniform while on the peninsula. Men were beginning to return from hospitals in both Malta and England. Others still remained scattered throughout the RAMC hospital system and were unlikely to reach the NZ&A Division for some time.

The Anzacs were reorganised and underwent intensive training for their next theatre of war – the "main theatre" of France. Some believed that they should have been sent there in June 1915 when the Gallipoli campaign began to flounder[162].

With the N.Z. Rifle Brigade now in Egypt and the arrival of large numbers of N.Z. reinforcements there were enough men to form two extra brigades. After political discussions and a commitment from the New Zealand Government to maintain a sufficient level of reinforcements to sustain its own Division in the field, the New Zealand Division was established[163], under the command of Major-General Sir A.H. Russell. This allowed the Australian 4th Brigade to be detached from the now disbanded NZ&A Division and integrated with the Australian 12th and 13th Brigades to form the 4th Australian Division.

General Godley had command of I Anzac Corps and retained control of the N.Z. Expeditionary Force as a whole. Godley was not popular with the men[164], particularly amongst the Gallipoli veterans and Private Norman Gray N.Z.M.C witnessed this when Godley officially opened the Moascar camp's YMCA hut in February and then decided to address the gathered men.

The immediate problem facing the new N.Z. Division was that the 1st N.Z. Infantry Brigade had all the experienced Gallipoli men. The Rifle Brigade had already been operating in Egypt for some time so it was decided to keep that brigade intact. To share this experience across the Infantry Brigades, it was decided that each 1st N.Z. Infantry Brigade battalion, being: 1st Otago, 1st Auckland, 1st Canterbury and 1st Wellington would establish another battalion, blending both the reinforcements and its veterans. In this way 2nd Otago, 2nd Auckland, 2nd Canterbury and 2nd Wellington were established. Many veterans chose to remain in the 1st Brigade possibly to stay with "mates" they trusted, in the belief that by looking after one another it improved one's chances of staying alive longer. Promotion was usually offered to entice veterans to transfer to the 2nd Infantry Brigade and those who accepted did so only after careful consideration.

There was now an urgent need to train and ready the Division, so with the reduced daylight available during the Egyptian winter months, all camps were ordered to be clear by 7:30am until 4pm daily. Lunch was provided by the mobile kitchens in the field most days, unless the Divisional Commanders ordered otherwise. Instruction courses were held on the newly issued .303 rifles, Mills bombs, and Lewis guns. Clothing, equipment and webbing was replaced or exchanged. The officers and NCOs underwent training in the new trench drills, battle order and tactics. These began at section level and introduced the deployment of the Lewis machine guns along with the new Stokes trench mortar. Training was then conducted at: platoon, company, battalion, and brigade level and then divisional manoeuvres began along with numerous night exercises.

The two Field Engineer companies were brought up to strength with the arrival of the reinforcements from New Zealand, and colleagues returning from hospitals in Egypt, England and Malta. Many of those from England arrived at the Moascar camp on the 2nd of January 1916, after spending Christmas at sea.

For the Engineers, their training became more technical. Whereas on Gallipoli wire entanglements were akin to fences, in France it was a science of interlinking barriers, gaps for the artillery or machine gunners to fire into, and channels for infantry to patrol in and out from. If wire was put up it had to be marked on a map and where gaps existed these were advised to the artillery and infantry battalion commander in that area of trench.

They also trained with Bangalore torpedoes in order to blow holes in the enemy's wire entanglements. British defensive works and fortifications were also being built in the desert to the east of the Suez Canal and the N.Z. Engineers were given the task of building floating bridges. These allowed men and supplies to cross the Canal at various points during the day, merely by assembling the barges wherever they were required. These were then connected together and after the military traffic had crossed were dismantled and the Canal shipping allowed to continue. The bridges varied in length. The three largest were around 400 feet and were erected at Ballah, El Ferdan and Serapeum.

The Field Companies not employed along the Suez participated in either the divisional manoeuvres or improving facilities and conditions around the New Zealanders' Moascar camp. Such work included laying water pipes for water supply and building ablution blocks, bath houses and barrack huts.

Careful not to repeat the mistakes of Gallipoli in fielding under strength formations, it was recognised that with three infantry brigades in the N.Z. Division, another field engineer company was required for the N.Z. Divisional Engineers. The only available engineering specialists were the Mounted Field Troop, so they became the nucleus of 3rd Field Company. Like all the newly formed units, they were immediately below the pre-requisite company strength. This situation was overcome when it was decided that the Divisional Cavalry, formed from the Otago Mounted Rifles, was to be reduced to only one squadron. As many of the Gallipoli veterans remained together in Divisional Calvary, the "new boys" became the surplus squadrons that were quickly broken up and disbursed to make up the shortages in the 3rd Field Engineers, the Field Artillery[165] and the newly formed N.Z. Pioneer Battalion.

Troopers Albany Thorp and George Pullar had only joined the Otago Mounted Rifles from the 5th Reinforcement; both became Engineers in 3rd Field Company. Suitable tradesmen were sought from the recently arrived Engineers' 10th Reinforcement and eventually, by such means, the N.Z. Division had its three complete, though not entirely trained, Field Engineer Companies – one for each Infantry Brigade.

The N.Z. Pioneer Battalion comprised those men remaining from the Native Contingent who had served on Gallipoli, along with their recently arrived 3rd Maori Reinforcements, Niue Islanders and Rarotongans[166]. As this only comprised half of the battalion; the other half was made up from the surplus Otago Mounted squadrons. Its commanding officer was Captain (later Lieutenant Colonel) GA King DSO.

The title "N.Z. Pioneer Battalion" would change on 1st of September 1917 when sufficient Maori reinforcements allowed them to fully man the Pioneer Battalion, and it was re-titled N.Z. Maori (Pioneer) Battalion[167].

As a result of this re-organisation, no New Zealand Engineers would accompany the N.Z. Mounted Brigade during its forthcoming desert campaign in the Sinai. Later, due to the cold climate in Europe a number of South Pacific Islanders would return to Egypt, eventually forming an Ammunition Column, also called the Raratongan Company, which helped to support the campaign in Sinai and Palestine.

Lieutenant-Colonel Pridham was appointed CRE and retained a number of his experienced officers; amongst who were: Major Barclay, Captain McNeill RE., Captain Skelsey, Captain Gibbs, Captain Hulbert, Captain Keenan, Lieutenant Salmon, Lieutenant Black, Lieutenant Newbold and Lieutenant Annabell.

On the 5th of April the advance elements of the N.Z. Division and I Anzac

Corps, commanded by General Birdwood, embarked for their voyage to France, arriving at Marseilles without incident on the 11th of April and entrained for the "nursery sector" of Armentières, in the northern part of France, being the British Sector of the Front. The II Anzac Corps, under General Godley, would arrive in France in June, when the N.Z. Division would be back under his command in II Anzac, swapping with the Australian 4th Division that would join I Anzac.

Remaining in Egypt were the New Zealand Base Depots containing the Stationary Hospital and Training Depots as reinforcements continued to arrive. These depots would remain in Egypt until June, 1916 when it was decided for war economy to transfer them to England.

Also in Egypt at this time was the New Zealand Mounted Brigade[168], now part of the Australian and New Zealand Mounted Division[169] under the command of Major General Harry G. Chauvel. They would eventually fight as mounted infantry across the Sinai and in Palestine. Their first of many victorious actions was at the Battle of Romani, east of the Suez Canal. Here on the 3rd of August 1916 the Turks attacked the railhead in another attempt to force their way through to the Suez Canal. The battle, commanded by General Murray, lasted two days with the Anzacs fighting fiercely around Wellington Ridge and Mount Royston before the Turks finally withdrew.

As the New Zealanders embarked for France, they heard the news that the advance by the British Army in Mesopotamia[170] had been halted. The Turks had been able to rush extra army divisions to that theatre from the now abandoned campaign in the Dardanelles. The city of Kut was still held by the British but was under siege from the Turks. The 13th Division, which had fought on Gallipoli, was again in action against the Turks as it tried to relieve that garrison. It was all in vain. On the 29th of April the garrison of around 8,000 men surrendered. Amongst them was Battalion Headquarters of the 1/4th Hampshire Regiment along with one of its companies and the Isle of Wight lads in the 1/5th Hants Howitzers Royal Field Artillery.

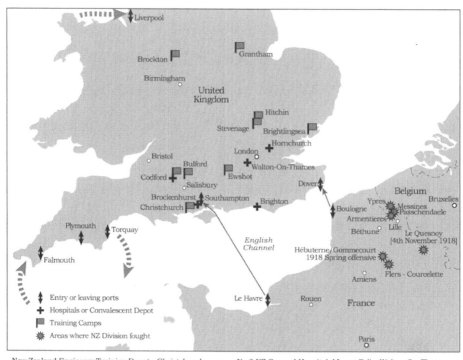

New Zealand Engineers Training Depot - Christchurch
NZ Command Depot, Codford
No.3 NZ General Hospital, Codford
N2 Army Service Corps. Depot, Codford
NZ Infantry Depot, Sling Camp, Bulford
NZ Rifle Brigade, Brockton
NZ Rifle Signal Training Depot, Stevenage
NZE Signallers Training Depot, Hitchin
NZ Convalescing Hospital "Greytowers", Hornchurch

No.2 NZ General Hospital, Mount Felix, Walton-On-Thames
NZ Artillery Depot and NZ Medical Corps Depot, Ewshot
Convalescing Hospital (Officers), Brighton
No.1 NZ General Hospital, Brockenhurst
NZ Evacuation Depot, Torquay
NZ Reinforcements Arrival, Falmouth
NZ Reinforcements Arrival, Plymouth
Machine Gun Training Depot, Grantham
Australian Engineers Training Depot, Brightlingsea

Location of New Zealand military establishments in England and sectors of France in which the New Zealand Division fought.

Drawing by Jenny Kynaston

Chapter Eighteen: The New Zealand Field Companies at Armentières, France

The troopships carrying the N.Z. Division arrived at Marseilles on the 16th of April 1916, and after unloading, the Engineers finally entrained for the British Sector in Northern France on the 17th of April. A selected number of long service men were granted a week's leave to England, while the remainder of I Anzac Corps spent the next few weeks re-equipping, getting their tin helmets, undergoing gas training and familiarising themselves with the front line trench routines.

Being billeted in French villages was a novelty for the men, even though it was colder than Egypt. There were two lasting memories during this time. One was of the crops still in the fields; the other was of the startling predominance of women wearing their long, black mourning veils. The men would later comment that this attire made the French war widows look very tall.

Eventually on the 12th and 13th of May the Division moved into a four mile section of front line at Armentières, near the Lys. Positioned in low-lying flats, the trench system that they took over was in a poor state of repair and it required extensive revetting, sandbagging and strengthening work by the New Zealanders. A "live and let live" attitude had prevailed in that sector until then. Earthworks, dugouts and wire entanglements had been ignored and the decayed sandbags on the parapets provided little protection from German bullets. One staff officer commented that "the damned place is positively dangerous!"[171]

The New Zealanders had no intention of following the "live and let live policy" of the previous British Divisions in the sector. They found the area to be relatively undisturbed. One scouting party found a ruined cottage with currant bushes and fruit trees[172]. They collected some apples and plums before starting back. As the Anzacs became more aggressive in the Armentières sector, this cottage would later became a range finder for the German artillery at the start of their daily bombardment of the trenches.

Throughout late May and June the Engineers began to raise and strengthen the earthworks, improve revetting, create drainage, construct dugouts and repair the wire entanglements. Due to the low lying nature of the terrain, "dugouts" were in fact sandbag and corrugated iron huts, similar to those used on Gallipoli.

The work took longer than expected. This was partially due to the distance the Engineers travelled daily from their billets near Armentières to the front line trenches. Then congestion in the trench avenues became a problem and caused delays in moving materials to where they were needed. Finally hostile shelling and minenwerfers caused considerable damage to the trenches. In response, the Engineers and Pioneers instigated nightly trench patrols and repair parties to keep the avenues open.

They found the work of continually rebuilding trenches which had been blown to pieces by German shelling very hard. On Gallipoli they had never seen what a modern artillery bombardment could accomplish. At Armentières they began to appreciate that their trenches and avenues, however well built, only existed because the Germans allowed them to remain.

Being in the trenches during an artillery bombardment was a terrifying experience. Lieutenant Thurow of the British 41st Division was inspecting his stretch of trench at night during an artillery duel when he heard something rushing down on him. He instinctively knew what it was. Having no time to go forward or back he dropped down onto the duckboard and crouched against the parapet, rolling into a small ball. The shell went into the wall and buried itself sending up a shower of water and mud. A dud he thought.

It started hissing and then there was a BOOM. Thurow was lifted 3 feet into the air and the parapet tumbled down. Reeling with the concussion he managed to extricate himself, dazed, dishevelled and with his ears ringing. He was astonished in the realisation that he was standing on the very edge of a new shell crater. He had escaped being killed due to the artillery shell burying itself in the soft ground, thereby lessening the force of the explosion. If the ground had been drier, he believed he would have been blown to smithereens.[173]

Malthus[174] and his colleagues in the 1st Canterbury Battalion were subjected to heavy German shelling, supposedly in retaliation to the Engineers exploding a camouflet charge in a German mine near their front line trenches, killing many of the German miners. During one occasion, two of his Gallipoli friends, sought available cover in a shelter constructed from timber, corrugated iron and sandbags. They all thought that it would provide sufficient protection until it received a direct hit killing both men.

Sapper Thomas Farrer, whose brother had been killed on Gallipoli the year before, was also killed during the same period in a bombardment while attached to the 2nd Auckland Battalion, leaving their mother in Oxford, England to now grieve for both of her sons.

The New Zealand Engineers soon realised that the trenches were very necessary protection against small arms and casual artillery fire, but to properly protect the men good trench supports and strong dugouts were needed. In fact, dugouts were soon considered essential for survival. They knew that the chance of anyone living through an intense bombardment without such protection was very slight.

In fourteen days, the Engineers and Pioneers turned 22,000 feet of timber into revetting "A" frames, at a rate of 50 a day as well as working on splinter proof frames for dugouts, high explosive shell frames, and supports for duckboard walkways. To achieve this they used around 900 infantry soldiers, as well as 45 Belgian civilians. The "A" frames would be placed upside down in the trench, the long feet helping to support both sides of the trench in order to lessen any inward collapsing. The gaps between each "A" frame could be further strengthened by revetting.

The duckboards would be placed along the bar of the "A" frames. In this way the resulting walkways were slightly raised and above the trench floor which provided stable footing and kept the men's feet dry. The space between the trench floor and the duckboards created the drainage course. These raised paths would then in turn lead to the properly re-enforced dugouts constructed in recesses along the sides of the trenches. All this material had to be transported to the front line trenches at night and by horse drawn wagons. This was the responsibility of the Field Engineers' drivers like Sapper Frank Appleton, who maintained the forward supply dumps with all essential engineering materials.

In addition to this strengthening work across their trench system, the Engineers also worked on trench drainage and built 2 brick observation posts.[175]

It was imperative that the parapet's height was maintained along the entire section of trench being occupied. As the parapet construction was effectively packed dirt and sandbagged it was subject to movement and erosion due to battlefield conditions, as well as rain or the effect of bombardments. The reason for maintaining the height was soon made self evident to those living in the trenches - enemy snipers. These men were hunters and would take advantage of any mistakes, gaps and exposure evident in the ground geometry.

An early incident in the 1st Otago Battalion's stretch of trench drove this lesson home to everyone - Engineers and Infantry alike. As part of Officer Cadets training, three former NCOs from Guards' regiments were in the New Zealand trenches late one evening. They were to undertake officers' night routine with the 1st Otago officers. Two were well remembered as they were both over six feet tall.

The New Zealand company commander with them, Captain Hargest, and the third officer cadet were both of medium height. After a tour of the trench position, they began walking back along the trench to the Company HQ dugout. At a single point the parapet must have sloped, eroded or had dipped, thereby robbing it of valuable height. Whatever the cause, it afforded a narrow view into the trench. The four men were moving in Indian file along the duck boards, their heads all in a line at just one spot. It was a fatal mistake. A single sniper round, fired skilfully through that slight opening hit both tall men in the head, killing them both and sparing Hargest and the other cadet by mere inches[176]. As a general rule, tall men did not fare well in the trenches.

The wire entanglements in front of the New Zealand trenches were in poor condition due to the prior occupant's lack of attention and the constant German bombardment. The barbed wire entanglements were mainly buried or blown away, with long grass having overgrown the barbed wire in places, thereby hiding the gaps in the wire used by patrols to enter and return safely from no man's land.

Locating and clearing these gaps became a priority, not just because they provided safe exit and entry points for patrols and raiding parties, but it was critical that these gaps be identified and marked on machine gunners and artillery maps to deny the enemy uncontested passage.

Once the grass was cleared, the entanglements were strengthened and in parts re-constructed in either a maze formation or by circular wiring that channelled the enemy into killing zones covered by machine gun posts. The gaps were marked with pegs painted white on the side facing the trenches so they could be seen by parties going out into no man's land at night, but not visible to anyone moving towards the New Zealand positions, including the returning patrols. The return routes and signals had to be pre-arranged with the sentries and forward listening posts before leaving the safety of the trenches to prevent being accidentally shot by their own side as they returned during the dark of night.

Wiring parties from the infantry were deployed at night to help the Field Engineers repair and extend the wiring into the design and shape they required. These techniques were developed in training grounds that had been created in the relative safety of the back areas of Armentières.

It was fortunate that many infantrymen were from the farms and back blocks of New Zealand, so were competent in bush-clearing and fencing. As a result the wire entanglements were expertly constructed despite the constant hazards of enemy fire, flares and the short summer nights. The methods they used allowed a wiring party of 12 men to make an obstacle thirty yards by 10 yards in twenty minutes[177].

153

Generally it was agreed to be dangerous, stressful work and as Sergeant Aitken who commanded one wiring party commented, there was "an attrition of the sense of humour"[178] brought on by the awkwardness of men working in darkness, coupled with the fear that any noise risked the Germans detecting and then firing upon the working party. This was warranted as Sergeant Courtney's wiring party from the 2nd Wellington Battalion were unlucky when they were surprised by a German machine gun which killed two men and wounded two others. The remainder of the party made their way back to their trenches as best they could, while carrying the wounded and one of the dead men.

Raids and counter-raids by night commenced at the beginning of July as did an increased intensity in German artillery bombardments and minenwerfers. The great British offensive at the Somme had begun at this time. For those at Armentières, news was heavily censored about this distant engagement. The fighting along the sector increased and on the 4th of July a heavy barrage fell on the Wellington Battalion in the Epinette sector, causing a large number of casualties in the forward trenches.

Then on the 3rd/4th of July, German artillery fired at the trench system called "No.2 Locality". In co-ordination with this artillery barrage, the Germans conducted a successful trench raid on that sector. The bombardment decimated a large section of trench. The Auckland Battalion suffered 110 casualties;[179] of which 35 were killed. Amongst those killed were the entire Advance Post who had resisted the German raiders. The prelude bombardment was so concentrated that men manning the front-line trenches were entombed, killed by the concussion or literally blown apart. Where there had been trench walls, there were only craters, piled dirt, shredded sandbags and the smell of cordite.

After a swift fight in no man's land and amongst the wreckage, the Aucklanders drove the German raiders off. Clearing away the debris and reconstructing the trench system took the Engineers several weeks of back-breaking work. The English newspapers reported that after a heavy bombardment of their position, the New Zealanders repelled a strong German attack after it entered their trenches.[180]

The Engineers were often asked to provide demolition specialists to accompany the infantry on trench raids. Each raid targeted a predetermined section of the German frontline trenches. The style of raiding favoured by 1916 employed a boxed artillery barrage technique that targeted all sides of the section of trench to be entered.

This artillery bombardment was intended to blow away the wire entanglements in front of the area to be raided, isolate the garrison and prevent them vacating the trench ahead of the raiders' arrival. It also harassed enemy reinforcements advancing up communications trenches and generally caused chaos in the area about to be raided. The raid's objective was normally to capture a pre-determined number of German prisoners for intelligence purposes, the destruction of equipment and demolition of defensive positions, such as machine gun posts.

The planning for every trench raid usually began some weeks prior to the actual event. It started with digging a replica German trench as shown on aerial photographs. This was constructed in detail and included dugouts, machine gun emplacements and listening posts in similar positions as shown on the photographs. The raiders rehearsed their various roles sometimes for up to two weeks beforehand or until they were proficient. As the raid would occur during the cover of darkness, the rehearsals were also performed at night, preferably at the same time as the raid was planned. The darkness would limit each man's depth of vision, so the training allowed them to adapt to the reduced visibility, cope with it and then use it to their advantage.

The training ensured that they had the aptitude for the job, could overcome the difficulties of operating in the conditions and were capable when executing the patrolling routines. As the Germans listening posts would be trying to detect them, silence was vital. There could be no noise until the artillery bombardment started and then hell would be unleashed.

The Engineer's role was to appraise the state of the enemy trenches and to destroy any equipment found. For practical purposes when working at night in an enemy trench, they carried revolvers as well as 6lb charges of wet guncotton. The guncotton was packed in a square box having holes in the lid corresponding with the primer hole.

Each charge was carried in its own individual sandbag which was perforated for the primers. They were put in small tins and boxes in one pocket and two three-foot lengths of safety fuse with detonators attached in another. Because of the bombardment preceding the raid, it was considered inadvisable to carry the guncotton charge with primers and fuse attached, just in case of shells dropping short. Tins of fuses and flash lamps were also carried along with small crowbars to open the steel doors that lead into the deep dugouts.

Once in the enemy trench, the Engineers stayed with their assigned assaulting party. Any Germans resisting were shot by the infantry. Some infantry rifles had electric torches taped to the top of them in order to give better vision when peering into dugouts and any dark corners enabling a better shot at the occupants. Bombs were thrown into dugouts, prisoners were handed up to "receivers" on the parapet, who then hand-cuffed them.

If too many prisoners were captured for the allocated handlers, the excess were usually disposed of. Papers and maps were swept into an empty sandbag while the Engineers searched for pumps, machine gun emplacements, concrete structures, air shafts and also mine tunnels.

Two Engineers accompanied the N.Z. Rifle Brigade's successful raid on 25th of June and also the 1st Wellington Battalion's raid on 1st of July. Lance-Corporal Milne and Sapper Frost accompanied the N.Z. Pioneers Battalion on 10th of July, but no way could be found through the German wire, so the raiding party returned before it was cut off by German Infantry active at the same time to their rear in No Man's Land.

On the 13th of July the 4th Otago Company was torn to pieces in No Man's Land by German artillery and machine gun fire during their raid. German flares lit up the night sky, just as the main group were about to rush the German trenches. The right and left groups were similarly shredded. Of around 200 men in the raiding party, around 180 men were either killed or wounded. Of the Engineers accompanying that raid, Corporal Caird and 2nd Cpl Perry were both severely wounded.

On the 19th-20th of July, Lance-Corporal Scrimshaw DCM, Sappers Willott and Prentice accompanied the 1st Auckland Battalion's raid but all were ordered out of the German trench before they had a chance to destroy anything.

These experiences of the Western Front continued unabated throughout July and August, as did the human wastage wrought by artillery bombardment and the high casualty rates from trench raids.

To provide an opportunity for rest amongst the men, the three Field Companies were rotated between frontline work and divisional tasks. One divisional role was to maintain the water supply in Armentières. This entailed pumping the deep well water and then distributing it through a pipe network to various points around the town. They continued to be employed in constructing bath houses, hospital buildings, ensuring proper sanitation in the billet areas and tending to the needs of the horses amongst other duties.

They also continued to operate the three woodwork factories near the Lys, where they made the frames, duckboards and other trench materials. The quantity of materials needed to ensure a steady output from their factories was sometimes procured more through stealth than the efficiency of the British Army ordinance system.

When French barges were spotted transporting materials up the Lys one of the New Zealand Engineering officers merely boarded them below the town, confirmed the cargo, and then simply changed the divisional labels[181]. When the barges eventually arrived at Armentières, the materials were unloaded, labels read, found to be mostly destined for the New Zealand Division and forwarded to their depots by the ASC. This invariably left the other Divisional Supply Officers with the headache of explaining to their superiors why nothing had arrived for their division. With the blame squarely laid on the supply system they would hastily re-request materials.

Being billeted in the back areas provided the Engineers with the opportunity to delouse, wash and enjoy some of the distractions provided by the various estaminets. The estaminets provided hot light meals, usually chips and eggs, as well as wine and beer. Breaches of discipline occasionally occurred and were swiftly dealt with. These ranged from the predictable, such as: drunkenness, absent on parade and insubordination, through to the careless or malicious. On one occasion, a driver left his horse and wagon unattended while he went into an estaminet. When he finally left, most of the stores and all the sandbags had been stolen. In another instance, an engineer broke into the Officers Mess canteen and helped himself to its contents. Both men were severely disciplined.

Punishments ranged from forfeiture of pay, demotion in rank, close detention through to the severe Field Punishment No 1, which had replaced flogging. This punishment resulted in the prisoner being tied in a standing position, to a post or gun wheel for up to two hours each day until he had served the sentence. The maximum period for this field punishment was 21 days.

As they become more familiar with the terrain and experienced in the enemy's practices, their field reconnaissance skills improved. This was important and made them capable of accurately assessing the amount of time, men, and materials needed to complete any given job. Being billeted in the back areas, they were close to the supply dumps and could properly plan the work.

The planning had to take into consideration the number of shifts required to complete the work, the availability of Engineers, the size of infantry work parties available and if this conflicted with work going on elsewhere. Once decided upon, the materials and tools would be ordered from their stores dump and then loaded onto their wagons. The drivers would be responsible for delivering it to the right place, where they would be unloaded. Here another important skill was honed; supervising infantry work parties who did not want to be there. If the infantry considered the work benefiting their immediate comfort and safety they participated wholeheartedly, otherwise their efforts were at best economic.

Earlier in late June 1916 the only desertion to the Germans of a New Zealand soldier had occurred. He was Private W.P. Nimot, serving with the Otago Regiment whose parents were German settlers living in New Zealand. He was later suspected of passing on information which led to a fierce German raid on the 8th of July on the vulnerable Mushroom outpost, which was in effect a salient held at the time by the 1st Canterbury Battalion. With most of the Canterbury's officers either killed or wounded during the fighting, the position was only regained when Lieutenant Kibblewhite led a mixed party of New Zealand Machine Gunners, Engineers from 1st Field Company and Infantry to successfully retake and occupy the salient[182]. Again, as on Gallipoli, the Engineers had proved their usefulness with the bayonet in a hard fight.

With the risk of loyalties being stretched and anti-German sentiment prevailing, the NZEF started a process whereby any soldier identified as being of "enemy extraction" was eventually transferred away from front line duty. Amongst these were two Engineers who had served on Gallipoli. Sapper Freidrich Reichardt was transferred to the ASC at Codford, England and Company Sergeant Major Otto Friedlander, who was in England at the time having just received an Imperial Commission, was posted to the Gold Coast Colony in Africa.

The Field Engineers had received all their reinforcements from Egypt and as August neared, they were expecting the first batch of much needed replacements from the Royal Engineer Depot in Christchurch, England. The first drafts of the men that arrived were mostly Gallipoli veterans now recovered from wounds and illnesses. They were a welcomed addition.

On the 1st of August the New Zealand Government passed the Military Services Bill that introduced conscription. Amendments to the Bill allowed that all those men who had been married between the Declaration of War in August 1914 and May 1915 were deemed single men, making them now eligible for conscription. An amendment exempting men from serving on the grounds of religious objection was rejected. The only exemption granted was to Maoris, in that they could not be compulsorily conscripted. Mr Massey the Prime Minister of New Zealand said that the Bill was the strongest ever introduced and he hoped its passing would produce a good morale effect elsewhere.

At the end of July the Rifle Brigade was relieved by the new 18th Division. This contracted the N.Z. Division's sector at Armentières. Later on the 13th of August 1916 after three months in the frontline, the N.Z. Division was finally relieved by the 51st (Highland Territorial) Division. This Division had been involved in the recent Somme fighting, where it had attacked, but failed to capture, High Wood. During the hand-over of the trenches to the Highlanders, the New Zealanders learned about the bloody fighting on the Somme.

The N.Z. Division moved back to a rest camp near Wardrecques and several days later they entrained to Abbeville, for further training and to take part in another major assault at an undisclosed destination.

The smart money was on them going to the Somme.

Chapter Nineteen: New Zealand training camps in England

With the N.Z. Division now in France, it was decided for reasons of war economy to transfer all training depots from Egypt to England. The 10th and 11th Reinforcements were the last troops trained and equipped in Egypt before being hurriedly despatched to France.

The main Training Depot in England was located at Sling Camp on Salisbury Plain, on the same site as occupied by the British Section back in October, 1914. The Canadians had then occupied the camp and due to their efforts the camp had an accommodation capacity for 4,000 men. The 12th Reinforcements, which had been held in Egypt, were the first to arrive at Sling Camp and by mid-June the 13th Reinforcements joined them. Thereafter reinforcement contingents[183] regularly arrived at British ports such as Plymouth, Falmouth, Liverpool and Glasgow from where they would entrain for the Bulford Camp siding. Tragically in September 1917 ten New Zealand soldiers were killed at Bere Ferrers station, when they were struck by the Waterloo to Plymouth express train as they went to collect rations[184].

From Bulford, the contingents would be marched the final two miles to Sling Camp, where the band played them onto the parade ground. Here they were allotted to one of the four training battalions: No 1 Canterbury, No 2 Otago, No 3 Wellington and No 4 Auckland.

Mingled in amongst these new men were veteran soldiers returning from hospitals and now awaiting return to active service. With the demands for reinforcements in France many of these men were only at Sling for one or two weeks, but from October 1916 only those who completed the full 30 day training course could be placed in a draft to France[185].

All cap badges were taken away and the men were issued with brass NZR[186] for their shoulder straps. As a privilege, those who had already seen service were permitted to retain their regimental badges. Any item considered unnecessary, such as extra tunics and blankets, were removed. The men then enjoyed a few days of light duties before the gruelling training routine began. The training was overseen by New Zealand instructors, who had already served on Gallipoli and in France, although there were some British Army instructors, mainly for physical training. Typical of the instructors was Staff -Sergeant Ted Baigent, who had served with 1ˢᵗ Canterbury on Gallipoli, at Armentières and at Flers-Courcelette where he had been severely wounded.

Features of their training were strict discipline, smartness and review order drill, also referred to as "Piccadillies". They undertook the usual long route marches around the countryside and were taught gas drills and trench routines. The gas training ensured that each man made several visits to the gas hut at Beacon Hill, fondly referred to as the "Chamber of Horrors". Here the men were exposed to chlorine gas, with their masks on.

Reinforcement officers joined this training regime and they were expected to carry a pack and rifle just like the men did. In addition to lectures on tactics, trench routines and raids the officers received training in map reading and in the use of a compass. Navigation was a vital skill when moving across ground made featureless by artillery bombardments and enveloped in thick smoke or when plotting enemy strong points and machine gun posts onto a map as potential artillery targets. They also had to appreciate and work with varying map scales; the distances on French maps were shown in metres and the British maps in imperial yards.

Musketry on the ranges was designed to sharpen up the men, as they had already been taught military shooting in New Zealand. Musketry covered barrage fire, covering fire, snap shooting and rapid fire. Also the men could qualify for their Marksman Badge during this phase of the training. Later the fusing and throwing of Mills bombs was practiced.

Finally the "bullring" awaited them. This had been introduced by General Braithwaite[187] while he was in command of the infantry training at Sling. Each day the instructors would organise a timetable of battlefield tasks. The men were then organised into groups to complete these set tasks while the instructors imposed a degree of pressure and urgency. The tasks could range from bayonet fighting with gas masks on, to having to rapidly advance across a mud and smoke filled battlefield with shell holes and wire entanglements. It was all meant to build confidence and to provide a taster for life on the front line.

When the 30 day course was finished, those serving with the Artillery, Signals, Machine Gunners, Pioneers and Engineers were sent onto specialised training camps to develop the skills that they would deploy at the Front, while the Infantry and Rifle Brigade (nicknamed "the Dinks" or "the Dinkims") continued with their more specialised training in tactics, bayonet fighting, wiring and the use of the Lewis Gun; trench digging, trench and listening post drills; reactions on enemy attacks, raids, enemy artillery barrages; and use of SOS flares. At this point they would have practiced trench raids and attacking a German trench position. The full training course took around nine weeks.

The N.Z. Field Artillery used the Larkhill ranges on Salisbury Plains with the Australian artillery until it was fortunate enough in August 1917 to be able to take over a section of the permanent Artillery camp at Ewshot, outside of Aldershot. Ewshot had been opened by the Kaiser during one of his visits to England before the war and had originally been called the "Leipsig Barracks"[188]. The artilleryman and their signallers undertook a six week course at Ewshot.

Most of it was similar to what they had learnt in New Zealand, with an emphasis on speed of the drills and managing the horse teams. Ewshot also possessed useful equipment for training observation officers. The observation officer with the artillery signallers practiced laying a gun line. This consisted of hut to hut communication with the instructions recreated on a model landscape in one of the huts. In this way, the accuracy of information was tested.

The observation officers also had to learn how to mark important reference points on their maps in raised crayon. In the dark of night, these bumps were "felt" to orientate the observer, who would then provide fire orders for the gun lines. Lights could not be shown for risk of attracting enemy fire, so these drills were essential to relay the correct instructions. During the German Spring Offensive of 1918, a young artillery observer mistook a mud grain on his map for a reference point. The artillery fire he called in destroyed a New Zealand machine post, killing the crew.

The N.Z. Medical Corps also joined the N.Z. Field Artillery at Ewshot. There they trained for work on hospital ships and as orderlies in UK based hospitals and advanced dressing stations in France. They even had a trench mock up built for them at Ewshot that allowed them to practice working in the confines of a dugout while treating battle and gas casualties, sometimes while wearing gas masks.

The signallers and machine gunners were originally grouped with the N.Z. Engineers and were sent to the N.Z. Engineers Training Depot at Christchurch in Hampshire. In August 1916 the Signallers moved from Christchurch to an established signals camp at Hitchin for more specialised training. The machine gunners went to Belton Park, Grantham for their seventy days training course. Grantham was the home for the British Machine Gunners, with around 50,000 men camped there by 1918. At Grantham they covered mechanical construction, gunnery theory as well as accuracy of fire. Once their specialist courses were completed, the signallers and machine gunners would return to Sling Camp and await a draft to France.

The Pioneers were trained at Sling Camp, until early 1917 after which they undertook a six week course organised for them by the N.Z. Engineers at Christchurch. Upon completion they returned to Sling Camp. This eventually changed when in mid 1917, Captain Keenan organised for the Pioneers to become permanently attached to the N.Z. Engineers Training Depot.

With low casualty rates amongst the N.Z. Division after its return to Armentières from the Somme no large drafts were dispatched from Sling Camp. By early 1917, the continual stream of contingents from New Zealand resulted in around 4,500 trained Infantry reserves and approximately 2,000 Rifle Brigade reserves awaiting deployment to France. Consideration was given to using these men to form a Brigade for the British Army, but this was rejected by the N.Z. Government who decided instead to form a 4th Brigade for the N.Z. Division. Normally only three brigades comprised a Division, so a fourth made the N.Z. Division a "heavy" Division.

That May, His Majesty the King inspected the New Zealand troops on Salisbury Plain and later a cinema film of this event was taken for exhibition in New Zealand[189].

With the congested conditions prevailing at Sling Camp, the Rifle Brigade relocated in August to Tidworth Pennings, four miles north of Sling. There, under the command of Major Rawdon St. John Beere[190], they established a tented camp for the remaining summer months, called the Tidworth Pennings Camp. The tents were fitted with wooden floors. Each man was issued with a straw mattress, a small pillow, and what was described as a liberal issue of blankets to keep warm during the cold nights. Hot shower-baths were installed in other tents.

The Rifle Brigade troops formed two battalions, under Capt. O. W. Williams and Capt. W. W. Dove, respectively and the "bullring" system was modified under the instruction of General Fulton[191]. The changes placed more responsibility on the officers to lead the men in the "bullring" tasks, not the instructors. The instructors were absorbed into the two battalions and the battalion commanders then personally directed the training of the troops under their immediate control[192].

As autumn began, the Tidworth Pennings Camp was vacated and on the 27th of September all 1,925 reserve troops of the Rifle Brigade entrained for the permanent camp at Brocton, approximately 130 miles north of Birmingham, near the country town of Stafford in Staffordshire[193]. The area was described by the troops as being bleak and dreary upland surrounded by countryside, although they did enjoy the old-styled thatched villages scattered across the locality. The Rifle Brigade took over a one hundred acre area that contained mainly open spaces. This terrain and the availability of the necessary equipment meant that Sling Camp could be by-passed and the brigade's reinforcements arrived instead at Brocton for their training.

At Brocton, an extended trench system was created for training in trench routines, attack and defence. The local soil when wet produced the same sticky mud as found in France which provided realistic training conditions. It was recognised that given the expected casualty rates certain specialists such as Lewis-gunners, signallers, scouts and bombers, were difficult to readily replace. Therefore the training programme was extended to develop more men with these skills and soon drafts were proceeding to France containing sufficient numbers of men with specialist skills.

Brocton camp had a Y.M.C.A that arranged concerts, talks and various evening amusements for the men, while the Rifle Brigade band, under Sergeant-Major Shardlow, held concerts for the local townspeople. Leave, when granted, was spent at Stoke, Derby, Birmingham and numerous other towns and cities that could be reached by train. Given the Staffordshire climate, the Rifle Brigade while at Brocton had one of the lowest sick-rates compared with the other New Zealand camps in England. The lowest sick rate was at the Engineers camp in Christchurch.

Once the N.Z. Division called for replacements, the various training camps would assemble a draft and despatch it to Southampton, Portsmouth or Dover for embarkation to France and then onto the British Army's main training depot at Etaples, where they awaited orders to join their regiments. Etaples was mainly a tented camp next to sand dunes where further infantry training was conducted by British Army instructors. They were generally remembered for their brutality. The training included gas drills, musketry, route marches and the generally hated "bullring" which aimed at hardening up the newly arrived soldiers.

The Anzacs, and in particular those veterans returning to the Front after being wounded, resented this treatment and questioned the experience of some of Etaples' British instructors. In September 1917 there was a major disturbance in the camp. Allegedly, a New Zealand artilleryman had been arrested and after a crowd gathered the man was released. This did not calm the pent up frustration towards the military police and scuffles broke out. Shots were fired by the military police and a Scot[194] was killed. Military authority broke down for several days before order was restored and the military police were withdrawn from the camp.

Two friends, Bert Grouby and William Wareham in England during 1918. Bert Grouby served with the 3rd Battalion NZ Rifle Brigade and was in hospital at Walton on Thames when this photograph was taken. As his personal baggage would not have been sent to him in hospital, he wears a "catch-up" uniform that was issued by the hospital clothing stores. As such he has no unit insignia. William Wareham was still undergoing infantry training at Sling Camp at this time, so was only entitled to wear the brass NZR badge on each epaulette, he has no hat badge and no regimental badge on his collars, also referred to as 'collar dogs'. He would later serve with the 2nd Battalion Otago Infantry Regiment in France.

Photo courtesy of Mr David Hall.

Chapter Twenty: Anzacs, Christchurch and Royal Engineers

The ancient town of Christchurch in Hampshire had first returned an MP in 1306 during the reign of Elizabeth I – so it was an old Borough with an economy based upon agriculture and fishing. It also boasted the eight hundred year old Priory Church. Since the start of the war, the Priory had been a popular attraction for visitors due to its association with Kaiser Wilhelm II and his visit there in 1907.

On the western outskirts of the town, by the River Stour was the Christchurch Barracks which had been built in the late 18th Century in response to the Napoleonic threat of invasion. Since then it had been home to Artillery batteries, Calvary squadrons and even temporarily to Rifle Regiments. It was now the depot for the Royal Engineers Training Centre for the Southern Command and possessed the necessary stores, equipment, instructors and training grounds for this task. Its official designation was "The Southern Command School of Instruction in Engineering" or SCSIE and Lieutenant Colonel Keen, Royal Engineer, commanded the Depot.

Engineering companies had begun to train at the Christchurch Barracks since the start of the war and it was home to the South Midland Royal Engineers and the Wessex Royal Engineers. The Canadian Engineers attended the Instructors' courses that were regularly conducted there. As elsewhere, the numbers of men in training quickly exceeded the available capacity at the barracks and congestion soon became a problem. To solve this lack of accommodation, tents were erected in military lines alongside the main camp and makeshift cookhouses were erected. The main tent lines were situated in the fields bordering on the bank of the River Stour between Iford and Tuckton, this was known as Jumpers Road Camp and the additional tent line beside the main road was called the Barrack Road Camp.

The Mudeford area was also used as a makeshift tented camp for Royal Engineers from early 1915. The camp was located at Mude Farm. The 152nd and 153rd Field Companies Royal Engineers trained there, practising bridging across the fast flowing Mudeford Run before embarking for France with the 37th Division in July 1915. Shortly after they had left, the 212th and 222nd Field Engineers of the 33rd Division arrived and took their place at the Mudeford Camp.

On the 22nd of June 1916 the first contingent of approximately 500 Australian Engineers arrived at RE Training Depot, Christchurch. An hour later, the smaller New Zealand contingent, under the command of 2nd Lieutenant Corkhill NZE, arrived and was attached to the South Midlands Royal Engineers for training, administration and rations.

After an address by Colonel Keen, the Anzacs were assigned tents along the River Stour at the Jumpers Road Camp. They soon made their tent lines as comfortable as possible with furniture and even a piano donated by a local family.

Australian troops[195] were already well known in the Bournemouth area, due to a visit by the AIF a year earlier in June 1915 were made very welcome. Back then, the newly arrived troops marched through the town to the Winter Garden – a glassed-in conservatory able to seat about 2,000 people and there an evening of musical entertainment was provided by the Municipal Orchestra, a number of local ladies and the Australians. Sergeant McSwaine of the AIF sang "Australia will be there" to a rapturous reception from the crowd. Included in the evening's selection was the New Zealand song "Far from the old folk at Home" and Canada's "The Maple Leaf Forever".

The Australians' commanding officer, Colonel Tunbridge, caused some consternation during his address at the interlude by stating that Australia was not fighting for Great Britain, but "defending itself as part of the great Empire"[196]. This aside, the loyalty shown by the Australians to the "Motherland" that evening was the one bright spot for many people after almost a year of war.

The town of Christchurch had a quaint custom relating to New Zealand. Its origins lay in Empire Day[197] 1911, when a map of the British Empire was given by the Mayor, Robert Druitt, to the Priory School for them to present to a visiting New Zealander, Dr Levinge[198]. Levinge was the Medical Superintendent of the Lunatic Asylum in Christchurch, New Zealand and may have presented a New Zealand flag to the Mayor in exchange.

Later that year, on the 22nd of June 1911 the New Zealand flag was hoisted by the Mayor on the occasion of the coronation of King George V. The significance of the event continued when the Borough Member, Sir Henry Croft Page[199] visited New Zealand the following year, where he was presented with a New Zealand flag by the citizens of the South Island city of Christchurch. Upon his return in 1912, the tradition began of flying that New Zealand flag from the Town Hall for special events[200].

One such event in which the New Zealand flag was hoisted in celebration was on the 26th of August 1916 when Mrs Page, Sir Henry's daughter in law, gave birth to a son.

Wessex Royal Engineers' Band plays in front of the small hospital at the Christchurch Barracks. In the foreground is an Australian Engineer, who would be training as a horse & wagon driver. A nurse is standing in the hospital doorway.

Photo courtesy of the Mrs Beryl King, Poole, Dorset

Chapter Twenty-One: Training at the Royal Engineers Depot, Christchurch Barracks – 1916

In New Zealand, the Engineers had undergone twelve weeks of basic military training covering matters such as: parade ground drill, route marches, musketry, field craft, entrenching and wiring, bomb throwing, semaphore and demolitions. This was conducted at Trentham Camp and included the notorious march over the Rimataka mountain range before embarking on the long boat ride to Egypt and then onto England. On-board the troopships, military training and lectures continued throughout the six week sea voyage. Those temporarily disembarking in Egypt would receive more military training including route marches, musketry and further inoculations.

Their three month course with the Royal Engineers at Christchurch began with a "refresher" in infantry training and musketry. The New Zealanders generally scored well with musketry and for later drafts, this aspect of the training was reduced to certification shooting. Parade ground drill was another matter. They could drill, but doing it in accordance with the British Army Training Manual was a totally different matter. Many of the Depot's instructors were ex-Regulars who had returned to duty for the duration of the war and were well versed in just what that manual said.

The New Zealanders had some memorable moments, as mentioned in Annabell's[201] account of the Depot. It would appear that one particular British NCO delighted in selecting a squad of recently arrived New Zealanders and after a spell on the parade ground he would stand them easy and then tell a story from his childhood. Apparently, his prized possession as a young lad had been his box of leaden toy soldiers.

Unfortunately during one of his family's many moves the box of toy soldiers was lost and his mother in consoling him promised that some day he would find them again. He would conclude his story with a growl "Yes and by God, I've found them again today!", leaving the men in no doubt that for the next nine weeks while they were on the parade ground they would be his playthings. Another postcard moment was his frenzied exhortations to his squad to turn on their toes; he could be heard roaring "Toes! I said, Toes! T-o-e-s don't spell 'eels."

Later in 1917 while at the Depot, the Maori Pioneers would mimic these antics for their own amusement and on one occasion Private Karapaina was awarded four days forfeiture of pay after being charged with "conduct to the prejudice of good order and discipline", in that he imitated a British officer giving orders – and got caught!

The Australians also had stories about their time in Christchurch. In a *Sydney Morning Herald* article[202] they commented on just how well they were behaving themselves and how the English officers and instructors could not make them out. "They growl because we don't keep stiff and stand still, and tell us what good soldiers ought to do; …at parade in the Barrack square, a corporal was called out. He is a good soldier, and doubled out, stood to attention and saluted the boss – and a bottle fell from his tunic [where he had hastily put it when called forward] as he had been holding it [throughout the parade] with his saluting hand."

After their time on the parade ground, the real experience was gained on "the Hill" as St Catherine's Hill was fondly known. St Catherine's Hill is a stony 35 hectares knoll rising 50 meters above sea level, about 2 miles north of Christchurch that overlooks the rivers Avon on the east and Stour to the west. In Roman times a fort and watchtower had occupied the high ground on the westerly facing ridge. Now astride the northern end of those slopes was an elaborate trench network where the entrenching instruction occurred.

British Army doctrine early in the war considered trench warfare as merely a temporary phase of war. To gain a decisive victory the enemy had to be driven out of his defences and his armies crushed in the open, presumably by the cavalry. Trench construction was therefore poor and inadequate for the troops living in them, especially when accurate Krupps artillery was bombarding them. By early 1915 the British and French had begun to imitate the German trench construction techniques and this change was noted by the "Morning Post"[203] when it reported that the British Army trenches were more comfortable, more sanitary than before and at least as protective as those of the enemy.

On Gallipoli, the trenches had been narrow and cut deep into the hard gravely soil. The model for the Western Front was to construct trenches with sufficient width to allow soldiers to easily pass each other, especially when carrying supplies or wounded men on stretchers. The floor of the trench was covered with a wooden grating called duckboards and at short intervals deep holes were dug to collect the surface water. This trapped water was then pumped out of the trench using hand pumps. The trench was dug with right angles every 18 yards into a 9 yard traverse, which created a right angle, zigzag or sawtooth design to minimise the effect of a shell burst and prevent enfilade fire should an attacking enemy capture a section of the trench.

The trench itself was usually dug to a depth of around four foot and had a high parapet on the fighting side that was created by piling the displaced spoils there. It was then topped off with sandbags, so the overall effect made the trench breastworks higher. It was all designed to protect the troops, limit the power of high velocity bullets, and provide some shelter from artillery bombardments. Ideally some form of revetting would line the trench walls to prevent the sides collapsing into the trench.

There were also narrow wooden, or steel framed loopholes every couple of yards which were reached by the man standing on the fire platform – also called a fire step. At irregular intervals machine-gun redoubts were built. In front of the trench the approaches were rendered difficult by entanglements of various sorts. The first line of these consisted of strong iron posts, carrying thick barbed wire; outside of that came the cheveux de frise; wooden hurdles locked tightly together and carrying a tangle of barbed wire.

Further out, the ground was probably sprinkled with small four-legged spikes several inches high and made in a star shape so that however they were thrown there was always a spike uppermost. All of these obstacles were intended to slow and injure attacking infantry or cavalry.

The trench organisation was maze-like, with cross passages, side trench exits to listening posts, dummy trenches leading to a dead end to trap attackers. The ammunition stores and other storage spaces were kept apart from the fighting trench. Once constructed, the Engineers had the continual task of maintaining the entire complex.

For the soldiers, songs were always a way of expressing their sentiments. Regarding trench life Private Robert Martin, who was serving with the Machine Gun Corps in France, penned a catchy insight in his original piece titled "My Little Sandbag Villa". It went like this:

"Excuse me, Mister Officer, are we getting relieved tonight?
I've got a nice little sandbag villa that just suits me all right –
With a corrugated iron and sand-bag roof, every things OK;
Come with me and I'll show you just where this dug-out lays.
Chorus:
Away down Communication Trench in the middle of Wizz-bang Lane,
I've got a nice little sand-bag villa,
Where the Krupps and Johnsons "rain".
Its very very close to Sniper's Post,
Where the aerial torpedoes visit us most.
We are going to give them machine-gun toast away down Whiz-bang Lane.

I went for a walk in Thiepval Wood, and I thought it was all right,
But the Officer said, as he scratched his head, "We go over the top tonight".
I said "If its true that you're going to visit Fritz, my word, that won't suit me;
Come with me and I'll show you just where I'd sooner be.

Chorus Repeats

On "the Hill" the instructors took the New Zealanders through all aspects of trench construction and maintenance. They dug shelters, shell slits, bombing posts, communication trenches, supervision trenches, fire bays and dummy trenches and even latrines. Each run of a main trench was given a familiar local name, such as Fisherman's Walk or Parkwood Road to make them easy to remember. On the Western Front, easily remembered trench names such as Piccadilly Circus, Elgin Alley, French

Lane and Waitangi conjured up familiar imagines and eventually a logical sequence of locations. It was similar to navigating through the London Underground stations and gave each trench its own character, as opposed to being just a cold, damp and sometimes lonely place.

Dugouts, deep dugouts, machine gun emplacements and strong points were constructed. The methods of wiring: trip, foil and barbed were taught along with trench communication methods, in particular the telephone. After several weeks of toil and instruction, the Engineers were knowledgeable on how the trench system was built, repaired, defended, expanded, strengthened, interconnected and lived-in. The training included night exercises in wiring and "sapping" as digging a stretch of trench was termed.

As well as the trench network, a grenade range was established on the western edge and a 600 yard north facing rifle range nestled on the eastern edge of the hill. It was all close by and self contained. Gas training was conducted either at Sling Camp or at Etaples, once they had arrived in France.

The other feature of "the Hill" was the daily presence of spectators, usually young ladies who had deliberately climbed the hill to inspect progress and reputedly stimulated the manual efforts of susceptible young Engineers. Often the Engineers would invite the girls to a local dance or meet them later while on an evening's leave.

As the war progressed trench construction would become an art form. New trench shelters were devised, such as the small, steel "baby elephants" shelters; deep dugouts became standard features, use of concrete became widespread. There was an appreciation that air spaces could cushion the effect of a direct hit by a shell and the design of a "bursting course" when constructing overhead cover was a necessary skill.

After they graduated from "the Hill", the Stour and Avon rivers provided opportunities for rapid bridge-construction and the ample mudflats around Christchurch helped the Engineers to gain extensive experience in pontooning. Like the Australians, they established several records in bridging, pontooning and entrenching work.

As well as engineering training, some men were detailed as drivers for the horse teams and lumber wagons or the motor trucks. Teaching the men how to drive the motor trucks occurred in the Royal Engineers' stadium, whereas driving wagons with harnessed horse teams occurred around St Catherine's Hill. This area had been used to help train the roughriders and gun teams of the Artillery batteries stationed at the Christchurch Barracks in the 1800's. Instructional periods were conducted on the nearby fields and then it was onto "the Hill", which yet again reverberated with men shouting and urging on their straining horse teams as they pulled a fully laden wagon along the shingle pits, slopes and pathways.

Just how much they had learnt would be tested on the battlefields of France and Belgium. There they would employ their skills night and day; in the heat, rain, cold, mud, moonlight and darkness; while being shelled, shot at or gassed. They would be tired, usually wet through, possibly sick and definitely scared.

After several weeks, the New Zealand Engineers were joined at Christchurch by a number of veterans who, after being discharged from hospitals in England, had spent some time at Codford Camp regaining their full fitness. They were now being posted back to France. It was soon evident by the daily charge sheets, that the Depot's old styled British Army discipline caused immediate resentment amongst these men. The Guard Room was busy with several of them charged with breaches of discipline ranging from refusing to obey an order to not saluting an officer.

By August, the Anzac numbers at the Training Depot reduced with the NZE Signallers moving to Hitchin to form a Signalling School and the Australian Engineer Training Depot (AETD) moved to Brightlingsea in Essex. The AETD would remain at Brightlingsea for the rest of the war, although due to a lack of stables there the Australian horse team drivers continued to train at Christchurch until mid 1917.

Chapter Twenty-Two: Integrating with the community

With leave granted most nights and weekends[204] the most favoured destination for the young men was Bournemouth which could be reached by tramcar or bus for one penny a trip. Bournemouth had been established in 1810 between the towns of Poole and Christchurch as a health resort. By 1841 it had a population of around 900 people, which by 1911 had grown to around 78,700 people[205] and known as the premier holiday resort in England. The architecture and seaside location would have been familiar to the Anzac soldiers who came from cities such as Sydney, Melbourne, Wellington and Auckland. The attractions of Bournemouth were the gardens, pier, promenade, concerts, stage shows, ice rink, movies at the Electric Theatre and Boscombe Picture House and dancing. They soon became enamoured with Bournemouth.

Bournemouth was at the height of the holiday season when the Australians and New Zealanders first arrived in the summer of 1916. It was full of visitors, mostly smartly dressed young ladies. With very few young men about the Anzacs quickly found partners for dancing, ice skating, music concerts, as well as the new motion pictures. The most watched film that August of 1916 was the picture documentary covering the July Battle of the Somme.

Before the war most ladies had a social and dress code that they generally adhered to. This gradually became more relaxed under the influence of the Suffragette movement that had been increasingly active over the recent years. The social etiquette expected that women did not keep the company of men unless with a relative present; their dress length was two inches above the ankle, they could not loiter in ice cream parlours, not smoke cigarettes in public and be home by 8pm.

With the economic freedom created through women being employed in factories and military establishments, many social conventions had disappeared by mid 1916. Not only were women now admitted to hallowed interiors of public houses, they tended to prefer to buy their own drinks. The Anzacs found it strange to see women employed as cleaners on railway carriages, being tram conductors, and even hotel porters.

Southampton was another destination for the men. It was known for its maritime history, theatres and a German prisoner of war camp containing some 5,000 POWs. When America later joined the war in May 1917, Southampton was used as a base area for them. The New Zealanders often enjoyed watching the Americans play the new sport of baseball. Eventually they would take the game back to New Zealand and it remained a popular sport amongst returned men through to the 1930's.

If they could locate and hire a bicycle, the soldiers could tour further into the country areas, along the Avon Valley and through the New Forest villages. Most of these places were accessible by taxi, bus and some by train. An essential piece of equipment while on leave tended to be the Australian's slouch hat. This was a much sought after item by New Zealanders as the ladies admired it, possibly because of its distinctive cavalier look.

A New Zealand lady from Auckland, formerly a Miss Reid who had married an English man called Downham, owned a large house two miles from Burley, in the New Forest near Christchurch. They kept an open house for New Zealand soldiers in the area throughout the war[206]. Apart from agriculture, Burley offered game shoots, mainly pheasant and partridge, and such occasions would have been on the social calendar for some of the Engineer officers.

The local military often arranged entertainment and encouraged the public to join in the various sports competitions. In July 1916 in Christchurch, the Australian and Canadian Engineers organised a Sunday school tea and sports day for the children and their parents and friends. Tea was provided at the Village Room in Stanpit, near Mude Farm and the beach. The sports were held at the nearby Mudeford Recreation ground with QMS George E. Jones, Sergeant Christies (both Australian Engineers) and Corporal Flumerfelt (Canadian Engineers) organising the various events for the children.

On the 27[207] of July, a large crowd was present at the Australian and New Zealand Military Sports[207] held at the Christchurch Barracks fields. Certain events were opened up to "outsiders". This type of an event provided the townspeople with a lovely day's entertainment and a nice distraction from the everyday hardships of the war. Flags flew and the band of the Wessex Engineers conducted by Sergeant-Major Haywood entertained the crowd. Several men were dressed in comic costumes, including one as Charlie Chaplin. With the competitors being drawn from the Australian, New Zealand and South Midland Engineers, the international aspect added to the overall occasion.

First blood went to New Zealand with Sapper Burns winning the 100 yard sprint, but the Australians came back strong with Sapper Allom winning the sack race. In the Tug-of-War final Australia won 2-0 against New Zealand. This was followed by Australian victories in the Pillow Fight won by Sapper Sydenham and the Obstacle Race clearly won by Sapper McSweeney. But the best was left until last and the deciding event went to New Zealand with Sapper Burns winning the 220 yards race. Later in the evening a dance was held for all soldiers, their partners and civilian guests.

The season of sports continued with the Barton-on-Sea Military Sports held on the 12th August which saw New Zealand Engineers win the Tug-of-War and the boat race, while the recently arrived No 1 N.Z. General Hospital based at Brockenhurst won the relay race[208] beating the Australian Engineers. There were pillow fights and sack races for the convalescent patients and a 50 yard Band Race, with the men playing their instruments. But the main event, the quarter mile with the prize of a wrist watch, was won by QMS Funnell of the Australian Engineers. Prizes were often donated to be presented to event winners. Apart from watches, other gifts would be tennis rackets, letter cases, safety razors, pens and the new Gillette razors.

With the summer sports season fading, the dancing season began. The ladies of the Southbourne & Christchurch Branch of the Women's Emergency Corps organised a dance at the Town Hall on the 2nd of September to provide some entertainment for the Australians and New

Zealanders who were so far from home.

Some of the dancers that night were the first N.Z. Engineers' reinforcement draft trained at Christchurch and about to leave for France that very evening. At 11pm they left the hall to catch their train to Le Havre via Southampton Docks. Their fellow dancers all began cheering and singing "For he's a jolly good fellow". The *Christchurch Times* newspaper faithfully noted that for many of the ladies present it was a tearful moment, reminiscent of their farewells earlier in the war for loved ones.

With the first group of trained N.Z. Engineers dispatched to France, the Christchurch depot became a staging area for subsequent replacement drafts. The casualties being sustained at Armentières had to be replaced and unknown then, the New Zealand Division was about to move from Armentières to the Somme to support the British offensive there.

The men forming a draft for France were "under orders", as it was termed. They would receive all their required inoculations, undergo a final medical check-up and had a full kit inspection - making up any shortages immediately. They were issued with identification tags – also known as "dead meat tickets". If they needed their boots mended or new boots issued, they had a chance to do so as well as buy a few luxury goods. The "old hands" would have sought out telephone wire to eventually replace rotten bootlaces, a trick learnt on Gallipoli. Then, depending on the timings for transport, they may be paid and granted local leave, or detailed for parade ground drill, or given camp fatigues. One draft spent their time laying water pipes to the makeshift cookhouse situated amongst their tent lines near the river, before embarking for France.

At the end of September 1916 an informal dance was arranged by Mrs Keen, the Camp Commandant's wife. Attending were the officers of the Royal Engineers, Australian and New Zealand Engineers[209] with a number of young ladies invited by Mrs Keen as dancing partners.[210] Providing partners at short notice was a speciality of a Miss Newridge.

The following Friday night, the N.Z. Engineer NCOs arranged their own impromptu dance. It began at 8pm and the last dance was at 1am. Miss Newridge again assisted with dancing partners. The event passed off as an unqualified success with about 50 couples present and the musicians amongst the New Zealanders provided the band music.

As an expression of their appreciation of the kindness which had been shown to them by residents of Christchurch, Southbourne, Pokesdown and Boscombe, the NCOs and men of N.Z. Engineers organised a Wednesday night dance on the 11th of October at the Gymnasium, Havilland Road in Boscombe. They covered all the expenses themselves and the gross receipts from sale of tickets were given to the British Red Cross Fund. The event was overseen by Lieutenant F.M. Corkhill and CSM Williamson. The organisers were Sergeants Body, Hannigan and Burt along with Corporal Smith and Sappers Huggins, Bennett, Donaldson. The Engineers again had their own dance band, which featured Corporal McIntosh (cornet), Sapper Hill (violin) and Sapper Huggins (piano).

These occasions provided the opportunity for the New Zealanders to invite young ladies they had met in town or on "the Hill". With a shortage of men and a chance to enjoy themselves, these events proved popular and soon a regular dancing calendar was established by the Engineers. There were also "khaki" dances, which meant only men in uniform could attend with their female partners. There was also dancing on both the Bournemouth and Boscombe Piers, which was popular and cost only two pennies for the girl and one penny for the soldiers. Music was provided by a military band until 10:30pm when the Piers closed under the light restriction imposed by the Light (England and Wales) Order. The dancing resumed with another band on the village green or other suitable places, like the promenades, until midnight[211]. Apart from the well known and formal dances, others were soon introduced from France and America. A dance called the "Bunny Hug" was popular during the war.

Amongst those attending the late September dance would have been Sapper Thomas Tester. Tester was a Gallipoli veteran with 1st Field

Company. He had contracted enteric fever in September 1915 on Gallipoli and had been evacuated back to England. After several months at 2nd London General Hospital in Chelsea he was moved to Hornchurch for recuperation and further tests. He met Miss Freda Thomas from South Norwood, London during this time and they married on the 24th of June 1916. In early July he was posted to Codford where he met up with some of his Gallipoli friends; Sappers Haynes and Mitchell as well as Willie Barrett, a relative now with the Auckland Battalion reinforcement training at Sling Camp.

At the end of August, Tester was posted to the NZE Depot in Christchurch as part of a draft for France. He was granted leave on his first weekend there, which he spent with Freda. The next three weeks were used in refresher training and being kitted out along with the rest of the draft.

On the 22nd of September, the reinforcement draft departed to the channel port of Folkestone, across to Boulogne and then marched into one of the many tented camps at British Base at Etaples. This was predominately an infantry training area, where troops would be hardened for the front line. The bullring became notorious, as were the route marches carrying full packs. It was not the environment for new or badly fitting boots.

They were also put through gas training; initially being exposed to tear gas in a chamber while wearing their box respirators, then a day in the bullring understanding the effects of gas. That day ended with the men running through a chlorine gas-filled trench with their respirators on and then moving through another filled with tear gas, this time without respirators.

When not training the Engineers had camp fatigues, levelling off the French roads, erecting fences, clearing blocked drains and having any shortage of personal equipment made up. If they were lucky, an evening leave pass would be granted to the town of Etaples. Entertainment in the camp was also provided by the YMCA and the N.Z. Concert Party. Generally, it was a matter of waiting until their name appeared on the next departure list to the Division.

Fortunately for Tester, he only remained at Etaples a week, undertaking general training before being sent onto the N.Z. Division, now engaged on the Somme, fighting near Flers.

Each Field Company had a compliment of various skills, such as: carpenter, bricklayer, blacksmith, surveyor, plumber and the like. The reinforcements were allocated by these trades to whichever field company had that particular skills shortage. The returning "old hands" were normally allocated back to their original field company.

The new men soon learnt how to travel light, quickly ditching excess kit rather than having to carry it. The field routine and standards while in billets was explained to them, which also meant that they could expect all fatigue duties for the next few weeks. They were given common sense advice on how to make themselves comfortable in their billets, especially when their clothing was wet. They were shown the pieces of equipment that they always had to have on their person. In the field they were told to always keep to marked tracks when moving in and out of trenches, especially during night work. On no occasion were they to step into the long grass for fear of kicking old rusting Mills bombs carelessly left lying about[212]. Other words of wisdom were that they should never linger in open spaces and when working at night not to look directly at the flashes of the guns. This caused a loss of night vision and increased the chance of injury as a result of bumping into obstacles or falling into the numerous water filled shell holes.

If they followed this advice, they had a chance of staying uninjured and alive longer in their new hostile world.

Chapter Twenty-Three: Christchurch in the War

The grim reality of war continued unabated with the Red Cross trains disgorging their grisly cargo of cot cases and walking wounded. In the middle of May 1916 the hospital volunteers at Christchurch were dealing with an influx of 108 wounded soldiers recently arrived from France. With the number of wounded increasing, there was an urgent need for more hospital helpers to join the Volunteer Aid Detachment. It was felt that many women were doing little to help the war effort and if they were unable to assist either full or part time in caring for the sick and wounded, then they could at least do something in their homes, such as the washing and rolling of bandages.

Hospitals continued appealing for: pillows, soap, matches, stationery, vegetable, fruit, cakes, jam, hand towels, bath towels and the most sought after item of all - cigarettes. Garden seats were even asked for, as it was found that those wounded men taking their first walk after a long period of injury were unable to go very far before they needed a rest. The public helped in every small way that they could, even down to collecting eggs. In July, some 1,831 eggs were provided to the Christchurch hospitals for the wounded.

At this time, news reached the Borough that after a resistance of 143 days and with supplies exhausted, General Townsend had surrendered Kut to the Turks. Amongst the British and Indian troops captured there were many local Hampshire Territorials serving with the 1/5th Howitzer Battery RFA under Major HG Thompson. This was an Isle of Wight raised company.

For their relatives the uncertainty as to their fate continued for several months. One such soldier was Lance-Corporal Joseph Barnes of Christchurch who had left for India in December 1914 with 2/4th Wiltshires. He joined the Ox and Bucks Light Infantry, fought in the Dardanelles campaign after which his battalion was posted to Mesopotamia. He was captured at Kut. His parents eventually received a postcard from him informing them he was alive and in a Turkish prison.

However their relief was short-lived as just before Christmas in 1916, they received a War Office telegram informing them of his death. No details were provided.

During the same campaign another local lad, Sergeant Valentine Read[213] had won the DCM. Read was a member of the Christchurch Company that had left for India shortly after the outbreak of War. Soon after arriving in India he had volunteered for service in the Persian Gulf and after a spell of garrison duty at Basra, he was involved in a number of clashes with the Turks as the British advanced to relieve General Townsend's force at Kut.

On the 6th of June 1916 the news of Lord Kitchener's death shocked the Nation. He was travelling on the HMS Hampshire when it sunk in a severe storm off the Orkney Isles. There were no survivors. A period of national mourning began. Flags flew at half mast throughout the country and Army band concerts planned for the Sunday evenings; entertainment at both the Bournemouth and Boscombe Piers were cancelled as a sign of respect to Kitchener. On the 13th of June a memorial service was conducted for Kitchener at St Paul's Cathedral[214].

Amongst all of this turmoil, people struggled to understand how Britain, with its vast Empire was so militarily weak and unprepared. One view[215] was that Britain was living on its past glories and had merely "muddled through". It had put its faith in the appointment of committees and political debate, and had relied upon a weak party system of civilians to govern military matters. It had underestimated Germany as a military power and accordingly had left itself unprepared as a nation.

Then in the early hours of the 1st of July 1916, a human storm broke over the Somme battlefield as the long awaited British offensive begun. The local newspapers were soon full of accounts of the battle as well as grim lists of the local Hampshire and Christchurch men killed, wounded or posted as missing during the opening days of the battle. The Reverend G.J. Ayre of Christchurch later learnt that four of his nephews had been killed that day. Three were serving with the Canadian Newfoundland Regiment.

They were 2nd Lieutenants Gerald W Ayre and Wilfred D Ayre, who were cousins, and Captain Ernie S Ayre of the same regiment. The Newfoundlanders suffered horrendous casualties that day, so much so that on the following morning a mere 78 men reportedly answered roll call amongst that decimated regiment. Also killed that day was Ernie's brother Captain Bernard Ayre who was serving with the Norfolk Regiment.

Local men's names continued to be printed in the daily "Roll of Honour" published by the *Christchurch Times* during July. Mr Lane of 140 Christchurch Road, Boscombe lost his son, Herbert, who served with 1st Hampshire Battalion during the Somme battle. He has no known grave.

Also killed on 1st July on the Somme was 2nd Lieutenant Gerald Henry Joseph Bramble, 3rd Hampshire Regiment, aged 21. On the 3rd of July his brother Bombardier John Bramble serving in the 109th Heavy Battery RGA aged 24 was also killed in action, leaving their parents, John and Rose Bramble of Avon, near Christchurch to mourn their loss. Gerald Bramble's name appears on the Thiepval Memorial, he has no known grave.

As a tribute to them, their parents had the following poem printed in the Christchurch Times:

> *"A little while – your grave will be o'ertrodden*
> *Soon the frail cross have fallen in the breeze*
> *No loving hands are there to tend and cherish*
> *Those graves in foreign soil across the seas.*
> *Somewhere in France! Oh Surely, my beloved*
> *Tho' sign and token all be swept away,*
> *It is not in that land of desolation,*
> *But in our hearts, that you will rest always. "*

Private Edward Adams, who had lived at Fairmile in Christchurch, had served with the 1st Hampshire Regiment during the Retreat from Mons, where one of his brothers had been killed and another taken prisoner. He had been posted as missing since July 1915 in the fighting around Ypres and after a year with no news, he was officially listed as "presumed killed" in July; so his name appeared amongst the lists of the Somme dead. He left behind a widow and four children. He has no known grave and his name is on the Menin Gate memorial at Ypres.

With local men now prisoners of war after the capture of Kut, and the horrific fighting during the Somme battle, relatives were keen to help them somehow. The Hudson Brothers of Bournemouth issued a price list of suitable foodstuffs and personal items that could be purchased from their store, which could be sent to either British prisoners or family members serving at the Front. Newspaper reports from British prisoners in Germany had referred to their lack of warm clothing and the poor quality of the food. Some prisoners mentioned that they almost entirely lived off the contents of these parcels, which encouraged families to send more. Additionally, summer fetes were organised to raise funds to buy parcels for prisoners of war.

That first week of August marked the second anniversary of the war and all the while the casualty lists from the fighting on the Somme continued to be published. To make sense of it all and provide some moral guidance, the vicar of the Priory Church, the Reverend R.R. Needham, held several services. The first was for the Christchurch Territorial Battalion's D Company in conjunction with their recruitment parade. In his address, the vicar reminded everyone that Britain had gone into the war with clean hands. It had wanted peace and had no ulterior aims or desires. It was fighting a just war to stop the Kaiser from imposing his will upon Europe, as Napoleon had done.

Afterwards, the Reverend Leslie B. Neale MA., Chaplain N.Z. Forces along with Right Reverend Bishop Taylor Smith DD., Chaplain General H.M. Forces conducted a service for around 1000 soldiers at the Depot. Australians, New Zealanders and British all attended. The sermon was taken from Genesis xxxiii 24 "And Jacob was left alone and there he wrestled a man with him until the breaking of the day." A second service was held later for the public and the Reverend Needham took as his text "The Lord hath been mindful of us and he shall bless us" (12th Verse 115th Psalm).

Sanger's Circus arrived in Christchurch during August and it provided plentiful entertainment with performing seals, clowns on trapeze and slack wire acts, "Pimpo" the Clown, and the trained elephants and horses. The final act was a patriotic display of the British Lion in the central circus ring.

Military concerts were also held through August and a local musical troupe of soldiers recuperating from wounds who called themselves "The WizzBangs" proved to be popular. Two of their more memorable performances were from Corporal Peter who spoke of his experiences before the Medical Board. It was not so much what he said that was funny, as the way he said it and the military members of the audience fully appreciated the humour. Sapper Brown sang "Me, Me, Me" and the risqué "Every girl is doing her bit" – both acts caused roars of laughter.

Amongst a world now changed by war, most children continued with their education and schooling. Sarah Williams, a widow was fined five shillings for her children not attending school. While at the local Christchurch Congregational Boys' School it was announced that Sidney Barfoot had been awarded an "A" County Council scholarship for Bournemouth School until he reached the age of 16; while his classmate Francis Tripp had been awarded a "B" scholarship for Brockenhurst School for Training Teachers. At the Church of England Girls' school Gladys May Preston, who was only 11 years of age, had won a "B" scholarship allowing her to attend Brockenhurst School for Training Teachers, much to the delight of Miss Shelford, the head mistress. While Miss Jessie Coley, of the Manse, Christchurch had succeeded in passing the Intermediate Art Exams at London University.

Chapter Twenty-Four: The changing fabric of life

With the mounting homeland threats from sea and air, the start of 1916 began with an appeal for raised public vigilance in coastal areas towards possible spies. The *Christchurch Times* reported that a large population of male enemy aliens still lived in prohibited coastal areas. It was estimated, which was soon made official, that around 7,449 Germans and 5,088 Austrian males, as well as an estimated 10,000 women of "enemy origin" were still at large[216].

The Defence of the Realm Act made it compulsory that all visitors to restricted areas were to register with the local police. This was not always observed and a farm foreman was fined in Norfolk for not registering several farm labourers from Lancashire[217].

Also failing to register was Mr. Belknap Battle, an American citizen and student at the Royal College of Science in Kensington. America had not yet joined the war, so Mr Battle was technically an alien and as he was staying at a Bournemouth hotel he was charged with entering a protected area without an identity book, and further failing to register. He claimed he was ignorant of the regulations. Regardless he was fined 5 shillings for not possessing identification and a further 2 shillings and six pence for failing to register; this was similar to being fined a week's wages.

Restrictions also applied to the use of cameras. Permits were required for the taking of photographs or the making of sketches in a prohibited area, which for the Bournemouth area was up to four miles inland from the coastline, and from Hurst Castle in the east to Lyme Regis[218] in the west.

There were also penalties for not keeping a list of employees. These lists were important for the recruiting authorities as labour tended to move around the country. Compulsory recruitment had started in March 1916 and was extended from May 1916 to include married men; so these lists aided the local military recruiters in knowing who was eligible for military service and where they were. To formalise this process Form 41

(Defence of the Realm Regulation) became law on the 22nd of December 1916 which made it obligatory for employers to keep a list of their employees and to send a copy of these to the local Recruiting Office. Failing to do so made the offending employer liable to six months imprisonment.

For those taking in lodgers, a "Lodger Form" officially known as "Form A.R.E", had to be completed and registered at the local police station. Many women, struggling on their husband's Army pay, were keen to take in paying lodgers for a few nights. Several fell foul of this regulation. Many lodgers were the wives of soldiers serving in nearby camps, such as Christchurch Barracks. For many men given a few days embarkation leave prior to leaving for France, having their wife nearby was usual; particularly amongst the newly married New Zealanders.

Mrs Annie Owen of Jumpers in Christchurch was charged with failing to obtain a lodger's form despite the fact that she did not keep a lodging house. She had never taken in lodgers before but on this occasion had agreed to let the wife of a young New Zealand engineer stay a few nights. She was found guilty and fined 2 shillings and 6 pence. There was an understandable degree of frustration with this regulation[219] as the householder's decision to accept a lodger was normally economic and spur of the moment. Dithering because of a form would result in people looking elsewhere for a room.

In early 1917 the local newspapers reported that Corporal A. Bendall and Private Moores had both been "killed in action", Private Francis Ferrey had been wounded by artillery fire while escorting German POWs back and had his leg amputated, while Private R.V. Prichard, who was the son of a Christchurch councillor, had been wounded in the knee. Lance Corporal George W. Scott, second son of the late Mr T.R. Scott of Castle Street, was reported as killed in action in France. He was well known in Christchurch. Sergeant Arthur Young[220] and Private George Adey[221] were reported as killed in Mesopotamia, while Sergeant Herbert Gossling had been awarded an officer's commission.

For many people, part of the daily wartime ritual was to read the local casualty lists in the newspapers to see if they recognised any names of school friends, neighbours or other local acquaintances claimed by the war. Such awareness would have helped the community to comfort grieving families.

For mothers worried about sons either wounded or still missing in action, reading those columns of casualties must have been a harrowing experience. They too were as much the casualties of the war as those involved in the actual fighting.

One morning along the railway lines near Staplecross Bridge, between Hinton Admiral and Christchurch, a platelayer found the body of a woman. The body was identified as being that of Mrs Lillian Slade aged forty-eight. Her husband had thought she had gone to the doctor in Christchurch as she had recently recovered from influenza, though still complained about pains in her head. She had been worried about their son who had been badly wounded in France. Dr Legate saw her body and a verdict of "suicide whilst of unsound mind"[222] was given. It was presumed that she had been struck by the foot guard of a passing train, after she most likely had lain down with her neck on the rail, as her skull was fractured.

An inquest was also held into the death of Mrs Clara Pitt aged forty-six whose body was found in the River Stour one morning. She had many abrasions on her face and other parts of the body, but no marks of violence to account for death. A young Arthur Stride aged fourteen stated that he noticed a woman near Iford Bridge who had spent a half hour looking over the wall of the bridge and wringing her hands. The inquests verdict was "death due to drowning".

Mary Coakes aged sixty-seven, a night nurse caring for the wounded soldiers sent to Christchurch hospital, was charged with attempting to commit suicide by throwing herself into the River Stour at Holdenhurst. She was saved by George Bellany, Lady Malmesbury's chauffeur who just happened to be driving wounded soldiers towards Holdenhurst when he saw something in the water. When charged, she replied "I had to do something, there's nothing to live for." She received three months hard labour at Winchester Prison. Attempted suicide was a criminal offence in England at the time.

The bravery of some became the envy of others who chose only to deceive. Stepping onto the railway platform at Christchurch station in April 1917 was a young soldier wearing three medal ribbons, including the Distinguished Conduct Medal, on his jacket as well as four gold wound strips on his left sleeve. He was spotted by a local policeman, Police-Sergeant Davies, who had won the DCM in France earlier in the war and possibly sensing a kindred spirit, started a conversation with the soldier.

Davies asked the man how he had won the DCM. He was told that the man had braved shell fire to bring in a wounded officer and captured a German machine gun at the same time. In the course of this action he was wounded in four places. The man mentioned that he was at the retirement from Mons and at the battle of Neuve Chapelle. Both actions had been fought in 1914, whereas the man did not enlist until 1915.

On checking the man's discharge papers Davies became suspicious and arrested the man as being an unauthorised person wearing a Distinguished Conduct Medal ribbon. The prisoner eventually pleaded guilty to both charges. It transpired that the man was Jesse George Gritt, aged 20, a labourer from Thorney Hill. When his military career was checked, it was revealed that he had deserted twice and on the last occasion was sentenced to six months' detention. He had been in France only three days before suffering from bronchitis and then returned to England where he was discharged as medically unfit. He was sentenced to three months imprisonment with hard labour on each charge, the sentences to run consecutively. Some may have thought he got off lightly given that many local lads had paid the ultimate price by not shirking their duty to their country.

The caring nature of the local community and the sharing of grief was on display in February 1918 when two bodies were discovered washed up on the beach at Hengistbury Head near Mudeford. The identities of the bodies could not be established by inquest, so the two men were buried as "Found at Sea No1" and "Found at Sea No2" at the nearby Christchurch Cemetery. Full military honours were afforded to the men and a firing party from the Royal Naval Division were in attendance. As the two coffins were lowered into the graves, three rifles volleys were fired and the Last Post sounded. The funerals were well attended by local people; and it must have been particularly symbolic for those who had already lost sons, husbands and relatives in far away places such as Gallipoli, France and Kut.

Their presence at the funerals allowed a respectful farewell; as they hoped their men folk had received. They knew that somewhere a mother, father, wife, brother or sister would never have the satisfaction of knowing the fate of those men. They would never be able to visit or to look upon the resting places and tend the graves. Soon there would be two more saddened homes in Britain when the "missing in action" telegrams arrived.

Chapter Twenty-Five: Military recruitment in Britain

The shortages of manpower were being acutely felt by a military system unable to rapidly replace its losses and maintain full-strength army formations in the field for offensive actions. Not only was there a continuing threat of a possible invasion, but also, political plight arose in Ireland following the Spring Uprising in Dublin, Easter 1916. The Army was completely stretched and with no more Regular Army units available, Territorial soldiers began serving in Ireland.

By July 1916 the impact of the Military Services Act was being felt within communities as all doctors under the age of forty-five years of age were called up which resulted in Christchurch losing two local doctors: Hartford and Robinson, who left to serve in the Army. It was soon estimated that 85-90% of doctors serving in the Army had been civilians less than two years before. [223]

Towards the end of 1916, there was a growing sentiment within certain public forums that Britain could not win the war without compulsory war service for all males between the ages of forty-one and sixty-one. "Compulsory volunteering" was the term used. *The Spectator* newspaper championed the Volunteer Movement[224] and observed that the whole manhood of Great Britain up to the age of forty-one, was either fighting or preparing to fight, with the exception of those men who were physically unfit or else doing important work in Britain and unable be spared for the Army. It was opined that these men, along with all those medically unfit, should be trained in their spare time and placed at the disposal of the Military Authorities for home defence in case of invasion or any other great emergency[225].

That Christmas, when delivering his annual lecture in his borough constituency of Christchurch, the local MP, Lieutenant-Colonel Page Croft, chose as his theme "Problems of the War and After". Here he stated his support for the sentiment that the war was about manpower. He believed that whichever Army possessed the most battalions would win. Manpower he believed would be the deciding factor. Britain needed more fighting men. Attritional warfare was now recognised as the path to victory.

Not everyone adhered to this belief, especially when it meant the ruin of a local economy because it had been deprived of essential and skilled workers. In addition, with a stalemate in the fighting, the lengthy casualty lists and the broken men returning home resulted in less allure to join the Colours, particularly when it meant leaving behind a family having to cope on a meagre Army pay. Notably, the fashion of giving a white feather to men not in uniform faded out around this time.

The Rural District Tribunal for Christchurch, manned by military officers, heard the appeals from those men seeking deferment or exemption from military service. Leniency was not one of the Tribunal's strong points. In September 1916 a thirty-seven year old man from the village of Bransgore, who described himself as a smallholder and stockbreeder, applied to have his enlistment date deferred. His reason was that he still had not finished his threshing and there were still root crops in the ground to be brought in. He stated that he was already working single handed and there was no-one to leave in charge. He was granted one month's postponement to complete gathering in his crops. A Burley farmer also appealed when his last remaining farm worker was conscripted. He was granted a three month exemption until the harvest was collected.

Inevitably, this haemorrhaging of manpower away from the fragile local economy forced employers to challenge the military over its unreasonable recruitment policy. The number of objections gathered pace throughout the early months of 1917 and Military Tribunals soon became increasing bogged down in appeal hearings. When a young meat salesman, aged nineteen was passed fit for military service his District Manager immediately appealed on his behalf. At the tribunal the District Manager stated that 130 branch shops had been closed nationwide as nearly six hundred of their men had been taken for military service. The tribunal was unsympathetic.

A Sopley employer applied for leave to appeal when one of his men, aged twenty-six, was called up. He claimed that the man should be exempt as he was the only one remaining who knew anything about the particular work undertaken. The Tribunal adjourned for one month to enable a medical examination of the man, after which time it would reconvene. Many other appeals were heard from bricklayers, agricultural smiths and market gardeners. All pleaded long hours and skill shortage. A local Bournemouth newspaper was granted a three month exemption concerning their last remaining print maker. They had argued that it was a certified occupation. Seven out of their thirteen printers had already joined the Army.

A boot repairer said that his wife could not carry on the business in his absence. Two businesses had already closed in Christchurch and he was engaged in repairing boots for the military, the entire town and the agricultural workers. He also helped his brother when possible on Sundays and Bank holidays. He had repaired over three hundred pairs of shoes for him during the last 18 months besides his own work. Accepting that vital war work was being undertaken, the military tribunal allowed conditional exemption for six months when the case would be reheard.

A local farmer asked that his son, who had just turned eighteen, might have his application adjourned for a short time. He had been at the Bournemouth Flying School and was applying now for a commission in the RFC. The tribunal agreed to allow one month's exemption to enable him to produce evidence of acceptance by the RFC, or to be medically examined if he were rejected by them.

One case which came before the Tribunal involved a married man serving with the 4th Battalion, Hampshire Volunteers as a Sergeant. He applied for future exemption stating that during the absence of the Officer he was in charge of the Christchurch Platoon. The man also happened to own a newsagent and tobacconist business in the town. The military Representative said that with his military knowledge he would be most valuable for the training of recruits. Somewhat grasping at straws considering he was already a member of a military unit, the man then explained that he had a fractured shoulder and could not carry the equipment. He further stated that being called up would mean losing his business as he could not leave it to be managed by the errand boys. The case was postponed for a month, during which time a certificate of his wife's health was to be obtained. If she was fit and able, then it would be up to her to manage the business while the man served.

Others were not treated as kindly and many businesses were lost during the war years. When the owner of Rose's Cash Store on the High Street in Christchurch was called up for Military Service, he was forced to close his business and sell all of his stock. He placed an advert in the *Christchurch Times* stating that he had large stocks of food which had to be sold immediately; his misfortune would benefit others. He encouraged the public to arrive early so as to get first choice.

The appeal of a conscientious objector, who was prepared to serve but not in a combatant role, displayed many of the flaws of the Bournemouth Military Tribunal. The man had earlier been granted a total exemption from serving, only for the military to appeal making him eligible for non-combatant service. The man was then arrested as a deserter which contravened section 3 of the Military Service Act, in that the man had an appeal pending. The Chairman of the Tribunal would not be swayed by argument, or seemingly the law of the land. He dismissed the man's appeal and had him lead away under military escort.

Conscientious objectors were not excused war duty and many volunteered to serve in the Army as non-combatants, while others were given war work on farms and wherever there was a labour shortage. In June 1917, the idyllic nature of Brockenhurst village was disturbed when a party of conscientious objectors arrived; presumably sent to the New Forest to help in felling the trees, wood cutting and supplying timber to the military camps. They were mobbed as they walked from the railway station and through the village. Women and children pelted them with clods of turf and booed them while other civilians hustled them out of the village. Two of them were ducked in the stream at Balmer Lawn, and the men's baggage which was on a lorry was thrown into the river.

This attitude displayed by townspeople and newspaper alike towards "conchies", as conscientious objectors were called, was not unusual. Although many served in France in Labour Battalions or as medical stretcher bearers with the RAMC, the greater view was that those who stayed at home were cowardly and disloyal to King and Country in this, its greatest hour of need. It was very much a belief in the slogan "My country, right or wrong". Private Alec Hutton thought that New Zealand had gone mad when he heard that conscientious objectors were being taught massage back home. He viewed them as beyond contempt and disloyal[226].

Captain Arthur Osburn, a doctor with the Irish Dragoon Guards, held a different view. He thought that at times they had greater moral courage than physical pluck, especially after seeing one of them threatened and taunted by what he referred to as a crowd of girls and loafers[227]. He thought that the war profiteers, who traded horses and those unmarried women who claimed separation allowances, were morally far worse than any conscientious objector.

Similarly, forms of social stigma were shown to those who had volunteered for military service, and for whatever reason were later discharged from military service. Mr Elman a teacher at the Christchurch Priory School enlisted in May 1916 and unexpectedly returned to his teaching position in June 1917. He had not served in France and presumably had been declared unfit for further military service. Five months later in November 1917, not even half way through the school year, he resigned his position at the school and left Christchurch.

The military demand for men did not relent and the *Daily Telegraph* on the 28th of July 1917 published an arousing appeal for volunteers by Lord French, who had commanded the BEF until 1915 and was now commanding Home Defences. The headlines set the tone by announcing: "Is there any man calling himself a man in this country who would not be prepared to do anything to save his country at such a time?"

By April 1918, the new Military Services Act raised the military age to fifty-one.

No. 1 New Zealand General Hospital at Brockenhurst, Hampshire. The local townspeople appreciated the agricultural skills the New Zealanders had and with the manpower shortages in England, the soldiers would often help on the local farms.

Chapter Twenty-Six: The Battle of Flers-Courcelette
15th of September 1916

The N.Z. Division was moved by train to an area around the lower Somme, arriving near Abbeville on the 20th of August for a period of rest and training. The N.Z. Engineers refreshed their skills in explosives, wiring, musketry and supervising work parties. There were also route marches. The bulk of their time was allocated to techniques that enabled them to rapidly dig trenches and consolidate captured positions. They had to be aware of the time required to complete the pre-requisite tasks and which method produced the best results. They took into account the nature of the ground, the men available, enemy bombardments and casualties incurred due to the battlefield conditions. Once the preferred approach was decided upon, it was then practiced until it was understood by each man.

Experience at Gallipoli and Armentières had taught them three major lessons. The first was that bombardments obliterated or badly damaged trenches; secondly the captured position would have been constructed facing the Allies lines with communication saps leading towards the enemy's trenches. The final lesson was that the enemy would counterattack quickly; using these saps as entry points back into the trenches system while an accurate artillery bombardment supported their assault. Knowing this, they calculated that the time elapsed between occupying the enemy position, creating obstacles and the new trenches that were capable of stopping a counterattack, was insufficient. The only solution available was to create strong points. A strong point was a small "fort" holding around fifty men and located slightly forward or on a captured position. It had a known shape, but no prescribed size.

The Engineers practiced constructing these strong points, beginning with understanding how to mark out the trench structure to be used. They then experimented with various digging and construction methods. The British Army engineering manual stated that a man could dig 80 cubic feet of earth in four hours. After several days of trial and error in the rear areas around the Somme, the New Zealanders believed that given the type of earth encountered that they could double that rate of work. Especially when "pressed by motives of personal safety or by a desire to be somewhere else".[228]

The routine established was that after an assault a series of strong points would be built, either in a circular or a cross shaped design. The deciding factors were the ground geometry and the immediate enemy threat. The circular design provided the easier pattern for fire command in all directions, although once it was enclosed with wire, enemy artillery could be ranged easily onto it.

The cross design required that the main length of trench was dug towards the enemy. Then at the central point, two smaller side arms were dug, running off at right angles making the cross. Machine guns were set-up on each of the four extremities. This provided effective cross-fire during any counterattack. The central stem of the cross design could then be extended to the rear providing a communications trench. The cross shape provided better concealment from overhead aircraft and it was also harder for artillery to range onto and completely neutralize.

The next phase was to sandbag the parapets, dig fire bays and finally place wire entanglements all around the strong point. Stores of munitions, bombs, food, water, sandbags, wire and timber would then be brought up. Telephone wires were laid to keep in contact with the battalion or brigade headquarters. It normally took only a few hours to complete the work. Despite the hasty construction, this structure was capable of withstanding a direct assault.

The final phase, which could be completed some time later, was to extend the side trenches until they joined up with the neighbouring strong points. As the trench lines gradually joined up, the line could be better consolidated, machine gun positions realigned and wire entanglements improved. Eventually the trench mortars would be brought forward.

Training continued until the 27th of August, when the N.Z. Engineers and N.Z. Pioneers marched towards Fricourt, near the new front line. They arrived that evening wet, weary and footsore. Proper rationing had not been organized for them, so they quickly besieged the YMCA shack buying hot drinks and food before setting up their bivouacs along the side of a road.

There was intensive activity for the next few weeks along the roads with trucks, troops and artillery continually moving along them. In the sky above the battlefield, were British aircraft and observations balloons. The fighting for the features known as 'High Wood' and 'Deville Wood' was still fierce, though neither could be called woods any longer as they had been reduced to bare stumps amongst a tangle of fallen tree limbs, smoke, shell holes and mud. The villages in the vicinity also testified to the extent of the determined fighting, merely comprising heaps of collapsed masonry[229].

The Field Companies were placed under the command of the Chief Engineer XV Corps. They were tasked with consolidating the old German second line on the 'Bazentin Ridge', near Longueval opposite 'High Wood'. Despite being captured a fortnight earlier it had not been properly maintained. As a consequence the trenches there were full of mud, water and decomposing bodies, both German and British.

Without adequate revetting and timber available for "A" frames, the sides continually crumbled into the trench space during the following days of wet and stormy weather. With the Engineers constantly working in the trenches and insufficient duckboards, the dirt and water was soon churned into knee deep mud.

Amongst this bog the toil continued. The Engineers described it as a "swine of a place" and the stormy weather hindered most of their construction efforts. For days they were continually wet and unable to dry their clothing. It was arduous work, but eventually they drained, repaired and reconstructed the trench system.

Given the working conditions, these advance trenches were incongruously renamed, 'Savoy' and 'Carlton' and were occupied on the 10th of September by the 2nd and 3rd Battalions of the N.Z. Rifle Brigade.

The flooded German deep dugouts were drained, eventually revealing numerous bloated German bodies. No one was keen to go down and remove them. The N.Z. Rifle Brigade's headquarters instead occupied a cellar near the village of Bazentin-le-Grand.

With the work on the trenches well advanced, the roads were repaired; muddy areas and holes filled in, brick rubble put on top and then drainage and sump pits dug to make the roads ready for the heavy traffic soon to use them. The next job was for the drivers to begin stockpiling stores at the newly established 'Green' and 'Thistle' dumps[230]. These were closer to the main trenches and necessary for the forthcoming offensive. They contained: wire, picks, shovels, wire pickets, sandbags, revetting, duckboards, telephone wire, timber, nails, corrugated iron and an array of other engineering tools and equipment. In amongst these dumps were Stoke mortar bombs, shells, ammunition, grenades, and numerous other essential munitions.

Stores dumps were prime targets for enemy aircraft and artillery, so each cache was disbursed to limit any destruction caused by a direct hit. The various items were stacked in a prescribed order to allow them to be quickly located at night. They were also camouflaged to conceal them from German aviators.

On the 3rd of September Delville Wood was finally captured by the South African Brigade and that day the N.Z. Engineers commenced the digging of two new communication trenches. This was the first occasion during the war in which the Field Companies were used in their prescribed roles, as opposed to operating alongside the Infantry Brigades.

The existing communications trenches were very shallow, blown in, full of dead German and British soldiers lying half buried in the watery, muddy bottom. In the heat of the September days the air was thick with the smell of putrefaction and flies; reminiscent of the swarms tolerated on Gallipoli a year ago.

These two new trenches were called 'Turk Lane' and 'French Lane'. The N.Z. Pioneers dug 'Turk Lane', allocating one platoon from each of the companies for the task. The construction of 'French Lane' was divided between the Field Companies, under the command of Major Barclay.

Both trenches began just to the north of the village of Montauban. At their entry points they were shallow, at a depth of two or three feet. They were dug steadily towards the low Longueval ridge, over a mile away. Once across the ridge the trenches became gradually deeper and both turned north-east. 'Turk Lane' snaked alongside 'Thistle Alley', through Caterpillar Valley and skirted the northern fringe of the rise leading up to 'High Wood'. The other trench, 'French Lane' was parallel to, but 400 yards to the south-east of 'Turk Lane', closer to Longueval and Delville Wood as it meandered along Caterpillar Valley.

Both were still roughly in parallel with each other, pointing in the direction of the town of Flers. 'French Lane' ended in the middle section of 'Black Watch Trench' 700 yards further on and faced towards the German trench system named 'Switch Trench'. 'Turk Lane' extended another 800 yards past the ridge to 'Black Watch Trench' and then another 500 yards ending at 'Worcester Trench'. At this point it had been dug to a depth of over six feet. This last section of work was hindered by the number of decaying German and British bodies that littered the area. These were merely removed to one side and then a layer of dirt was shovelled over them to reduce the smell. The urgency to complete the trench meant that there was no time to properly bury any of the dead.

Most of the work was conducted at night. As the trenches neared the front line, the German artillery began bombarding them with high explosives and gas shells. This caused numerous casualties, especially amongst the N.Z. Pioneers. Digging ceased during the bombardments as the men sought whatever shelter was available or else withdrew along the trench away from the shelling. Hot meals were occasionally provided, but the main ration during this time was: bread, tinned meat and petrol flavoured water.

Despite the weather, aggressive enemy bombardments and other interruptions, the Engineers and Pioneers managed to complete the two trenches in nine days. Each were six foot deep and three foot wide, duck boarded with timber shelters every 500 yards and telephone lines cleared and fixed to one side of the trench. On the nights of the 12th and 13th of September they laid out two lines of wavy, assembly trenches with the help of around 800 infantry soldiers. They were four foot deep and two foot wide, located between 'Elgin Alley' and 'French Lane'. On the first night, 600 N.Z. Infantry managed to dig 1200 yards of trench. Somehow that night another 200 N.Z. infantry had managed to "escape" the job, so they were tasked to finish the remaining 400 yards on their own during the second night. Altogether, 1,600 yards of trench were completed within two nights, despite the darkness, rain, shelling, and bodies that they disinterred along the route of the trenches.

While the assembly trenches were being completed, 2nd Lieutenant Russell employed another 500 men from the 1st Battalion N.Z. Rifle Brigade, to make a serviceable road from Mametz, near Fricourt, along Caterpillar Valley and up to 'Thistle Dump'. The infantry also continued to act as fatigue parties helping to carry logistical supplies forward for the stores dumps, prior to the offensive.

The Germans anticipated a major attack and began to heavily bombard the entire frontline area. Both 'Turk Lane' and 'French Lane' were severely damaged during these high explosive onslaughts, with the last 800 yards of 'French Lane' being reduced to nothing more than mounds of broken earth and smashed duckboards. That night, the heavily laden infantry stumbled through this devastation, ensnaring themselves on dislodged and low hanging telephone wires as they moved up to their assembly trenches.

The battle of Flers-Courcelette began in the early hours of the 15th of September. The weather was fine and warm. The N.Z. Division quickly captured 'Switch Trench' and the 1st Field Company allocated to support the 2nd Brigade, moved forward at 1:30pm to build their first of many strong points. Infantry work parties carried the barbed wire, sandbags and other stores needed to complete these.

The new strong points were constructed seventy yards past the captured 'Switch Trench' position. Soon the German Artillery, having pre-plotted

'Switch Trench', began bombarding the entire area that had been captured, believing this to be where the assaulting troops had dug in.

Only the dead still occupied that thin ridge line. The German bombardment did little damage to the New Zealand position, although German fire from High Wood, which still had not been captured by the 14th (London) Division, caused many casualties on the left flank of the 2nd Otago Battalion. With their flank exposed to the German fire coming from High Wood, they sustained heavy casualties throughout the day.

The advancing N.Z. Division soon got ahead of the flanking 47th and 41st Divisions and a salient was formed along their divisional area. The 41st Division had the new tanks in support and they captured Flers with the help of the N.Z. Rifle Brigade, but they got no further that day. The 14th Division took the whole day to capture High Wood.

The salient soon placed extra demands on the Field Engineers. Deep dugouts were constructed in the captured area for battalion and brigade headquarters. One particular dugout for an advanced Brigade's headquarters was constructed sixteen feet below ground level with the help of a detached Tunnelling Company.

'Turk Lane' was extended by the N.Z. Pioneers from 'Worcester Trench' over the ridge through 'Switch Trench' and towards Flers. They even laid duckboards, supplied by Green Dump, to provide easy passage across the rough ground. This trench became the main communication trench during the offensive and it was greatly appreciated by the troops. It provided a protected route for supplies and reinforcements going forward and the wounded coming back.

The 17th and 18th of September brought heavy rain. There was no shelter available in the barren, pot marked landscape. The Engineers housed dressing and aid stations, machine gun positions and the artillery signallers as best they could in either freshly constructed dugouts or else under temporary overhead cover made from corrugated iron and sandbags. The infantry soldiers used waterproof sheets or pieces of corrugated iron to keep themselves dry, or at a minimum, less wet.

Although the road from Fricourt was kept open, it was targeted by artillery and with the wet weather it was not long before the mud soon trapped the wagons, limiting the movement of materials and supplies. With the Division in the midst of consolidating the captured ground and preparing for further offensive action, getting adequate supplies of food, water, ammunition, shells, bombs, telephone wire and barbed wire were essential. When there was time, the dead were buried and the grave sites marked.

As a rough guide, each battalion needed around three ton of supplies a day. For the N.Z. Division that totalled some thirty ton that had to be moved forward each day, preferably at night to limit the disruption from enemy artillery. To overcome this problem, pack animals were brought in to move supplies to collection points and stores dumps such as 'Green Dump'. The infantry fatigue parties would then gather up their supplies and once fully loaded, they trudged back to their positions. The 3rd Field Company laid a road from 'Thistle Dump' to the now captured 'High Wood', thereby providing an extra route for re-supplies. To provide some relief to the supply problems, the 2nd Field Company laid a small gauge Decauville light railway line to Delville Wood to supply shells for the heavy artillery. They also located water in the town of Flers and established six wells that provided drinking water.

The Engineers moved forward each night with the supplies necessary to undertake specific jobs; such as extending trenches, fast wiring or supporting infantry assaults. With the congestion in the communication trenches, getting forward took some time as the Germans continually bombarded the forward areas with gas and high explosive shells. Getting caught in the open was akin to suicide.

Safe movement across open ground was made possible through luck and alert observation by the New Zealanders. It became apparent that although the German bombardment was accurate, it was always within the same grids because two German artillery batteries had not overlapped their fire plans. This omission created a fire-free, safe corridor that was about a hundred yards wide and went all the way to the front line area. Once the situation was confirmed, compass bearings were taken and each night the Engineers strolled above ground and along this unintentional safe zone. Only on one occasion did a shell land in the lane.

To straighten the line and remove the salient, the N.Z. Division continually attacked the flanking German trench systems. Two of these were on their left: 'Grove Alley' and 'Goose Alley'.

On the night of the 19th of September, the 2nd Auckland Battalion was pressing an attack through 'Flers Trench' and into 'Drop Alley', supported by two Stokes mortars. Their aim was to work up the 'Flers Support Trench' and seize the southern end of 'Goose Alley'. Once this was gained, two Engineering sections from 1st Field Company would block-up the ends of the captured trench with sandbags, undertake necessary repairs and consolidate the defences.

The manoeuvre started with the infantry advancing along 'Flers Trench' and up to 'Drop Alley'. The Stokes mortars commenced their bombing of the German positions. Soon artillery shells rained down on the whole area: German and British. The air was quickly saturated in shrapnel, high explosives, tear gas and anything else that was available to the Germans.

Major Barclay, who had recently been presented with the Montenegrin Order of Danilo by the Corps Commander, was unceremoniously blown into a muddy shell hole where he remained for several hours as the heavy barrage continued. The German's intention was to disrupt any troop movements supporting the assault. The Engineers stayed as low to the ground as they could in their hastily dug two foot trenches.

Corporal Fear, who had won the DCM on Gallipoli, was killed during this bombardment. The other three men who shared the same trench with Fear were also killed by the airburst shrapnel. They were: Sappers William Fotheringham, George Kay and Charles Ross. Ten other men were wounded and acting-Sergeant John Woodhall was awarded the Military Medal in daring the bombardment to rescue the wounded.

A map showing the New Zealand Division's sector during the Battle of Flers-Courcelette which began on 15th September, 1916.

Drawing by Jenny Kynaston

The Engineers carried their wounded back and returned to bury their dead, carefully marking the location of each grave. The action caused Colonel Pridham, their CRE to remark "The poor old Sapper, they don't get any awards until they get into a mess!"[231]

On the 21st of September, the 2nd Canterbury Battalion eventually captured that section of 'Goose Alley' after a brutal counter-attack by Bavarian troops. This attack was eventually stopped by Captain Fred Starnes and his company, who realized that the only way to clear the Bavarians out of the trenches was to risk an attack over ground and bomb them out. This was successful and Starnes was recommended for the Victoria Cross, eventually being awarded the DSO for his actions.

Later on the 25th of September, the 1st Otago and the 1st Canterbury Battalions captured a further stretch of 'Goose Alley'. The Engineers dug T-head saps over the crest in which they positioned and fortified machine gun posts. They then prepared the deep, narrow pits for the Trench Mortar platoon near 10th Otago Company's position. The trench mortar arrived with their ammunition already fused, set up their Stokes mortars in the newly dug pits and began firing.

Trench mortar positions were enemy artillery magnets and it was normal protocol to warn the infantry when they were about to commence firing, so as to give them a chance to get under adequate shelter. Soon the nearby 10th Otago Company was suffering heavy casualties from the German bombardment on their position. Private Alfred Towns, who was operating one of the Stokes mortars, was wounded by German shrapnel and lost three fingers as well as sustaining other puncture wounds.

The Engineers continued with their routine of trench repairs and they supported the continual assaults around 'Grove Alley' and then 'Factory Corner'. At 'Factory Corner' they found a large supply of German engineering equipment and a deep well with good drinking water. This helped relieve some of the Division's supply problems.

Sapper Thomas Tester's reinforcement draft from Christchurch joined the Field Engineers on the 30th of September. He noted in his diary that the Engineers were living in barns. Given the continual deterioration in the weather, this was far better than the bivouacs in the roadside fields that they had occupied two weeks earlier.

The N.Z. Division was readying itself for an attack on the 'Grid Trench' system that same day and a new aspect of warfare was being tested during their assault. It was managed by a detachment from the Special Brigade, R.E. They were using mortars to project thirty-six explosive oil containers at the German trenches prior to the N.Z. Division's attack. Thirty of these containers burst and exploded on the German position, covering the area in flames and smoke. The effect was terrifying on the German troops. The New Zealanders took the position and with the assistance of their Stokes mortars repulsed the German counterattack. The Engineers then moved up and consolidated the captured trenches by building strong points.

After twenty-three days continually in the front line, the New Zealand infantry were relieved by the 41st Division. The N.Z. Engineers and N.Z. Pioneers had been in the front line for a total of thirty-six days. The N.Z. Division became the Corps Reserve for another attack proposed for the 5th of October. The fierce fighting in wet conditions and wearing damp uniforms, left men in a weakened state and unable to march very far, nor for very long, on the hard French roads.

The weather worsened and so the attack was postponed. Eventually on the 10th and 11th of October the N.Z. Division entrained to rejoin II Anzac Corps at Armentières on the Lys. Once out of the line, several Engineers managed to get very drunk, which would normally carry a harsh field punishment. Their commanding officer was lenient, and taking into account their long service, what they had endured at Flers-Courcelette and their feats amidst such hardships, they were instead severely reprimanded.

Captain McNeill R.E. left the N.Z. Engineers after splendid service on Gallipoli, Armentières and Flers-Courcelette for which he was awarded the Military Cross. He returned to the Royal Engineers where he served with the 2nd West Lancashire Field Company in France. He was killed on the 10th of January 1917.

On the 7th of October, General H. Rawlinson, Commander of the 4th Army praised the N.Z. Division on its gallantry and success in capturing and holding its objectives.

New Zealand wounded at Lady Malmesbury's Convalescing Hospital at Heron Court, near Christchurch in September 1916. The men are enjoying their afternoon tea on the grass after helping with a garden fete organised to raise funds for "smokes" for the convalescent soldiers. The local villagers and townspeople enjoyed such day's outings partaking in the entertainment stalls such as: "Bombing the Kaiser", Cake Weight Guessing, Aunt Sally Stall, Dipps, Ball Quoits or they could take a rowboat ride around the little island in the lake.

Photo courtesy of The Red House Museum, Christchurch, Dorset

New Zealand wounded at the Priory Church at Christchurch with Mr HE Miller, a guide at the Priory Church (standing third from left) and an unknown lady helper. The men are wearing "hospital blue" uniforms and on such outings were always accompanied by a nurse. She is standing second from the right. The Priory Church became a popular attraction as Kaiser Wilhelm once attended Sunday service there in December 1907 and signed the Visitors' book.

Photo courtesy of Mrs Barbara Jones, Christchurch, Dorset.

New Zealand wounded outside the Priory Church at Christchurch.

Photo courtesy of The Red House Museum, Christchurch, Dorset.

Chapter Twenty-Seven: The New Zealand Engineers Depot at Brightlingsea, Essex

At Christchurch, winter was approaching and competitive sport was soon being planned by the NZE Reserve Depot. The local *Christchurch Times* published a challenge from the New Zealanders to all local sports teams. It simply read:

Hehoe Tenakoe (Listen. Greetings.)
"We hear that the New Zealand Engineers have formed "Rugger" and "Soccer" Clubs and are open for engagements for any Saturday afternoon.
They open the season this afternoon at King's Park, Boscombe with a Rugger match against the "All Blacks" (New Zealanders) from Sling Camp.
Kick off 2:30pm"

Although they could find plenty of opposition for soccer matches, the New Zealanders found it difficult arranging rugby fixtures, so their early matches were against teams from the N.Z. Infantry Training Depot at Sling and the N.Z. Artillery at Ewshot.

As with all the other training companies camped in Christchurch, the New Zealanders could not remain under canvas during the cold winter months, so billets in the local area were sought. As the townspeople had billeted the Loyal North Lancashire Battalion during the prior winter, a similar arrangement was expected.

Rumours were soon circulating that some of the townspeople did not want the colonial Australians and New Zealanders lodging in their houses. Conscious of the harm such attitudes could cause, the local newspaper ran a full comment column reminding the townspeople that the Anzacs had come a long way to fight for the Empire and a debt of gratitude was due.

Eventually the topic of billeting was discussed at the Town Hall Council

Meeting. The Mayor, Dr A.H.B. Hartford, reported that 280 men from the camp, including some of the Royal Engineers, had so far been billeted in the town, with another 170 men billeted in empty houses which had limited heating and cooking facilities. The South Midlands Engineers had been billeted at Twynham Lodge on the edge of town. He alluded to the rumours that he had heard about the billeting of soldiers in the town and he reported that in the past, the soldiers had behaved themselves extremely well with only one prosecution for drunkenness the whole time.

The main conversation centred on the economics of the matter. The majority view expressed at the meeting was that with the extra costs, households would lose money billeting one or two soldiers. To make it worthwhile at least seven to eight soldiers would have to be billeted in each household and this was impractical. Eventually, it was pointed out that the whole town benefited not only by the money paid for billeting, but also by the money which the soldiers spent in the town. The council was reminded that many tradesmen had been able to keep their heads above water owing to the presence of the troops.[232]It was a peculiar situation that was never properly resolved.

On the 22nd of October 1916 the N.Z. Engineers went into their winter billets at Christchurch. It proved an unsatisfactory arrangement and after a mere four days Lieutenant Corkhill paraded the entire company, minus the drivers. They entrained for Brightlingsea to join the Australians. The Australian and New Zealand drivers however remained in Christchurch and continued their training with the horse teams as Brightlingsea had no stables.

The train journey from Christchurch to London was uneventful and after their arrival a new challenge soon presented itself, as the soldiers did not know how to get to the District Line for their onward train connection to Brightlingsea. A Coldstream Guardsman generously offered his services that eventuated in the New Zealanders arriving safely at the wrong railway station.

Brightlingsea in Essex was the first yachting centre in England, and the home of the "Shamrock" crew that had competed for the America's Cup. To the New Zealanders it was a cold, windswept, unattractive little town. Upon their arrival they were immediately allocated their winter billets. These had recently been vacated by 11th and 10th Australian Field Companies who were now back on Salisbury Plain, preparing to embark for France.

The last word on the billeting matter is best summed up by the insight of Major Donaldson, the CO of the 11th Australian Field Company after they had left their billets in Brightlingsea. He wrote that:

"Some surprise was expressed ... both the military authorities and the townspeople were agreeably surprised to find their lives and property were not appreciably jeopardised by the wild colonial soldiery" [233]

The training facilities at Brightlingsea were not as expansive as those offered at the SCSIE at Christchurch. Yet it did provide a different environment for bridging, pontooning, defensive earthworks, infantry training and musketry. One valuable training aspect was that the pontooning was carried out over an arm of the sea, with a tidal rise and fall.

On the 16th of November, Captain Keenan[234], who was in England recuperating from sickness contracted during the Somme campaign, assumed command of the NZE Training Company. Keenan was a career soldier and military engineer who had served in Africa during the Matabele War and the Mashona Rising of 1896. He was appointed Staff Officer to the Director of Railway Transport (N.Z. Railway Battalions) in 1913, and on the 5th of August 1914 he was recruited to the NZEF, and served with the 2nd Field Company at Gallipoli, commanding the mining operation at Quinn's and later the 2nd Field Company at 'Rhododendron Ridge' and the 'Apex' on Gallipoli after the August offensive. He had recently served as the adjutant to the CRE at Armentières and the Somme. He was an experienced officer and a solid choice to command the N.Z. Training Depot.

Reinforcements were arriving monthly from New Zealand and they were joined by veterans convalescing after being released from English hospitals. The Training Company quickly numbered over 300 officers and men, so on the 20th of November, less than a month after arriving in Brightlingsea, the strength for the Training Company was exceeded and the available billets were exhausted. To alleviate the situation, fifty men were posted for training to the Machine Gun Depot at Grantham.[235]

The training at Brightlingsea was supervised by two Royal Engineer officers, being Major Stewart and Captain Lawson, and was best suited for Corps Engineers. The Australians had a Corps, whereas the New Zealanders were Divisional Engineers and often deployed in combat roles. Hauling on ropes during a frosty December while erecting, dismantling and then re-erecting a three hundred foot bridge across the Ayresford Creek[236] must have been considered pointless training to the veterans of Gallipoli and Flers-Courcelette.

During one bridging exercise the "old hands" took to imitating an Egyptian labour gang while hauling on the ropes. This irritated Major Stewart and after delivering a lively assessment of the men's work practices, he stopped the exercise. On their pretend "Western Front" the Australians and New Zealanders also practiced map reading, laying minefields, clearing wire entanglements with Bangalore torpedoes and trying to keep warm in the bleak autumn winds. The wily veterans found plausible reasons to visit the storeroom where they passed the time warming themselves around its fire.

The start of that winter in England was hard for the men and they clearly disliked the isolation and the lack of distractions in the small village. Sports were organised, with rugby and soccer played against the 66th Division, the ASC, and the Naval men stationed nearby. Still the Wesleyan Chapel seemed to be the most popular of all the attractions,[237] possibly because of the dances organised there.

Another officer at Brightlingsea that December was the newly promoted 2nd Lieutenant Cyril Lawrence, a New Zealander who had joined the AIF at the start of the war and had served with 2nd Australian Field Company on Gallipoli and in France. As a sergeant on Gallipoli, he had distinguished himself during that last night of the evacuation in

December 1915, leading one of the demolition parties that destroyed all abandoned guns and equipment[238]. He described the drab town of Brightlingsea as being the "most deadly place in England"[239].

Enjoying a walk through the New Forest near Brockenhurst. They are from left to right:
Lieutenant Peter Painter, 2nd Canterbury Battalion (in the wheelchair), Miss Constantine, the N.Z. Nurse accompanying them, Captain A.L. McDowell, N.Z. Rifle Brigade, (standing and holding the lunch bag), Major F.G. Massey, 2nd Battalion N.Z. Rifle Brigade (seated).

Photo courtesy of Mrs JM Walker

Thorney Hill Ancillary Hospital at Avon Tyrell, where many New Zealanders and Australians convalesced. To help raise money for the Red Cross, the men would make children's wooden toys, marketed as "Chunky Toys". These also became popular in the United States.

The Brightlingsea Depot was in the special defensive area of England and formed part of the East Coast garrison. Early in the war the German Navy had shelled coastal towns, and German airships regularly crossed the channel to bomb towns and factories. The Engineers were to help repel any attempts of invasion, so drills were conducted with the men manning their trenches, although it soon became apparent that without a sufficient quantity of weapons and munitions, they would have little impact in deterring a determined enemy force.

The Engineers continued their training at Brightlingsea despite the cold weather experienced during the late December period. The harsh weather caused several interruptions to training and a higher incidence of sickness was reported. By Christmas the rumour was in full flow that they were returning to Christchurch; news which was well received.

Back at Christchurch, the ladies of one of the War Committees extended a Christmas party invitation to the New Zealand wounded at the No 1 N.Z. General Hospital at Brockenhurst. Local entertainment was always appreciated by the wounded New Zealanders, especially as for most men it was their first Christmas in England.

So on the 23rd of December, around 100 New Zealanders from the Brockenhurst Hospital arrived at the Christchurch Town Hall for an afternoon's entertainment and tea. The event had been organised by Mrs Russell, Miss Russell and Mrs Porteous who worked hard to transform the bleak Town Hall into an inviting and hospitable entertainment hall. They decorated it with colourful flags, including the New Zealand flag sent from New Zealand as a present to the Borough back in 1912. Tables were set for tea and decorated with flowers, Christmas crackers and little New Zealand flags.

The guests arrived at about two o'clock and were given a cordial welcome by their hostesses. Cigarettes were handed around, while other ladies helped wounded men to a table.

The *Christchurch Times* reporter who attended the event, commented that the musical entertainment provided was exceptional. It consisted of

Sapper Wright, RE who sang well with a fine bass voice and was a great favourite. Mrs Porteous sang most artistically. Miss Beaumont and Miss Watkinson received vigorous encores, and Miss Rae, who sang with great charm, was also given a cordial reception; while Miss Vaghan delighted the audience with her violin. It included a Maori song by Private Whititei NZASC with "a weird accompaniment of gestures and facial expressions". One of the New Zealanders said that he was the sort of man who did so well at Gallipoli. The Turks could not stand up against them and their uncanny war songs.[240]

At four o'clock the tea, which was catered for by Mrs Smith of the Priory Tea house, was served. Then the Christmas crackers were popped and the headdresses found inside were worn for the rest of the afternoon by the soldiers, in true Christmas fashion. A bran tub or "lucky dip" had been organised, which provided a small present for each man. The afternoon's entertainment continued with games and Christmas carols until six o'clock; when the men had to depart for the Christchurch railway station and return back to Brockenhurst.

The efforts made by the ladies had made the New Zealanders feel welcomed. Before leaving they expressed their thanks for an enjoyable afternoon by singing "For they are jolly good fellows" and then gave them all three cheers, followed by the National Anthem.

This would not be the last time that the town of Christchurch would host New Zealand soldiers and as Christmas 1916 drew nearer, the NZEF had altered its training policy.

Training Depots now became Reserve Depots and would be responsible for the training of the newly arrived reinforcements as well as administering those men returning from hospitals. Brightlingsea was not suited as a N.Z. Engineers Reserve Depot. It was a small depot in a small town, suited possibly for three or four 4 Field Companies[241] comprising altogether about 1,000 men. The Australians had established their Training Depot there, with Lark Hill on Salisbury Plains as the AIF Reserve Depot. Other factors against Brightlingsea may have been: lack of space; variety of training; and lack of control of the training content.

With the SCSIE facilities available at Christchurch, it was decided that the Reserve Depot for the N.Z. Engineers would be located there.

On the 2nd of January 1917 the N.Z Training Company paraded and entrained for Boscombe, which is about two miles away from Christchurch. Upon their arrival, they immediately went into winter billets.

Their allocated billet area was from Pokesdown station, along Seabourne Road to the east, Woodside Road in the south which bordered the Wentworth Estate and then along Parkwood Road, across the main Christchurch Road and down Gloucester Road on the western edge of the area, finishing at the railway line near the cemetery and King's Park. This area was estimated to billet over 400 soldiers. The houses in this area were predominantly three bed roomed terraced or semi-detached houses. The area had the normal array of small shops in both Southbourne and Pokesdown which catered for the various domestic needs: tobacconists, cobblers, general provision stores and a post office. There were also several pubs in close proximity.

The New Zealanders returning to Christchurch and Boscombe included men who had fought at Gallipoli and in France. These men were billeted with families whose men folk had also served in these same theatres. To those families, it must have been comforting to hear first hand both the humorous and the grim stories of Gallipoli and France. It would have created a closer bond and ensured a warmer welcome than that experienced several months earlier.

Chapter Twenty-Eight: Winter in the Lys sector
near Armentières 1916/1917

The immediate problem facing the N.Z. Engineers in their new sector of Armentières was the low lying water which threatened to flood the trenches. To keep this to a minimum, drainage became a priority and regular patrols ensured that communication trenches and drainage ditches were kept clear of blockages to prevent flooding.

Concrete dugouts had been constructed in the trench system, but these were not waterproof. The Engineers repaired them and built extra concrete dugouts. These new dugouts were known as heavy explosion shelters and provided additional cover in the trenches for the men[242]. Materials were supplied by river barges and the tram lines from the forward dumps to the front line.

With the increase in hostile activity, each deep dugout was provided with two entrances to ensure that the garrison did not become trapped during a raid or by a bombardment. It also had the added advantage in that it provided the dugout with fresh air. A second shaft was constructed for those dugouts which were twenty feet below ground. They were further reinforced with timber beams and then gas proofed.

With the continual wet weather and intensive German bombardments; general repairs, drainage, reclaiming of trenches and revetting continued unabated. To minimise the impact of enemy artillery, a section of reserve trench was designated as a dummy front line. In this section, fires were occasionally lit and occupation simulated. This attracted enemy bombardments onto these non-vital areas of trench, leaving more strategic sectors undamaged and lessening the burden of repairs.

In addition to the work in the front-line trenches, the Engineers were busy in the billeting areas that were located behind the front line, keeping them sanitary, constructing bath houses with a hot water supply, building drying rooms, repairing burst water pipes, providing stabling for the divisional horses and experimenting with Bangalore torpedoes. These explosive devices were used to blow gaps in wire obstacles.

When there was free time, the Engineers could take a hot bath, get a clean uniform, play sport and visit the towns and local estaminets. The various YMCA buildings usually provided nightly entertainment and concerts. With the high incidence of venereal disease, the men were warned against over fraternisation with the local women.

During the wet and stormy night of the 8th - 9th of November, the 3rd Field Company supervised some three hundred men in making twelve dams constructed from sand bags and timbers. The natural geometry meant that several creeks in no man's land drained their water into the Lys. The intention of the raid was to stop this natural drainage, allowing the water to back-up sufficiently so as to eventually flood the German trenches. One man was wounded during the operation, but all dams were successfully completed.

After several days of heavy rainfall the Lys rose, restricting the drainage and eventually causing the German trenches to flood, as intended. With the nuisance now apparent, a German raiding party attempted to destroy one of the dams, but were detected, fired upon and forced to withdraw. With the continual heavy rain, a lake had formed; so on the night of the 17th of November the Field Engineers heightened two of the dams. This caused further flooding amongst the German trenches. Eventually the sandbags rotted and the structures weakened, losing their effectiveness.

The Engineers continued to accompany raids and participated in major daylight raids in early 1917. The first of these occurred on the 7th of January when eighty men from the 2nd N.Z. Rifles Brigade, with four Field Engineers, attacked a German strong point destroying the machine gun emplacements there.

Later on the 21st of February, five hundred men from the 2nd Auckland Battalion, with sixteen Engineers attached, undertook an early morning raid on the German front and support trenches. A heavy mist quickly turned the raid into a shambles, with assaulting parties failing to locate their targets. Heavy fighting ensued and although several dugouts were destroyed, the Engineers destroyed little else. Of the sixteen Engineers involved in the raid three were killed and seven were wounded.

The Division eventually left the Lys area in mid March 1917 and moved north towards the Ypres sector, near to the town of Messines.

Back in Christchurch, the Bournemouth Natural Science Society held a series of New Year lectures, in early January entitled "New Zealand and the War" which were delivered by the Right Honourable Sir Joseph George Ward, the late Prime Minister of New Zealand.

The Chairman, Sir Daniel Morris, opened by remarking on how magnificently the overseas Dominions had come to the help of the Mother Country in the war to oppose the bogus "kultur" of the Prussian enemies.

Sir Joseph Ward, in his lecture stressed that the overseas Dominions were in the war to support the British Empire for the general benefit of their descendants and to make the Empire even more successful than it had been so far. Sir Joseph emphasised the unity of the New Zealand people in this crisis, and their desire to see that there was a change in British policy after the war to ensure that the Dominions had a proper voice in matters of vital interest to the British Empire, not merely a constitutional duty. He described the scenic beauty of New Zealand, its equable climate and prolific rich soil that had allowed record quantities of food to be exported to Britain during 1916, and which would be repeated in 1917. He spoke of New Zealand's commitment of men and finance to ensure that the war was won. His address was appreciated by his audience and it ended with a picture show of New Zealand scenery, buildings, and various industries.

For many people, everyday life improved slightly when at the end of February 1917, a new Order was issued; permitting the ringing of Church bells across England between sunrise and 9pm. This presumably reflected the lessening of the risk of invasion, and to provide a degree of cheer and pre-war normality for the public.

Chapter Twenty-Nine: The New Zealand Engineers Reserve Depot, Boscombe

After their short spell at Brightlingsea, the battlefield experienced New Zealand Depot staff decided upon their training priorities. They knew which parts of the War Office Training Syllabus should be taught and which aspects were obsolete; they were well aware of the reality of a Field Company operating on the modern battlefield. They knew that some of these hardships could be minimised if certain skills, short-cuts and tricks were passed on, so know-how become a key component in the training syllabus.

The Allies were adapting their frontline trench design and tactics in response to the German methods of trench raids, gas attacks, concentrated artillery bombardments and aircraft observation. The training had to reflect these changes and soon construction methods for gas shelters, trench design and deep dugouts became a vital part of the syllabus along with bridging, pontoon building and infantry skills.

On their return to Christchurch the New Zealanders wasted no time in establishing their own N.Z. Engineers Reserve Depot, which officially came into being on the 31st of January 1917. It was designated as part of the Christchurch Station, Southern Command and under the command of Major P. Keenan. It had an original authorised establishment of two Officers and seven Other Ranks being:

> Officer in Command Major P. Keenan
> Adjutant 2nd Lieutenant C.W. Chilcott MC
> 4/58b RSM A.A. McMasters
> 4/391 RQM Sergeant H. Dyson
> Orderly Room 23653 Sergeant H. Christmas
> Sergeant Bootmaker 23676 Sergeant H. Curran
> Sergeant Tailor 23688 Sergeant C.R. Farrant
> Sergeant Cook 4/1783 Sergeant P.E. Geary
> Provost Sergeant 9/1838 Temporary Sergeant Albert Franz[243].

Keenan was a hands-on leader and many of his instructors were New Zealand officers and NCOs who had seen service on Gallipoli, at Armentières and most recently at Flers-Courcelette on the Somme.

His adjutant was 2nd Lieutenant Chilcott MC originally from Auckland. Chilcott had served with the Mounted Troop on Gallipoli and had been commissioned in the field in February 1916 when the N.Z. Division was formed in Egypt. He received his Military Cross for exemplary leadership during the early days at Flers-Courcelette when the Engineers were under constant heavy German artillery bombardment. He was posted to Boscombe in March 1917 from France to take up the post of Adjutant.

At the outset, the Depot had 473 NCOs and men undergoing training – 100 at the SCSIE[244] and 373 NCOs and men at the NZE Depot. The instruction and lectures at the NZE Depot were conducted by Major P. Keenan, assisted by Lieutenants Lush and Collier.

The weather for the first three months was almost spring-like with only one day's training a month being lost in January and February. Despite the snow storms, no training days were lost in March and April. This was impressive and certainly justified the N.Z. Engineers decision to return to the Christchurch area.

When they first arrived at the Depot, every man underwent a medical and dental examination. Then battle fitness and general PT standard was assessed, followed by instruction in infantry training and musketry. Personal training cards were created for each man, disclosing their administrative matters and training standard achieved.

The NZE Depot would parade twice a day. The first parade was at 8am at which the band played under the conductorship of Corporal Amos. The second parade, depending upon their training schedule, was usually at 1.30pm. After each parade they were detailed to their various jobs or training centres, depending on which of the three categories applied to them: "Under Training", "Fully Trained" or "Deploying".

Those classed as "Under Training" would proceed either to: "the School" being the SCSIE in Christchurch, Littledown Common, the Bridging Ground, or "the Hill". All were reachable within thirty-five minutes from the parade ground. Each party would take lunch with them and remain on their jobs until 3.45pm when they marched back to Camp.

New Zealand Engineers entrenching on St Catherine's Hill as part of their three month course at the Southern Command School of Instruction in Engineering at Christchurch. The trench in front has reed rivets put in place; these were used to stop the soil collapsing into the trench.

Photo courtesy of Alexander Turnbull Library, Wellington, New Zealand and Royal NZ RSA Collection.   Reference number: 1/2-013870-G.

When the training day had ended, the men would be assigned camp duties such as guard duty or fatigues. The drivers had their horses to feed and groom; their harnesses to clean and repair, as well as keep the stable area clean.

During the summer months at Christchurch, dinner was served at 5pm. This messing routine had been instigated after the return from Brightlingsea while the men were in their winter billets. Then, the men's daily rations were issued to the householder, who would prepare the meals for the soldiers. With food being scarce this soon proved to be a flawed approach. A number of men complained of not receiving their full ration. To remedy the situation, a formal Soldier's Mess was established in a large converted garage in Boscombe and a cookhouse building was attached to it. Table and chairs were obtained from the Ordnance Stores; a sergeant was placed in charge of cooking, while a corporal distributed the meals. This was found to be a more suitable arrangement.

The schedule devoted four days of the week to engineering training and this was conducted in two phases.

The first phase comprised a full nine week course for thirty hours of actual engineering training each week, at the Southern Command School of Instruction in Engineering (SCSIE) at Christchurch Camp, as had been conducted the previous year. The content of this course often varied depending upon the current battlefield emphasis which needed to be included into the syllabus. Such a change occurred in 1917 when the infantry training was reduced to a confirmation shoot on the range, in favour of river pontooning.

Pontooning had become an important skill after the Somme battle and one which the Field Engineers in France had lacked time and opportunity to train in. Extra instruction was provided at any available moment throughout the SCSIE course.[245] After the German Spring Offensive in 1918, another change occurred when infantry training was reintroduced as an essential skill. In September 1918, in response to the more prevalent open warfare strategy, an extra week was added to

Earthworks training to allow further instruction on deep dugout construction.

This more flexible approach in altering the training programme given the changing battlefield conditions was an improvement from the rigid attitude that had been encountered in June 1916.

The Earthworks phase of their training taught field geometry and field levels, how to construct overhead cover, camouflage, building shelters and gun emplacements; as well as siting and then constructing a trench. In the demolition exercises they made up the charges, fixed them and then fired them, with and without electricity.

Bridging instruction ranged from using boats for improvised bridges to the more substantial spar, suspension, frame, tension or railway bridges. After this, they still had to learn about: obstacles, the defence of localities, use of flares and alarms, map reading and the use of various engineering instruments. They completed musketry and bombing courses and learnt how to work with the infantry at outposts and as guards.

Instruction was also given in constructing wells and testing water to ensure that it was drinkable. With the death and destruction strewn across the battlefield, there was a high risk of contamination entering the wells and waterways. Testing these was essential in ensuring that clean or treated water was provided to the soldiers. In this way the spread of disease and sickness caused by drinking foul water was reduced.

The second phase of the course was held at the NZE Depot. The New Zealanders had obtained a portion of waste ground at Queen's Park which was part of the Littledown Common. In 1917 this area was less populated than it is now, so was ideal for the type of training intended. It was here that they established their Advanced Training School.

The ground was similar to that fought over during the Somme. It was not overly hilly; there were slopes, dips and some areas of flat ground. It provided two essential elements: variety and space. The training conducted was confined to the latest designs in fire, communication and support trenches used on the Western Front, together with demolitions, bombing and revetting.

A one hundred yard rifle range was also set out on this site. A number of small scale tactical exercises around infantry skills were held, including trench raid routines. Night work occurred every Thursday for 2½ hours. The night exercises were an important aspect to allow the men to practice their skills of wiring, repairing damaged trenches and construction tasks while in darkness.

All men at the NZE Reserve Depot, including those returning from hospital and the "tour of duty men" were required to complete the Advanced Training School training. Battle experienced Field Engineers, often recently arrived from France, assisted in providing instruction and realistic situations for these training exercises.

Draughtsman and surveyors were occasionally excused this training when they arrived at the Depot, usually because they joined the next draft for France.

This regime ensured that veterans worked alongside men who had recently finished their SCSIE course, as they all completing a common task. In this way battlefield knowledge was passed on, new techniques practised and awareness honed. The Advance Training School also allowed the Pioneers to work with the Field Engineers, thereby making the training exercises battlefield centric.

One day each week was allocated to a route march, where the entire NZE Depot, including the NZ Pioneers, was paraded in full marching order. The route march included packhorses, tool carts, lumber wagons and pontoon wagons. The men carried 20lbs in their packs, usually comprising greatcoat and clothing. The "old hands" started the practice of placing inflated air cushions in their packs instead. This trick was soon adopted by the new lads. The route march proceeded to the north of the camp, through the forest villages and then back to the barracks.

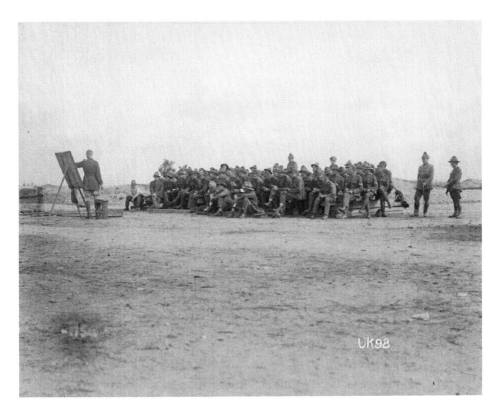

New Zealand Engineers at an open air lecture on St Catherine's Hill. The officer standing and leaning on the walking stick is Colonel Barclay.

Photo courtesy of Alexander Turnbull Library, Wellington, New Zealand and Royal NZ RSA Collection. Reference Number: 1/2-013893-G.

New Zealand Engineers laying a light railway track on St Catherine's Hill as part of their training course. In the distance are the towns of Christchurch and Bournemouth and the Southbourne water tower is visible on the skyline.

Photo courtesy of Alexander Turnbull Library, Wellington, New Zealand and Royal NZ RSA Collection. Reference Number: 1/2- 014029-G.

New Zealand Engineers training on setting up and camouflaging a machine gun post on St Catherine's Hill. Notice the opening at the back of the gun position where another engineer is standing. This was probably a tunnel opening connected to a communication sap, which would allow the gunners to move back and forwards between shifts and be re-supplied as needed.

Photo courtesy of Alexander Turnbull Library, Wellington, New Zealand and Royal NZ RSA Collection. Reference Number: 1/2- 013872-G

There was also general fitness training which included a battle efficiency test called the Engineer's Run, which would have been based upon the infantry equivalent. It entailed each man running a course of one mile carrying specific equipment along with his field pack. This event was included in the public sport events as a race against other Engineering Companies, with Sergeant Body of the N.Z. Engineers often winning this particular event.

Saturdays were devoted to pay parade, CO's inspection, infantry drill and then sports in the afternoon. The remainder of Saturday was employed in camp tasks and duties. Church parades were held each Sunday, after which local leave was normally granted.

At the completion of each training phase there were exams in: earthworks, demolitions, bridging and pontooning to ensure that the designated standard was met. Their training card was signed and dated by a Training Officer and finally authorised by the NZE Reserve Depot Adjutant. Only then would the soldiers be classified as "Fully Trained" and the completed card pasted inside the man's pay book, giving a certified record of the training levels achieved by the Engineer.

For the Officers and NCOs classed "Fully Trained", they could apply to attended Royal Engineer Instructor courses. There were a fixed number of places allocated to every Reserve Depot.

These specialised courses were held at the Military Engineering School at Esher, Infantry Training at Tidworth, Musketry at Hayling Island and the Area Gas School at Chiseldon. Other courses were held at Gosport, Woolwich, Aldershot and Weybridge. Soldiers not occupied on courses, were assigned "special employment" until classed "Deploying". This usually denoted carpentry, maintenance or building duties at one of the numerous N.Z. camps, such as Hornchurch, Walton-on-Thames, Codford, Sling Camp or Brockenhurst. If they remained at the Depot, then their time was occupied on fatigue parties, more training and helping to clear up on "the Hill".

In this way, around a third of the Depot were "available but not under orders" or "likely to become available within 14 days". Both categories meant that they were available for deployment to France whenever needed.

At any one time there were normally around one hundred and eighty N.Z. Engineers at the SCSIE undergoing training out of a total NZE Depot strength of some 500 officers and men. With reinforcements constantly arriving from New Zealand, several SCSIE courses were run simultaneously often comprising only of New Zealanders in order to clear the backlog.

The N.Z. Tunnellers, under the command of Lieutenant Thorne-George RE were also stationed at Christchurch. All the Tunnellers underwent a four week infantry course at the NZE Depot. From the early days at Falmouth in 1916, the mixture of N.Z. Tunnellers and parade drill did not bode well[246], so it can be assumed that while the Tunnellers were at Christchurch that this tradition continued. The short infantry course ensured that they had sufficient awareness about operating in the front line areas. The remainder of their training was focused on the techniques and materials used in shafts, galleries and deep dugout construction.

They also trained on the laying, charging and tamping of underground mines. Many of the men had worked in coal or gold mines, so were familiar with working underground. The only death recorded during the Tunnelling Company training was that of Sapper C. Febey. He was buried with full military honours in Boscombe Cemetery on the 15th of February 1918.

The Light Railway Operating Company (LROC) was based at the NZE Depot from mid 1917. They would train on St Catherine's Hill and the Stanpit Marsh laying 9lb and 20 lb tramlines as well as Decauville small gauge railway. These were used by the Tunnellers in moving the spoil from the underground works and often in the divisional area to transport supplies to the forward stores dumps around a battlefield. Tractors would assist in towing the small rail wagons and presumably the tunnel spoil was useful to the Engineers for road repairs. Normally around twenty LROC men would be training at the NZE Depot at any one time. In March 1917, the NZE Depot relocated from winter billets in Boscombe and into white bell tents along the banks of the River Stour, this time in the Barrack Road Camp. To make it more comfortable, the Engineers built a makeshift wood and corrugated iron cooking hut next to their tent lines and used large marquees as the mess halls. On their parade ground the flagpole was towards the southern corner, so the men would face towards New Zealand.

The normal routines continued whether they were camped at Christchurch or billeted at Boscombe. The camp at Christchurch did provide the extra space needed to cope with the added requirements surrounding the formation of the 4th Field Company and to accommodate the N.Z. Pioneers' training company.

A camouflaged machine gun post on St Catherine's Hill. Camouflage helped to prevent the position from being spotted from the air or some high point. Machine gun positions were prime targets for enemy artillery. Notice the barbed wire braces and other obstacles placed out in front amidst the pretend "no man land".

Photo courtesy of Alexander Turnbull Library, Wellington, New Zealand and Royal NZ RSA Collection. Reference Number: 1/2- 013871-G

Another style of trench, designed for a medium trench mortar. The walls and part of the roof are reinforced by planks of wood and sandbags. These would be camouflaged over. The trenches were deliberately narrow as trench mortars attached retaliatory artillery barrages. The design was meant to limit the target area and possible damage.

Photo courtesy of Alexander Turnbull Library, Wellington, New Zealand and Royal NZ RSA Collection. Reference Number: 1/2- 013121-G.

Constructing pontoons across the River Avon, near Christchurch in Hampshire. The steel structure in the background is the railway bridge crossing the river; the pontoon is the lower structure supported by boats and with men standing on the decking.

Photo courtesy of Alexander Turnbull Library, Wellington, New Zealand and Royal NZ RSA Collection.   Reference Number: 1/2- 013885-G.

Another advantage of being at the Christchurch Barracks was that there was a small hospital in the camp, containing around thirty beds and was staffed by British nurses and local VADs. It coped with minor injuries and sickness, such as dysentery. The more serious illnesses, such as tuberculosis or training accidents, would be treated in the Christchurch Red Cross Hospital or at the New Zealand Hospital at Brockenhurst.

On the return of the Depot to Christchurch a Regimental Band had been organised, originally under the conductorship of Corporal Amos. It proved to be very popular, despite great difficulty in maintaining its strength owing to the constant departure of men for the Front. With the increased status of the Depot, permission was given to draw permanent bandsmen who had long service overseas from hospitals and other Depots. With the appointment of a Bandmaster, the Regimental Band then became a recognised institution in Bournemouth and the surrounding district. As well as playing on route marches and parades it performed weekly at the New Zealand Hospital at Brockenhurst. Its performances were soon extended to include Crag Head Hospital in Bournemouth, Cornelia Hospital at Poole, as well as the Bournemouth Pier, the Boscombe Pier and at the opening of the NZYMCA Hostel. In July 1918 it played at the Mayor's War Fund Horticultural Show as well as the Baby Week Celebration at Meyrick Park.

Discipline at the New Zealand Engineers Depot

Many of the camp duties and fatigues were assigned to those men on CB or "confined to barracks". The punishment of "confined to barracks" meant initially no leave, and undertaking fatigues once the normal day's work was completed. The punishment would continue well into the night and involved any task, including cleaning the coal stores, shifting manure, cleaning the cookhouse or any other tasks that needed to be undertaken.

Their "crimes" ranged from being late for, or absent from a parade, being absent without leave, absent from a billet after hours, being slovenly dressed or slovenly conduct outside of camp. Insolence to a NCO and neglect of duty were severely punished. For not saluting an officer the offender would incur either two to three days CB or forfeiture of pay. One group of Engineers who were all late for a 7.30am mobilisation parade were awarded one day CB – a parting gift from the NZE Depot.

Three days CB was awarded to Driver R. Delaney for being improperly dressed in that he was wearing the wrong puggaree[247] having just that day transferred from the Light Railway Operating Company to the Engineers. Thirteen Engineers were awarded two days CB for being improperly dressed in that they had no belt on parade. On that occasion, the "old hands" like Sapper S. Ross and Sapper C.S. Vial should have known better whereas the new men such as Sapper A.F. Healey had to quickly learn.

Being absent from the CO's Inspection, being absent from a Church Parade, being absent from duty, being inattentive on parade would all warrant seven days CB. Failing to obey a sentry when called upon to halt was an offence which earned Sapper C.G. Gregg and Sapper J.R. Matheson both of the N.Z. Tunnelling Company two days CB each. Although the more interesting charge of "irregular conduct on parade" earned Sapper S. Dickey an admonishment.

Having no means of identification was a fineable offence; as this contravened the camp's Standing Orders. Discipline was constant, and the charges always stated "when on active service" leaving no doubt that while in England the men were serving in an active war zone. Other breaches of discipline could result in detention in a military prison. Disobeying an order was not tolerated and would generally result in 168 hours detention and one Pioneer received twenty-eight days detention for being absent without leave for eight days. When he was eventually apprehended in Boscombe, he had missed his draft for France.

Sapper Jim Williamson volunteered to escort one of the Maori Pioneers who had been awarded fourteen days detention at the military prison on the Isle of Wight. The Pioneer had absented himself from a night exercise on Queen's Park and had instead gone into Boscombe to meet his

English girlfriend. Possibly thinking the punishment a little harsh, the escort and the prisoner stopped off for a few beers while waiting for the boat to the Isle of Wight from Southampton[248].

The local police also had powers of detention over military personal. One morning in June 1917, Constable Gould found three Australian soldiers asleep in the Christchurch Recreation Ground. Privates Arthur Charles Goodwin, Ernest Cunningham and Alfred Donaldson were charged with being absentees from their regiments. The court remanded them to await an escort.

On another occasion, two other Australians, Privates A. Callen and W.G. Brown, were similarly charged with being absentees from their regiment and were remanded to await escort. They confessed that they had been absent for nine days, and were only having a look around the country. They had no intention of deserting.

By early 1917, venereal disease (VD) had become a major social concern and incidences of the disease had increased. Statistics gathered that year amongst the NZEF recorded that in a six month period 1,238 cases occurred, of which 223 came from France, the rest were contracted in England and of those, half were contracted in London[249] while soldiers were on leave there. The NZEF treated the disease seriously and prophylactics were on sale in the New Zealand canteen, lectures were given and men warned of the effects of the disease. Those who did contract VD were sent to isolated hospitals and it was usual for their pay to be stopped until they were cured. Having their pay stopped was a deterrent, as many families back home depended upon monthly allotments from Army pay.

Apart from the social stigma and personal discomfort, it was published that of 1,100 children in the London County Council schools for the blind, 268 children had been blinded from gonorrhoea, and 343 from syphilis.

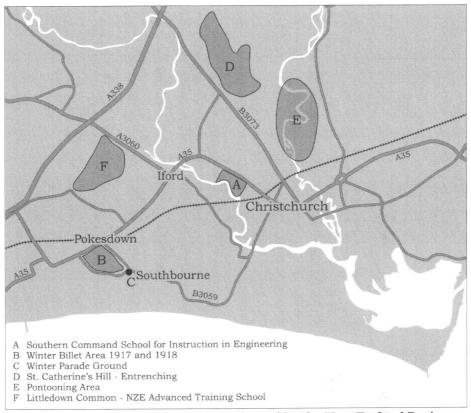

A Southern Command School for Instruction in Engineering
B Winter Billet Area 1917 and 1918
C Winter Parade Ground
D St. Catherine's Hill - Entrenching
E Pontooning Area
F Littledown Common - NZE Advanced Training School

The areas of Boscombe and Christchurch used by the New Zealand Engineers for training and billeting throughout 1917 and 1918.

Drawing by Jenny Kynaston

The English actor, Mr Reid Patterson, during his tour of the Front was asked one evening to visit the wounded at a base hospital. He addressed a group of "Tommies", telling them that it was an inspiring sight for him to see men from every corner of the British Empire doing the same job. This provoked an unexpected roar of laughter which confused him. His biggest laugh came when he told the men that he knew all of them would see the job through. Afterwards he was told that that he had just visited a venereal disease hospital.[250]

One of the main problems in controlling the disease was that those who contracted it often attempted to conceal the condition rather than have it treated. This was addressed in 1917 by medical health officers who were invited to attend local Town Council meetings to brief officials on the recommendations of the Royal Commission looking at the matter. In summary, the remedy lay in: prompt diagnosis, treatment of the early stage of the disease, and education within the community to diminish the spread of the diseases. Venereal Disease clinics were soon established in public hospitals where the necessary treatment was provided.

Prostitution, termed "keeping a disorderly house", existed in Christchurch and was clamped down on by the police. In March 1917 Bessie L. Shearing, of 83b Purewell, Christchurch was charged with allowing a house to be used as a disorderly house. Agnes Crow was also charged with aiding and abetting. They were observed by a police constable stationed four feet from the window, behind a fence, keeping observation.

He observed them bringing soldiers back around 10pm, having supper, singing and dancing. The soldiers eventually left at 4.45am. Shearing, the wife of an Army driver with four children, said that although she had been in the company of soldiers she had never kept a bad house. Mrs Crow said she had nothing to say except that she had never accepted money from any man. Both had been previously cautioned by police. Of Mrs Crow's five children, four were already with guardians, and only one was still in her care. Each woman was sentenced to three months hard labour.

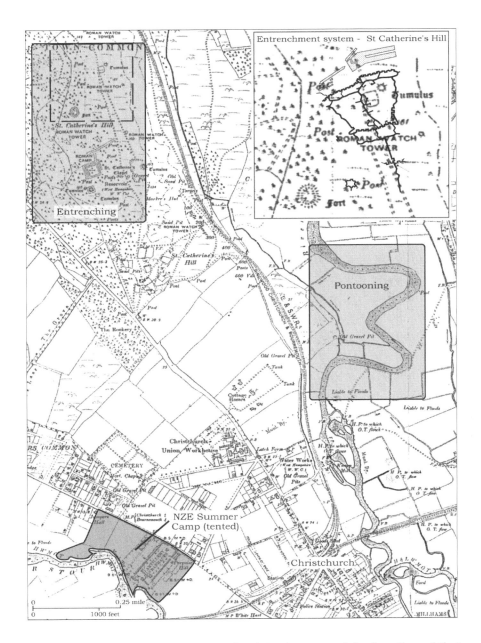

Training areas used by the New Zealand Engineers and the location of their summer tented camp at the back of the Christchurch Barracks near the River Stour. The insert shows the location of the entrenching school on St Catherine's Hill, the trench system used for training with the wiring to the front.

Drawing by Jenny Kynaston

"Tour of Duty" Men

For the British Army fighting on the Western Front, soldiers were entitled to one week's home leave to visit their family after twelve months service in France. Leave for officers was more regular. This was not practical for the Dominion troops, given the distance and logistics involved in getting home, instead they were granted leave in Paris or England. Those men qualifying for leave generally spent it in Paris or else in England; sightseeing or visiting relatives. Ireland was "out of bounds" after the Spring Uprising of the Irish Nationalists in 1916.

In March 1917 it was decided at Divisional level that an exchange of personnel between the Field Companies in France and the Reserve Depot in England should occur. The reason was twofold; it permitted those men who were chosen to have a rest away from the fighting and with their experience they could assist with the training back in England. Trench warfare and battlefield tactics were constantly changing and this had an impact on the demands placed on the Engineers. Replacements were arriving in France with good trade skills, but the outdated training they had received in England on inadequate equipment and with limited stores hindered their effectiveness.

Their field craft often let them down, which meant their casualty rate was too high. It was therefore considered a better approach to leverage the experiences of veterans by placing them for a spell at the Depots. In addition, it allowed them to become familiar with the calibre of replacements and tune essential battlefield skills. There was another advantage, in that these veterans could attend specialised courses thereby raising expertise and qualifying them for further promotion.

The first "swap" involved 2nd Lieutenant G.V. Russell, who would later be awarded an MC for his calm leadership at Passchendaele, and two sergeants who had been continuously with the 1st Field Company since 1914. These were Sergeants William Jones, one of the original British Section, and John McKay, who had joined the Engineers in Egypt in 1915. Both had fought at Gallipoli, Armentières and Flers-Courcelette. All three proceeded to England on the 22nd of March 1917 and 2nd Lieutenant

Lush and two Sergeants from the 12th Reinforcements were posted to France in their stead.

These exchanges were termed "Tour of Duty" and were granted to those soldiers who had served for a long period on active service. Upon arrival, the men were usually given a period of leave and then assigned camp duties, including instructing at the Advanced Training School. There they observed what was being taught then advised and demonstrated techniques and trench routines that the replacements would be expected to know once in France. They also provided whatever extra realism they could to training scenarios.

In December 1917, the newly promoted Lance Corporal Bert Tuck, who had completed three years of war service, and Corporal Albert Brockenshire proceeded to England for a two months exchange. They were tasked with the training of the Maori Pioneers in engineering work that was required in the trenches, but first they were granted fourteen days leave which they spent in Scotland.

The Canadian Engineers also had a similar rotation scheme, whereby every two months they would exchange experienced with inexperienced officers and NCOs. This scheme was suggested to the British and Australian Engineers at the Rouen conference in July 1917.

The scale and frequency of the rotation was enlarged by the CRE N.Z. Division by July 1918 when the Reserve Depot welcomed the first of two exchange drafts of sixty Engineers from France. They were put through a week of infantry training and then attended the Advanced Training School before being granted leave and later assigned jobs at the Depot.

They returned to France in October 1918 and were immediately replaced at the NZE Depot by another exchange, comprising sixty Engineers and ten N.Z. Tunnelling Company other ranks. This was the final exchange of men, as a month later the war ended.

Reinforcement Non-Commissioned Officers (NCOs)

By the middle of 1917, the Depot faced the problem of the regular arrival from New Zealand of NCOs. They were part of the reinforcement drafts and had obtained substantive rank by either attending trade courses or else were instructors, prior to embarkation. The 22nd reinforcement consisted of one Sergeant Major, one Sergeant, one Corporal and one Lance-Corporal and ten other ranks. It was becoming increasing difficult to place these NCOs[251] in Field Companies, given their lack of battlefield experience.

During May and June the NZE Depot sent eight new NCOs to the Field Companies in France, rotating the same number of experienced NCOs back to the Depot as instructors. By July, it was reported by CRE, N.Z. Division that only one of these new NCOs had justified his rank. There were grumblings that such inexperienced senior ranks should not be put in charge of more seasoned NCOs and men. Even the unit commanders did not entrust certain tasks to these men[252]. The NCOs in question were keen and willing, but certain circumstances required experience. It was becoming a major concern.

The Engineers were not unique in this matter, as the N.Z. Field Artillery at Ewshot had exactly the same issue. The view held was that an army of NCOs was being built-up.[253] At Sling Camp, all Infantry NCOs arriving from New Zealand "went down" a rank. This affected their pay scale as well. They were placed in an instructor's class and at the end of the course they had an examination. If they passed they retained their reduced rank, if not then they reverted to the ranks and became privates.

The obvious remedy was for all engineer reinforcements to revert to the ranks prior to joining Field Companies in France. The exceptions being those men returning from hospital or from leave. For temporary rank this was possible, but for substantive rank it was not permissible under NZEF Order No. 299, paragraph 16. To change this would have an impact across the whole N.Z. Division and not solely restricted to the Engineers[254]. Frankly it would have been unfair on the men involved who felt they had earned their rank.

On average, four new NCOs arrived at the Depot from New Zealand a month. Normally, after the situation had been explained; only one on average would revert to the ranks. The remaining three would then have to attend an NCOs course at the School of Military Engineering, Esher before proceeding overseas as NCOs. The NZE Depot was only allocated three places on each six week course.

This created a backlog of NCOs within the Depot with no role to fill. The situation was further exasperated by the Depot's custom of making temporary promotions to men given positions of authority. This happened with the Bandmaster, Instructors sent to Sling Camp, Orderly Room Clerk, Medical Corporal and the Provost Sergeant. By July there were twenty-five NCOs at the Depot that had been awarded substantive rank or were qualified for it. None of them had seen service at the Front[255].

Colonel Keen was approached about this growing number NCOs at the NZE Depot and he offered to organise a six week course to the same standard as that at Esher for these NCOs, thereby allowing them to obtain their certificate and become available for overseas deployment.

One of the "tour of duty" men, Corporal Bert Tuck, disliked many of them during his stay at the NZE Depot. Tuck had only received his Lance Corporal rank on the anniversary of completing three years service in the NZEF, so he was one of the few surviving, long serving Engineers. He viewed the NZE Depot NCOs as child-like; he disliked their attitudes and knew that a "rude awakening" awaited them in France. He kept taunting them by asking when they planned to "join the Allies"[256] and get involved in the fighting in France.

Eventually, on the 17th of July 1917 NZEF Order No 100 was issued which instructed the "Relinquishment of NCOs Temporary Rank". This went part way in solving the problems. Effectively, all NCOs of reinforcement drafts from New Zealand holding temporary rank only would relinquish it on arrival at a Reserve Depot. By October, there were only two temporary NCOs remaining at the Depot: Canteen Sergeant E.H. Jamieson, who was too old for overseas service and Quartermaster

Storeman Corporal H.J. Saxton, another old soldier.

The last act on this matter was played out when Staff Sergeant Major Yarrow who was an Engineer Instructor in New Zealand with no battlefield experience, was sent to France on the 26th of December 1917 with the intention of being either attached to a reinforcement camp or sent to the Front if an opening could be found for him. In this way it was hoped he could gain some experience.

Thereafter, the Depot instigated a policy which required a reinforcement NCO to revert to the ranks prior to proceeding overseas. This practice was immediately observed by Sergeant Ferran, Temporary Sergeant Mackereth and Lance Corporal R. Paoromati when they proceeded to France in March 1918 as part of Lieutenant Hetet's draft, all as either newly made-up privates or sappers.

The Barclay era at the New Zealand Engineers Depot

On the 21st of August 1917 Major G Barclay took over command of the Depot and Major Keenan left for France. Major Barclay, a Boer War veteran, had fought on Gallipoli in command of the 2nd Field Company and was awarded the Montenegrin Order of Danilo, Fourth Class. He had later commanded the 3rd Field Company at Flers-Courcelette. Barclay had a relaxed style of command which was appreciated by the men. In January 1918 he was promoted to Lieutenant Colonel and commanded the NZE Depot for the remainder of the war.

Officers were allowed to have their wives join them in England and Mrs Barclay did so, finding suitable rooms in a private house in Southbourne, near to the town of Christchurch.

Barclay altered some of the camp routines; the first was to instigate the monthly War Diary for the NZE Depot. Administration was tightened. Brigadier General Richardson[257] was invited several times to award gallantry medals. The first being the Medals Parade in April 1917 and then again in November 1917 Richardson returned to inspect the N.Z. Engineers Reserve Depot parade at King's Park, including the N.Z. Maori (Pioneer) Battalion now established there. On this occasion he also presented medals to: Sapper C. Lovell-Smith N.Z. Engineers – Serbian Medal of Merit and Zeal for his work at Salonika and to Sapper J. Williamson N.Z. Tunnelling Company, the Military Medal for his work at Arras.

During this visit, Brigadier General Richardson officially opened the NZYMCA Club at The Grange, in Boscombe. This was a large house next to the Post Office and offered: games, reading room, canteen as well as a small hostel for visiting New Zealanders spending their leave period in Bournemouth. The facility proved very popular. Finally in May 1918 the NZYMCA acquired two houses alongside each other at The Crescent, off Christchurch Road in Boscombe. These became known as 'Khartoum House' and were for recreation and accommodation purposes, catering for New Zealand soldiers in the Bournemouth area or else used as accommodation for visiting sports teams.

In January 1918 Barclay presented Military Medals for bravery in the field to: RSM John Woodhall, Sergeant Nicholas Higginson, Sergeant Harry Fricker and Corporal Roland Knight.

Barclay arranged that all engineer replacement drafts to France would report to the Royal Engineers Depot at Rouen for further training, effectively by-passing the infantry depots at Etaples.

The RE Training School in Rouen was laid out over several acres of ground and catered for all obstacles, both physical and mental, that the Engineers could expect to encounter on the Western Front. There were training areas dedicated to: wiring, entrenching with zig-zag and saw-tooth designs, machine gun posts, heavy and medium trench mortar positions, concrete deep dugouts, normal deep dugouts, sniper posts, and observation posts. There were shelled areas resembling the front line areas where the men were taught how to move with equipment and how to seek cover in such ground – all useful skills that would help keep them alive a little longer; and it ensured that they were versed with the latest battlefield techniques for the conditions expected at the Front. There they trained with the standard equipment and stores that would be available to them in France. The days of using aged, surplus equipment was now left behind at the Christchurch Depot.

During 1918 the NZE Depot had its permanent establishment strength increased by an additional ten personnel with the arrival of a Medical Officer, Dentist, Medical orderlies, Chaplains and Mr A. Lascelles who was the Field Secretary for the NZYMCA.

The Reverends who served at Christchurch were the Reverends L.B. Neale who proceeded to France and was replaced by Mr A. Mitchell and the Reverend P. Hakiwai who was later replaced by the Reverend W. Wainohu of the N.Z. Maori (Pioneer) Battalion.

Besides the drafts arriving from New Zealand, long serving soldiers from other New Zealand battalions were granted transfers to the Engineers, the Pioneers, the Tunnellers or the Light Railway Company. Some such transfers were: Private Bowler who transferred from the Wellington Infantry to the Engineers, while Private R.A. Carruthers of the Otago Infantry, Private Thorpe from the Auckland Infantry and Private A.F. Tepene of the N.Z. Machine Gun Company, all joined the Light Railway Operating Company. There were also transfers out. Several Pioneers transferred to the N.Z. Raratongan Company which was serving in Palestine. Private Heeney transferred from the Pioneers to the N.Z. Field Artillery, while Driver H. Maka transferred from the ASC to the Raratongan Company. As he was still at the NZE Depot in May 1918 he was instead posted to the N.Z. Maori (Pioneer) Battalion.

The busiest that the NZE Depot reached was during July 1918 when 31 officers and 598 other ranks were stationed in Christchurch.

The New Zealand Engineers at the Barrack Road Camp at Christchurch, Hampshire conducting an early morning parade. The band is playing and the officers and men are saluting as the New Zealand flag is raised. Note the tented camp in the background.

Photo courtesy of Alexander Turnbull Library, Wellington, New Zealand and Royal NZ RSA Collection. Reference Number: 1/2- 013867-G

New Zealand Engineers at their camp at Jumpers Common in Christchurch, Hampshire undergoing musketry drills.

Photo courtesy of Alexander Turnbull Library, Wellington, New Zealand and Royal NZ RSA Collection. Reference Number: 1/2- 013875-G

New Zealand Engineers at their camp at Jumpers Common in Christchurch, Hampshire practising sighting drills, under the watchful eye of their instructors. Although proficient when they left New Zealand, this aspect of training was often ignored in favour of other instructions, such as pontooning.

Photo courtesy of Alexander Turnbull Library, Wellington, New Zealand and Royal NZ RSA Collection. Reference Number: 1/2- 013874-G

Drivers of the New Zealand Engineers with their wagon teams on the
Christchurch Barrack fields.

*Photo courtesy of Alexander Turnbull Library, Wellington, New Zealand and
Royal NZ RSA Collection. Reference Number: 1/2- 013887-G.*

Chapter Thirty: The 4th Field Company at Christchurch

On the 25th of March 1917 orders were given by NZEF Headquarters that a 4th Field Company would be raised, along with a 4th Field Ambulance to support the 4th Infantry Brigade that was being formed at Sling Camp for the N.Z. Division. With the large number of New Zealand reinforcements at Sling Camp, the British Army had suggested that a Brigade be formed and attached to a British Division.

This was rejected and a 4th Brigade for the N.Z. Division was agreed upon. Forming a second N.Z. Division was suggested but it was thought that maintaining two Divisions in the field was beyond the resources of New Zealand, especially after its losses at Gallipoli and in France thus far. A heavy Division of four Brigades was considered sustainable.

Captain F. N. Skelsey, of 1st Field Company and Corporal Ernest Smith, both original British Section men, proceeded to England with orders to raise, equip and train the 4th Field Company. This company had to be ready for overseas duty at the same time as the new 4th Infantry Brigade. The N.Z. Engineers Depot contained a large number of men who had already completed the engineering course at the SCSIE at Christchurch Barracks.

Many had first arrived at the NZE Depot in June 1916 and despite completing their training, had still not been selected for a reinforcement draft to France. It was these men that the newly promoted Major Skelsey had assigned to his new command and by the 2nd of April 1917 the 4th Field Company began its full field training. Captain H. H. Fischer was appointed as Skelsey's second in command.

The training schedule was prepared by the newly promoted Major P. Keenan. It included exercises and topics outside of the normal Depot syllabus, such as night bridging, laying out of works, constructing strong points and controlling working parties by night. The intensive training continued throughout April and May, gradually moulding the men into an efficient Field Company. During this period the 1st Field Company were complaining that they had no carpenters amongst the latest batch of replacements from the NZE Depot – presumably Skelsey had already claimed all of them for his 4th Field Company.

On Anzac Day, 1917 Brigadier General G.S. Richardson visited the Depot where he inspected the 4th Field Company and presented gallantry medals for Flers-Courcelette, including the MC to Captain Chilcott. Later that evening, an Anzac Day social dance was held for the men and their partners at the Boscombe Assembly Rooms and around two hundred people attended the function. Major Mitchell, the Chaplain of the N.Z. Forces, organised the entertainment and presided over the evening.

Being a Social Dance, the evening was in two parts. The first part of the evening was the "social" element consisting of vocal, instrumental and elocutionary entertainment. Major Keenan read a cablegram from the recently formed N.Z. Returned Mens' Association and also a telegram from the High Commissioner in London, offering his best wishes to the men. Afterwards there was a twelve dance programme until midnight, and a supper served. The dances were: Waltz, Lancers, Valetta, Waltz (Franchise), Two-Step, Waltz, Lancers, La Rinka, Waltz, Schottische, Chain Medley and the evening ended with a last Waltz.

The 4th Field Company completed its final preparations and departed for France on the 29th of May 1917. Upon its arrival in France, it was immediately deployed into the Messines area as the N.Z. Division made preparations for the forthcoming battle. It undertook essential road mending to keep the lines of communication open for artillery, troops, and supplies being brought forward by wagons and mule trains. During the battle for Messines it supported the other field companies in consolidating the captured ground, which entailed trench reconstructions, drainage, preparing machine gun and trench mortar positions, wiring and building deep dugouts.

After Messines, the 4th Field Company was deployed in mid September to assist with the preparations for the Battle of Passchendaele. The Field Company was tasked with repairing roads, creating supply dumps, painting the signs to help troops identify key locations, such as aid stations, YMCA area, and stores dumps. More critically, it constructed deep dugouts for field hospitals, casualty clearing stations and for infantry brigade and battalion headquarters. They undertook water pumping operations to keep these dugouts serviceable and as the weather worsening during the battle, this became a constant struggle. After the Battle of Passchendaele, the 4th Field Company entrained for Ypres with the 1st and 3rd Field Companies. At that time, Major Skelsey was not aware that it was his Field Company's last action.

A makeshift cookhouse designed and built from corrugated iron, by the New Zealand Engineers & Pioneers during their summer stay under tents at Jumpers Common camp.

Photo courtesy of Alexander Turnbull Library, Wellington, New Zealand and Royal NZ RSA Collection. Reference Number: 1/2- 013879-G.

Chapter Thirty-One: The Battle of Messines, June 1917

Since February, preparation for the attack at Messines had been underway and the Field Engineers were busy as they had been at the Somme in preparing the area for the arrival of the N.Z. Division. Stores dumps were set up and camouflaged from German aircraft flying overhead, roads repaired, tramways to move supplies were laid, trenches dug, water supplies established, deep dugouts constructed and bridges repaired. As the German artillery and machine gunners knew the ranges for static features, such as bridges and road junctions already, much of this work was subjected to accurate enemy fire. Night work was especially dangerous.

Lessons from the fighting at Flers-Courcelette were observed and extra attention was given to removing and rounding off the corners of certain communication saps, termed OUT saps, so that stretcher bearers could move freely along them while carrying the wounded back from the fighting. Iron shelters, topped with earth and gas-proofed were constructed as Aid Posts[258]. "Burster" layers were completed above the supported roof and the structure finished off with sandbags full of broken bricks. This layer of loose fill around air was found to prevent the risk of the roofs collapsing under the weight of an explosion. During this period, aware of the Allied build-up and the inevitability of a major offensive happening soon, the Germans continued to bombard the area with high explosives and gas. In addition to the inevitable disruption and damage caused, the constant enemy activity, made sleep difficult for the Engineers during the day and the night and added to their fatigue.

A daylight raid was undertaken by the 1st Otago Battalion on the 5th of June 1917, under the command of Captain J.W. Bevis against La Plus Dovre Farm, to the south of Messines and on the right flank of the intended advance. The raiding party of one hundred and fourteen men attempted to destroy three heavy concrete dugouts occupied by the Germans in their forward trenches. Eight sappers, working in four pairs and armed with three charges of 20lb guncotton and two charges of 10lb guncotton[259], accompanied the raiding party. It was a dicey affair. Sapper

John Drysdale was wounded during the raid and later died.

Captain Bevis was also wounded during the raid and Sapper Bert Tuck had to nervously wait until the raiding party had retired from the trenches before firing his charge. One charge demolished one dugout; another dugout was severely damaged, while the third was rendered uninhabitable. One charge did not explode due to faulty fuse and this was recovered on the 8th of June after Messines had been captured.

The attack on Messines began on the 7th of June 1917 with the usual preliminary heavy artillery bombardments and then nothing happened. This gave the Germans time to occupy their trenches. An hour later when the relieving German troops began filtering into the German defensive positions, twenty-one British laid mines exploded killing large numbers of the defenders and destroying many of their fortifications. A second British artillery bombardment commenced and the Anzac and British troops advanced, easily overrunning the stunned German opposition and capturing the vital road network around the village of Messines.

The Field Engineers followed up the infantry assault and constructed strong points in the devastated ground. Then they located wells, built new roads forward for mule traffic and bridged the Steenebeck canal. The N.Z. Pioneers were tasked with digging new communications trenches from the strong points. Tramlines were laid to the new artillery battery positions, allowing supplies and munitions to be brought up across the artillery ravaged ground.

Over the next few weeks, despite German counterattacks, the area was consolidated. Tracks, light railway tramlines, water supplies, supply dumps and even electric lighting systems were installed.

The strain of the fighting and the exhaustion of the Anzac troops at Messines were described by Mr Reid Patterson, an actor touring the area entertaining the troops. Patterson passed a big detachment of Australians just out of the trenches marching to their billets. He described how they all had that half bewildered desperate look of those who have come through a grip with death. One Australian wandered uncaringly in the direct line of Patterson's motor vehicle. The mounted Australians, he thought looked extra-ordinarily picturesque, with their rifles slung across their shoulders, over the long cloaks with either their slouch hats or steel caps worn generally very one-sidedly. Captain Eustace Smith his military escort, told Patterson that the New Zealanders "are simply magnificent fellows – many over six feet tall with fine features, especially the Maoris".[260]

The N.Z. Division was relieved on the 10th of June by the 4th Australian Division and it proceeded to the Le Touquet sector near Armentières. The 4th Field Company remained behind in the Messines area to assist with road mending and rejoined the NZ Division several days later.

Once out of the line, 2nd Field Company, along with the N.Z. Rifle Brigade and the N.Z. Pioneer Battalion, were detached to the 1st French Army in the Woesten area in Belgium. There they helped to construct gun pits and roads[261] while the 1st, 3rd and 4th Field Companies enjoyed a period of rest, sport and training before returning to Divisional duties.

The Engineers' training agenda began with physical drill at 6.30am, followed by: musketry, infantry drills, semaphore signalling, bridging, demolitions, laying out work, gas drills, draining and ending each day with a nine mile route march and swimming in the cold waters of the nearby canal. Extra instruction was provided to NCOs and section officers on demolitions, bridge and road construction. Additional practice at bridge building and pontoon work was also provided on the River Lys, resulting in an impromptu pontoon race one evening.

The 1st Field Company organised three instructional courses for its NCOs with special attention to reconnaissance, reporting, map reading and the use of a compass. The replacements were given special instruction in laying out and the siting of strong points and trenches[262]. They were also given instruction on the use of screw pickets and what was described as antagonistic barbed wire[263]. They had not been trained on this wiring at Christchurch Depot due to the lack of war materials.

Discipline was strict and defaulters were dealt with by having to run around a field at night with their gas masks on. It was not a pointless punishment as gas shells were a feature of the forward areas and the Engineers often worked at night wearing their respirators, so it was practical discipline.

As well as the additional training, the 3rd Field also provided four NCOs for a raiding party on a German trench.

On the 15th of June the N.Z. Division was back in action as it began to push patrols forward across the Lys to determine the Germans' intentions.

That sector was not liked by any of the N.Z. Field Companies. They took over all engineering tasks from 3rd Australian Division and commenced road mending, trench and wire repairs, burying the dead that they came across, building supply dumps, supervising working parties, finding water and generally keeping the line of communication open amidst the constant shelling.

On the 18th of June, Sapper Thomas Tester, the Gallipoli and Flers-Courcelette veteran who had been married in England the year before was caught in the open by a machine gun. He was severely wounded in the leg, chest and shoulder. He later died of his wounds.

Chapter Thirty-Two: The Royal Engineers Rouen Conference July 1917

In late July 1917, a Royal Engineers' conference was held at the RE Training Depot at Rouen, France and representatives for all the Reserve Field Companies, Training Centres and Schools of Military Engineering gathered, for the main purpose of inspecting the Royal Engineers' training school there. Attending were: Colonel H.F. Chesney RE Commanding Reserve Groups and School of Instruction at Esher; Major P. Keenan Commanding NZE Reserve Group in Christchurch; Major H. Agar Engineer Training Centre at Deganwy; Major C.J. Stewart School of Military Engineering at Brightlingsea; Lieutenant D.H. Holly School of Military Engineering at Chatham; Captain K.I. Gourlay Engineer Training Centre at Newark; Captain C.E.W. Turner Canadian Engineers at Shoreham and Lieutenant E.H. Fraser Australian Engineers at Brightlingsea.

The Commandant at RE Rouen let it be known that the training standard of Engineer replacements arriving in France were below his expectations. Training standards had to improve and quickly. The Canadians, Australians and New Zealanders did not send their replacement drafts to Rouen at that time. Their men went to the holding area around Etaples before they were sent forward to join the various field companies. Regardless, they still felt some of the comments were pertinent to them.

The main deficiencies highlighted were that the men were not sufficiently conversant with the materials used at the Front. In England they trained on what was made available, which was normally old, worn and of insufficient quantity. This greatly reduced the effectiveness of training that could be given. The other issue raised was that both the officers and men needed to have more practise in working with the tools and vehicles used by a full Field Company.

At no stage in the training syllabus did the mounted and the dismounted men work together. The other main criticism tended to apply to the British Training establishments. There the demand for replacements meant drafts were hastily organised and sent at short notice to France. This resulted in the men who were sent across being untrained or only partially trained. A card system to record training of each man was recommended and given the type of conscripts the British Army was receiving; they felt that this would prevent men from pleading ignorance or insufficient training to evade active service.[264]

Upon his return to England, Keenan requested from NZEF Headquarters at Southampton Row in London, modern trench stores: including screw pickets for the wire, French wire, galvanised iron pipe for making Bangalore torpedoes, trench "A" frame supports and an ample supply of sandbags, which was possibly the one item always in short supply throughout the war; as well as full equipment and horses for a Field Company.

Responding to this request given the restrictions of the war economy, Brigadier General Richardson suggested it inadvisable to incur the expenditure for the full equipment and horses needed for a full Field Company, solely for the NZE Depot's use[265].

Despite these wartime restrictions, new supplies were made available to Keenan, which included: French wire, Calais pattern shelters, Bangalore torpedo tubes, machine gun loopholes and mounting pivots, screw post for wire, steel gabion hurdles, camouflage rolls, and various building materials were procured for the NZE Depot. The availability and use of these new training materials soon produced a marked improvement in the standard of training.

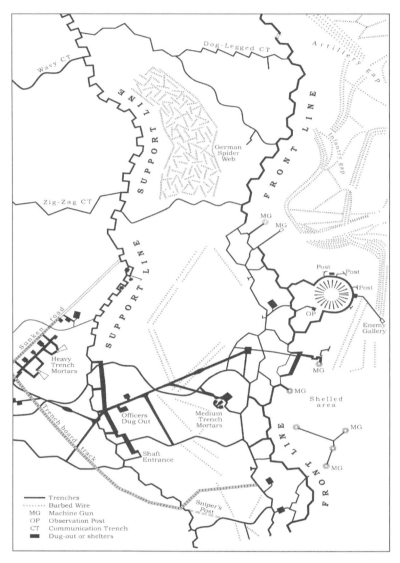

Map modified from the original "Plan of RE Training School (Rouen)". Rouen was a more extensive training area than St Catherine's Hill in Christchurch. The New Zealand Engineers would spend several weeks at Rouen becoming familiar with the conditions they would work under in the front line. This was believed to be more beneficial than the infantry styled, "hardening-up" training conducted by the British Army at Etaples.

Drawing by Jenny Kynaston.

Chapter Thirty-Three: The N.Z. Pioneer Battalion, later N.Z. Maori (Pioneer) Battalion

On the 9th of May 1917 Major Keenan arranged for one hundred and forty-two pioneers from the N.Z. Pioneer Battalion, whose depot was at Sling Camp, to undergo four weeks of training in military engineering at the Advanced Training School on Littledown Common.

This proved successful and after their return to Sling Camp another detachment was sent to Christchurch. With better weather on the coast there was less sickness and fewer training days disturbed by the weather. This soon became a regular training event for the N.Z. Pioneers and eventually the N.Z. Pioneers Depot moved from Sling Camp and became permanently established at the NZE Depot. The largest draft of N.Z. Pioneers to leave from the NZE Depot consisted of sixty pioneers and was under the command of Lieutenant Hetet. They left for France on the 27th of March 1918 – during the German Spring Offensive.

A typical weekly training schedule in July, 1917 for the N.Z. Pioneers arriving at the Advanced Training School would have been:

Monday	6:45 to 7:15	Physical Drills	Camp
	8:15 to 9:30	Lecture	Camp
	9:30 to 3:45	Field Works (lunch to be taken)	Queen's Park
Tuesday	6:45 to 7:15	Physical Drills	Camp
	8:15 to 9:30	Lecture: Materials and Sources of Supply	Camp
	9:30 to 3:45	Procuring Materials for Field Works (lunch to be taken)	Queen's Park

Wednesday	6:45 to 7:15	Physical Drills	Camp
	8:15 to 4:45	Route March, Swimming and Parade for Foot Inspection. (lunch will be taken)	Band will parade
	1:00 to 2:15	During Route March a Lecture on the Organisation for the Attack.	
Thursday	6:45 to 7:15	Physical Drills	Camp
	8:15 to 10.00	Lecture: Revetments & Fascines[266]	Camp
	10.00 to 3:45	Field Work: Revetments – Brushwood, Trench elements, Sand bagging (lunch will be taken)	Queen's Park
Friday	6:45 to 7:15	Physical Drill	Camp
	8:15 to 10.00	Lecture: Obstacles a) Light: Chevaux de Frise, Gooseberries, Light wiring, Row wiring, Blocks – earth and wire. b) Heavy: heavy wiring, strategic wiring, land mines	Camp
	11.00 to 3:45	Rapid Wiring Drills (lunch to be taken)	Queen's Park
Saturday	6:45 to 7:15	Physical Drills	Camp
	8:15 to 9:30	Squad drills, Rifle Exercises and Rifle Inspection	Camp
	10.00	CO's Inspection	Camp
	10.30 to 12.00	Knotting & Lashing	Camp
	12:30	Half day Holiday	

An Orderly Lance-Corporal of the NZ Maori (Pioneer) Battalion
at the NZE Reserve Depot in Christchurch, Hampshire, with the tea.
He is wearing the original Native Contingent collar badges and has four
service reverse chevrons on his right sleeve, indicating four years of service,
so he would have served on Gallipoli as well as in France. This photograph
would have been taken in late 1918.

Photograph courtesy of the Auckland War Memorial Museum.
Reference Album 413 p.23

The Maori soldier was a novelty in the area. They were well known for their ability at military drill and they were often invited to give drill displays at public gatherings in the Bournemouth area. They also provided concerts where they entertained the audiences with Maori dances and songs.

At the request of the Countess of Malmesbury a concert was given by the Maoris in September 1917 as part of the British Red Cross fund raising drive. They received such a hearty reception at their first performance that it was requested that another be arranged soon. Tickets quickly sold out in the small YMCA Hall at Barrack Road and the concert raised £15. In the Haka Party were Privates Hodge, Amohu, Hingston and Wehekore, who also performed a Poi dance.

Soon Maori concerts were in demand. That November one was arranged at the Boscombe Assembly Rooms. This time it was advertised as a "War party in native dress". The evening's entertainment was of exceptional interest to the local inhabitants. The hall soon proved insufficient to satisfy the demand for seats and by seven o'clock it was packed. The programme had been arranged by Lieutenant Woodward, the officer in charge of the Maori Contingent, and all proceeds were given in aid of the Southbourne War Hospital Supply Depot.

Woodward began by mentioning that the men had made the costumes themselves, using maize that they had found near Tuckton, as opposed to flax and toi-toi grass. The weapon it was explained was the mere and was made of whalebone or greenstone. Their head-dress was made from the feathers of Huia which is a bird like an English crow, with white tipped tail feathers. Woodward went on to mention that of the one hundred and fifty Maoris who had enlisted first in 1914, there were unfortunately very few left, but they made up part of a battalion in France doing important work as pioneers.

The original N.Z. Native Contingent motto, *Te Hoko Whitu A Tu Mata Uenga* was printed in the programme. Woodward explained how this was taken from a Maori legend which dated back to the days before the European discovered New Zealand. He then recounted the legend:

Some of the Maori tribes were continually at war with each other. They had Gods whom they used to pray to for good crops and anything they needed. *Tu Mata Uenga* was the God of War of this particular tribe which had been reduced to one hundred and forty or "twice seventy" as they would express it, of the old original fighting braves. In their desperate straits they turned to their God, and he smiled on them. With his aid they were able to drive the other tribes over the cliffs into the sea. This motto was used on the original black badges of the Maori soldiers, who were the direct descendants of the "Twice Seventy". Translated it reads "The twice seventy fighting braves of the invincible War God Tu Mata Uenga".

The programme opened with a performance of the Haka – the Maori War Cry, by the Haka Party whose appearance upon stage was greeted with prolonged applause. The effect must have been inspiring, as the reporter attending the event described:

"With their "kilts" of rustling grass, their gleaming and splendidly developed bodies, brilliantly coloured sashes, and quaint headdresses and their meres in their hands, they looked formidable enough as they filed on to the stage; but when they had got worked up in the excitement of the dance, one was quite glad that such a fierce-looking party was only "play-acting". The rhythmic beat of the right foot, the weird cries and violent gesticulations produced a thrilling effect, and little imagination was needed to realise the sensations of an enemy when a thousand braves of this description were charging recklessly to the fray."[267]

Private Hodge sang "Somewhere a Voice is calling". A Poi dance by the Haka Party followed, the peculiarity of this dance, it was explained, was that the movement is practically confined to the arms and the body with no leg action at all. The music for this dance was provided by Private Rihia on a mouth organ. Private Amohau followed with a song "And a little Child shall lead them", Private Wehekore gave a solo Poi Dance. A Maori love ditty "Hoke Hoke" was sung by the party. It was considered effective as music, but from an English point of view it was considered slightly mournful as an expression of love. Corporal Hingston scored a great success with his rendering of "My Soldier Boy". There were musical contributions from Privates Hodge and Lawson. The Haka Party performed the action song, "Hoe te Waka" (canoe song).

After the interval the Maori Love song "E Kore E Mutu" was sung by the entire party without accompaniment. Then there was another action song, "Ope Tuatahi". Corporal Hingston sang "Little Sam", and in response to a vigorous encore, gave a patriotic song, "We shall get there in time". "Gallipoli" was performed and Private Lawson sang "All Territorial Soldiers," and "Sands of the Desert", while Private Hodge scored conspicuously with "God send you back to me", and as an encore gave a parody on "The Long, Long Trial." The hymn, "Lead Kindly Light" was sung, and a final Haka gave a thrilling and appropriate finish to the programme. At the end of the performance, Mrs Backhouse the President of the Southbourne War Hospital Supplies Depot thanked everyone. It had been a great success.

The attraction for these performances by the Maori Haka party was in part due to their contribution of men to the war effort, considering that their population was estimated at 49,796[268] at the time. So it was recognised and greatly appreciated by the people of Christchurch. There was also a belief that this was a dying culture, so such public displays became "must see" events. The allure of the Maori having been fierce cannibals was intriguing to imagine for post Victorian society at that time.

The Maori soldiers were also remembered for their humorous oratory. One memorable moment was when the Maori soldiers helped with the "Flag Day" in Christchurch. A "Flag Day" was a fund raising event.

Although there were the traditional stalls, most monies were habitually raised through the energy and persuasiveness of young ladies with coin boxes. On this occasion, the New Zealanders manned the various stalls and one cheerful Maori installed himself at the tram terminals. Soon a large crowd of amused onlookers had gathered as he appealed to passengers on each arriving or departing tram for donations. His persuasive banter and beaming smile had the desired effect and soon the coins poured in.

One tragedy befell the Maori, when on the 14th of May 1918 the body of Private Tuheke Matenga was found floating in the River Stour, at the back of the summer camp area. The verdict recorded was: "found drowned". It appeared that he had attempted a "short cut" to camp at night, possibly after curfew. He had tried to swim across the river to the camp on the other bank but had got into difficulties. He was buried with full military honours at Brockenhurst Cemetery on the 16th of May 1918.

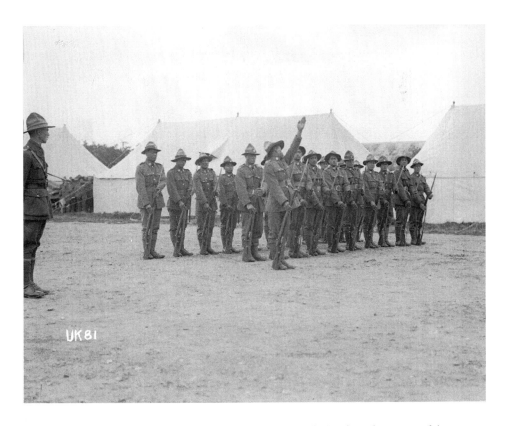

Maori Pioneers at Barrack Road Camp in Christchurch, Hampshire undergoing rifle drill having just fixed bayonets. They became very proficient at rifle drill and were often invited to local fetes and fairs to provide demonstrations.

Photo courtesy of Alexander Turnbull Library, Wellington, New Zealand and Royal NZ RSA Collection. Reference Number: 1/2- 013876-G

Maori Pioneers practising their wiring skills. Along with entrenching, road and bridge repair this became a major skill, especially during the 1918 Spring Offensive when they erected up to 6,000 yards of defensive wiring each day.

Photo courtesy of Alexander Turnbull Library, Wellington, New Zealand and Royal NZ RSA Collection. Reference Number: 1/2- 013882-G

Chapter Thirty-Four: Food Production

Britain's traditional supplies of wheat, grain and cereals were from Russia and refrigerated shipping of meat and dairy products from the colonies had commenced back in 1867. Hay's Wharf was known as "the larder of London" due to the cheese and butter delivered there. This reliance on imported foodstuff was exposed at the commencement of the war and the new world producers being America, Canada, Australia and New Zealand were relied upon to fill the warehouses. If the Gallipoli campaign had been successful, then Russian grain and wheat would have flowed again as in the pre-war commerce and it would have been available to the Allies. Britain only produced $1/5^{th}$ of what it needed[269]. The rest was imported. This dangerous state of the British agricultural policy would become a growing burden on the nation during the long years of war.

Matters had not been helped at the outset by the display of panic buying at the beginning of the war, the calling up of many of the young agricultural workers and the requisitioning of horses and wagons by the military. As a result farmers lacked the skilled manpower necessary to successfully farm, so less land was cropped, the harvest was slow to gather and this all contributed towards a lower than expected annual tonnage to feed the military and civilian population. The soldiers' rations were first reduced in October 1915. A soldier's daily ration of fresh or frozen meat went from 1¼ lb to 1lb per man per day, while preserved meat was reduced from 1lb to ¾ lb per man per day.

In 1916, the Imperial German Navy escalated its submarine offensive against Britain's shipping lanes. The Royal Navy countered by detailing destroyers to escort merchant shipping. A great number of ships did get through, despite the German Navy's best efforts to disrupt shipping, and during a ten day period in July 1916; Australian refrigerated ships managed to land 13,000 ton of frozen meat for Army purposes.

Regardless, around 1,700 merchant ships were sunk in 1917 by German submarines. The merchant fleet could not sustain these losses and keep the Nation fed. As less food arrived, the Government tried to persuade the public to eat less. Posters prominently displayed ships on the high sea with the patriotic caption "We are doing our bit, are you?"

Foodstuffs were always made available to the Army, Navy and the Royal Flying Corps. Donations made by members of the public to the various voluntary organisations were used to buy the necessary foodstuffs and women gave their time free to prepare and serve tea, cakes and sandwiches. These women were often fondly remembered by the soldiers as they distributed the small food parcels when the troop trains stopped at the various railways stations. Many railways stations had free "tea and bun" stalls for soldiers and sailors. At Waterloo Station a free buffet operated on the subway leading to the Underground stations. During the course of the war, this one buffet alone provided over one million cups of tea to the men.

Such free buffets were fondly remembered for the warmth of the welcome, if not as much for the quality of the tea. They were especially liked by men on a much treasured week's leave from France. Here they could get a mug of warm tea before rushing off to get the connecting train to their home town.

Eggs were always being collected from households for the wounded at Red Cross Hospitals, along with numerous other items requested such as blankets, soap, matches, fruit, vegetables, cakes, cigarettes, tobacco, hot water bottles and even brandy.

In early 1916 a plea was issued by the small farm holders in Hampshire who had joined the Colours. They asked if someone could take care of their land while they were serving. Many had only their wife to care for both the family and the farm. Tending the animals and crops was a demanding enough role, and then there were all the other farming jobs that needed attending to, such as maintaining streams and watercourses so as not to cause damage to the land. The War Agricultural Committee insisted that fallen and overgrown trees, bushes, weeds, reeds and other obstructions were removed to ensure all water channels were kept open. Women on their own struggled to cope with all of these tasks and became increasingly reliant upon any remaining male relatives and the goodwill of their neighbours for help in undertaking labour intensive farm work.

To address this labour shortage in rural areas, workers from the cities were enticed onto the land. Newspapers reported how six men, five women and a boy, freed from school owing to the war, received 15 shillings a week for haymaking, milking, ploughing and general farm work. They were provided with a cottage and paid 4 pence each for overtime. They had ½ hour for breakfast, 1 hour for lunch and if working overtime, ½ hour for tea.

The farmers came under public criticism as being a barrier to agricultural reform[270]. Before the war many foodstuffs were imported so a low dependency existed upon farmers. This had now changed and the nation placed a heavy reliance upon them to make up the shortages. Their difficult nature, stubborn attitudes and independent views were often at odds with officialdom, especially when the Daylight Saving Bill was introduced in 1916. This mandated that clocks be changed by two hours in summer time. This meant that milking times were earlier than normal, to ensure smooth distribution of the milk to railway stations and delivery to the towns as the train operated according to the new daylight saving timetables.

The introduction of the National Register in July 1915 had made it compulsory for all males and females aged between fifteen and sixty-five to register. It recorded each person's age, occupation and if they would volunteer for any other form of labour. Women made themselves available for employment although the process of allocating them to war work was haphazard. Women began to gradually fill the roles in shops and factories vacated by those men now in military service. At International Stores women had replaced over 2,000 men by 1916.

It was not until the Women's Land Army (WLA) national campaign of February 1917 that women were directed into a specific economic sector. The WLA, which was funded and controlled by the Board of Agriculture and Fisheries, asked for 10,000 women volunteers for farm work. The

WLA intended to place women on farms as milkers, field workers and carters. They were paid 18 shillings a week, provided with accommodation and a free clothing issue consisting of boots, breeches, overalls and a hat.

New Zealand Engineers tending their fields of vegetables, grown at the back of their camp at Jumpers Common. Originally the New Zealanders had a 2½ acre field to grow food in, but with food shortages increasing across England during 1918, an additional 5½ acres was planted out and beehives also became a feature in the fields.

Photo courtesy of Alexander Turnbull Library, Wellington, New Zealand and Royal NZ RSA Collection. Reference Number: 1/2- 013878-G.

This campaign was more successful in the north of Britain where women were more used to working on the land. In the south, this was met with resistance from the farmers. They were outspoken in their criticism of women engaged in agricultural work. Notwithstanding the opposition, the WLA eventually employed some 113,000 women – one third of all labour working on the land[271].

Prisoners of war were also employed on the land throughout the later part of the war, assisting with the labour intensive tasks of; sowing, weeding and the eventual harvesting and threshing of the crops.

On the 18th of November 1916 *The Times* newspaper reported the rise in prices charged by teashops around the country. Bread and butter were 2½ pence with the bread thinly cut. Steak puddings were now six pence and two poached eggs on toast cost almost a shilling. This was unaffordable to most soldiers on leave who earned one shilling, plus allowances, a day.

In an attempt to address spiralling prices, on the 18th of December 1916, the Board of Trade Order came into force. It immediately restricted all hotels and restaurants from serving any more than a three course meal. At the same time, the military commander for the London district also required hotel and restaurants to limit the prices charged to members of the military. Non compliance resulted in those establishments being placed out of bounds to all military personnel, thereby restricting their trade. The prices were to be set so as to check unnecessary extravagances. The meal price for a military person was set at: Lunch three shilling six pence, Tea one shilling and six pence, Dinner five shillings and six pence and Supper three shilling and six pence[272].

On a civilian wage, these prices may have seemed reasonable, but on British Army pay they were not. Factory workers' were reputed to earn as much as £1 per day (the same as 20 shillings) in some industries. Feeling this inequity, it became a regular saying amongst the resentful soldiers that 'the Tommie in the trenches got one shilling a day, while a worker in the factory earned £1 a day'.

Shortages amongst other essential food items soon occurred. In one incident the potato dealers in Bournemouth would not accept orders for small quantities, so the orphanage in Christchurch went without potatoes and sugar for three weeks because of this.

The suppliers were merely responding to the restrictions placed upon them by the local War Committees. Besides, there was plentiful demand for their produce within the easier reaches of the Bournemouth area without troubling themselves travelling to rural Christchurch.

With no room to manoeuvre, Christchurch Council authorised the Superintendent to purchase potatoes at £14 and 10 shillings a ton if they were delivered to Christchurch. It was pointed out at the time that this equated to 1½ pence per lb; the highest retail price possible. There was no alternative if the orphanage was to be supplied.

Soon coal supplies were being affected in the same way. Part of the reason for this was that the merchants themselves relied upon horses and wagons to carry the goods. With most healthy animals commandeered by the military and a shortage of ample oats and barley to properly feed those remaining working horses, they determined that it was unsustainable to continue carting what they considered to be a small order to individual households.

The only recorded price reduction in 1916 was Puritan Olive Oil Soap which reduced by one halfpenny per pound.

The effect that these shortages were having upon the national diet was first divulged when "The Medical Officers Report on the Children of England" was published by Sir Henry Newman in September 1916. In his report he made it known that of the six million children in schools, approximately one million were "defective, so that they were unable to derive their full amount of health or education"[273]. It was a worrying percentage for the Government authorities, with few options available to remedy the situation.

National food rationing had not existed in the early years of the war. The

British Government's policy was to fix the price of those essential food items where they had efficient control at all stages, from the producer down to the retailer. This intention was to allow retailers to make a reasonable profit, but prevent speculation.

It was left to the local War Committees to enforce governmental policies as they saw fit for their areas and many food items were distributed under license and supervised by the local Food Controllers.

Ration Order Forms were gradually instigated which required each household to register with a named grocer, who would provide the household with a pre-set daily quota of flour, sugar, butter and meat. Other food items could be purchased, but the price was often an inhibitor to consumption. In Christchurch and Bournemouth, tea, jam and cheese were soon added to the quota system.

The approved weekly allowance for those items already restrictively distributed was three pounds of flour, 2½ lbs of meat and ¾ lb sugar. This provided about 1,350 calories a day, if all the meat was butcher's meat. The best food available to make up the recommended daily intake of 2,500 – 3,000 calories per person were lard, margarine, butter, suet, bacon, bread, beef, nuts, eggs, plums, herrings, grapes, milk, banana, parsnip, tinned salmon, vegetables and tomatoes. Cost was often the issue in obtaining these items. Tiny oranges which pre-war sold at four for a penny, now cost three pence each in 1917.

The N.Z. Government provided a meat ration of twelve ounces a day to each NZEF soldier in England. A similar arrangement existed for the Australians, Canadians and Americans who each had their own ration scales for their troops, which were often greater than the rations provided to the British troops.

The meagre British ration had caused an unexpected reaction amongst the N.Z. Tunnellers in early 1916 while training in England and attached to the Royal Fusiliers in Falmouth. They described the food provided as being "scarce"[274]. Being a hard-bitten lot they soon staged what they called a "bit of a strike", which resulted in the intervention of the New

Zealand High Commissioner to resolve. He immediately ensured that the Tunnellers were placed on the greater NZEF ration scale.

In their ranks the N.Z. Tunellers could boast seventeen ex-secretaries of Labour Unions, as well as members of the 'Red' Federation of Labour, all knowledgeable in labour strikes from their activities back in New Zealand during 1912. So a "bit of a strike" would have been a total misstatement and a shock to the military good order practised by the Royal Fusiliers. There would have been some resentment amongst the English troops when they saw the increased rations provided to the N.Z. Tunnellers as well as a morale problem for the Fusilier's commanding officer to confront.

The start of 1917 heralded the days of self denial in Britain. There was a growing demand from the Government for greater food economy. An Order which came into effect from March 26th 1917 required that any flour being sold could only contain a maximum of 81% wheat flour. Other cereals such as rice, maize or barley could be added but they could comprise no more than 10% of the total content. The remainder was sawdust or other junk produce. The soldiers' daily rations of cheese and bread were reduced in January 1917 and by April that year the jam ration was also cut[275]. Butter, which had always been an extra ration for the soldiers, was stopped in July 1917.

The reduced supply of potatoes meant that the civilian population could only eat these every other day unless they grew their own potatoes and vegetables. Restaurants served potatoes on alternate days. In Christchurch, the price was so high that many people could only manage to eat them once a week.

Although the newspapers tried to adopt an upbeat mood at the start of that third year at war, the severe snowstorms that were experienced throughout April dampened peoples' spirits. Frustration soon grew to outspoken criticism. Food shortages touched everybody personally.

Speaking in the House of Commons in February 1917, the local Christchurch MP; Colonel H. Page-Croft stated that wheat and sugar production must be encouraged. In his view, it was the duty of everyone through the length and breadth of Britain to do everything possible to bring the land under cultivation, although he recognised that farmers needed to achieve an economic price for their produce. Increasing production required more than fine words and as the British Government wrestled with ways of increasing food production, the local Christchurch War Committee's solution, in April 1917, was to begin by asking people to save sugar by taking fewer lumps in their tea.

The people of Christchurch began criticising the profiteering of food distributors and specifically complained that most of the fish caught in their rivers and off their beaches, were sold to Bournemouth restaurants. Local inhabitants rarely saw salmon or other fish for sale in the local town shops. Many rural dwellers did have rabbits and pigeons to eat. There were also eggs if they had chickens and those bordering country estates could still acquire pheasant. There was an active barter system for butter, milk and some cheese amongst rural folk. It was the cereals, meats, manufactured and imported goods that created the hardships for them.

The bickering and comparison between rural versus city food supplies continued for some time until the shipping losses were eventually published. Then everyone began to understand the seriousness of the national problem. The merchantmen and sailors of the Royal Navy were doing their best to keep the nation fed; although with over 1,700 food carrying ships[276] being sunk each year by long range German submarines the food problems would not be quickly resolved, particularly as Germany could build submarines quicker than the Royal Navy could sink them.

With the realisation that responsibility for the food situation had to be shared by all, articles on the spraying of potatoes and caring for gardens and allotments appeared. Articles advising how to preserve fruit and vegetables and recipes for bread making became regular features in local newspapers. The Countess of Malmesbury took up the challenge and organised a "Food Economy Exhibition" at Sandhills in Mudeford aimed at ways to reduce food waste. People soon realised that the only way out of the problem was to get involved and solve it themselves.

In May 1917 a meeting was held to debate saving bread. The outcome was that the War Committee proposed that a Food and Bread Saving Committee be formed for Christchurch and District. This was in line with the national campaign to eat less bread. Soon a campaign was underway to urge people to avoid waste in all ways, especially cooking, over-eating and what they fed to babies. The main aim was to save bread although economising on the use of oatmeal; barley and wheat were also included. As a result, the price for a loaf of bread was increased that month by 50%. It rose to one shilling and nine pence. At the start of the war a two pound loaf of bread cost a mere three pence, now in just over two years of war the price had increased an astronomical 633%. This was staggering inflation.

Another restriction actively policed concerned bakers. By law, they were not allowed to sell their bread until 12 hours after it had been baked. The idea being that stale bread would cut down consumption. They were also prevented from supplying yeast to the public which effectively prevented home baking. It was believed that home baking was not economical, as it wasted ingredients and required a disproportionate amount of fuel to warm the household oven, as opposed to bulk, commercial baking.

Bread consumption become such an issue that the Christchurch Mayor read out at a public meeting a pamphlet, prepared by a local dignitary Mr John Druitt, that summarised the recent Proclamation from The King. The Royal Proclamation called on the people to reduce the consumption of bread by at least one-fourth of the quantity consumed in ordinary times, to abstain from the use of flour in pastry, and wherever possible to abandon its use in all food items other than bread. It also instructed people who owned horses to stop feeding oats or other grain to them, unless they were licensed to do so by the Food Controller.

It was decided to have the Proclamation printed and distributed by the Boy Scouts. The use of posters had by this stage of the war become ineffective as with so many now on display on walls and billboards, the public hardly noticed them anymore.

Two months later in July, at a public meeting in Christchurch Town Hall, war bread was criticised as being unpalatable. Children could not eat it, so much of it was wasted and other people complained that it caused indigestion. The advice given by the Ministry of Food specialists was to eat no more than you really need and chew every mouthful slowly. It soon became a standing joke that it was considered disloyal to have indigestion. A "win-the-war" cooking book soon began to sell locally in an attempt to encourage different habits. The cookbooks sold for two pence each, nothing seemed to be given away free in the war years.

By September 1917 the food situation continued to be a major topic of conversation. It even surpassed news on the operations at the Front and the weather. Its importance was heightened when the Director of Food Economy appealed to the nation for food economy as a matter a national safety. He stressed that in 1914 the need was for Men; in 1915 it was for Munitions; in 1916 for Money; and now in 1917 it was for Men, Munitions, Money and Economy in Food.

Soon milk prices were increasing monthly, rising ½ penny in December 1917 to 7 pence a quart. An 8% increase in one month. It was ½ penny cheaper if it was collected from the retail shops, farm or cowshed by the public. The logic being that horses were a scarce resource, more usefully employed in agriculture than in the delivery of goods to householders.

Beer quality and prices were also impacted, when in November 1917 "The Beer Order 1917" set the maximum price for beer sold in a public bar at either four pence per imperial pint for beer of an original gravity of 1036% or five pence if the specific gravity did not exceed 1042%. Each barrel had to be clearly marked with four pence or five pence depending on which quality was being sold.

The Army camps in Christchurch also come under criticism, as a rumour circulated that twenty tons of potatoes had arrived there and most of them had been wasted. It was felt by the public that the distribution was unequal and that there was a lot of waste in these camps.

The local Christchurch Red Cross Hospital was not immune from rumours either. Word circulated that the hospital was getting more vegetables than it knew what to do with. This was emphatically denied by the hospital commander, who pointed out that with over two hundred men to provide for, it was hardly likely that too much was ever wasted, let alone given away.

Feelings amongst the public began running high and any gossip pertaining to food was quickly seized upon as if it was a truth. The danger in such behaviour became apparent when one hundred and fifty Royal Engineers arrived at Mudeford for billeting. Initially the householders refused to take the men in, preferring to believe the gossip circulating that each Engineer had been issued a full week's ration; when the civilian population still faced food scarcity on a regular basis.

The military soon refuted these wild claims. They pointed out that the rations issued to each Royal Engineer were their first issue of the day and comprised ten ounces of meat per man, which was less than their daily ration quota. For the rest of the day each man had to procure what he could. The military pointed out that there were several cases where the men had no daily rations at all to put in their haversacks.

In another incident after Christmas there were whispers that some people had plum pudding for Christmas. It was pointed out that probably those that did have plum pudding had preserved the fruit in the summer months when the fruit was available, with the intention of using it at Christmas time.

Unfortunately as desperation became more widespread, the disparity between rumour and truth widened. This would continue for the remainder of the war.

By 31st of December 1917 the futile attempt to restrict sugar consumption stopped. In its place ration cards were issued. Sugar was distributed to the public in accordance with the Rules of the Food Controller. A card was issued to each householder by the local Food Committee and sugar was given only to those persons named on the card. An application for a

Sugar Card was made by a Declaration Form issued through the Post Office. The card covered all persons, including servants, who slept in the house. If a servant slept elsewhere, then they were excluded from the household's sugar card. These cards were presented to the grocer who provided each registered member of a household with a Retailer's Sugar Ticket, which was exchanged when buying sugar.

Despite these and other local and National measures, food shortages increased as did the length of the food queues outside of the grocery shops. People waited to buy restricted items such as butter, cheese, margarine and bacon. Compulsory rationing on all food items was soon being talked about. With leather classed as an essential war product, acquiring a pair of war-time boots became just as uncertain. One leather delivery for Christchurch had been expected for over four months and still no-one knew when any would arrive. People just had to mend and make do.

It was an offence under the Hoarding Order 1917 to buy and store excesses of food. Any householders found to have done so were charged as food hoarders. One couple, the husband being a London solicitor, were charged with hoarding 298lb of Quaker Oats, 518lb rice, 134lb Sugar, 48lbs tea and 20lbs of Scotch Rolled Oats. They were fined £25 in respect of the Quaker oats, £25 in respect of the rice, £10 in respect of the sugar, and £10 for the tea, plus costs. The provisions were confiscated.

In Christchurch, warnings were issued that food hoarders should send their surplus provisions to the Red Cross Hospital before the Food Controller caught them. There was an official name and shame policy as hoarding was seen as a mean and selfish offence.

In March 1918 the local Food Control Committee had received urgent instructions from the Ministry of Food to do all in its power to encourage the production of local food. It was urged that all available land be cultivated to its utmost capacity. It was also requested that: potatoes, haricot beans, broad beans, cabbages and other vegetables be grown by everyone who could use a spade. Allotment gardens were made available across the Christchurch Borough, although experienced gardeners were encouraged to apply, as opposed to those with mere patriotic zeal. Experience would guarantee that the maximum output could be achieved.

All cottagers were urged to keep a pig and by so doing increase their own meat supply. Children were also encouraged to rear rabbits. There was a suspicion though that these home-reared animals may be commandeered by the Government, but this was emphatically denied.

In January 1918 to assist with the supply of vegetables for their troops, the N.Z. Engineers were provided with a 2½ acre plot of ground next to their camp on the River Stour. This was expanded by an additional 5½ acres in February. The land was ploughed using their wagon horses. Later the tractors of the N.Z. Light Railway Operating Company found a suitable role in ploughing the agricultural fields and provided their drivers with vocational training. By April, the planting of potatoes and other vegetables was underway.

The effort was taken seriously and the Engineers were allocated to agriculture duty one day a week to assist in weeding, watering, tending and harvesting the crops. In June a hive of bees became the latest addition and as in prior years, in September the men were busy collecting blackberries from the hedgerows which the cooks soon made into jam. This jam was prized by the Field Companies in France and when reinforcements from the NZE Depot arrived, there was an anticipation of a fresh jam ration.

The vegetables were used within the NZE Depot camp, with any surplus supplies forwarded to the other NZEF training camps and hospitals in accordance with Brigadier General Richardson's instructions. This all helped to make the NZE Depot self-sufficient and contributed in some way towards alleviating the food shortages being experienced elsewhere. When the NZE Depot closed after the war the agricultural area continued to be used as an Agricultural School until the mid 1920's.

Chapter Thirty-Five: Social Events and Sports

Sports continued to be an important aspect of the men's pastime and the NZE Depot arranged rugby games against the N.Z. Rifles Signal company at Stevenage, which the Engineers won; in their next match they drew against the Artillery Cadet Depot at Exeter and on Good Friday 1917 they played N.Z. Headquarters, London losing 9-3.

Since their return to Christchurch in 1917, the New Zealanders had become involved in the organised boxing contests that periodically occurred at the camp. Sergeant T O'Briant, the ex-Champion welter-weight boxer of Australia, was stationed at Christchurch with the Australian drivers. He provided boxing lessons every Monday and Wednesday evening at the Drill Hall on Portfield Road.

Boxing was a popular sport in Christchurch before the war, with weekly bouts arranged on most Market Days. The prospect of it being revived by the military, with the quality of boxers available, was keenly welcomed, along with the opportunity for some betting.

The YMCA Hut was the venue in January 1917 for the first contest involving the New Zealanders. It opened with a three-round bout between two evenly matched Royal Engineer boxers. That was followed by a five round contest between Corporal Stevens of the Devon Hussars and Driver McIvor NZE. In the first round Stevens with his long reach got in some telling blows despite slipping. McIvor got in with some good body blows. The next two rounds were even. In the fifth round McIvor did some smart dodging and put up a good defence but just before the close was floored and although he was up before being counted out he was saved from further punishment by the call of time and Stevens was declared the winner.

The next contest was a three round contest between Drivers Carey RE and Thornton NZE. Carey finally won. A five round contest between Sergeant Monagatti NZE and Trumpeter Keenan (Devon Hussars) ended in a victory for Monagatti in four rounds.

Monagatti and Stevens then started a three round contest, but the fight was stopped when Monagatti was knocked down. Stevens was awarded the victory. The evening sport finished with a bout between Drivers Picken (NZE) and Tout (SMRE) in which the New Zealander carried off the honours.

The next military contest occurred on the Christchurch Barrack field on 9th June, 1917 and was noteworthy as it featured for the first time Maori boxers. They were described as being sturdily built men, who could take any amount of punishment.

The "star turn" of the evening was the appearance of Staff-Sergeant Instructor Jimmy Wilde, the Fly-Weight Champion of the World and also the outright winner of the Lord Lonsdale Belt. He fought two opponents, the first being Private Collins of the Machine Gun Corps, who had won 13 out of 15 contests and with whom he gave a two round exhibition. The next opponent was Private Morgan NZE. Wilde won both bouts.

The other fights that evening were:
Private Amatawa (N.Z. Pioneers) v Driver George RFA declared a draw.
Private Kihi (N.Z. Pioneers) v Driver Martin Wessex RE resulted with Kihi getting in a knock-out body blow in the first round.
Private Morgan (N.Z. Pioneers) v Driver Brewer Wessex RE resulted in Morgan winning.
Private Simpson (N.Z. Pioneers) v Private Ward DCM, MM Queens Regiment, resulted in Ward winning.
Sergeant Rawlings SMRE v Private Johnson (N.Z. Pioneers) resulted in Johnson winning with a Knock Out in the first minute.
Private Wi (N.Z. Pioneers) v Private Johnson (Cheshires). Johnson was declared the winner. Wi was only sixteen years of age.

Military dances were arranged for the men and the 1917 dance season began with a khaki dance (military only) with partners in February. The Masters Of Ceremonies for the evening were: Sergeant-Major Howard RE, Sergeant H.A. Shepherd RE and Corporal J. Smith NZE. The band was the newly formed N.Z. Orchestra – conducted by Sapper Huggins, and consisted of Corporals Chesswas, McIntosh and Hill.

With the addition of the "Tour of Duty" men and the N.Z. Pioneers now at Christchurch Camp, the New Zealanders were becoming more involved in the local community. It was therefore decided in July, to organise a summer event and invite the neighbouring community.

An Aquatic Sports Day was held, to be concluded in the evening with a dance. The main events advertised were a catamaran race, followed by a water polo match between an Imperial Team captained by Sergeant T Thould of the Wessex RE and an Overseas Team, captained Corporal Leeder of the New Zealand Engineers. These international competitions always proved popular with the public.

At the conclusion of the sports events the prizes were presented in the officers' enclosure, with the event winners being:

Special Catamaran Race – 1st Sapper Blezard WRE.
Double Canoe Race – 1st Tapene and Tipane, N.Z. Pioneers.
Tub race – 1st Curtis N.Z. Pioneers; 2nd Hawira, N.Z. Pioneers.
50 yards Swimming Race – Sergeant Thould WRE and Private Wharepapa N.Z. Pioneers (dead heat).
100 yards Swimming Race – 1st Sergeant Thould WRE, 2nd Sergeant Deen N.Z. Engineers.
Water Derby – 1st Sapper Gregory WRE, 2nd Sapper Curtis N.Z. Pioneers.
Tug of War in Punts – Won by the N.Z. Pioneers: Henare, Tipane, Edwards, Aperahama, Hawira and Petaine.
Walking Greasy Pole – 1st Private Edwards, N.Z. Pioneers; 2nd Private Tipane N.Z. Pioneers; 3rd Private Denby WRE.
Obstacle Race – 1st Sergeant Thould WRE; 2nd Corporal Mitchell SMRE.
Water Polo match – won by the Imperial team.
Water Tournament – won by Private Hawira and Private Petane, N.Z. Pioneers.

The last presentation was a bouquet of flowers that was presented by Major Bamford to Mrs Keen and the ladies who assisted at the concert.

Throughout the day, the band of the Wessex RE played selections of music. The concert parties from both the South Midland RE – the Pierrot

Troupe and the Wessex Engineers Troupe entertained from a pontoon raft by the river's edge. The evening concluded with a Grand River concert, which featured:

Song: "Tow-the row-row" The Wessex Entertaining Engineers (WEEs).
Song: "Blighty" Miss G.M. Breeze.
Song: "Consolation" Sapper Babbington N.Z. Engineers.
Comic item: "Parody" Rickens' Party N.Z. Engineers.
Recitation: "The Hell Gate of Soissons" Lance Corporal Sweeney WRE.
War dance: "Maori Haka" N.Z. Pioneers.
Violin solo: Captain G.H. Simpson SMRE.
Duet: "The Fisherman" Lance Corporals Sweeney and Green WRE.
Humorous item: "Uncle Joe" Rickens' Party, N.Z. Engineers.
Song: "When the great red Dawn is Shining" Miss Madeline Barlow.
Song: Sapper Dixon N.Z. Engineers.
Song: "Link, Red Sun" Miss Mary Wall.
Concert item: "They all lived happily afterwards" WEEs.
Song: "An Old-Fashioned Town" Miss MC Berry.
Humorous song: Sapper Jinks WEEs.
War Dance: "Maori Haka" N.Z. Pioneers.
God Save the King.

Later that week the local *Christchurch Times* published a "thank you" to the New Zealand Engineers, by way of a poem:

An Echo of the Military Sports
To the Royal Engineers and the New Zealand Engineers.

A thousand thanks, for Saturday's fun –
Well worth doing, most worthily done!
The Barrack field was a goodly sight,
Full of colour, rhythm and light,
Flags a-flutter, and music's joy
Gem-like clearness of arching sky;
Mind and muscle, prowess and tact –
For your game endeavour nothing lacked!
Anzac! The British Lion roared,

And with answering thunder you leapt aboard,
With your kin-at-arms take now the salute
From your guests whose lips, perforce, are mute

One who was there.

In late September 1917 the N.Z. Engineers held an invitation ball at the Town Hall as the opening night of their dancing season. Nearly one hundred and fifty dancers were assembled and included men of the N.Z. Maori (Pioneers), now stationed at Christchurch. Regimental-Sergeant Major M.J. Woodwall and Corporal O.F. Wells were the Masters of Ceremony for the night and along with Sergeant H. Christmas, they had all assisted in organising the event.

During the winter of 1917/18, the sports season was renewed with more familiarity of the local teams than the Engineers had in the prior year. The rugby team won against the RAF at Beaulieu 75-3 and then lost to the Officer Training Cadets team at Exeter 14-8. Hockey was now being played regularly against local teams. In their opening game the N.Z. Engineers' hockey team beat the Tank Corps at Bovington.

The new draft of "Tour of Duty" men that had recently arrived formed a soccer team, which promptly lost its first two matches to the Wessex Royal Engineers, but as their fitness and physical conditioning returned they won their third game against Bournemouth Tramways 8-0!

The after-match functions were held at the NZYMCA building known as 'Khartoum House' at The Grange in Boscombe.

Members of the Women's Army Ancillary Corps near the River Stour in Christchurch. The women undertook roles such as clerks, drivers, cooks and administrators in Army establishments, thereby allowing more men to be made available for the fighting in France. Many also served in similar roles in France.

Courtesy of the late Mrs Olive Samuel

Local women competing in a skipping event at one of the numerous summer festivals organised by the New Zealanders. This event is likely to be at Codford, on Salisbury Plain.

Photo courtesy of Alexander Turnbull Library, Wellington, New Zealand and Royal NZ RSA Collection.   *Reference Number: 1/2- 013825-G.*

Local townspeople enjoying tea and cake during a summer sports festival organised by the New Zealanders at Codford.

Photo courtesy of Alexander Turnbull Library, Wellington, New Zealand and Royal NZ RSA Collection. Reference Number: 1/2- 013829-G.

Playing cricket at a New Zealand sports event at Codford, near Salisbury.

Photo courtesy of Alexander Turnbull Library, Wellington, New Zealand and Royal NZ RSA Collection. Reference Number: *1/2- 013823-G.*

Winning the Three Legged Race event at Codford Camp, near Salisbury.

Photo courtesy of Alexander Turnbull Library, Wellington, New Zealand and Royal NZ RSA Collection. Reference Number: *1/2- 013824-G.*

Chapter Thirty-Six: The Battle of Passchendaele and a cold winter at Ypres

After the success of Messines, General Haig and his senior officers believed that one more Offensive against the Germans could be completed before winter set in. The tactical high ground and ridge near the village of Passchendaele became his next objective and the Anzacs were included amongst the troops who would help take it.

Throughout August and September, the N.Z. Field Companies were employed with rear area work, building hospitals, bath houses, collecting material from the railway heads, working in the trenches, repairing roads, creating supply dumps and map making. The rear areas were constantly harassed by artillery bombardments and air raids. They began working on deep dugouts in the forward areas and by October the Engineers were gas proofing dugouts as the N.Z. Division readied itself for the next major offensive. On 4th October, the Battle of Passchendaele commenced.

To get to their assembly areas, the N.Z. Infantry had to wade through knee-deep mud caused by wet weather and the heavy shelling. The mud clung to everything. Even the maps had to be cleaned with a pen knife before they could be read[277].

The thick mud did have one benefit. German artillery shells buried themselves in the soft ground before exploding, thereby reducing the number of otherwise fatal casualties.

The Engineers constructed a stream crossing across the swollen Ravebeck and waited to be called forward to consolidate captured ground. The attacking infantry could not breach the unbroken aprons of wire in front of the German positions, nor compete against the carefully sited machine guns protected by their concrete emplacements. Throughout the day the exhausted N.Z. Infantry were cut to ribbons as they fought from shell hole to shell hole, captured German trenches, and stormed pillboxes with bombs and bayonets. Yet they achieved their first objective – 1,200 yards of ground up to the strategically drawn Red Line as well as part of their second objective, which was a further 1000 yards up the ridge to the equally iniquitous Blue Line just below the village of Passchendaele, although some of this ground had to be given up.

During the fighting Lieutenant Colonel King, who commanded the 1st Canterbury Battalion during the battle was killed. King had been the first commander of the N.Z. Pioneer Battalion when it was formed in Egypt. Upon hearing of his death a detachment of his Pioneers came up and retrieved his body for burial[278].

The Engineers managed to extend the duckboard tracks across the morass and towards the forward areas. With little shelter and cover available, the Engineers were busy with the repair of captured German pillboxes for use as dressing stations or infantry headquarters, despite the entrances facing the wrong way.

The German machine gunners on Bellevue Spur made this work nearly impossible, so the Engineers were withdrawn to the rear to assist with the major task of road mending, maintaining mule tracks, pulling guns out of the bog, and continuing to repair and extend the duckboard track ways across the waterlogged ground full of shell holes that in some places were sixteen feet deep[279].

All the time it rained and the roads and store dumps continued to be targeted by German artillery. Amidst the cold, the rain and the mud, no amount of effort or timber could keep the supply routes operating to the capacity needed. Regardless of the conditions, the Engineers persevered as best they could. This effort helped in the evacuation of the wounded and went some way in lessening their suffering, though the heavy traffic along the muddy roadways soon caused congestion which in turn attracted German artillery fire.

The N.Z. Division was withdrawn on 6th October, though the N.Z. Engineers and N.Z. Maori (Pioneer) Battalion remained and continued with their efforts to keep the roads operating. Another attack was planned for the 12th October and the N.Z. Engineers were detailed to help consolidate captured ground, then clear out and reinforce captured pillboxes so that they could be used by the British. Despite the muddy terrain, the attack went in with infantry struggling across the ground under effective German machine gun fire, only to be halted by wide unbroken entanglements of wire that the artillery had again failed to destroy.

With the advance halted, the Engineers were not required to consolidate captured ground; instead they continued to extend and improve the roads and communication routes.

On the 13th of October, the Engineers were still in the field continuing with maintaining lines of communication and helping to bring in the wounded from the sea of mud. This continued until the 22nd of October when they were finally relieved by the Canadian Engineers. After a weary march they entrained with the N.Z. Division to the 2nd Army Training Area at Bainghen-Le-Comte near Ypres, while the drivers proceeded back along the busy roads with their wagons and exhausted horse teams. The Engineers' history notes that some horses showed signs of twitching limbs due to being too close to bursting shells, while others were near to collapse.

1200 men from the N.Z. Division were killed and 1,400 wounded during the fighting for Passchendaele. Reinforcements arriving after the battle were termed "rainbows"- as rainbows only come out after the storm is over.

At Bainghen-Le-Comte, the Engineers received training on some new topics: construction of dugouts, their resistance to shellfire and reinforced concrete. Other instruction sessions were intended to revise old skills such as: gas drill, guard mounting, road construction, musketry, trench construction and demolitions. Training in the various types of wire entanglements was undertaken, including the newly developed apron and double apron fast wiring techniques. This short period of rest and retraining also allowed the Engineers to reorganise after Passchendaele and allowed replacements and newly promoted NCOs to integrate into their new roles.

The N.Z. Division spent that winter at Ypres; and it soon became evident during those first few weeks in the front line that there was a distinct lack of overhead shelter in the trenches for the N.Z. Infantry Brigades. This was caused by an extreme shortage of most materials and being new to the area, it took some time before the New Zealand Engineers became familiar as to which supply dump had what materials.

So they used their initiative to resolve the situation, as was bitterly recorded by Captain E.T. Vachell of the British 41st Division in his diary. He remembered the New Zealanders in the Ypres area during that cold December. He wrote of how his divisional stores had a lucky escape one particular night when a group of sixteen New Zealanders decided to pay it a visit. Ignoring the objections of the four armed British sentries on guard, they had begun to remove timbers and corrugated iron.

Vachell wrote that "these Anzac people are devils to have about. Its not safe to leave anything even for five minutes out here in the ordinary course of events, but people will usually pinch things from under your very eyes."[280] Soon the problem of inadequate winter shelter and drainage in the New Zealand sector of the trenches was remedied. As it transpired, that winter of 1917/1918 it was one of the coldest winters experienced and "trench foot" became a common ailment amongst the Allied soldiers in that sector.

Trench repair, "double apron" wiring, constructing defensive machine gun positions, building pillboxes, providing overhead shelter for artillery batteries, road repairs and drainage kept the Engineers occupied during the cold winter months at Ypres. Most work occurred in the forward areas, especially repairs to roads and wiring which was performed at night with the Engineers often supervising infantry work parties.

There was no let up from the German machine gunners, heavy artillery bombardments and gas shelling. On clear nights German Gotha bombers flew overhead bombing the rear areas, the camps, store dumps and horse lines.

These interruptions forced the working parties to disperse into whatever cover was available. It then took time to reassemble the working parties, despatch any casualties to the aid stations and then complete the work assigned. All of this resulted in the pace of work in the front lines being slow, unless some risks were taken. Amongst those killed that winter were two experienced Gallipoli veterans; 2nd Corporal Edward St George-Gorton and Sapper John Ramsey; both died from multiple gunshot wounds most probably as a result of machine gun fire. They are buried side by side at the Ypres Reservoir Cemetery.

At the end of February 1918, the N.Z. Infantry Brigades began moving back to the reserve rest areas at Staple, west of Hazelbrouck. The N.Z. Engineers remained engaged in Army Corps work such as: constructing concrete dugouts that were electrically lit; erecting Nissan huts to accommodate the troops; erecting barbed wire entanglements; laying railway tracks and constructing reserve positions for the heavy artillery in case of withdrawal, as well as their other duties around Ypres. To allow some respite, the Field Companies were rotated between the trenches and the rest areas[281].

With the need for replacements amongst the infantry brigades, the 4th Brigade was disbanded and the men allocated to the other brigades. On the 16th February, 1918 the 4th Field Company was also disbanded. It was renamed the "N.Z. Reinforcement Field Company Engineers".

It was attached to N.Z. Entrenching Group, where the Engineers became a replacement pool for the remaining three Field Companies. Their equipment was drawn upon to make good shortages amongst the remaining Field Companies. They were initially employed mending roads, wiring, extending duckboard tracks and digging trenches often with those 4th Brigade Infantrymen not posted as replacements to the other Brigades. The men resented their new role and morale dropped accordingly, which was unfortunate considering the German storm that was about to break over the Somme area.

Chapter Thirty-Seven: New Zealand Engineers Depot 1917-1918

With the winter of 1917-1918 approaching, the question of building huts at the summer camp area instead of going into winter billets was raised by Colonel Barclay. The War Office was unable to assist, so consequentially on the 29th of October 1917 the NZE Depot struck camp and with a company strength of 13 officers and 414 other ranks went back into winter billets around Boscombe and Southbourne. The only men billeted near the Christchurch Barracks over that winter were the mounted section drivers, who were quartered in an empty house "Girlsta" close to the camp so that they could continue to care for the horses and equipment.

The billeting arrangements were similar to the prior year, whereby two or three men were allotted to each household and the householder was responsible for supplying the men with a comfortable bed, light and fuel.

The officers were billeted around the Cromwell Road and Oxford Avenue area of Southbourne. This area was tree lined and populated with large villa styled houses. The senior officers were permitted to have their wives join them in England. Mrs Keenan and later Mrs Barclay made the long journey from New Zealand to be with their husbands.

Three former houses on Christchurch Road, Boscombe were used for administration purposes with the NZE Depot Headquarters situated at number 231 Christchurch Road, while house numbers 223 and 227 accommodated: the Senior NCOs mess, Details and Maori Orderly Rooms, Tailors', Boot makers' and Butchers' shops as well as Medical, Dental, Postal, Observation Hospital and Quartermasters' Stores. The Headquarters were situated at 30 Cromwell Road.

The large converted garage at Granville Road, which had been used as the messing hall the previous year, was used to store materials belonging to the Field Company, Blacksmiths, Carpenters, Painters and it also housed a cycle shop. Each night a guard was posted to prevent pilfering.

The NZE Reserve Depot has been mentioned in many military references as being located at both Christchurch and at Boscombe. There was only ever one NZE Reserve Depot; the differentiator was merely the season – summer at Christchurch, winter at Boscombe.

Junior NCOs and men had to be in their billets by 10pm, while senior NCOs had the privilege of an 11pm curfew. If found absent from the billet or reported to be so by the householder after the designated time, then the punishment awarded was forfeiture of one days pay for the first offence, then two days pay for the second offence and so on until the behaviour was remedied. Undoubtedly some deals were made with the house owners to overlook certain misdemeanours.

Drunkenness in a billet or elsewhere was not tolerated and if found guilty this resulted in three days punishment being awarded and a fine of usually ten shillings, although Sapper E.W. Hampton set the record when he was charged for being drunk in Boscombe. He was fined £1 and awarded seven days punishment.

For the house owners it would not have been easy having soldiers in their house, particularly some of the battle hardened 'tour of duty' men and those released from hospitals. Those men from France would have been restless, used to sleeping on the ground, in rough barns, dirty cellars, open fields or the semi-destroyed farm buildings of northern France. There would be the nightmares and talking in their sleep, the tensing at sudden loud noises, the need to be outside to smoke or just to move and pace. They would have been early risers and possibly the first into the kitchen to start the stove fire and have a warm mug of tea.

Sometimes the women in the billets, or their friends, would accompany the soldiers for an evening's entertainment while other times they would stay in with the soldiers and talk. For men whose only contact with normal life was through letters received from home, these times would have been appreciated and fondly remembered.

New Zealand Officers at the NZE Depot, Christchurch in late 1917. There is a mixture of Engineers, Pioneers, 3rd Auckland, Machine Gunners and 11th Taranaki (fourth man standing from right) in this photograph. Some of the men can be identified; seated first from the left is the RMO Captain Ward, Captain Tura Horoti MC; then the chaplain the Rev A. Mitchell; in the middle is Colonel Barclay. Captain Chilcott MC, the adjutant, is seated second from the right.

Photo courtesy of Alexander Turnbull Library, Wellington, New Zealand and Royal NZ RSA Collection. Reference Number: 1/2- 013890-G

Brigadier General Richardson, commander of the New Zealand Forces in the UK, inspecting Pioneers of the NZ Maori (Pioneer) Battalion at King's Park near Boscombe, Hampshire in November 1917, prior to awarding gallantry medals to Sapper C Lovell-Smith NZ Engineer the Serbian Medal of Merit and Zeal for his work at Salonika and to Sapper J Williamson NZ Tunnelling Company, the Military Medal for his work at Arras. Later that day Brigadier General Richardson officially opened the NZ YMCA Club at The Grange, in Boscombe.

Photo courtesy of Alexander Turnbull Library, Wellington, New Zealand and Royal NZ RSA Collection. Reference Number: 1/2- 014071-G

At Boscombe, a more convenient parade ground was provided by the Salvation Army. It was located on the edge of the Southbourne town and towards the sea end of Fisherman's Walk. This was sufficient for six hundred men to be on parade and was close to the billet area.

A better messing arrangement was instigated to avoid some of the problems encountered the winter before. Several messes were created around Boscombe. The Mess rooms and Cookhouse for the men were established at St James Institute, Stourfield Road which also doubled as wet and dry canteens. The Sergeants and senior NCOs had a house with a kitchen allocated to them in Dean Road, Southbourne.

With rationing and food shortages, the public were often in need of animal fat for food and cooking. So every evening, women would come around to the cookhouses where the cooks would distribute brown paper parcels containing the left over fats or dripping[282] from cooking the meals. These parcels were highly sought after for the nutrition value alone, with bread and dripping being an evening meal in some households. Occasionally, the cooks would also provide hot meals to the children of people that they knew, as long as they ate the meals in the cookhouse area.

The N.Z. Soldiers' Club was established at the Technical School on Christchurch Road alongside Pokesdown Railway Station. It was managed by the NZWCA[283] under Mrs McCalmott and Miss Birch with the Rev A Mitchell acting as manager. Concerts and Whist Drives were held at the club, as well as a free cinema three times a week. The Dance Committee ran a dance every Friday at the Assembly Rooms, Boscombe and this helped to raise funds to operate the N.Z. Soldiers' Club.

Church Services were held each Sunday at 10am at the local Cinema Theatre at Boscombe, or else the men were free to attend any of the regular services at the various denomination churches in the area.

On Christmas Day 1917, the entire NZE Reserve Depot dined at St James Institute with the NCOs acting as mess orderlies for the men. Married men were allowed to bring their wives. For the festive celebrations, the

New Zealand Government had supplied the entire NZEF with extra Christmas rations and the Engineers' Christmas Dinner consisted of turkey, duck, chicken, roast pork and vegetables, along with Christmas pudding.

With the arrival of warmer weather in March 1918 the NZE Depot vacated their billets at Boscombe and moved back to the Barrack Road camp on the River Stour. Two large marquees were joined together and erected at the camp to house the Soldiers' Club, which had been relocated from the Technical School. Mrs MacCalmott and her assistants stayed on and managed it. A water supply, ablutions and a cookhouse were constructed by the Royal Engineer Billeting Committee so that tea could be served and concerts organised for the men.

During these summer months tennis, bowls and cricket were played. In one cricket game at Wareham the Tank Depot was all out for 46 and the New Zealanders were 45 for 2 wickets when rain stopped play.

In keeping with Brigadier General Richardson's education initiative, NZEF Headquarters in London suggested that educational lectures should be provided to all ranks. After approaching several prominent townspeople, a long series of lectures covering scientific, economic, social and agricultural topics were arranged, covering subjects entitled: "Natural Wonders of America" by Mr C. Lyon, "Caterpillar Camouflage" by N.R.J. Neale, "Five months in Bolshevik Russia" by Mr A.L. Williams. There was only ever one compulsory lecture for the entire NZE Reserve Depot. Its content was considered far too important to be missed. It was "Supplies in France" and was presented by Captain Tadclyffe of the N.Z. Army Service Corps.

A French class was held every Monday evening, but as the class size quickly quadrupled an extra class was added. English classes were begun to help some men with their reading and writing. Other topics such as fruit farming, electrical engineering, sanitary science, agriculture, bee and poultry keeping and woodwork were taught in camp as evening activities. The Bournemouth Municipal College also arranged classes in engineering, shorthand and typewriting, chemistry and art.

During the summer of 1918, the NZE Depot band and the Maoris entertained full houses at the Winter Gardens in Bournemouth and then later at the military gymkhana at Meyrick Park.

The last draft of reinforcements left Christchurch around the 12th October of 1918. There were fifty-four men in the draft which was commanded by Lieutenant Hulbert. It was comprised of mainly experienced men, like Sapper Jim Kelly, returning to the N.Z. Division in France.

A wedding day photograph of Lily Eyears and Staff-Sergeant Frank Appleton NZE, who were married on 28th December 1918 at St Alban's Church, Bournemouth. Frank was an instructor at the NZE Depot, and had served on Gallipoli with the Auckland Mounted Rifles where he was wounded. After he had recovered, he served in France for two years with the Engineers as a driver before being posted to NZE Depot as an instructor.

Photo courtesy of Mr Keith Bennett

Chapter Thirty-Eight: War Brides and War Widows

Inevitably, romances sprung up wherever the New Zealanders happened to be: training depots, hospitals or leave periods in various British towns and cities.

In Christchurch, introductions were made at the military dances, through acquaintances, the winter billets they roomed in, chance encounters around the local towns and villages, or on St Catherine's Hill when entrenching exercises were underway. Sapper Walter Williamson met his future wife, Miss Annie Bolton, at St Catherine's Hill when she and some of her friends came up to talk with the toiling Engineers.

Corporal George Swadel, at the time a "tour of duty" man back from France, met his future wife Ethel who was a nanny, while she was pushing the baby's pram along Convent Walk behind Christchurch Priory. Another "tour of duty man" was Staff Sergeant Frank Appleton who met and soon married Miss Lily Eyears of Bournemouth. Appleton, born in Nottingham, had been wounded on Gallipoli and had served in France until May 1918 when he was posted to Christchurch. After the war he was discharged in Britain where he settled, never returning to New Zealand.

In order to marry, the soldier applied to the NZEF Headquarters in London for a special licence and once granted, the couple could have a religious marriage service or else a civil service at a registry office. Entering into marriage with a New Zealand soldier usually meant that at the end of the war, if the man survived, the bride would follow her husband to New Zealand.

This was a major commitment, as once the bride left England she realised that she may never see her family again. New Zealand was too far away, the duration of the trip too long and the passage too costly.

Many relationships ceased on this single reality, although some soldiers chose instead to marry and then discharge in Britain at the end of the war and live near the wife's family. This meant securing a good civilian job that would still be available after the local men demobbed at the end of the war. The wages in Britain by 1918 were high due to the manpower shortages, and this added to the attraction of being discharged in the Britain.

In the Christchurch and Bournemouth area, marriage services were conducted at the Christchurch Priory, Roman Catholic, Methodist and Presbyterian Churches and other chapels. Some soldiers married in Registry Offices, with the Christchurch Registry Office being the nearest to the camp.

New Zealand female nurses serving in the hospitals formed close friendships with some of the NZEF soldiers that they cared for and these relationships occasionally resulted in marriage. Nurse Irene Ancell, a N.Z. Army staff nurse serving at Brockenhurst married Major Philip Ellis MC at Brighton in 1918. Ellis, a Field Artillery officer had been severely wounded in France and evacuated to England where his leg was amputated at Brockenhurst hospital. Irene nursed him during his dark days. Ellis was eventually moved to a convalescent hospital at Hornchurch and had an artificial limb fitted, during which time Irene was posted to the N.Z. Stationary Hospital in France. They remained in contact and in October 1918 Irene resigned from the N.Z. Army to marry Phillip Ellis. They returned to New Zealand in January 1919 and lived in Auckland. They had no children.

Another nurse from Brockenhurst who married a soldier was Sister Marie Wilkie. She was a theatre nurse and married Major James Hargest at the Christchurch Priory in September 1917. Hargest had been at Gallipoli and would go on to become the youngest NZEF battalion commander in the war, commanding the 2nd Otago Battalion. In the Second World War he served as a Brigadier with the N.Z. Division.

Sapper Vincent Peters, a young veteran of Gallipoli and of Flers-Courcelette, married Miss Gertrude Foote, a seventeen year old VAD working at Brockenhurst hospital. They left for New Zealand in 1919, with their newly born son. Gertrude died in her early 30's while in New

Zealand and certainly would have missed her family.

Sapper Freidrich Reichard, a soldier of "enemy extraction" spent the final years of the war with the NZASC at Codford Camp. He met and married Miss Florence Perry at Salisbury in September 1918. They returned to New Zealand in February 1919 and after discharge they set up home in Taihape. He died in Rotorua in 1978.

As the New Zealand Divisions' casualties mounted during the fighting in France, so did the number of widows. One was Kitty Langridge, from Bournemouth who married Leonard Maisey in July 1917. Kitty and Leonard had a daughter, Phyllis Mary, who was baptised on the 16th of June 1918. Leonard never saw his daughter. He was posted from the N.Z. Engineers to the newly formed N.Z. Entrenching Battalion, a unit generally disliked by most who served in it. He managed to be transferred to the 1st Wellington Battalion in July 1918. He was killed by machine gun fire on the 31st of August 1918, aged 23.

As a footnote, one of Leonard's friends, Sapper John Francis married Kitty's sister – Miss Emily Edith Langridge on the 14th of November 1917. John survived the war. He and Emily eventually embarked for Hamilton in New Zealand with their daughter Kathleen Joan in 1919.

Sapper Thomas Tester, the Gallipoli and Flers-Courcelette veteran, who had taken part in two trench raids at Armentières, was killed by machine gun fire on the 18th of June 1917. His wife Freda most probably received the telegram advising her of Thomas's death the week of their first wedding anniversary, which fell on the 24th of June. No children are recorded from the marriage. In 1923 Freda signed for Thomas's war medals. She had not remarried.

As well as the marriages, there were also instances of bigamy. One was when Mrs Edith Staples married Driver James Kelly, a Gallipoli veteran who was at Christchurch recovering from illness contracted in France. They were married at the Southampton Registry Office in November 1917, the only problem being that she was already married to an English Royal Engineer, Driver Henry Staples. She had married Staples at the

Christchurch Registry Office the previous March. He was still very much alive, despite rumours of his death and was serving in France. Edith received three months hard labour at Winchester jail.

After she was released from Winchester; she and Kelly remained in contact. Kelly's discipline declined in the months following her release from Winchester jail. His absence from parades became more regular and on one occasion he was absent for several days. It soon became a problem for Staff Sergeant Frank Appleby, who was in charge of all the drivers at the NZE Reserve Depot. Both men were Gallipoli men and had served together in France, so they would have known each other quite well; but Frank Appleby could not ignore the breach of discipline forever.

Eventually Kelly was transferred back to the 1st Field Company in France and did not return to the Britain until early 1919. Upon his return he found a job as a blacksmith in the Christchurch area and was discharged from the NZEF. He moved back into Edith's house where they lived together until his death in 1932. Edith continued to visit his grave, often taking her grand daughter Marlene to help lay flowers on his grave. He was remembered by Edith's children as a kind and caring man.

One of the mourners at his funeral may have been another of his old acquaintances from his Gallipoli days; Sergeant Ellis Wrigley. Wrigley was living in Highcliffe, Hampshire about 5 miles from Christchurch and had been medically discharged in the UK back in 1917. Presumably he and Kelly had met several times since the end of the war to reminisce and commemorate Anzac Day.

Wrigley, an ex-professional rugby player, died in 1936 and is buried at St Mark's in Highcliffe.

The wedding of Kitty Langridge to Sapper Leonard Maisey NZE at All Saints, Southbourne in July 1917. The bestman is Sapper Iuan Funnell NZE. Leonard was killed a year later while serving with 1st Battalion Wellington Regiment in France. He left behind a young widow and daughter Phylis who he had never seen. One of Kitty's sisters, Emily Edith Landridge, who is standing second from the left beside the boy, married Sapper John Francis NZE, another New Zealand Engineer, in November 1917. They lived in Hamilton, New Zealand.

Photo courtesy of Mr Keith Bennett

Chapter Thirty-Nine: The German Offensive Spring 1918

At the beginning of March 1918, the N.Z. Division was in the Ypres sector. In addition to their front line responsibilities, the Engineers and Pioneers were employed in building a new defensive line in the rear areas, assisted by a half company of the 6th Siege RE Mechanical Engineers (REME). Rumours were circulating of a major German offensive brewing in the Somme sector.

These were taken seriously, particularly as the Royal Engineers' Store was issuing around 170 tons of material daily for the various defensive works. Soon infantry work gangs of up to 450 men were assisting each Field Company with building tasks and on the 19th of March the Germans shelled the rear area to disrupt progress. Two days later the N.Z. Division was put on notice to move and the 6th Siege REME were left to continue the work. The long awaited German Spring Offensive had begun on a fifty mile front in the Somme area and a continuous line of defence was impossible to establish as the German advance had not yet been checked.

The N.Z. Division, along with the Australian Corps, entrained for the St Roche area near Amiens. Their orders were to plug the hole that had developed between the British 3rd and 5th Armies following the early successes of Ludendorff's storm troopers. A mile wide gap had been opened up between the retreating British Armies, which the Germans were taking advantage of.

With the railway lines east of Amiens cut by bombs, the New Zealand troops detrained and began a 25 mile[284] march with full packs to their new defensive line being established north of Albert near Mailly-Maillet and Colinscamp. The N.Z. Field Engineers and the N.Z. Maori (Pioneer) Battalion arrived at the village of Pont Noyelles exhausted in the early hours of the 26th of March.

The N.Z. Division was assigned two urgent tasks, the first to check the German advance through the gap between the British Armies; which the

N.Z. Rifle Brigade succeeded in doing. The next was to close the gap and link up with 4th Australian Division on their left. They did this with a composite brigade led by Lieutenant Colonel A.E. Stewart.

The Engineers and Pioneers had already begun constructing a series of mutually supporting strong points, referred to as defence line posts, each able to contain 40 men and six machine guns. These were revetted and duck boarded. Drainage and wire entanglements were also completed[285]. The infantry made further improvements once they occupied them. Eventually, by working day and night, the Engineers and Pioneers managed to complete sixty of these posts within just five days.

With an acute shortage of engineering stores, all Royal Engineers' stores dumps in the vicinity were scoured for suitable supplies. The store located at Colinscamp was a virtual Aladdin's cave containing such engineering treasures as: 35,000 sandbags, 5,000 screw pickets and 5,000 angle iron pickets amongst other essential stores for defensive works.

Once the N.Z. Infantry Brigades had linked up with the Australians and closed the gap, the Engineers and Pioneers began to connect the strong points to form a continuous defensive line. To achieve this given the volatile situation, they changed the trench design.

Instead of the right angle traverses in the standard saw-tooth design, they used oblique angles. This allowed an extra 30 percent of trench to be dug in the same amount of time. Given the urgency of the situation, these were constructed to a depth sufficient to fire from, but would need further deepening and improvement at a later stage. The trench width was also increased in the belief that advancing German tanks would find the greater width more of an obstacle.

The effectiveness of the wider trench was never tested. Judging from the successes of the British tanks in crossing the German trenches later in 1918, it was highly doubtful that this new design would have actually stopped a tank.

The N.Z. Divisional area was divided into sectors and each sector was assigned its own Field Company[286] with Pioneers to support them as needed. Stores dumps were established and in the early days the supply of war materials arriving from Amiens was meagre. This was improved once more men were allocated to road repairs.

The next task was to locate sites for deep dugouts and commence construction. Then the Engineers earmarked objects for demolition should there be a need to delay further German advances. It was important to deprive the enemy use of road networks, water wells, buildings, bridges and vital railway lines.

Water wells for suitable drinking water were investigated including the local caves, roads were repaired and drained and the gas proofing of all dugouts got underway once sufficient supplies arrived. Artillery positions were prepared using heavy timber platforms to prevent the guns sinking into and then becoming bogged down in the mud as had happened during the Passchendaele offensive. The N.Z. Maori (Pioneer) Battalion managed to erect from 4,000 to 6,000 yards of barbed wire entanglements daily and these obstacles significantly strengthened the NZ Division's defences.

So much wire was laid, that it prompted a British officer to ask one of the Maori Pioneers why they were putting up so much wire. The alleged answer was to stop the Tommy soldiers from running away, which did not amuse the British officer.

Despite repeated German attacks, the new defensive line held and by mid April the N.Z. Division was moved to the Hébuterne sector where they relieved the 42nd Division. The Engineers soon commenced work on constructing more deep dugouts for brigade and battalion headquarters, building bath houses and drying areas and providing drinking water and water troughs for horses, while the Pioneers started their usual tasks of wiring, burying telephone cables, repairing the roads and trenches across the new sector.

With the Germans having using vast quantities of mustard gas during their assault in late April in the Armentières area, the construction of more deep dugouts became a priority. Troops from the 179th Tunnelling Company were attached to the N.Z. Division to help with construction. This work continued into May as a shortage of mining frames slowed the work down. Despite these delays, one hundred and twenty-two deep dugouts managed to be constructed in the N.Z. Divisional area, of which four would be used as machine gun posts.

In June, two N.Z. Tunnelling Company officers: Lieutenants Ronayne and Leeds, were attached to provide further assistance in constructing more deep dugouts.

June also saw the arrival of American soldiers on the frontline. Two U.S. Engineer officers: Captain Simmonds and Captain Crawford along with several senior American NCOs were attached to the New Zealand Engineers for instruction. The Americans had entered the war in April 1917 and their commander General Pershing had to overcome three initial problems: lack of experienced Staff Officers, shortages of equipment and better training for his men.

The approach adopted by the American commander was to assign officers and senior NCOs to the various divisions already serving on the frontline, such as the N.Z. Division. This was a sensible approach and allowed the Americans to gain much needed experience as well as become familiar with, and develop cooperation amongst, their new Allies.

Chapter Forty: The Final Act

On the 7th of June 1918 the N.Z. Division was relieved by the 42nd Division and the N.Z. Engineers moved to Pas en Artois while the N.Z. Pioneers went to Coigneax. At Pas en Artois, American Army Officers and NCOs continued to be attached to the Engineers for instruction. The Engineers also received extra training in bridging, demolitions and the gas-proofing of dugouts. Training continued throughout that summer whenever the Engineers were out of the front line or in rest areas.

Most of this training was aimed at ensuring that their skill levels were maintained, new techniques were properly taught so that the reinforcements possessed the correct degree of training for the tasks ahead. An example[287] of a typical training schedule from June 1918 is below and highlights those skills considered essential, especially musketry.

Monday	8:00 to 9:00	Inspection of equipment, clothing
	9:00 to 10:00	Infantry Training
	10:15 to 11:15	Saluting
	11:15 to 12:00	Bombs and
	& 1:00 to 2:00	Bomb Throwing
	Afternoon	Cricket Match
		Lecture: Deep Dugouts
Tuesday	8:00 to 8:15	Inspection
	8:15 to 9:00	Lecture on Musketry
	9:00 to 12:00	Musket Training
	& 1:00 to 2:00	Musket Training
	Afternoon	Cricket or Rugby
		Lecture: Lewis Gun
Wednesday	8:00 to 8:15	Inspection
	8:15 to 9:00	Musket Training
	9:00 to 12:00	Map Reading
	1:00 to 2:00	Cricket or Football
		Lecture: Deep Dugouts

Thursday	8:00 to 8:15	Inspection
	8:15 to 10:15	Infantry Training
	10:30 to 12:00	Lecture: Working Parties & Tasks,
	& 1:00 to 2:00	Tracing out works and Distributing
		Work Parties
	Afternoon	Cricket or Football
		Lecture: Gas
Friday	8:00 until	Musketry on Rifle range
	complete	Grouping Practice
		Application practice
		Snap practice
		Rapid firing
Saturday	8:00 to 8:15	Inspection
	8:15 to 9:15	Infantry Training
	9:30 to 12:00	Lecture: Revetting, Wiring, Draining, etc
Sunday	10:00	Church Parade

By now, the battlefield emphasis was beginning to move away from the old style static trench warfare and towards a more mobile warfare, influenced by the battlefield deployment of the tank and the arrival in the field of General Pershing's American Army of approximately one million men.

By the 5th of August, the N.Z. Division was back in the field, supported by American Field Engineers from the 2nd Battalion 305th Regiment working under the command of the New Zealanders. The Americans were often involved in reconstructing trenches, clearing avenues for machine gun fire and making revetting hurdles from the scrub that had been cut away.

Although rumours of peace talks abounded, the fighting was not over. Under the new open warfare tactics, where several miles of ground could be captured in a single day, the emphasis moved to constructing strong points that could sustain bombardments, gas attacks and infantry assaults. For the rest of the time trench construction became a rough, shallow affair with the infantry sometimes occupying captured German trenches or deep dugouts for a day or two before moving off again, as the advance resumed. Only the reserve areas continued to have properly constructed trenches, deep dugouts, and pill boxes that could sustain a direct attack from German tanks.

As the N.Z. Division's advance continued through France, the labyrinth of static trench systems were left far behind and the Engineers' efforts were quickly switched to: bridge building, pontooning, road repairs, construction of water points, the creation and then camouflaging of stores dumps. All this became crucial in sustaining the forward momentum of the Allied offensive. The Engineers were also attached to the infantry during assaults to help the infantry entrench, construct strong points, reconnoitre for wells and assess the usability of the bridges and road networks in the area captured.

During the action near Puisieux au Mont, on the 21st of August 1918 Lance Corporal Bert Tuck was killed by machine gun fire while undertaking a reconnaissance of the roads in the area just captured. He was in charge of three other sappers, all of whom managed to get clear. He was the longest serving members of 1st Field Company and the next day after the Germans had been cleared from the area, his friends recovered his body and buried him, setting a proper wooden cross on his grave. Later the men of his section wrote a letter to his mother, expressing their sincere sympathies at her loss.

The Allied advance continued, and from the 5th of August until the 4th of November 1918 the N.Z. Division advanced over sixty miles though towns and villages such as: Bapaume, Bertincourt, Metz, Lesdain, Beauvois and Viesly. Aware of their pursuers, the Germans destroyed road junctions and bridges. The N.Z. Engineers became proficient at building new bridges or temporary roads to by-pass obstructions. At Selle they constructed a road bridge in thirteen hours while under constant artillery fire. The next day they built a heavy traffic bridge alongside the first bridge in fifteen hours which allowed heavy tanks to pass over and sustain the offensive.

Demolition charges were removed from bridges and the Engineers were often busy late into the evening helping to site and then assisting the Infantry in the digging of trench positions, constructing shelters and gas proofing them as German artillery bombardments became concentrated. Numerous booby traps were encountered during this period as the N.Z. Division passed through the French towns recently vacated by the Germans. Souvenirs were highly sought after by the soldiers, so books on tables, bayonets, badges and helmets could be rigged with pull wires attached to explosive charges. Entrances to dugouts and doorways to buildings or shelters were equally dangerous for the same reason.

On the 28th of October the N.Z. Field Engineers and the N.Z. Maori (Pioneers) were busy building footbridges, semi permanent traffic bridges, dismantling trestle bridges, erecting sign posts, gas proofing and creating store dumps, prior to the assault of Le Quesnoy planned for the 4th of November. This was the last major action for the N.Z. Division in the Great War and saw the New Zealanders take the ancient town and push on to Herbignies on the outskirts of the Foret de Mormal. This area was a major communications route and used by the Germans as one of their main lines of retreat, so its capture was strategically important.

On the 11th of November 1918 the Armistice was declared and the fighting stopped.

On that same day the N.Z. Division left the front line at Le Quesnoy and marched back towards Beauvois, where Divisional Baths were provided and the men underwent a period of rest and training. On the 13th of November the New Zealand Division's commander, Major-General Sir A. H. Russell, announced that the N.Z. Division was to form part of the Allied Army of Occupation of Germany.

On the 28th of November the N.Z. Division, accompanied by the 37th Division, began its long march towards Germany. Because most of the railway bridges had been destroyed, thereby disrupting any possible movement by rail, the first one hundred and seventy miles would be covered on foot. It rained almost continuously that week and the only relief along the route was at night when they were billeted in civilian houses. This gave them a chance to get warm and dry.

Boots soon wore out on the French and Belgium cobbled roads and to ease the men's burden, their greatcoats and steel helmets were left at Montignies-sur-Sambre along the route. Eventually on the 20th of December the German border town of Herbesthal was reached. Here they entrained for the final sixty miles of the journey to Cologne. After crossing the River Rhine they marched to Mulheim, where they joined the Allied Army of Occupation.

Their role was to guard German war material and factories. In addition, they practiced occupying defensive positions around bridgeheads, factories, railway stations, and vital public buildings in case of civil disturbances. River excursions and visits to the centre of Cologne were organised, where men often took photographs of each other on the steps of Cologne Cathedral.

Within three weeks of arriving at Cologne, the first drafts began to be withdrawn back to England for embarkation to New Zealand. This gradually accelerated and by the end of March 1919 the New Zealand Division had left the Western Front.

The final act for the New Zealanders in Europe occurred towards the end of 1919 and involved General Sir Ian Hamilton who had commanded the Mediterranean Expeditionary Force on Gallipoli. He had just crossed the German frontier and was waiting on the railway station at Düren, near Cologne. It was November 1919 and there amongst the crowd on the railway platform he recognised the letters N.Z.M.R (New Zealand Mounted Rifles) on the shoulder straps of an officer. He had not seen those regimental letters since Gallipoli. The wearer was Lieutenant Colonel John Studholme, who had served on Gallipoli and he recognised Hamilton. The circle was complete. Hamilton had launched the New Zealanders into their first major campaign of the Great War and now he bid farewell to Studholme, the last member of the NZEF to leave the European theatre of war.

The NZEF's involvement in the Great War had ended.

New Zealand Expeditionary Force as part of the Triumphal March of Overseas Troops marching past Buckingham Place on 3rd May, 1919

Photo courtesy of Alexander Turnbull Library, Wellington, New Zealand and *Royal NZ RSA Collection. Reference Number: 1/2- 014232-G*

Chapter Forty-One: Returning Home

With the cessation of hostilities on the 11th of November 1918, the NZEF confronted other problems, these being to dismantle their infrastructure in France, Egypt and England and to return all the men back to New Zealand.

By January 1919, men began to return from Germany and these drafts were housed at Brocton, Sling and Larkhill. The Maoris had marched out from NZE Reserve Depot Christchurch to their new Depot at Larkhill, from where they returned to New Zealand in January 1919, via the port of Liverpool. The camps were reorganized for demobilization and the men categorised according to length of service and the provincial area in New Zealand where they would disembark. After months of waiting, they would be sent to one of the various British ports for embarkation and home. Difficulties in arranging shipping back to New Zealand caused delays and frustration amongst the long serving men keen to return home.

The amount of military training undertaken in the camps was gradually reduced and the emphasis was on ensuring that the men remain healthy and smart. So "spit and polish" routines and route marches continued, while educational classes replaced field training and helped to prepare the men for a return to civilian life.

Several of the British camps experienced breakdowns in military discipline, with men refusing to parade. When meals were stopped riots erupted and food stolen. The men's mocking chant was "Lies, Damned Lies, Demobi-lies"[288]

The slow pace of demobilisation caused resentment and at Sling, the repetitious activities eventually caused disruptions. Parades held at 0900 hours and 1330 hours were ignored by many soldiers. This resulted in forfeiture of pay and men being "Confined to Barracks". Still, they could not lock the whole camp up. Eventually attempts were made to ease the tension, although the men were still restless as they wanted to go home.

The carving of the Bulford Kiwi in the chalk hills overlooking their camp was one remedy. This was no minor feat. Sergeant-Major P.C. Blenkarne of the N.Z. Education Corps made the drawing of the Kiwi. This was then plotted out on the hillside and digging to expose the chalky soil began. When completed, the Kiwi was 420 feet long, its beak being 50 feet and the adjoining letters "NZ" were 65 feet high. Altogether it covered an acre and a half of the hillside.

On the 3rd of May a large contingent of New Zealand troops participated in the Triumphal March by Overseas troops through the streets of London and past Buckingham Palace.

The N.Z. Rifle Brigade[289] held its final parade at Stafford on the 10th of May 1919. As a farewell gesture to the people of Stafford, Lieutenant Colonel Shepherd presented a New Zealand flag to the Mayor. In return the town presented to the N.Z. Rifle Brigade the Union flag and a New Zealand flag. Both were in silk. They also presented the N.Z. Rifle Brigade with a musketry challenge-shield, in sterling silver.

On the 14th of June, the remaining troops left Brocton for Codford Camp, where they joined around 3,000 New Zealand troops awaiting embarkation. By this time there were an estimated 70,000 Australian troops still at Bulford and Tidworth also awaiting transport home. A common sense attitude seemed to have prevailed from June 1919 onwards, especially as the congestion eased, although it was not until October 1919 that the last New Zealand troops finally left for home.

N.Z. Headquarters in London instructed the NZE Reserve Depot to undertake all constructional and repair work in connection with the hospitals and various other buildings occupied by the New Zealanders in England. They also constructed and erected crosses for all New Zealand graves in the UK.

The local villages at Brockenhurst recount the story of when the N.Z. Engineers were dismantling the hospital at Tin Town. As a cricket pavilion was needed for the local village cricket team, one of the hospital buildings was dismantled and then reassembled on the cricket ground, to the delight of the local villagers. Similarly, the Kia Ora NZYMCA Hut in Brockenhurst located near the railway station was not dismantled. It was instead given to the local Free Masons as their Masonic Lodge[290]. It remained there until January 2005 when the land was sold and the Lodge was demolished. A housing development now occupies the site - which is called "Silver Fern".

The last public appearance of the New Zealand Engineers was as the Guard of Honour for her Royal Highness, Princess Beatrice at the opening of the new Bournemouth Art Gallery where Brigadier General Richardson presented the Mayor of Bournemouth with a New Zealand flag and asked that this be placed in some public institution. The New Zealanders were known for their good conduct and the N.Z. Band had almost become a local institution. The NZE Reserve Depot eventually closed on the 20th of June 1919 and with the town of Bournemouth's best wishes the New Zealanders left for Torquay and then home.

During the time at Christchurch two New Zealand deaths were recorded. The first was Sapper C. Febey from the N.Z. Tunnelling Company who was killed in a training accident. He was buried with full military honours in Boscombe Cemetery on the 15th of February 1918. On the 14th of May 1918 the body of Private Tuheke Matenga of the N.Z. Maori (Pioneer) Battalion was found floating in the River Stour, at the back of the summer camp area. He was buried with full military honours at St Nicholas's Churchyard at Brockenhurst amongst the other New Zealander soldiers who had died throughout the war at N.Z. No1 General Hospital located at Brockenhurst.

There was a general criticism voiced that the new men arriving in France from the NZE Depot never showed the same grit and those men trained in harder schools, such as Egypt and Brightlingsea.[291] This opinion suggested that the location possibly offered too many distractions. This was generally true as there was regular leave to various lively towns like Bournemouth, Southampton and Poole. Lance Corporal Williamson definitely thought that it was the best camp in England and "the best holiday" he had ever had.

To create some perspective, the original 1ˢᵗ Field Company and the Mounted Troop (later 3ʳᵈ Field Company) were originally trained as Infantry or horse Mounted Infantry. Their NCOs were promoted based upon experience, long service and their ability to lead men. Gallipoli had moulded these men from enthusiastic civilians into hardened, battlefield savvy soldiers.

This process could not be repeated at Christchurch, where the training was influenced by British Army regulations, probably more so than at Brightlingsea. This is evident by the number of veterans charged for breach of discipline while at the NZE Reserve Depot. It should also be remembered that the men trained with war materials that were out-dated and of insufficient quantity. Therefore, exercises were always going to be limited in their scale and never able to replicate the conditions experienced on the Western Front. Field craft, gas drills and infantry skills were not prominent in the training schedule, often being replaced by extra instruction in other subjects such as pontooning or the construction of deep dugouts.

Advancement in rank was through trade qualifications or instructor courses passed, not battlefield experience. Corporal Bert Tuck who was at the NZE Reserve Depot during his 'tour of duty' rotation in 1917 felt that many of the NCOs there were naïve and lacked the necessary mental maturity. He believed they were all in for a rude awakening when they joined the Field Engineers in France and that some were only there because they had been conscripted.

Of the new men who joined the N.Z. Engineers in France after 1917 only three managed to receive official recognition for gallantry. One was awarded a Croix de Guerre and two received MIDs (Mentioned in Despatches). This amounts to 2% of all New Zealand Field Engineers decorated throughout the war. Possibly this was because the opportunity for gallantry did not exist while repairing roads, building bridges or working in divisional rear areas. Although they may not have displayed the same grit, their training was of a high standard. The Advanced Training School created by Major Keenan along with the practice of rotating experienced men between France and the NZE Reserve Depot would have had a positive effect in passing on practical skills. It should also be noted that unlike the British Field Engineers, the New Zealanders had to complete their entire training course before being considered for a draft to France. This resulted in only fully trained Field Engineers ever being sent to the N.Z. Division. The training provided by Colonel Keen RE., Major Keenan and Lieutenant Colonel Barclay at Christchurch was of the highest standard and helped the N.Z. Division to achieve the feats at arms proudly displayed today on each of the various Infantry battalions' Regimental Colours.

The NZEF returned to the south coast of England twenty-one years later at the start of World War Two. A New Zealand Artillery company was formed in England in 1939 and they encamped in the Christchurch area, near to Highcliffe Castle. In 1940, they provided a twenty-one gun salute with their 25 Pounders to King George VI at the nearby town of New Milton, before leaving to join the 2nd NZEF that had recently arrived in Essex. The 2nd NZEF had been sent to England to defend the South Coast against the threatened German invasion.

New Milton was the venue for another notable New Zealand event at the end of World War Two, when Captain Charles Upham VC and bar, married Miss Mary (Molly) Eileen McTamney at the New Milton Catholic Church. Upham was the most highly decorated New Zealander of the Second World War.

Major Hargest, who married Sister Wilkie at the Christchurch Priory in September 1917, also returned to England during World War Two. In the inter war years he had become a prominent local N.Z. politician and served as a Brigadier with the N.Z. Division before being captured in Libya. He escaped from a POW Camp in Italy and managed to arrive in Switzerland from where he was repatriated to England. He wrote "Farewell Campo 12" about his experiences as a POW and his escape. In England he was attached as an observer to the 50th Division during D-Day. He was killed by German mortar fire in August 1944. His son Geoffrey had been killed earlier in the year while serving with the N.Z. Division at Monte Cassino in Italy.

Appendix One: No.1 Field Company, New Zealand Engineers (April 1915)

This is not an official NZEF Nominal Roll. It has been compiled by the author through research from diaries, books and other records. It may contain some inaccuracies. There are 197 names contained in this list many of whom fought at Gallipoli.

Original Unit	Regimental Number	Surname	Christian Name	Known Rank
Royal Engineers	British Loan Officer	PRIDHAM	GR	Lieutenant-Colonel
Royal Engineers	British Loan Officer	FERGUSION	SA	Captain
Royal Engineers	British Loan Officer	McNEILL	AG	Captain
British Section	4 642 a	SIMSON	Donald	Captain
NZ Engineers	4 448	WAITE	Frederick	Captain
British Section	4 194 a	SKELSEY	Frederick Walter	Lieutenant
Royal Engineers	British Loan Officer	BUTLER, the Honorary	Robert Thomas Rowley Probyn	Second Lieutenant
British Section	4 28 a	NEWBOULD	Maurice George Robert	Second Lieutenant
Mounted Troop	4 429	PAINE	Sydney William	Second Lieutenant

British Section	4	15	a	FREIDLANDER	Otto Albert	Sergeant
British Section	4	75	a	JONES	William Meirion	Sergeant, HQ Section
British Section	4	112	a	MASTERS	George	Sergeant
British Section	4	115	a	NEWMAN	Horace William	Sergeant
British Section	4	22	a	ROSS	Daniel Angus	Sergeant IC Horse Lines
British Section	4	1	a	ABBOTT	William Warrener	Sergeant
British Section	4	72	a	WALLACE	Alan	Sergeant
2nd Reinforcement ex Wellington Infantry Regiment	4	1356	a	TURNER	Ernest Charles	Sergeant
British Section	4	143	a	WRIGLEY	Ellis	Corporal, Driver
British Section	4	85	a	ABBEY	Alexander William	Corporal
British Section	4	188	a	FEAR	Francis John Herbert	Corporal
British Section	4	40	a	FYSON	Albert Kernball	Corporal

British Section	4	a	KILBRIDE	John Kelvin	Corporal
British Section	4	a	SAUNDERS	Charles William	Corporal
2nd Reinforcement ex Wellington Infantry Regiment	4	a	CONNERY	John	Second Corporal
British Section	4	a	CRIPPS	John Southern	Second Corporal
2nd Reinforcement ex Auckland Infantry Regiment	4	a	McLAUGHLIN	William George James	Second Corporal
Main Body ex Wellington Mounted Rifles	11	a	JOLL	Bruce Langdon	Lance Corporal
British Section	4	a	O'BRIEN	Martin	Lance Corporal
Main Body ex Auckland Infantry Regiment	4	a	HALL	Lionel William Baird	Lance Corporal
British Section	4	a	SNODGRASS	John Graham	Lance Corporal
British Section	4	a	THOMAS	Acland Withiel	Lance Corporal
British Section	4	a	WOODHALL	John	Lance Corporal
Main Body ex Otago Infantry Regiment	4	b	KELLY	James	Driver

2nd Reinforcement ex Auckland Infantry Regiment	4	1516	a	TESTER	Thomas Launcelot	Driver
2nd Reinforcement ex Otago Infantry Regiment	4	1297	a	McCOLL	Donald Alexander	Driver
2nd Reinforcement ex Canterbury Infantry Regiment	4	1369	a	PALMER	Leonard James	Driver
2nd Reinforcement ex Otago Infantry Regiment	4	1382	a	PICKERING	Charles Augustus	Driver
British Section	4	171	a	SULLIVAN	William David	Driver
British Section	4	222	b	VICKERS	Frank Henry	Driver
British Section	4	74	a	GLASSE	Alfred Onslow	Sapper
2nd Reinforcement ex Auckland Infantry Regiment	4	1137	a	ALCOCK	William	Sapper
2nd Reinforcement ex Auckland Infantry Regiment	4	1139	a	ALLEN	Lawrence	Sapper
2nd Reinforcement ex Auckland Infantry Regiment	4	1325	a	ARNELL	Robert Anderson	Sapper
British Section	4	4	a	ASTLEY	Eric Henry	Sapper
British Section	4	87	a	ATKINSON	Theodore	Sapper

Unit		Number	a/b	Surname	Name	Rank
British Section	4	90	b	BANKS	Harold Kirby	Sapper
2nd Reinforcement ex Canterbury Infantry Regiment	4	597	a	BARKER	Ernest Christopher	Sapper
2nd Reinforcement ex Canterbury Infantry Regiment	4	1238	a	BARRIE	Charles Seymour	Sapper
2nd Reinforcement ex Otago Infantry Regiment	4	1189	b	BARTLETT	George Roach	Sapper
British Section	4	220	a	BATHAM	Guy Symonds Meacham	Sapper
British Section	4	35	a	BEAMISH	Richard	Sapper
2nd Reinforcement ex Auckland Infantry Regiment	4	1146	a	BEDLINGTON	Roy Percy	Sapper
British Section	4	91	a	BELLINGHAM	Arthur	Sapper
2nd Reinforcement ex Auckland Infantry Regiment	4	1152	a	BLAKER	Charles Major	Sapper
British Section	4	84	a	BLEW	Kennersley	Sapper
British Section	4	150	a	BLO(O)MFIELD	Edwin Hoffman	Sapper
British Section	4	207	a	BONSOR	Eugene Alfred	Sapper

2nd Reinforcement ex Auckland Infantry Regiment	4	1157	a	BOWLES	Edward	Sapper
2nd Reinforcement ex Wellington Infantry Regiment	4	1188	a	BRICKELL	Ernest Burnett	Sapper
2nd Reinforcement ex Auckland Infantry Regiment	4	1159	a	BRIDGE	Sidney William	Sapper
2nd Reinforcement ex Wellington Infantry Regiment	4	1189	a	BRIDGEWATER	Frederick James	Sapper
British Section	4	88	a	BURFORD	Herbert	Sapper
British Section	4	49	a	BURTON	Frank	Sapper
Main Body ex Otago Infantry Regiment	4	168	a	BUSBRIDGE	William Joseph	Sapper
2nd Reinforcement ex Wellington Infantry Regiment	4	1198	a	CAIRD	John	Sapper
2nd Reinforcement ex Auckland Infantry Regiment	4	1166	a	CAMERON	Frederick Thomas	Sapper
2nd Reinforcement ex Canterbury Infantry Regiment	4	1255	a	CAMPBELL	Harold Wesley	Sapper
British Section	4	152	a	CARGILL	William Walter	Sapper
2nd Reinforcement ex Otago Infantry Regiment	4	911	a	CARLYON	Samuel	Sapper

Surname	Forename		Number		Unit	Rank
CHAPMAN	George	10	1205		2nd Reinforcement ex Wellington Infantry Regiment	Sapper
CHENNELLES	Eric John	4	228	a	British Section	Sapper
CLIFTON	Ernest Charles	4	1210		2nd Reinforcement ex Wellington Infantry Regiment	Sapper
CODLING	Thomas	6	1074	a	Main Body ex Canterbury Infantry Regiment	Sapper
COLLINS	Robert Walter	6	1267		2nd Reinforcement ex Canterbury Infantry Regiment	Sapper
COOKE	Thomas Purdy	4	37	a	British Section	Sapper
COOKSLEY	Bertie Victor	4	1086	a	2nd Reinforcement	Sapper
CORBETT	Joseph	4	198	a	British Section	Sapper
CORNELIUS	Archibald	4	189	a	British Section	Sapper
COSGRAVE	Norman	4	1179	a	2nd Reinforcement ex Auckland Infantry Regiment	Sapper
COTTON-STAPLETON	George C	4	213	a	British Section	Sapper
CRAWFORD	Sidney Black	4	92	a	British Section	Sapper

Main Body ex Auckland Infantry Regiment	4	b	DE MONTALK	Alexander Stanilas	Sapper
British Section	4	a	DENNAN	William Francis	Sapper
British Section	4	a	DRAPER	Thomas	Sapper
British Section	4	a	DRYSDALE	Thomas John Hirst	Sapper
2nd Reinforcement ex Wellington Infantry Regiment	4	a	DUGGAN	John	Sapper
British Section	4	a	ELKINGTON	Archibald Gordon	Sapper
2nd Reinforcement ex Auckland Infantry Regiment	4	a	ELLIS (Ellice)	Peter	Sapper
British Section	4	a	ELSOM	Charles Henry	Sapper
British Section	4	a	FAIR	Charles Patrick	Sapper
British Section	4	a	FARRER	Thomas Culling	Sapper
British Section	4	a	FIELD	Henry George	Sapper
2nd Reinforcement ex Wellington Infantry Regiment	4	a	FINN	James	Sapper
Main Body ex Canterbury Infantry Regiment	4	a	FISCHER	Albert George	Sapper

FOOTE	4	41	a	Harry Arthur	Sapper	British Section
FORBES	6	1284		John Henry	Sapper	2nd Reinforcement ex Canterbury Infantry Regiment
FOSTER aka Facer	4	27	a	Frederick Charles	Sapper	British Section
FOX	4	99	a	John Ignatius	Sapper	British Section
FOX	4	155	a	Humphrey	Sapper	British Section
FRASER	4	1287	a	William	Sapper	2nd Reinforcement
FROST	4	196	a	Cyril de Beaupre	Sapper	British Section
GIBBS	10	1241	a	Percival Francis	Sapper	2nd Reinforcement ex Wellington Infantry Regiment
GILES	4	214	a	William Joseph	Sapper	British Section
GOODMAN	4	1419	a	Garnet Granville	Sapper	2nd Reinforcement ex Auckland Infantry Regiment
GORDON	4	98	a	James A	Sapper	British Section
GOSSET	4	19	a	Charlwood Henry	Sapper	British Section
GORTON	4	212	b	Edward St George	Sapper	British Section

Unit/Section	No.	ID		Surname	Forename	Rank
British Section	4	18	a	GREEN	Albert	Sapper
2nd Reinforcement ex Wellington Infantry Regiment	4	1247	a	HALIBURTON	Borthwick	Sapper
British Section	4	103	a	HAMILTON	James William	Sapper
2nd Reinforcement ex Canterbury Infantry Regiment	4	1306	a	HANCOCK	William	Sapper
2nd Reinforcement ex Wellington Infantry Regiment	4	1249	a	HARDYMENT	Albert James	Sapper
2nd Reinforcement ex Canterbury Infantry Regiment	4	1307	a	HARLAND	John William	Sapper, HQ Section
2nd Reinforcement ex Auckland Infantry Regiment	4	1426	a	HAYNES	Arthur	Sapper
British Section	4	107	a	HELM	Herbert Walter	Sapper
British Section	4	158	a	HEWLETT	Claude Stephen	Sapper
Samoa Advance and 2nd Reinforcement ex Canterbury Infantry Regiment	4 6	112 1440		HUTCHINS	Albert Richard	Sapper
British Section	4	203	a	HODGES	Edgar Arthur	Sapper
British Section	4	162	a	HODGSON	Francis Joseph	Sapper

British Section	4	217	a	HOLT	John	Sapper
Main Body ex Auckland Infantry Regiment	4	56	a	HOPKINS	Richard	Sapper
British Section	4	83	a	HULBERT	Walter	Sapper
2nd Reinforcement ex Auckland Infantry Regiment	12	1439	a	HUNT	Bert	Sapper
British Section	4	43	a	HURLBUTT	Patrick Edward	Sapper
2nd Reinforcement ex Canterbury Infantry Regiment	4	1322	a	INGLIS	Archibald	Sapper
British Section	4	205	a	JAMESON	Alfred Barrett	Sapper
2nd Reinforcement ex Otago Infantry Regiment	4	1373	a	JONES	George	Sapper
Main Body ex Otago Infantry Regiment	4	58	a	KEATING	John Dudley	Sapper
British Section	4	191	a	KENNEDY	William Alexander	Sapper
British Section	4	218	a	LINDSAY	Alan Crawford	Sapper
British Section	4	46	a	LOW (originally as LOWE)	Norman Kwongtsu T.	Sapper

2nd Reinforcement ex Wellington Infantry Regiment	4	1284	a	MANEY	Vivian Richard	Sapper
British Section	4	145	a	MANNING	Henry John	Sapper
British Section	4	219	a	MANNING	Frank Victor	Sapper
British Section	4	192	a	MATTHEWS	William John	Sapper
Main Body ex Otago Infantry Regiment	4	424	a	McDONALD	Malcolm	Sapper
2nd Reinforcement ex Otago Infantry Regiment	4	1298	a	McGREGOR	Duncan	Sapper
2nd Reinforcement ex Wellington Infantry Regiment	4	1300	b	McKAY	John	Sapper
2nd Reinforcement ex Otago Infantry Regiment	4	1300	a	McKENZIE	Murdock	Sapper
2nd Reinforcement ex Auckland Infantry Regiment	4	1473	a	McINTOSH	Archibald	Sapper
British Section	4	58	b	McMASTER	Alex Adair	Sapper
British Section	4	113	a	MITCHELL	William George	Sapper
2nd Reinforcement ex Canterbury Infantry Regiment	4	1339		MITCHELL	William John	Sapper

British Section	4	26	a	MOORE-JONES	Horace	Sapper
British Section	4	38	a	MORIARTY	John Ferris	Sapper
British Section	4	48	a	MUIRHEAD	Malcolm	Sapper
British Section	4	233	a	NAYLOR	Walter	Sapper
2nd Reinforcement ex Canterbury Infantry Regiment	4	1364	a	NOBBS	James	Sapper
2nd Reinforcement ex Canterbury Infantry Regiment	4	1365	a	NUTTALL	Alfred	Sapper
British Section	4	117	a	OTTERSON	Greffory David	Sapper
British Section	4	121	a	PEACE	Ernest	Sapper
2nd Reinforcement ex Otago Infantry Regiment	4	1309	a	PEARSON	Francis George	Sapper
2nd Reinforcement ex Wellington Infantry Regiment	4	1314	b	PEDDIE	Thomas Adam	Sapper
British Section	4	229	a	PERRY	Corran Masters	Sapper
2nd Reinforcement ex Wellington Infantry Regiment	10	1316		PETERS	Vincent	Sapper

Main Body ex Otago Infantry Regiment	8	271	a	QUAYLE	Angus David George	Sapper
British Section	4	123	a	RAE	Thomas	Sapper
British Section	4	125	a	RAMSAY	John Ker	Sapper
2nd Reinforcement ex Canterbury Infantry Regiment	6	1383		RAMSEY	Ernest	Sapper
British Section	4	165	a	REICHARDT	Frederick	Sapper
British Section	4	52	a	REID	Lestock Henry	Sapper
2nd Reinforcement ex Canterbury Infantry Regiment	4	1392	a	REID	Edward Herman	Sapper
British Section	4	164	a	REYNOLDS	William	Sapper
British Section	4	232	a	RIDGLEY	Thomas Angus	Sapper
British Section	4	210	a	ROBERTSON	Allan David	Sapper
British Section	4	154	a	ROONEY	Reuben Robert	Sapper
British Section	4	29	a	ROSS	Hugh MacPherson	Sapper
British Section	4	51	a	ROUNTREE aka Mountree	Edward Gilbert	Sapper

British Section	4	2	a	ROWE	Thomas Northcott	Sapper
British Section	4	124	a	RUDDOCK	Edward Oliver	Sapper
British Section	4	208	a	SALMON	Cedric Whitby	Sapper
British Section	4	226	a	SAVAGE	William	Sapper
2nd ex Canterbury Infantry Regiment	4	1399	a	SCRIMSHAW	Eric George	Sapper
2nd Reinforcement ex Wellington Infantry Regiment	10	1332		SELWYN	Philip Austin	Sapper
British Section	4	33	a	SHAW	Leslie Raymond	Sapper
British Section	4	57	a	SHAW	Robert Hetherington	Sapper
British Section	4	70	a	SHEARWOOD	George	Sapper
British Section	4	130	a	SIMMONDS	Frederick Thomas	Sapper
2nd Reinforcement ex Otago Infantry Regiment	4	1334		SKINNER	Vincent Victor	Sapper
British Section	4	131	b	SMITH	Ernest Vincent	Sapper
British Section	4	169	a	SNELGROVE	William Leonard	Sapper

Surname		No.		Unit	Forename	Rank
STOKES	a	55	4	British Section	George	Sapper
SUTHERLAND	a	53	4	British Section	Ernest	Sapper
THETFORD	a	186	4	British Section	Felix Harry	Sapper
THOMPSON	a	137	4	British Section	Albert Edward	Sapper
THURLOW	a	62	4	British Section	Reginald	Sapper
TREZISE	a	135	4	British Section	Theodore	Sapper
TUCK	a	1355	4	2nd Reinforcement ex Wellington Infantry Regiment	Herbert James	Sapper
TURNER		1356	10	2nd Reinforcement ex Wellington Infantry Regiment	Ernest Charles	Sapper
ULRICH	a	138	4	British Section	Gerhardt Adolphus Chapman	Sapper
WARBURTON	a	63	4	British Section	Piers Acton Eliot	Sapper
WHITMORE	a	144	4	British Section	Ernest Harvey	Sapper
WILLIAMS	a	193	4	British Section	Aubrey Lewis	Sapper
WILLIS	a	176	4	British Section	Thomas William Pitt	Sapper

British Section	4	141	a	WILLOTT	James	Sapper
British Section	4	178	a	WOOD	Alan Carruthers	Sapper
British Section	4	139	a	WRIGHT	Robert Henry	Sapper

Appendix Two: The New Zealand War Contingent Association

The New Zealand War Contingent Association was formed in London on the 17th of August 1914, under the chairmanship of Lord Plunket, a former Governor General to New Zealand. Its aim was the care and welfare of the New Zealand troops who were expected to arrive in England. It comprised New Zealanders living in England and those with a link to New Zealand. The Association was soon involved in a myriad of activity.

In the opening months of the war, many towns across New Zealand had organised gifts of clothing, blankets, mutton, flour, wheat, barley, cheese and eggs to be sent to England to assist in the war effort.

The sheer scale of the gifts sent from New Zealand was quite staggering. In one shipment alone there were 30,622 boxes of butter and 17,920 crates of cheese. The responsibility of just what to do with all of these goods fell to the Ladies Committee of the New Zealand War Contingent Association. This was chaired by Miss McKenzie, the High Commissioner's daughter. A portion of the clothing and blankets was distributed to the Belgian refugees and a quantity of the food went to the National Food Funds. The remainder was divided between existing charities; namely the Church Army, the Salvation Army, the Friends of the Poor and the Soldiers and Sailors Association, who distributed it to the poorer parishes in the East End of London and some provincial towns.

With the departure of the British Section and with no other New Zealand troops in England apart from those serving in British Regiments, the Association found itself conducting a long distance welfare programme for the NZEF in Egypt. The sewing committee continued to provide socks and a small post office managed thousands of letters and parcels which had been sent to England for the men. The organisation also had a branch in Scotland which helped with sewing, knitting and fund raising.

As the Gallipoli campaign intensified, more New Zealand wounded began to arrive in England. The first group arrived at Southampton from Alexandria in Egypt on the 23rd of May aboard the hospital ships 'Ghurka' and 'Delta' and were transferred onto Red Cross trains. Under the RAMC (Royal Army Medical Corps) distribution system, the wounded were labelled and sent to any hospitals that had spare capacity. Consequently, the New Zealanders arrived at various hospitals across Britain.

As there was no New Zealand Military Representative in England, the administration of these soldiers was undertaken by the New Zealand High Commissioner's staff through the Military Records Office. As the New Zealand wounded were scattered throughout the British hospital system it was difficult to know where all of them were. The Association relied upon the Military Records Office for such information, who in turn relied upon receiving some notification from the RAMC, the hospital's administration or from the soldiers. Obviously delays, oversights and mistakes were made by such a chaotic system. Once a soldier was located, the N.Z. War Association began addressing the soldier's needs and general welfare.

They arranged for each located soldier to be visited. The visits were organised by Mrs Muir from Balclutha and Mrs Scholefield from Wellington, who mobilised all available resources at their disposal. Even the New Zealand nurses serving in various London hospitals were asked by the Association to visit the men. The Association would send each soldier a small parcel containing a shaving kit, writing paper, stamps and other small personal comforts. Those men missed by this system often felt neglected, particularly when they were semi-illiterate or unable to communicate due to their wounds.

The numbers of New Zealand sick and wounded continued to arrive in England throughout June and July 1915 and the Association recognised that they could not properly cater for the large number of soldiers now in various parts of Britain. The Association decided that a New Zealand hospital was the solution. Lady Islington soon found such a location at Mount Felix, a manor house with various buildings at Walton-on-Thames, outside of London.

The Association began fund-raising to purchase the property and eventually the manor house was converted into a hospital. The surplus funds were placed into the Lord Liverpool Fund. This money, along with N.Z. Government funds, would maintain the hospital. It was officially opened by the High Commissioner on the 1st of August 1915 as "The New Zealand Military Hospital at Walton-on-Thames". In addition to the hospital facilities, the Association often arranged motor buses and river launches for the wounded to have daily excursions, away from the hospital. Items of clothing, as well as necessities such as razors, soap, shaving brushes, newspapers and cigarettes were provided free to the soldiers.

By the middle of 1916, the N.Z. Division was fighting in France and N.Z. hospitals and training depots had arrived in England from Egypt. The Association expanded its services to cope with this influx of New Zealand troops. In addition to maintaining the Walton-on-Thames hospital, they also managed the Soldiers' Canteens and the Nurses' Rest accommodation. Their most popular effort was reportedly the "Aotearoa" club at Codford. It was claimed to be the best equipped club on Salisbury Plain boasting: a library, reading and writing rooms, a games room and billiard tables. The soldiers could also buy tea, coffee and something to eat. The proceeds were then channelled back into the club. It had a staff of ten ladies to help managed it, arrange concerts and other entertainment.

For those on leave in London, the Association would sometimes meet soldiers at the railway stations, provide them with local information or even personally take them to where they needed to go, although this service seem to be absent when Lance Corporal Wilfred Smith arrived at Paddington station. He wandered around London for well over an hour until he finally asked directions and found the N.Z. Soldiers' Hostel at Russell Square. The Association did come under criticism in newspapers back in New Zealand for not doing enough for the soldiers on leave and Smith's experiences would have been a case in point.

In addition to the guides at railways stations, the Association arranged tours to places of interest, such as Hampton Court, the Zoological

Gardens and the Botanical Gardens. At night they had regular "patrols" in central areas to direct the men to suitable accommodation. There were two NZEF accommodation buildings for N.Z. soldiers on leave in London.

One was the N.Z. Soldiers' Club located along Southampton Row, off The Strand which was run by New Zealand ladies. It contained 200 beds and a canteen for light refreshments which was open all day and night. Dinner was 1 shilling[292]a night and bed, breakfast and tea were 8 pence each. The other was the New Zealand Soldiers' Hostel at 17 Russell Square. The Union Jack Club near Waterloo station was also popular, being situated close to Westminster Bridge and the River Thames.

When available, the Association distributed free theatre or concert tickets to the soldiers. These were obtained by the New Zealand actress Miss Rosemary Rees, who used her contacts throughout the theatres of London. She also provided concerts in the hospitals and Soldiers' Clubs. Yet some men still managed to get into mischief. They had a large amount of back pay, there were many public houses and prostitution was rife. Pickpockets were also a known problem for soldiers travelling on the crowded London buses.

Hospitality at country homes and private residences was also organised to help the soldiers see more of England and mix with local civilians. These encounters were popular with the soldiers, though such encounters did not always go well as Sapper Eric Miller found out. His friend had received an invitation to a local home, in which there were two young ladies. The parents were from Cornwall and their conversation was dominated by stories of smuggling and ship wrecks, while the young soldiers told of life in New Zealand. The young ladies contributed tales of the heroic feats performed by their male friends, all of whom happened to be officers serving in the Army or Naval Air Force. The New Zealanders soon tired of this and were glad to eventually leave.

As the war dragged on and food production became a national concern, the Association provided the hospital at Walton-on-Thames with vegetable seeds, some land for a vegetable garden and a fund to purchase chickens. This gave the convalescing wounded a familiar, productive pastime and helped the hospital to provide extra food for the men.

Sometimes the Association volunteers found themselves the object of the wounded men's frustration. One particular instance occurred when a Miss Grant found herself arguing with Riflemen Alec Hutton[293] who was an amputee at Oakland Park at Walton on Thames. His injury and the inability of the medical authorities to supply him with a prosthetic leg after several months had made him bitter and angry. The fact that she had no envelopes left for his letter home was enough for his outburst, in which he expressed his frank opinion of the hospital and its organisation.

The Association also occasionally clashed with Brigadier General Richardson, who was responsible for all New Zealand Forces in England. It was unclear as to where his responsibility began towards the soldiers' wellbeing and where the Association's ended. Some areas of disagreement occurred over food production, nurses pay and comforts for the soldiers.

The Associations accounts showed that they spent on average £2,000 a month on soldiers' personal comforts compared with Brigadier General Richardson's discretionary military fund which spent on average £100 per month. It tends to indicate that without the Association's contribution of money and helpers, any homely comforts amongst the khaki of military life would have been scarce.

Appendix Three: New Zealand Hospitals in Egypt

On arrival in Egypt in December 1914, the a N.Z. Field Ambulance had been established to cater for up to two hundred cases of illness amongst the NZEF camp at Zeitoun, with the hospital at Abasseyeh available for those cases considered more serious.

Throughout the fighting on Gallipoli, the wounded and those sick with malaria, dysentery or enteric fever were sent to hospitals at Mudros, later these men would be again moved again to Alexandria General Hospital, Egyptian Government Hospital, Ras-el-Tin Military Hospital, No.5 Indian General Hospital, Bombay Presidency Hospital, the PHD Hospitals No.1 and No. 2 in Alexandria, the Red Cross Hospitals on Malta and Gibraltar or else onto England and through the Royal Army Medical Corps (RAMC) clearing system.

During the early stages of the Gallipoli campaign, transporting the wounded to the hospitals by sea was a harrowing experience. The men lay on bare decks, in their torn and blood soaked clothing. There was a lack of proper food for badly wounded men and insufficiently trained orderlies to properly care for the wounded. Generally the Australian, New Zealand and Indian orderlies on the hospital ships were well liked by the soldiers as they tried to make them comfortable and provided them with hot drinks and something to eat.

In May 1915, the NZEF had 7,928 sick and wounded officers and men distributed across a wide geography of hospitals. New Zealand had neither Stationary nor Base hospitals in Egypt to care for their own casualties, although the Egyptian Army Hospital at Pont de Koubbeh in Cairo was made available to the New Zealanders. This had been staffed by an RAMC Medical Officer, along with some NZMC medical officers and orderlies.

The first group of thirty-one New Zealand military nurses was not sent overseas until June 1914; almost two months after the fighting on Gallipoli had begun. When they arrived in Egypt, they were immediately posted to various Imperial hospitals throughout Cairo and Alexandria. Although welcome, they suffered what they termed "colonial cringe" from the British hospital staff, who thought that colonial nurses were better than nothing at all. After several months, the skill and dedication of the New Zealand nurses earned the respect of their British colleagues. Attitudes rapidly changed. On the other hand, the New Zealand nurses were not impressed with British military hospitals. They thought the administration was poor, that the Army officers in charge jealously guarded vital equipment, and that the food was inadequate.[294]

Nurse Fanny Speedy hoped never to work in a military hospital in peace time. She thought their systems to be outdated with no vestige of humanity[295] Other nurses commented during their time at the General Hospital at Abbassia that the food served to the wounded men was rough and crudely prepared. They often found themselves having to tempt the patients to eat it.[296]

This situation was not isolated to hospitals in Egypt. After becoming sick on Gallipoli, Sapper Farrer had been sent to No.1 Australian Stationary Hospital on Mudros, which he thought was well run. His problems started once he began to recover and was sent to the RAMC hospital on the island to fully recuperate. He tells of the hospital's disorganisation throughout the entire time he was there. At breakfast one morning they had mugs with no handles and not enough food for everyone there. Bread was served and then after a long delay bacon was produced. Later still a cup of tea was provided, which was so bad one Australian kept it to show a doctor that it was quite undrinkable[297]. Farrer's immediate view was that they would be better off back on the Gallipoli Peninsula.

In July 1915, 1st NZ Stationary Hospital[298] was formed and located at Port Said. It contained around five hundred beds and although the conditions were more basic, the food was better. Lady Godley also established a convalescent hospital there with fifty beds and it was visited daily by an RAMC officer. Discipline was strict and although well run, it was never a popular hospital amongst the soldiers.

Two non-military convalescent hospitals were established. One was at

Helwan and was run by two New Zealand nurses who had travelled to Egypt at their own expense. The area had sulphur and saline springs and selected patients went there to bathe in the springs. The other was the Aotea Convalescent Hospital at Zeitoun. This was established by three New Zealand nurses from money raised by the people of Wanganui[299]. Later military convalescent hospitals were used at Port Said and Luxor.

The Pont de Koubbeh hospital was taken over by the newly arrived 2nd NZ Stationary Hospital in July 1915, and the bed capacity increased to eight hundred patients. It was immediately staffed with seven NZMC medical officers, twenty-seven trained NZANS nurses and eighty-seven NZMC medical orderlies[300]. The wounded men responded well to being cared for by fellow New Zealanders. Corporal Ray Perkins, dangerously ill with both dysentery and typhoid fever, was in a room that overlooked the parade ground. Every day he saw a stretcher covered with a Union Jack being wheeled across the parade ground to the mortuary and the thought occurred that it may be his turn soon. When the NZMC staff arrived he was visited by Captain Fred Bowerbank, a medical officer from Wellington who knew Perkins's father. Bowerbank told Perkins that he would be treating him. For Perkins, whose will to live had waned, those simple words were like a tonic and he made a good recovery.

During the August 1915 offensive on Gallipoli, casualties arrived at hospitals in Malta and Alexandria. Many of the wounded men still wore the original battlefield dressings, which were by then several days old[301] and in most cases the wounds had become putrid. There had been little or no care given to them aboard the hospital ships. This was addressed on the 23rd of August, when a number of New Zealand nurses left for the Dardanelles aboard the hospital ship *Maheno*.

One of the nurses onboard, Lottie Le Gallais, had asked a British officer about Gallipoli as her brother, Leddra, was fighting there with the Auckland Regiment. Everyone she asked would say nothing about the conditions on the peninsula[302]. It gave her a bad feeling, but in no way prepared her for what she was about to encounter. Off Anzac Cove they helped to load and treat the wounded, change dressings, wash men with what water was available and help in the operating theatres as they transported the men to Mudros. Her memories were of awful wounds, of men wasted away and broken down for want of food, their mangled bodies covered with fleas and lice.[303]

The assistance given by the nurses was found to be invaluable and the NZEF instructed that nurses would continue to accompany all transporters returning with wounded.

As the hospitals became better organised, so did the casualty treatment on the beach at Anzac Cove. By October the wounded were being cleaned up and bandaged at beach hospitals before being loaded onto the barges and sent aboard the hospital ships. At the same time Nurse Lottie le Gallais received a welcome bundle of three month old mail. In one from her father she learnt that Leddra had been killed in Shrapnel Gully on the 23rd of July 1915.

More nurses and medical staff arrived from New Zealand and the Pont de Koubbeh hospital became a 1,040 bed General Hospital. With such a large, fully utilised hospital there was an urgent need for hospital helpers. The Red Cross Society and the Order of St John of Jerusalem assisted as much as they could, but eventually an appeal was made in England by the Red Cross Society for VADs[304]. In November 1915 a number of English VADs arrived in Egypt. Their duties were to undertake general tasks around the hospitals. These included: making beds, changing bed pans, keeping the wards clean, washing the men, serving meals, assisting in the quartermaster's store and undertaking any other hospital tasks so that the nurses could cater to the medical needs of the men.

One event which marred this period was the sinking of the SS Marquette on the 23rd of October 1915 by a German submarine while bound for Salonika. Aboard was the 1st N.Z. Stationary Hospital from Port Said, which had been instructed to establish a military hospital at Salonika. Also on board were military munitions, English troops and approximately six hundred mules, all of which made the Marquette a legitimate military target under the term of naval warfare. Ten out of the thirty-six New Zealand nurses onboard were drowned.

The survivors were eventually landed at Salonika and 1st NZSH became a Casualty Clearing Station. Once it had been re-supplied with new medical equipment it reverted to being a Stationary Hospital. In December 1915 Lord Plunkett, the chairman of the New Zealand War Association, visited the New Zealand hospital at Salonika[305], following the torpedoing of the *SS Marquette.* There he met the medical staff; seeing for himself the work that they performed close to the frontline and amidst the occasional aerial bombardments from German Taube aircraft. He also met and had dinner with Brigadier General George Richardson, a New Zealander serving with 12th Corps.

The New Zealand medical and nursing staff remained at Salonika until the 7th of March 1916 when they returned to Moascar in Egypt as the New Zealand Division prepared to leave for France.

As well as managing the hospitals, the NZMC was responsible for NZEF camp sanitation in Egypt. They ensured latrines were cleaned to reduce the incidence of flies and that hygienic practises were used in storing and preparing food. In February 1916, venereal disease become prevalent with fifty to seventy cases admitted to hospital each week and an unusually large number of cases of scabies were also treated. There was also a mild outbreak of meningitis amongst the newly arrived reinforcements from New Zealand. This was rapidly contained.

On the 9th of April, the NZ Field Ambulances and other NZMC units entrained for Alexandria and France, leaving the newly formed No.1 New Zealand General Hospital in Egypt.

Appendix Four: The New Zealand Hospitals in England

The first New Zealand hospital was at Mount Felix, Walton-on-Thames. It was opened in August 1915 and was a well equipped hospital, not a convalescent home. It originally had a total of one hundred and ten beds, with space to expand to one hundred and seventy beds. It had an operating theatre, staff accommodation and eleven wards: Auckland, Hawkes Bay, Wellington, Taranaki, Nelson, Marlborough, Canterbury, Westland, Southland, Dominion and Otago[306]. There was also the Hinemoa wing which contained a piano and once a week a concert was held there for the soldiers' entertainment. It also acted as a club for the wounded men, where they could meet friends and relatives, write letters home and read. The Wellington Ward had views across the lawns and the bank of the River Thames.

Corporal Thomas Phillips[307] was the first death in a New Zealand hospital in Britain. He had received over forty shrapnel wounds to his legs and arms, as well as gunshot wounds during the fighting on Gallipoli on the 15th of August.[308] He died of pneumonia at Mount Felix hospital on the 18th of October 1915 after five weeks in hospital, aged 20.

The limited capacity at Walton-on-Thames was soon unable to cope with the increasing numbers of New Zealand wounded arriving, so the RAMC sent these wounded to other military hospitals, some of which were: Royal Surrey County Hospital in Guildford, First Southern General Hospital Birmingham, 3rd London General Hospital, 2nd London General Hospital Chelsea, St Thomas's Hospital London and hospitals in Oxford, Warrington, Netley, Liverpool, Lincoln and even as far away as Edinburgh.

As in Egypt, there was a general dislike of British military hospitals and the nurses there. They were felt to be too formal and excessively disciplined. What would pass as cheeky banter in an Anzac hospital was viewed as being akin to insubordination in the British hospitals.

As one wounded man from Gallipoli put it when admitted to the British

Naval Hospital on Malta; "the forbidding doors ... opened and swallowed up the protesting forms of Colonial soldiers... The whole place was like a battleship, and the nurses were armour-plated too".

The men were happier when they were discharged and reached the Anzac Base[309] at Weymouth, Dorset where the Australians had four convalescing hospitals. As at Walton-on-Thames, the familiar surroundings, relaxed atmosphere and the inspiration from the medical staff benefited the men's recovery.

Also, the food was better and there was plenty of it, particularly as the New Zealanders received an extra 5 ½ ounces of meat ration per day over the standard British ration. This was paid for by the New Zealand Government. Once fully recovered, they were transferred back to NZEF bases in Egypt, though by mid-1916 this practice had stopped.

By early 1916, there was an estimated two thousand [310] New Zealand soldiers convalescing or in hospitals across England. There were also an estimated four hundred soldiers still suffering from enteric fever. They were waiting for bacteriological tests[311] and if it was found that they were carriers of the disease, then they were to be sent back to New Zealand for discharge.

It was recognised that a better structured administrative process for the sick, wounded, convalescing and fully recovered New Zealanders in England was urgently needed. In January 1916 Hornchurch was nominated as the N.Z. General Depot, which included the Command Depot and Infantry Training Depot with accommodation for five hundred men, many billeted out.[312] The New Zealanders still at the Anzac hospitals in Weymouth were transferred to Hornchurch.

With France now the next operational theatre for the N.Z. Division, there was a need for a much larger base establishment in England, with a New Zealand officer of senior rank to command it. Colonel J.J. Esson, 5th (Wellington) Regiment was initially given this task, but he was soon recalled by the New Zealand Government for special civil and military duties. Despite this, during his brief spell in command he commenced the re-organisation process.

In February 1916, the New Zealand Government had requested that Brigadier General George Richardson – then at Salonika with 12th Corps - was appointed as the New Zealand Military Representative at the High Commission in London, a role had held before the war. He would undertake liaison duties with the War Office and become the Commandant of the N.Z. General Depot at Hornchurch. He had the responsibility to map out the future organisation of the N.Z. Forces in England.

The first step was to expand the capacity at Mount Felix hospital to cope with more casualties arriving from the fighting in France. It was also designated as No.2 New Zealand General Hospital in accordance with military order. The bed capacity was increased to 1,040 with the building of huts and the erecting of marquees. With the pressure on Mount Felix during the battle of Flers-Courcelette in September 1916, the New Zealand Medical Board acquired a historic hotel, Oatlands Park just a few miles along the road. This new hospital catered for medical, limbless and tuberculosis cases.

The plastic surgery unit for facial and limb reconstructions was opened there as well. Later at the insistence of Her Majesty Queen Mary, the "jaw centre" as it was fondly referred to, relocated to the Queen's Hospital for Facial Injuries at Sidcup. There the famous plastic surgeon Sir Harold Gillies, also a New Zealander, was in charge. They formed "The New Zealand Section" at Queen's.

Hornchurch was at this time the only operating New Zealand base. It was better known as "Grey Towers". The "Grey Towers" manor was built in 1874 as the home of Henry and Emilie Holmes. After their deaths in 1914, the house was sold and in November 1914 Grey Towers became the Headquarters of the First Sportsman's Battalion, the 23rd Fusiliers[313]. In March 1916, the New Zealand Forces in England made Grey Towers their main depot after Brigadier General Richardson arrived from Salonika.

Richardson considered the buildings inadequate for his Headquarters. This may have been because of the lack of space, or else Hornchurch was too far from the War Office in London and the other NZ Depots established on Salisbury Plain and along the south coast of England. His headquarters were relocated to 31 Bloomsbury Square, London, WC1.

The "Grey Tower" buildings were converted for use as the main New Zealand Convalescent Hospital and later the New Zealand Section of the Convalescence Camp at Epson was transferred to "Grey Towers". The hospital had good facilities consisting of large mess rooms run by the VADs, a canteen and a swimming pool. Later an Auxiliary Hospital was added to cater for amputees and in 1918 a School of Massage was opened. Eventually it could accommodate around 2,500 patients.

The YMCA, N.Z. War Contingent Association and the Church Army each ran a recreation hut there, which had: games, picture shows, billiards, concerts and reading and writing rooms. There were also education facilities, particularly for those classed as unfit for duty and were waiting embarkation to New Zealand. The YMCA ran workshops on carpentry, elementary engineering as well as various arts and crafts.
Using the model developed in Egypt, the four phases of each man's recovery process was: hospital care, convalescent care, the period between convalescence and fitness and then the final stage for men sufficiently recovered that need to be retrained for active service.

It was a graduated process that allowed the men to progress to a degree of fitness after long periods of hospitalisation. Those classed as still recuperating started with fifteen minutes of physical drill in the morning. This was gradually increased to thirty minutes of physical drill and a two mile route march in the afternoon. Finally the men would undertake thirty minutes of physical drill and a four mile route march. Once they achieved this level of fitness they were discharged and sent to the N.Z. Command Depot that had been relocated to Codford, on the Salisbury Plain. It had a three hundred and thirty bed capacity, although by early 1918 it had been extended to accommodate around 3,200 men.

For Sapper Jim Williamson, his initial experiences at Hornchurch were not fond ones. Williamson was a Tunneller who was gassed during the construction of the mine shafts used to denote the large mines at the start of the Battle of Arras and had been awarded a Military Medal for his work. He had been posted back to the NZE Reserve Depot at Christchurch as a result of gas inhalation and as he also suffered from a hernia he was sent to Walton-on-Thames for an operation to correct it. From there he was sent to Hornchurch to convalesce, though at Hornchurch this meant doing work fatigues, drill, and route marches - intended to help the men regain their full fitness. His first day of convalescing was spent being issued with various military items and then queuing for everything else that he needed. The following day he was required to parade for morning physical exercises, which he thought ridiculous given the operation he had just had. True enough, after a mere five minutes of military exercises the hernia gave way and he was back in the ward.

The NZEF remained at Grey Towers, Hornchurch treating patients suffering from the Spanish 'flu pandemic. Grey Towers eventually closed in June 1919. Afterwards the grounds and buildings became a training ground for the Girl Guides. The buildings were finally demolished in 1931.

The Mount Felix part of No.2 N.Z. General Hospital closed at the end of June 1919. On the 3rd of June a function was held for staff, patients and other helpers to celebrate the hospital's work. They were addressed by Sir Thomas Mackenzie who stressed the valuable work which had been carried out at the hospital by its dedicated staff. It had been the longest operating New Zealand hospital in England and had treated around 25,486 patients and had around one hundred and fifty deaths, of which seventeen were buried in the Walton Cemetery.

Three medical staff were buried at the small hospital cemetery, one being Wilmet Annie Bennett, a VAD working at the hospital who died on the 21st of November 1918. She most probably contracted Spanish 'flu and died as a result of that influenza pandemic. The other two were medical officers: Colonel Charles Mackie Begg and Captain Charles Ward.

Around eighty beds were still operating at Mount Felix until August 1919 and there were still amputees at Oatlands awaiting fittings for their artificial arms and legs.

By the 10th of October 1919, Oatlands hospital had closed and the last of the wounded, being the limbless patients, left England for New Zealand, aboard the *Arawa*. In 1921 a plaque was erected to the New Zealanders. After the demolition of Mount Felix in 1966 following a fire, the plaque was moved to the Walton Town Hall in New Zealand Avenue.

Appendix Five: NZ Command Depot, Codford and the Evacuation Depot, Torquay

Following the relocation of the N.Z. Command Depot from Hornchurch to Codford Camp and the N.Z. Infantry Depot at Sling Camp there were some 2,500 New Zealanders on Salisbury Plain. There was no General Hospital initially, just a small camp infirmary. In July 1916, the Codford Camp Infirmary was taken over to become No.3 NZ General Hospital. It was expanded and eventually contained beds for ten officers and nine hundred and eighty soldiers[314]. Apart from servicing the needs of those still convalescing or undergoing training, a dental hospital and a venereal disease section were also established there.

Upon arrival at Codford, the men would receive a classification from the doctors. Generally the men were classed A or B, although there was a class C. This classification indicated the intensity of the route marches, physical training and bayonet fighting that they would undertake. The route marches started from four to six miles a day, then eight to ten miles a day and finally fourteen miles a day, at which point they would be classed as A and sent to a reserve unit as fit. Classifications would be held weekly. In addition to the physical training the soldiers could expect to receive further medical treatment, such as physiotherapy, massage, electrical treatments and special baths.

Those classed as C went before medical experts of the New Zealand Travelling Board, who regularly visited all the New Zealand camps. They decided if they should be "boarded", which meant that in the Travelling Board's medical view, the soldier was no longer physically fit for active duty and assigned some other duty. Given the war economy at the time, unless they were capable of performing another duty, such as an instructor or an administration role, then they were sent to the Depot at Torquay, in Devon, for embarkation to New Zealand. Once in New Zealand they would receive further treatment before being discharged from the NZEF.

The Torquay depot consisted of nine large houses or villas. The men were grouped according to which provincial area in New Zealand they would disembark. Auckland men were No.1 Company and allocated a villa called "Hampton". Littleton and Port Chalmers were No.2 Company and allocated a villa called "Daison". Wellington was No.3 Company and being the largest group they were allocated a collection of small houses. No.4 Company was composed of married men, orderlies, Headquarters staff and others detailed to the Depot.

While at Torquay, a soldier could apply to be "loaned" out to a local industry. Many took this opportunity working in the cider industry or else the flour mills. With a labour shortage, this extra help was welcomed by the factory owners and the men would be paid wages on top of their Army pay. It also taught them a new skill.

Educational classes were organised by the NZYMCA and an eight hundred acre farm was leased by the NZEF, to assist in preparing the men for civilian life back in New Zealand. Trade and clerical classes were held, as well as agricultural skills such as ploughing, agriculture, shearing, wool classing and bee keeping. Classes were also available for the English wives accompanying them to New Zealand. These classes tended to have a domestic focus on such topics as child care, cooking and household skills. Some of these women did not make a great impression on Lance Corporeal Williamson. He thought they were the roughest lot of women he had ever seen[315].

One unusual session of the Travelling Board occurred in January 1918, when most of the 31st and 32nd Reinforcements, which had recently arrived from New Zealand, were paraded. Due to the large number of gross foot deformities and other chronic physical defects many were immediately returned to New Zealand. The percentage was so high that the Board wondered if there were any fit men left back in New Zealand.

Those C class men assigned to other duties were posted to the N.Z. Divisional Employment Company. From here they would be assigned a suitable role given their skills and experience.

Sapper Felix Thetford after suffering a compound fracture to his left leg at Gallipoli was invalided back to England where his leg was amputated. He remained in England for the remainder of the War working at the Base Records Office at Hornchurch and later in London. He finally embarked for New Zealand on the 8th of December 1918 as a Sergeant.

Sapper Reginald Thurlow, the Essex carpenter with the N.Z. Engineers, was evacuated from Gallipoli with dysentery and after he had recovered in England he was sent to France, where he was gassed at Armentières. After he had recovered at Hornchurch, he was employed as the NCO in charge of the carpenters there, and later at Codford. He remained in the UK until 1919 and was awarded a Meritorious Service Medal in 1919 for his valuable war work. He embarked for New Zealand, with his bride Edith Ashton from Brecon.

Sapper Williamson, the Tunneller who was gassed at Arras, became a cook at the NZE Reserve Depot at Christchurch and regretted having turned down the Sergeant stripes offered to him while serving in France. The No.3 NZ General Hospital, Codford closed in July 1919 although the venereal disease wards remained open until August 1919 when it too closed. The two hundred patients still being treated at that time were transferred to the British hospital at Chiselden[316].

There are sixty-six New Zealand graves at Codford.

Appendix Six: No.1 New Zealand General Hospital, Brockenhurst

In early June 1916, the No.1 New Zealand General Hospital at Pont de Koubbeh was instructed to prepare for departure overseas. They arrived in England later that month at Southampton docks and after logistical hold-ups they disembarked and a steam train took them the fourteen miles to Brockenhurst in heart of the New Forest in Hampshire. Upon arriving, they took over the Lady Hardinge's hutted hospital. The choice of Brockenhurst was because of its proximity to Southampton, the principal port for disembarking the sick and wounded from France.

The medical orderlies were marched up the hill; past St Nicholas's Church and onto their new home, while the officers and nurses followed on behind in motor transport. The locals referred to the hospital as "Tin Town", due to the main building material being corrugated iron. It was built in 1915 as the General Hospital for the Lahore and Meerut Divisions, who were fighting on the Western Front. It was constructed in the shape of a capital E and contained a headquarters and administrations area, two wings with ten wards each with thirty-six beds to a ward, operating theatres, x-ray room, dental surgery, dispensary and a large cookhouse. The officer quarters were to the front of the building and the Other Ranks quarters on a slope below the main block. The nurses had their quarters on the other side of the road.

As well as the General Hospital buildings, two local hotels, Balmer Lawn Hotel and Forest Park Hotel, were requisitioned to expand the bed capacity that was needed. Both had two hundred bed capacities and were within a mile from the main hospital, on the other side of the village.

Under Lieutenant Colonel D.S. Wylie, who had commanded No.1 Stationary Field Hospital at Salonika, the N.Z. medical staff quickly set about getting the hospital ready to receive patients.

There were two memorable moments during this time. One was when Captain Bowerbank, a senior medical officer, was setting up his office.

He found two boxes with screwed down lids in an office cupboard. Both had silver plates bearing the name and rank of an Indian soldier along with an inscription in Urdu. On closer inspection these were found to contain the ashes of two Indian servicemen. They had been cremated so that their ashes might be sent home and cast on the sacred Ganges River. Both boxes were despatched to the War Office for their attention to the matter. The other, was when the New Zealand medical orderlies were given a night's leave to go to the local village pubs. Being use to drinking the Danish lager beers in Egypt, the English ale proved far more potent. At closing time the men staggered back in twos and threes, one man having to be wheeled back in a borrowed barrow[317].

In the first fortnight after the Brockenhurst hospital was opened, two hundred and eighty patients were admitted. Thereafter for the next six weeks admissions averaged over one hundred a week. The majority were New Zealand sick and wounded transferred from English hospitals[318] to Brockenhurst and by September 1916, the majority of hospital ships carrying the wounded from France arrived at Southampton, so the RAMC would despatch the New Zealanders immediately to Brockenhurst.

Although Forest Park hospital was supposed to be a hospital for officers, this was ignored when casualties needed beds. Private Bert Jennings who was serving with the 2nd Canterbury Battalion had received about a dozen shrapnel wounds during an intensive German artillery barrage on their trenches at Armentières in July 1916.[319] He was evacuated to Brockenhurst and spent the next five weeks recovering at the recently constructed huts at Forest Park.

By the first week of October the New Zealand wounded from the Somme battle of Flers-Courcelette began to arrive at Brockenhurst. By now there were over 1,200 patients housed across all three hospitals. For many of the men it was like a homecoming; seeing familiar faces, talking to New Zealand doctors and sharing jokes with the nurses. The letters back home told of the good treatment being received, the fun they had and the hard work put in by all of the medical staff at Brockenhurst. It seemed that no-one was allowed to feel gloomy.

While being treated at hospitals and various convalescence homes in the New Forest area, the men were initially issued blue jackets and trousers, with white shirts and ties. These were supplied by each hospital. There was a practical side to this as it identified the men as patients needing care and also their own clothing would have been blood strained, torn and filthy from their battlefield experiences. Tunic, shirts and trousers would have been cut away when the casualty clearing medical staff treated the injuries.

Any remnants of a uniform would have been burnt by the medical staff either in France or later in England. It could take weeks before their base kit containing spare uniforms, extra clothes and other personal belongings caught up with the wounded men, if at all. So the quartermaster's store, the N.Z. War Contingent Association and the NZYMCA provided them with personal items until then. Wearing the blue uniform also meant that they were not allowed to be served alcohol in a public house. Once they were convalescing, they would revert to wearing khaki.

When men felt well enough, they could go for walks in the forest, across the heath land or into the village of Brockenhurst. At the top of the main street through the village was the NZYMCA *Kia Ora* hut where the men could get away from military life for awhile; have a cup of tea, read books and write letters to friends and family. Further afield were the towns of Lyndhurst, Beaulieu, Lymington, Southampton and Christchurch, all reachable by train. They could visit theatres, tea rooms, bookshops and historical sites.

They could also travel to the seaside resort of Bournemouth which offered a beach, promenade, restaurants, an ice rink, concerts in the Winter Gardens and well dressed young ladies. Outings were only permitted if a nurse was in charge of the party, which usually meant arrangements had to be made around when nurses had an afternoon off.

Once in the town, the nurses would generally leave the men to their own devices, as long as they all met up again at the agreed time. Not wanting to get the nurses into any trouble, the men respected these arrangements.

Some unfavourable experiences did occur though. Sergeant Cecil Malthus, a classics scholar, had visited Bournemouth on one occasion with his friend and company commander, Captain Dron. Both had served at Gallipoli and they had been wounded at Flers-Courcelette. On their first visit to Bournemouth, they had enjoyed a particularly good lunch at one of the restaurants. Dron returned to France and several weeks later Malthus, still on crutches, returned to the same restaurant.

There he was met at the door by the manager and was refused entry. He was not an officer and therefore could not be served. It transpired that he was only served on the previous occasion because he was with an officer. Such attitudes were bewildering to the colonial soldiers and ignited their social sensitivities.

After the Somme offensive, there was a fall in weekly admissions to Brockenhurst until the winter months. During this time, Captain E.H. Rawson, who ran the dental section, had applied to join the Royal Flying Corp. While he waited for news of his transfer he would go alone into the New Forest armed with a borrowed drill book. There he would find a quiet spot and rehearse the necessary words of command. Soon a rumour spread around the village that a mental case from the New Zealand Hospital had been heard in the forest, shouting at the trees and giving orders in a loud voice. His transfer was granted in December 1916 and silence once more descended upon the forest.

Early December 1916 saw the sisters, nurses and VADs all preparing for Christmas. Rivalry developed between the wards as to the most original decorations. Some of the walking patients were sent into the New Forest to gather branches and wild flowers, but managed to wander into Morant Park and returned with numerous branches still covered with coloured leaves and blossoms. Later a complaint letter was received by the New Zealand commander stating that a number of prize shrubs had been mutilated. Lady Morant graciously chose to overlook the incident.

At Brockenhurst on Christmas Day 1916, the Medical Officers went into their wards to carve the turkey and other meats provided for Christmas lunch. Christmas puddings that had been sent all the way from New

Zealand were a treat and even the duodenal ulcer patients ate some, declaring later that it was worth the subsequent pain. For some, it was their first proper Christmas since they had left New Zealand two years before.

It snowed that winter and became so cold that ponds iced over. These were novel conditions and many of the patients and staff amused themselves with snow fights and attempts at ice skating. It appears that the ice skating was the most enjoyable to watch, as the out of control skaters slid about the ice, clutching onto anything before falling into confused heaps.

It was also especially cold in France, particularly in December 1917 and January 1918. This resulted in a rise in respiratory diseases amongst the New Zealand troops in the Ypres trenches. Hospital admissions at Brockenhurst during the next few months were mainly due to bronchitis or bronchopneumonia due to gas poisoning.

The hospital continued to develop specialist departments, such as: Bacteriological, Radiology, Dental and Eyes, Ears and Nose. Orthopaedic surgery was also developing in England at the time and a specialist centre was considered for Brockenhurst. In addition to three NZ General Hospitals, the NZEF continued use of other specialised military hospitals such as King George Hospital as a Fever Hospital and the Queen's Hospital at Sidcup for plastic surgery.

No.1 NZ General Hospital, Brockenhurst treated 21,004 patients[320] during the war and was the first to close. On the 11th of March 1919 the last of the patients housed there embarked on the *Maheno* for New Zealand. Left behind were the graves of 94 Anzacs. Most had died at the hospital, including one Australian.

Appendix Seven: Clearing the battlefield casualties in France and Belgium

The physical injuries inflicted upon the men would range from: gunshot wounds, bayonet wounds, bone fractures, shrapnel wounds, burns, bomb blasts, concussion, effects of gas, trench fever, trench foot, frostbite, pneumonia, appendicitis, bronchitis, septic wounds, mumps, dysentery, influenza, shell shock, traffic accidents, horse accidents and nervous malaises. They did not have to be in the front line trenches to be injured. Long range artillery, aerial warfare, or mere accidents in the rest areas caused injury.

For those attending a sick parade there were three medical classifications: MD meant given medicine and continue with their duty; ED being excused duty; or LD being light duty. This would not result in the man necessarily being evacuated. Those evacuated to a hospital would have to display: high temperature, rapid pulse, breathing difficulties, severe discomfort or something that the famous No.9 pill could not cure. The clearing system for sick and wounded men was generally the same once they had reached a Casualty Clearing Station or Hospital.

When a man was wounded, the medical care and evacuation system started with the initial treatment administered by a comrade, a medic or by themselves with a field dressing. Once safe, the casualty would be taken to the Regiment Aid Post (RAP) for further treatment. Stretcher bearers from the Field Ambulance would collect the wounded from the RAP and take then to the Advanced Dressing stations (ADS). Those considered walking wounded would be directed to the ADS, while stretcher cases were carried through the trenches, sometimes with assistance from captured German prisoners to the ADS. There the wounded would be re-assessed; wounds re-bandaged or some treatment given to ease the pain and then they were documented. The next move was further back from the frontline to a Casualty Clearing Station (CCS).

This occurred by motor ambulance, light railway carriages, stretchers or walking, which is also why having serviceable roads was important to evacuate the wounded. The CCS would normally be staffed by six medical doctors, several nurses and medical orderlies. There the casualties were sorted; urgent cases operated on and dubious cases held on to for observation. It was also somewhere warm where sick men could rest and recover under medical supervision. When it was safe those casualties to be "cleared" were moved further down the lines of communication to a Base Depot.

Depending on the seriousness of their injury, the casualty was sent on to a Stationary Hospital for additional medical treatment and recovery care, thereby remaining in France. The more seriously sick or wounded were sent to a General Hospital, possibly in England. A "blighty" wound, as it became known, necessitated being sent to England for such medical treatment. This was the type of wound most men hoped for, serious enough to get home but not debilitating.

The NZMC had No.1 N.Z. Stationary Hospital operating in France in support of the Fourth Army and later the Second Army. It was stationed at Amiens and treated British soldiers wounded from the Somme fighting and later New Zealand wounded from Messines. They often endured aerial and artillery bombardments as they were close to the front line. Later the hospital relocated to Wisques, near St Omer, where a distinctive Maori carved gateway provided a sense of home.

Those destined for England were placed on hospital trains usually bound for the French ports of Boulogne or Le Havre. The lucky ones travelled the few miles to Boulogne and then the short crossing to Dover. The unlucky ones had a roundabout trip to Le Havre and then onto Southampton.

The rail system was always over used so delays often occurred. The hospital trains tended to be very bumpy and had jerky brakes all of which made the trip very difficult for the wounded. Morphine was often administered to ease the effects of travel. In winter, the carriages were unheated resulting in the nurses and medical orderlies having to distribute blankets and hot water bottles in an attempt to keep the patients warm. Such conditions inevitably caused deaths, particularly amongst those with head injuries or already weak from loss of blood. In the summer months the men complained about the stuffiness in the carriages. Throughout the war, bloody bandages and pieces of clothing were thrown from the hospital trains. These articles would festoon tree branches and the countryside alongside the railway tracks as evidence that a hospital train had recently passed.

Hospital trains could be delayed for hours in sidings. In the summer months if there was no shade, the hot sun would soon raise the temperature inside the carriages making it unbearable for the wounded. In these circumstances, there was little that the medical staff could do to alleviate the men's sufferings. When the train was eventually unloaded at the port stations, the stench of septic and gangrenous wounds, unwashed bodies and sweat-soaked uniforms would permeate the railway platforms. The walking wounded would be loaded aboard the hospital ships using the gangways, while the stretcher cases would be loaded by either stretcher bearers carrying them up the gangway, or else by a hoist that placed them into the ship's cargo bays.

In the early months of the war, these sights and smells greeted the reinforcement drafts arriving from England who disembarked at the same ports used for medical evacuation. This sometimes affected the morale of these newly arrived troops, so eventually different ports were used to embark the wounded, well away from the disembarking fresh troops.

The evacuation policy with New Zealand wounded was that those arriving at Dover were brought to Walton-on-Thames, while those arriving at Southampton were taken to Brockenhurst. The efficiency of reaching the correct hospital was dependant upon the medical embarkation staff in France, where they grouped together New Zealand soldiers and labelled them for a New Zealand hospital in England. This did not always happen, especially when large numbers of wounded were being evacuated.

Being aboard a hospital ship did not guarantee safe arrival in England.

On the 3rd of August 1918, the Hospital ship A69 *HMAT Warilda*[321] was torpedoed by the German submarine UC-49. The *Warilda* was fully laden with 614 wounded, 70 RAMC, nursing staff and crew. It sank off Selsey Bill, as it entered Southampton waters with a loss of 123 lives. One of those drowned was Private James Joseph McGrath, serving with the 2nd Otago Battalion who had suffered a severe fracture to his upper left arm and shoulder during hostile artillery fire on the New Zealand trenches in the Rossignol Woods area.

His mother never accepted his death and even as an elderly lady she would still ventured down to the Wellington docks in New Zealand to see if her son Jimmy was on one of the recently docked ships.

Appendix Eight: Voluntary Aid Detachment (VADs)

VADs had existed prior to the outbreak of war in 1914. Generally they were educated young ladies who would assist in the hospitals. There they would make beds, change bed pans, clean floors, serve food, clean up any messes, cook, launder and undertake all other roles that supported the smooth running of a hospital.

The NZMC employed VADs in Egypt in late 1915, due to a shortage of nurses. The nurses and VADs who worked in the New Zealand hospitals came from England, Scotland, South Africa, Australia and New Zealand. They were all volunteers. The colonial nurses and VADs generally were already in England when the war broke out, or else they had come over later to join husbands who were officers. One was the wife of Captain Bowerbank, a NZ Medical officer. His wife, Maud, had sailed to England at the same time that he had left New Zealand with his medical unit for Egypt. She volunteered for service in Egypt and administered the Red Cross store in the Pont de Koubbeh hospital.

Also, young ladies who volunteered in New Zealand for VAD duty in England were permitted to travel there with their mother, given the great need for hospital helpers in England especially as the fighting in 1916 and 1917 brought greater numbers of wounded into the hospitals. On average, a thirty-six bed ward needed a full time staff of three sisters and five VADs to care for the patients, feed, bathe them and keep the ward clean.

The uniform for the New Zealand VADs was a blue dress, white apron with "New Zealand" worked in red on the bib and a white cap with a Red Cross on the front. New VADs were initially assigned to the dining rooms and kitchen for duties and if they were shown to be capable they moved onto the wards where the discipline was strict. They were expected to have loyalty to the ward sisters, care for the welfare and comfort of the patients, take pride in their ward and help their fellow VADs. They learnt how to dress and undress wounds, assist nurses, tell "white lies" especially to the amputees, be good listeners when the men wanted to talk of home, try to keep back their tears and not become too fond of their charges.

But they did tend to build friendships with the men. Cecil Malthus accepted an invitation to visit the Lyndhurst home of his VAD nurse, Mrs Beaver. Having the chance to go somewhere away from a military environment, even for several hours, was an opportunity not to be missed. Friendships did develop and some of the men married their ward VAD. Sapper Vincent Peters, a young veteran of Gallipoli, married Gertrude Foote, who was a VAD at Brockenhurst. They left for New Zealand in 1919, with their newly born baby son.

Bert Jennings also remembered his VADs when he was convalescing at the Somerley estate, near Ringwood. Both were the daughters of the Countess of Normanton, who had kindly opened up part of her home as a convalescent hospital. Both ladies cared for the men and even umpired the cricket match that the men held. In return, the New Zealanders put on a concert for the Countess and her family. Although their singing was not a strong point, the main feature of the performance was a Maori haka which the men had practiced. The Countess's young children enjoyed it so much that it was performed three times.

The VADs had half a day off a week and one and a half days once a month. Some would use their off duty time meeting the trains carrying the wounded and distribute cups of hot cocoa to the wounded[322]. There was always something to do.

To some sisters and qualified nurses, the VADs were regarded as silly, incompetent, upper-class women who were allowed to nurse wounded and sick soldiers. They had a frivolous, cute image compared to the starched stereotype of the stern nurse[323]. The reality was that where there was a shortage of trained nurses, the VADs were capable of replacing them on the wards. To the soldiers, the VADs were indispensable.

Private Alec Hutton, a New Zealand amputee at Walton-on-Thames, made his views clear in a letter home[324] after the war had ended and the VADs were being disbanded and about to leave Oatlands. He thought that the Oatlands hospital would soon become "very rough" with regards to the care provided. He knew that the sisters and nurses did not like making beds or keeping the wards clean, so he feared the worst. To the sick and wounded soldiers, the VADs were angels on earth.

The *Christchurch Times* published a poem in the "Our Soldiers Poets' Corner" in February 1918. It was entitled "The V.A.D. – by one who knows" and was by a Royal Engineer at Christchurch Barracks, whose initials were H.L.E. It went:

Who is put on to scrub the floor,
While ratings will not soil their paws,
And clears up, really, all the stores,
Why the VAD
Who is it works from seven to one,
Without the comfort of a bun,
Kept all the time upon the run?
Why the VAD
Who is it always finds the time
To shift the bed, yea, nine time
With patience that is quite subline?
Why the VAD.
When I to move was far too ill,
When shells burst round, who stayed quite still
While others bolted up the hill?
Why the VAD
Who when I said "Do save yourself"
You've youth and looks and love and wealth,"
Replied "I am not here for my health"?
Why the VAD
Who when the shelling bout was o'er,
Instead of swooning on the floor,
Brought me back to life once more?
Why the VAD

Many sisters and qualified nurses were also held in high regard by the men at Brockenhurst and a number of genuine friendships developed between nurses and patients. Nurse Speedy was given a new pen for

Christmas from "the boys of Ward 17". When she told them that she did not deserve it, the men, with their New Zealand humour, agreed with her. Still, they all wanted to thank her and show their appreciation. In her diary Nurse Speedy wrote that she had not been too nice to those boys either, "which probably shows what jolly good fellows they are"[325].

She also wrote of the departure of eight men who had been boarded to return to New Zealand. In her diary she mentioned that she would miss them all. Of one in particular, Cargill, she noted that the romance that she thought had been growing must have only been in her imagination, as he was already engaged. [326]

Appendix Nine: Convalescent Hospitals

In the early part of the war, the main convalescent hospital for NZEF soldiers was at the Anzac Depot in Weymouth, although not all Anzacs found themselves at Weymouth. Some convalesced at the Epsom War Hospital, after being discharged from the No.3 General Hospital near London.

Epsom was an odd establishment and there seem to be little care for the mental as well as physical well-being of its patients, who were alone with no relatives or army friends to visit them or any entertainment. In one incident, Private Patrick Ryan of the 4th Battalion, AIF who had only been at the Epson War Hospital for four days, was involved in a hit and run incident when a motor vehicle knocked him over while he was crossing the street. As he was drunk at the time, the local police detained him in a cell overnight. He had three fractured ribs, a heart injury and a ruptured spleen[327]. He died in hospital four days later on the 13th of December 1915. The coroner's verdict was accidental death.

The New Zealand hospitals recognised that good facilities were needed to keep the soldiers occupied and when they established themselves in England, both the N.Z. War Contingent Association and the NZYMCA helped to cater for the men's needs. It was important to make them feel comfortable and keep them entertained.

Hornchurch became the main N.Z. Convalescent Hospital with all the appropriate facilities; Brighton was the convalescent home for officers with two houses in Lewes Crescent, with tennis courts and located near the sea for bathing and boating. In the New Forest, convalescent hospitals seem to spring up wherever there was a large house and a piece of land. These were located at: Heron Court, Avon Tyrell at Thorney Hill, Somerley near Ringwood and Lymington.

Barton-on-Sea was set aside for those recovering from dysentery and also had the popular entertainment troupe called The "Whiz Bang" Costume Concert Party for any patient with musical talent. The troupe gave performances at the Union Jack Club in Christchurch and at various

Town Halls. All proceeds from the performances helped to provide extra comforts for the wounded in the hospitals and for a time, their business manager was a Private Wallace of the New Zealand Regiment.

Lymington was the favoured convalescent hospital for the New Zealander. It was consider very comfortable, near to the town with shops, restaurants and a small, yet busy port.

Heron Court Auxiliary Hospital was opened and operated by the Countess of Malmesbury[328] in November 1914 to accommodate twenty patients. By mid 1916 New Zealand soldiers were sent there. The hospital staff consisted of: Dr Shell, Sister Hughes and eight VADs. Activities for the patients were constantly being organised by Lady Malmesbury. Using her influence, the Sailing Club arranged a picnic tea for the wounded men. It was held one Sunday afternoon in August, amongst the sand hills at Mudeford Quay.

In September 1916, a garden fête was organised in the grounds of Heron Court to raise funds for "smokes" for the convalescing soldiers. These events gave the villagers and townspeople a day's outing and allowed the wounded soldiers to invite relatives and friends.

The band of the 10th East Lancashires provided the musical entertainment and there were stalls such as Hoop-La run by Private E. Lisk with Nurse Lane. Lord FitzHarris, who owned Heron Court and Scout H. Haskell, managed the "Bombing the Kaiser" stall, which would have been interesting as Lord FitzHarris knew the Kaiser personally, and the Kaiser was his son's godfather.

There was a Cake Weight Guessing competition, an Aunt Sally stall, "Dipps" ran by Scouts H. Skinner and C. Frazer, and Ball Quoits run by Scout G. Scragg. For the more adventurous, Sergeant Sherwood & Scout Dennett had a rowboat to take people around the little island in the lake.

The nurses provided humorous entertainment in a clever dialogue called "Hints" in which Nurse Barnes played a newly-wed man and Nurse Lane his bride. The nature of the characters' confessions caught the imagination of the audience. Some of the more musical amongst the patients dressed up and provided songs and dances as the "Orange Girls". One of them, Private C.F. Hoare, had been told that morning that he had received the Military Medal for valour in the Battle of the Somme.

The speaker then went on to say that he was pleased to see that "girls" were also being awarded medals now.

Several miles away from Heron Court, past the village of Bransgore, was Avon Tyrell where the Thorny Hill Auxiliary Hospital was located. It housed New Zealand and Australian patients. In mid September, they also held a Garden Fête at which toys that had been made and painted by the New Zealand patients at the hospital were sold.

The proceeds went towards a small workshop where the men could work during the winter to continue developing their skills. The style of toys being produced by many disabled soldiers and sailors at the time was marketed as "CHUNKY" Toys.

Appendix Ten: Salonika

Salonika was very much a sideshow for the Allies, but interlinked with the strategies on the Western Front and Gallipoli.

The seeds of this conflict were planted in 1912 after Italy and Turkey had fought a year long war for the control of Turkey's North African territories. Turkey was defeated and ceded Libya, Rhodes and the Dodecanese Islands to the Italians. The ease of their defeat encouraged the small states of the Balkan League[329] to claim territories from Turkey.

This led to the First Balkan War of 1912 to 1913 that ended with further Turkish territory being ceded. Tensions then arose amongst those victorious Balkan League states over the division of Macedonia, resulting in Greece and Serbia forming an alliance against Bulgaria. The Second Balkan War followed in 1913 and after two months of fighting Bulgaria was defeated. Macedonia was divided up mostly between Greece and Serbia; Bulgaria was left with a lesser share.

An uneasy peace settled across the region and by 1915 Bulgaria, which had been watching Germany's successes in Russia and the failure of Italy's offensive against Austria at the Isonzo River was beginning to be influenced by the Central Powers.[330]

Bulgaria possessed the strongest of the Balkan armies and more importantly the eastern section of the Berlin to Constantinople railway which ran through the middle of Bulgaria. If the supply route to Turkey could be opened then Germany could send artillery and other war supplies to Turkey and the Middle East; and in return Germany would have access to raw material from Asia for its war production. This made Bulgaria strategically important to Germany, although there was one problem concerning the 200 miles of railway which ran through the north of Serbia – a pro Allied country.

While Serbia controlled this area, the Berlin to Constantinople railway was closed. The Austro-Hungarian army had attempted to invade Serbia the year before, in August 1914 and then again in September 1914. Serbia had repelled both of these assaults.

Earlier in the war, both the Entente Allies and the Central Powers had begun political bargaining with all the Balkan states for their support, Bulgaria's price included Serbian territory, which the Entente Allies could not persuade Serbia to agree to. The matter was resolved on the 6th of September when Bulgaria secretly signed a pact to join with the Central Powers.

Germany withdrew several divisions from Russia and concentrated them on the northern Serbian border along with the Austro-Hungarian divisions still on the northern Serbian border. Bulgaria positioned four divisions on its border with Serbia. By the 19th of September Belgrade, the capital of Serbia was already being bombarded.[331] Faced with such overwhelming odds, Serbia looked to invoke the treaty it had with Greece. The countries had earlier agreed that if Bulgaria attacked Serbia, and Serbia was able to field a military force of 150,000 men, then Greece was committed to come to Serbia's aid.

The pace of regional events quickened and the Greek Premier Venizelos succeeded in having the King of Greece mobilise his army. On the 22nd of September, he asked the Allies if they would provide the 150,000 men instead of Serbia. This would meet the treaty's stipulations and allow Greece to meet its obligations given Bulgaria's aggression.

The Allies had a problem in that two major forthcoming offensives[332] were about to commence on the Western Front, so neither the British nor the French could free up any divisions at that time, so instead a smaller British and French force[333] was instructed to be dispatched from Gallipoli. As Serbia was a landlocked country with no ports of its own, the Allied force was instructed to sail to Salonika - the Greek port in the Aegean Sea nearest to Serbia. Confusion then reigned.

With the obvious dangers in joining the European war, the majority of Greeks, including a portion of the Greek Army[334], argued that as Serbia had been attacked by Germany and Austria, and not solely by Bulgaria, the treaty did not apply. With the allied force approaching Salonika, a political debate erupted as to whether the Greeks had actually asked for the force to be sent or merely enquired as to its feasibility.

The King of Greece wanted to secure the safety of his country by remaining strictly neutral, so initially the Allied troops were refused permission to land, but eventually on October 3rd the small Allied force disembarked at Salonika under the written permission of the Greek authorities there.

A few days later, the King of Greece informed Premier Venizelos that he could not support his policy to help Serbia, so Venizelos resigned.[335]

With Greece now officially a neutral country and having no intention of joining the Allies against the Central Powers, the reason for supplying Allied troops had vanished. The British Government attempted to disengage its Divisions from what was now viewed as a futile enterprise. But a wave of "Save Serbia" sentiment was sweeping the French people and it caught on in England. How, the people asked, could two great nations allow their small ally, Serbia, which was fighting so bravely, to be overwhelmed without apparently reaching out a hand to help?[336]

The matter was settled on the 7th of October when the German and Austrian divisions launched their attacks on Serbia. On 11th October Bulgaria declared war on the Allies and also invaded Serbia from the north and south.

The Allied troops were still at Salonika awaiting additional troops and equipment that had been dispatched from Egypt.

It was not until late November that the combined British and French force was able to move north to link up with the Serbs. It was too little, too late. The Serbian Army had already suffered heavy losses in men and equipment during October, losing 500 guns[337], and the Bulgarian Army had cut communication links with Greece. Then by late October, the railway line to Salonika was cut, which effectively prevented the Allies from supplying the Serbian Army. Finding their army isolated and with no possibility of re-supply, the Serbs recognized the situation as hopeless. They put up little resistance[338] choosing instead to withdrawing towards Albania and the sea, where French transport ships evacuated them to Corfu and then eventually Salonika.

By mid December 1915, the Allies had withdrawn back to Salonika and had begun fortifying the port against the Bulgarians and the Greeks. The Greeks were threatening to intern the French and British divisions[339] which the previous Government had invited to Salonika.[340] These threats ceased after Lord Kitchener, who happened to be in the theatre assessing the possibility of a Gallipoli evacuation, diverted to Greece and meet with the King and the Premier of Greece.

As Greece was neutral, the Allies had difficulty in controlling people traffic in and out of the Salonika area, particularly German and Bulgarian diplomatic staff. This and the thousands of Greeks employed for road making made secrecy impossible. German aircraft over flew the area on reconnaissance flights or on bombing raids, which soon became a regular feature at Salonika. On several occasions the New Zealand Military Hospital[341] tents were peppered with shrapnel. In retaliation to the air raids, all enemy consuls were arrested by the Allies and shipped to Marseille.

The Anzacs initially deployed a few Engineers for map making duty and ASC personnel to manage the packhorses, to Salonika during those early months while it was being fortified. Most of the Anzac units were withdrawn by early 1916. The No.1 New Zealand Stationary Hospital at Lembet Camp was relieved by Canada Field Hospital on the 3rd of March 1916 and the New Zealanders proceeded to England, leaving behind them what the Germans dubbed 'the greatest Allied internment camp in Europe'.

The 10th (Irish) Division, along with the 22nd, 26th, 27th and 28th Divisions would continue to hold the defensive line at Salonika, combating the ravages of malaria, until eventually attacking the Bulgarians who surrendered unconditionally in September 1918.

Appendix Eleven: Major-General Sir George Spafford Richardson

Richardson began his military career as an eighteen year old gunner in the Royal Regiment of Artillery. He attended the Shoeburyness Gunnery School[342] in 1886 and served four years at Gibraltar. In 1891, he was posted to the New Zealand Forces as a Gunnery Instructor with the rank of Master Gunner. Upon retiring from the Imperial British Army on the 16th of April 1907 he was commissioned as a Captain in the New Zealand Militia and became the Director of Artillery. In 1912, he returned to England and attended Staff College at Camberley, graduating in 1913 and was then attached to the Imperial General Staff in London as New Zealand's Military Advisor at the War Office.[343]

When war broke out in 1914, he joined the Admiralty Staff, accepted a Royal Marine commission and served with the newly formed Royal Naval Division during the defence of Antwerp, along with another New Zealander, Lieutenant Commander Bernard Freyburg.

In 1915 he was promoted to Lieutenant-Colonel and served at Cape Helles throughout the Gallipoli campaign as the Quarter Master General to the Royal Naval Division where he was awarded a CMG in October, 1915.

While at Gallipoli he experienced the fighting first hand, regularly touring the trenches and having a few near misses, one in particular was when a young Lieutenant[344] he was speaking with was suddenly shot, presumably by a sniper. Later he had a bullet go through his dugout and penetrate his canvas bath – it is uncertain if he was in it at the time. At Cape Helles, he became familiar with many senior New Zealand officers, including Lieutenant-Colonel Malone of the Wellington Infantry Battalion and Chunuk Bair fame and observed the lack of battle effectiveness resulting from poorly trained officers and men, particularly amongst the civilian-soldiers of the Kitchener's New Army who he did not highly rate. In his diary he even noted the rumours from France that in October 1915, a Brigade of "K's Army" had surrendered and two other brigades had run away[345].

He eventually left the peninsula when the Royal Naval Division evacuated on the 20th of December, 1915. The following day he learnt that he had been promoted to Brigadier-General and posted with immediate effect to Salonika as Deputy Adjutant and Quartermaster for 12th Corps. He arrived just before Christmas and after living the past eight months in dugouts, he enjoyed the luxury of a hotel room – for the highly inflated price of £1 per night[346].

In late February 1916 he was formally appointed Commandant New Zealand Troop in England. After only two months with 12th Corps, he left Salonika and proceeded to England to take up his new command. He continued in that role until 1919 and was posted back to New Zealand as the General Officer in Charge of Administration at the New Zealand Army Headquarters, Wellington.

He became a prominent member of the N.Z. Returned Servicemen's Association and in March 1923 he was appointed New Zealand's second Civil Administrator to Western Samoa, a posting in which he had little success. He received his knighthood in 1925.

Sir George Spafford Richardson died in 1938.

Appendix Twelve: New Zealand Marriages at the Priory Church, Christchurch 1916-1919

Date of Marriage	Groom's & Bride's Name	Age	Occupation	Address	Father's Occupation
25 October 1916	Kolbjorn Thoroaldsson Jenssen	31	Lieutenant, NZ Engineers	The Camp, Christchurch	
	Rose Newdick	33	Nursing Sister	NZ General Hospital, Brockenhurst	
13 November 1916	Joseph Donnell	26	Driver, NZ Engineer	Raven Court, Jumper Avenue Christchurch	Farmer
	Edith May Perkins	23		Raven Court, Jumper Avenue Christchurch	Warrant Officer
27 March 1917	Albert Edward Robertson	21	Driver, NZ Engineers	7 Portfield Road, Christchurch	Master Mariner
	Leavinia Jane Spencer	19		28 Livingstone Rd, Christchurch	
10 April 1917	James Stuart Cummings	31	Corporeal NZ Engineers	The Barracks, Christchurch	Station Master
	Beatrice Lucy Boorman	26		Ashford, Kent	
25 April 1917	Donald Mckenzie	24	Driver, NZ Engineers	Handyside, Portfield Road, Christchurch	Gentleman
	Dorothy Kate Betenger	23		11 Millhams Street, Christchurch	
27 September 1917	Ernest John Champ	28	Sapper, NZ Engineers	NZ Camp, Christchurch	Farm Bailiff
	Daisy Marian Freeman	20			
29 September 1917	James Hargest	26	Major, NZEF - 1st Otago Regiment	The Vicarage, Christchurch	Farmer
	Marie Henretta Wilkie	31	Sister, NZANS	NZ General Hospital, Brockenhurst	Farmer
31 October 1917	Frederick Nicholas	29	Sapper, NZ Engineers	The Camp, Christchurch	Railway official

Date	Name	Age	Rank, Regiment	Bournemouth	Post Office official
	Vera Chalotte Bolton	18			
17 November 1917	Walter Richard Williamson	32	Sapper, NZ Engineers	The Camp, Christchurch	Carpenter
	Annie Akte Bridle	26		12 Church Lane, Christchurch	Gamekeeper
27 February 1918	Albert Edward Petherwick	23	Driver, NZ Engineers	The Barrack, Christchurch	Tailor
	Lottie Barrow	22		Bitterne, Oak Avenue, Christchurch	Butcher
1 June 1918	Harold Litchfield Green	26	Sapper NZ Engineers	NZ Camp	Farmer
	Mary Breach	27		The Coburg, Terrace Mount, Bournemouth	Gentleman
20 June 1918	Michael Tomas Priestley	32	Sapper, NZ Engineers	5 Portfield Rd, Christchurch	Farmer
	Lily Hebert	22		5 Portfield Rd, Christchurch	
1 August 1918	Henry Charles Schroder	23	Driver, NZ Engineers	6 Clarendon Rd, Christchurch	Farmer
	Bertha May Atkins	26		6 Clarendon Rd, Christchurch	Clerk
18 October 1918	William Norman Walter Bain	26	Driver, NZ Engineers	NZ Camp	Electrician
	Florence Evelyn Dibley	18		Hengistbury Cottage, Christchurch	
9 November 1918	Ralph John Black	26	Captain, NZ Engineers	HQ, NZE Boscombe	Accountant
	Dorothy Kathleen Phillips	22		Kilston, Princess Ave, Christchurch	Draper
12 January 1919	David Joseph Eagleson	29	Driver, NZ Engineers	The Homestead, Jumpers, Christchurch	Farmer
	May Hilda Whiting	25		109 Bargates, Christchurch	Miller
25 January 1919	David William Galvin	22	Private, NZ Pioneers	54 Purewell, Christchurch	Farmer
	Gertrude Dorothy Hiscock Stokes	20		54 Purewell, Christchurch	Dairyman

References

[1] Ernest George King, A diary of the War, 2nd Reinforcement, 19th Battalion, 5th Infantry Brigade, AIF – February 12, 1916.

[2] Letters from World War 1 Part 6 – Diary of Alister Robinson, letter 10.

[3] The Jameson Raid consisted of 600 irregular militiamen from the British Cape Colony. Their aim was to take Johannesburg and provoke an uprising of the British expatriate workers in the Transvaal. Around 30 raiders were killed in a series of engagements before they surrendered. The Kruger telegram sent by Kaiser Wilhelm II to Stephanus Kruger, president of the Transvaal read:

"I express to you my sincere congratulations that you and your people, without appealing to the help of friendly powers, have succeeded, by your own energetic action against armed bands which invaded your country as disturbers of the peace, in restoring peace and in maintaining the independence of the country against attack form without." It was the reference to "friendly powers" which elevated this from a colonial matter to an international incident and is believed to have contributed to the Second Boer War in so far as the Boers believed Germany would assist them against the British.

[4] Anglo-French Entente Cordiale (1904) and the Franco-Russian Alliance (1892).

[5] Prince Buelow, German State Secretary, address to The Reichstag on 29th March, 1909.

[6] November 1907.

[7] Princess Auguste Victoria Friederike Luise Feodora Jenny of Schleswig-Holstein-Sonderburg-Augustenburg.

[8] The Christchurch Times 16th November 1907.

[9] Punch cartoon titled "The Triple Alliance" from 11th July 1891 narrative notes that they disliked each other passionately.

[10] The Battle of Dorking: Reminiscences of a volunteer published 1871 by George Chesney.

[11] Spies of the Kaiser – Plotting the downfall of England, published May 1909; by William Le Queux. The Invasion of 1910, serial story in the Daily Mail in March 1906 by William Le Queux.

[12] Questions asked by Colonel Mark Lockwood, Member of Epping in mid 1908.

[13] Colonel Stuart Wortley was promoted Major General in 1913 and commanded the 46th (North Midland) Division in France during the Battle of the Loos in October 1915 and later on the opening day of the Battle of the Somme - 1st July, 1916. He was the only divisional commander to be sacked after that battle as it was believed that because the 46th Division had suffered the least number of casualties on that day, it had shown a lack of offensive spirit.

[14] near Wimborne Minister.

[15] http://www.martinstown.co.uk/WEBSITE/OBJECTS/STURTPICS/GUESTS/keppel.htm.

[16] In the county of Southampton had the additional title of Viscount FitzHarris of Heron Court until 1950.

[17] William Harris, 6th Earl of Malmesbury born 18th November, 1907.

[18] The Christchurch Times, December 1907.

[19] The Christchurch Times, December 1907.

[20] The Christchurch Times, November 1907.

[21] The Christchurch Times, November 1907.

[22] The Christchurch Times, November 1907.

[23] The Battle of Leuthen was fought on 5th December 1757 during the Seven Years' War. It was a decisive victory for Frederick the Great, ensuring his control over Silesia from the Austrians.

[24] Sermon of the Rev TH Bush BA - Advent Sunday 1907.

[25] Sermon of the Rev TH Bush BA - Advent Sunday 1907.

[26] This can still be seen today in the Priory Church at Christchurch, Dorset.

[27] The Christchurch Times, December 1907.

[28] The Admiralty had appointed Samuel Franklin Cody their Chief Kiting Instructor.

[29] The airship *Nulli Secundus* flew over London, achieving an average speed of 24 mph and reached a height of 1300 feet. It flew for 3 hours and 20 minutes eventually landing at Crystal Palace.

[30] http://www.geocities.com/aleph135/NAVY.HTML.

[31] http://www.worldwar1.co.uk.

[32] The Balkan League comprised: Bulgaria, Greece, Montenegro and Serbia.

[33] New Zealanders at War, Michael King – World War One.

[34] The Guardian, Bournemouth, Saturday 15th August 1914.

[35] The Guardian, Bournemouth, Saturday 15th August 1914.

[36] from 3d to 4d a 2lb loaf.

[37] The Christchurch Times Saturday 15th August 1914.

[38] The Christchurch Times, Saturday 15th August 1914.

[39] The King's message to the Fleet, The Guardian, Saturday 8th August 1914.

[40] The Guardian, Bournemouth, Saturday 15th August 1914.

[41] The Christchurch Times, Saturday 15th August 1914.

[42] The Guardian, Bournemouth, Saturday 15th August 1914.

[43] The Christchurch Times, Saturday 15th August 1914.

[44] The Guardian, Bournemouth 5th September 1914.

[45] The Guardian, Bournemouth, Saturday 15th August 1914.

[46] Unwilling Passenger by Arthur Osburn p34 – Faber & Faber Limited, London 1932

[47] Resolute would defeat Shamrock IV by 3 races to 2.

[48] The Guardian, Bournemouth, 5th September 1914.

[49] Unwilling Passenger by Arthur Osburn. London Faber and Faber Limited page 249

[50] The "Rush to the Colours" means enlisting in the Army

[51] The Wessex Division were Territorial troops comprised of the Devon and Cornwall Infantry Brigades, the South-Western Infantry Brigades and the Hampshire Infantry Brigade.

[52] Bournemouth and the First World War – The Evergreen Valley 1914 to 1919 MA Edgington – Bournemouth Local studies Publication 1985.

[53] Dr Maitland Scott, Dr St John Harris, and Dr Margaret Vivian.

[54] The Bournemouth Guardian 3rd October 1914.

[55] The ANZAC Experience – Christopher Pugsley, Reed Publishing (NZ) Ltd 2004.

[56] New Zealanders at War, Michael King.

[57] New Zealanders at War, Michael King – World War One.

[58] The New Zealand Medical Service in the Great War 1914 – 1918, Lieutenant Colonel AD Carberry. Whitcombe and Tombs Limited, 1924.

[59] Anzac A Retrospect, Cecil Malthus, published by Reed Books, Auckland, NZ page 17.

[60] The Great Adventure edited by Jock Phillips, Nicolas Boyack and E.P. Malone, page 195

[61] New Zealanders at War, Michael King – World War One.

[62] Lee was a New Zealand writer. In 1918 he was awarded the DCM for gallantry at Messines Ridge where he lost his left forearm after being injured by a German hand grenade.

[63] The ANZAC Experience – Christopher Pugsley, Reed Publishing (NZ) Ltd 2004 page 63

[64] Queen Alexandra's Imperial Military Nursing Service Reserve was formed in 1902 and during WW1 around 100,000 women served in the unit as nurses in France, Italy, Salonika, Russia, India, East Africa, Mesopotamia Palestine and Egypt,.

[65] Captain Henry John Innes Walker survived the opening months of the war, but was killed at Ypres in April 1915 – he has no known grave and his name appears on the Menin Gate Memorial.

[66] The German East Asia Squadron, consisting of the cruisers *Scharnhorst* and *Gneisenau* and the light cruisers *Nürnberg, Leipzig, Dresden* and *Emden*. The *Emden* conducted a raiding campaign in the Pacific until it was eventually destroyed by HMAS *Sydney,* in the Cocos Islands, while the remained of the squadron engaged the British West Indies Squadron on 1st November 1914, off the coast of Central Chile, sinking *HMS Good Hope* and *HMS Monmonth*. When the Squadron attempted to return back to Germany via the Altantic, it was surprised by a force under the command of Vice Admirmal Sir Doveton Sturdee off the Falkand Islands, and the squadron was destroyed on 8th December 1914.

[67] Memorandum from the NZ High Commissioner to the Honourable The Prime Minister of New Zealand – 14th September, 1914.

[68] Plain Soldiering – NDG James – The Hobnob Press page 159.

[69] Evening Post, 5th August 1915 article "On Salisbury Plains".

[70] Volume 1 The Story of ANZAC by C.E.W. Bean page 110.

[71] Volume 1 The Story of ANZAC by C.E.W. Bean page 112.

[72] The Bournemouth Guardian, December 1914, article German Raid on North-East Coast.

[73] Plain Soldiering – N.D.G. James – The Hobnob Press.

[74] The steamers owned by the Bibby Line Group were requisitioned by the British Government at the outset of war in August 1914. These ran a regular service from Burma and Colombo to Liverpool, servicing the tea and rubber trade as well as passenger traffic.

[75] During the training in the desert of Egypt in December, 1914, the "Australian and New Zealand Army Corps" was formed. The initial composition was to have been two Infantry Divisions - 1st Australian and the "2nd" or New Zealand Division, as well as a Mounted Division formed from the 1st, 2nd and 3rd Australian Light Horse Brigades and the New Zealand Mounted Rifles Brigade. Eventually, the Corps was organised into two divisions only, the second being formed from the New Zealand Infantry Brigade, the 4th Australian Infantry brigade, and two mounted brigades (1st ALH and NZMR). These four were placed under the command of General Godley, commanding the New Zealand Expeditionary Force. The new division was thus almost equally divided between New

Zealand and Australian troops, except that New Zealand provided all its artillery. The title chose for it was "New Zealand and Australian Division.

[76] Volume 1 The Story of ANZAC by C.E.W. Bean.

[77] The Great War, Les Carlyon. Picador 2007 ISBN 978 1 4050 3799 0 page 53.

[78] When the Main Body left New Zealand 1st Field Troop NZE numbered 3 officers and 74 men, the NZ Signals Troop, NZE 1 Officer and 32 men and the NZASC 4 Officers and 125 men. http://www.nzetc.org/tm/scholarly/tei-WaiNewZ-b3.html.

[79] Volume 1 The Story of ANZAC by C.E.W. Bean page 59.

[80] *Memories of Sapper Beamish.*

[81] On The Anzac Trail – being an extract from the diary of a New Zealand Sapper, by "Anzac", London: William Heincmann, 1916, page 36.

[82] On The Anzac Trail – being and extract from the diary of a New Zealand Sapper, by "Anzac", London: William Heincmann, 1916, page 70.

[83] History of the New Zealand Engineers, N&M Press, page 11.

[84] Anzac A Retrospect – Cecil Malthus, published by Reed Books, Auckland, page 39.

[85] The ANZAC Experience – Christopher Pugsley, page 72.

[86] The ANZAC Experience – Christopher Pugsley, page 73.

[87] King's College London – Hamilton Collection 16/8 Preface to Gallipoli Volume of NZ History of the War.

[88] Kings College London – Hamilton Collection 16/11.

[89] After being pursued by the British Navy, the *Goeben* a battle cruiser and the *Breslau* a light cruiser entered the Dardanelles on 10th August and were transferred to the Navy of the Ottoman Empire, raiding the Russian Black Sea ports of Sebastopol and Odessa in October 1914.

[90] Les Carlyon, *"Gallipoli"*, Pan MacMillan Australia Pty Limited, 2002, pages 65 to 73.

[91] The National Archives CAB 45/251.

[92] Christchurch Times Saturday 8th May 1915.

[93] ANZAC – A retrospect Cecil Malthus p64.

[94] Christchurch Times Saturday 8th May 1915.

[95] Grey River Argus, 9th September 1915 titles "Our Boys at War".

[96] Volume 1 The Story of ANZAC by C.E.W. Bean, page 598.

[97] On The Anzac Trail – being an extract from the diary of a New Zealand Sapper, by "Anzac", London: William Heincmann, 1916, page 151.

[98] Chatham and Portsmouth Battalions.

[99] Official History of Australia in the War 1914 -1918 Vol I The story of ANZAC by C.E.W. Bean page 601.

[100] Diary of 4/129a Sapper TC Farrer CAB 45/251 The National Archives page 26.

[101] Evening Post 15th December 1914, articles titled "Home-made Grenades".

[102] John (Jack) Simpson Kirkpatrick (6th July 1892 to 19th May 1915) was a stretcher bearer during the Gallipoli Campaign. He soon established a reputation for evacuating the wounded, using his donkey Murphy. He immortalised the selfless attitudes shown by many during the Gallipoli campaign.

[103] Official History of Australia in the War 1914 -1918 Vol II The story of ANZAC by C.E.W. Bean page 99.

[104] Stanley.P. (2005). *Quinns post, Anzac, Gallipoli.* Crow's Nest, Australia: Allen & Unwin.

[105] A camouflet was a countermine not sufficiently powerful to break the surface, but still powerful enough to collapse the enemy tunnel.

[106] Guncotton is a mild explosive substance.

[107] Ammonal is a low explosive and as such provides a lifting or pushing effect. It was ideal for use in counter mining and from 1915 Ammonal was used by the military to detonate mines under enemy positions with great effect.

[108] Grey River Argus, 9th September 1915 "Our Boys at War" – a letter written by Driver William Sullivan.

[109] ANZAC – A retrospect Cecil Malthus page 89.

[110] Diary of 4/129a Sapper TC Farrer CAB 45/251 The National Archive page 17.

[111] Bournemouth Echo, 19th May, 1915.

[112] Diary of 4/129a Sapper TC Farrer CAB 45/251 The National Archive.

[113] On The Anzac Trail – being an extract from the diary of a New Zealand Sapper, by "Anzac", London: William Heincmann, 1916, page 174.

[114] On The Anzac Trail – being an extract from the diary of a New Zealand Sapper, by "Anzac", London: William Heincmann, 1916, page 183.

[115] Wellington Evening Post, Volume XC, Issue 88, 12th October 1915, page 8.

[116] Grey River Argus, 9th September 1915 "Our Boys at War" – a letter written by Driver William Sullivan.

[117] The letter was published in the Christchurch Times, 3rd July, 1915 titled "Cheerful New Zealanders".

[118] The Great Adventure, Edited by Jock Phillips, Nicholas Boyack and E.P. Malone. Allen and Unwin Port Nicholas Press page 59.

[119] History of the New Zealand Engineers, N&M Press, page 32.

[120] History of the New Zealand Engineers, N&M Press, page 36.

[121] Diary of 4/129a Sapper TC Farrer CAB 45/251 The National Archives page 52.

[122] Captain Hulbert suffered heart problems on Gallipoli, his pulse being 120. He returned to New Zealand in late 1915 and was posted back to France with the 35th Reinforcements. He was awarded the DSO for War service.

[123] ANZAC – A retrospect Cecil Malthus page 66.

[124] MS257 Transcript of Diary Major General Sir George Richardson, Auckland War Memorial Library.

[125] Christchurch Times Saturday 23rd October 1915.

[126] The Guardian, August 1915 article titled "Life in the Dardanelles".

[127] Grey River Argus – 8th February 1916 titled "N.Z. Engineers".

[128] The NZ Native Contingent is used here as opposed to the NZ Maori Contingent, which has been used in various publications, which has added to the confusion of naming. Although the men were enlisted as "Maori Contingent", this was never an actual military formation, whereas the NZ Native Contingent did exist as a military formation originally formed in the Land Wars in the 1860's and incorporated into the NZEF.

[129] The New Zealanders at Gallipoli, by Major Fred Waite, page 194.

[130] Auckland Weekly News 13th January, 1916 page 31.

[131] Grey River Argus – 8th February 1916 titled "NZ Engineers".

[132] Gallipoli – LA Carlyon – Banton Book 9780553815061 page 566.

[133] Grey River Argus – 8th February 1916 titled "NZ Engineers".

[134] Auckland Weekly News 11th November 1915, page 17.

[135] ANZAC – A retrospect Cecil Malthus page 105.

[136] Armentières and the Somme – Cecil Malthus – Reed Publishing (NZ) Ltd 2002

[137] Christchurch Times 14th August 1915.

[138] The Turkish word is "anzak" which means "only just".

[139] The Guardian, August 1915 "Life in the Dardanelles"

[140] Evening Post 15th September 1915 article headed "Total Casualties – The official estimates".

[141] Official History of Australia in the War 1914 -1918 Vol II The story of ANZAC by C.E.W. Bean page 785.

[142] General Monro's own order of countries as per C.E.W. Bean Vol II, page 785.

[143] Official History of Australia in the War 1914 -1918 Vol II The story of ANZAC by C.E.W. Bean page 785.

[144] Christchurch Times – Saturday 4th December 1915.

[145] Christchurch Times – Saturday 4th December 1915.

[146] ANZAC – A retrospect Cecil Malthus page 140.

[147] Official History of Australia in the War 1914 -1918 Vol II The story of ANZAC by C.E.W. Bean, page 908.

[148] Three years with the New Zealanders. Lieutenant Colonel C.H. Weston, page 46.

[149] Hamilton, who was against evacuation, estimated 35% to 45% - Official History of Australia in the War 1914 -1918 Vol II The story of ANZAC by C.E.W. Bean page 781.

[150] Christchurch Times – Saturday 25th December 1915.

[151] ANZAC – A retrospect Cecil Malthus page 150.

[152] The Great adventure edited by Jock Phillips, Nicolas Boyack and E.P. Malone. Allen and Unwin/Port Nicolas Press page 78.

[153] The ANZAC Experience – New Zealand, Australia and Empire in the First World War Christopher Pugsley, Reed Publishing (New Zealand) Limited 2004.

[154] The New Zealanders at Gallipoli by Colonel Fred Waite published Whitcombe and Tombs, 1919, Christchurch.

[155] Diary of 4/129a Sapper TC Farrer CAB 45/251 The National Archives – Appendix titled Newspaper Cutting.

[156] A Doctor's Story by Fred Bowerbank, The Wingfield Press 1958, page 110.

[157] The Army and Navy had their own trained pilots and it would not be until May 1915 that the Royal Flying Corps was formed. It drew pilots from both services and originally comprised three squadrons: 1 Squadron was airships, kites and balloons; 2 & 3 Squadrons with aeroplanes.

[158] Christchurch Times – 19th June 1915 article titled "Air Raid into Germany".

[159] First Blitz, Neil Hanson page 51.

[160] The German Air Raids on Great Britain 1914 to 1918 by Captain Joseph Morris. The Naval and Military Press. Preface section.

[161] Billies were the bushman's pot, which could be suspended over a fire to boil water, making tea or cook a stew in.

[162] M257 A Gallipoli Diary by Major General Sir George Richardson, Auckland War Memorial Museum Library page 21.

[163] On the 1st March 1916 authority was given for the title "The New Zealand Division" to be used.

[164] The Great Adventure edited by Jock Phillips, Nicholas Boyack and E.P. Malone. Allen and Unwin/Port Nicolas Press page 80.

[165] The You-shot No2 published on 25th April 1918.

[166] The official history of New Zealand's efforts in the Great War, Volume 2 France by Colonel Stewart, published by Whitcombe & Tombs, page 9.

[167] Used by NZE Reserve Depot War Diary May 1916 to December 1917. This is consistent with other unit naming such as 14th Northumberland Fusiliers (Pioneer) battalion; although is at odd with "The Maoris in the Great War" by James Cowan, page 123 where it is referred to as the N.Z. (Maori) Pioneer Battalion.

[168] Formed from the Canterbury, Auckland and Wellington Mounted Rifles Regiments which had fought dismounted at Gallipoli as well as Field Engineers, Signals, Veterinary, 2 Camel Companies, Field Ambulance, ASC, Raratongan Company, 1 Machine Gun Company and the Auckland Mounted Rifles Band .

[169] In June 1917 this was renamed the Anzac Mounted Division.

[170] Now modern day Iraq.

[171] Armentières and the Somme, Cecil Malthus, page 48.

[172] Gallipoli to the Somme, Alexander Aitken, 1963 London, Oxford University Press, page 88.

[173] Diary of 04/5/1 C Thurow. Imperial War Museum, London.

[174] Armentières and the Somme, Cecil Malthus, ISBN 07900085103 Reed 2002 page 77.

[175] Extract from War Diaries NZE No 1 Field Company 1 June 1916 to 30 June 1916 Public Records Office Kew Gardens WO95/3675.

[176] Gallipoli to the Somme, Alexander Aitken, 1963 London, Oxford University Press, page 96.

[177] Gallipoli to the Somme, Alexander Aitken, 1963 London, Oxford University Press, page 92.

[178] Gallipoli to the Somme, Alexander Aitken, 1963 London, Oxford University Press, page 92.

[179] Gallipoli to the Somme, Alexander Aitken, 1963 London, Oxford University Press. Page 91.

[180] The Christchurch Times, 10th July 1916.

[181] Annabell, History of the New Zealand Engineers during the Great War 1914- 1919. Evens, Cobb and Sharpe Limited, page 74.

[182] The official history of New Zealand's efforts in the Great War, Volume 2 France by Colonel H. Stewart, published by Whitcombe & Tombs, page 54.

[183] New Zealand raised 51 Reinforcement contingents during the war, but not all were sent overseas as the war had ended by 11th November 1918.

[184] On 24th September 1917 New Zealand soldiers from the 18th Reinforcement were killed and injured when they were struck by the Waterloo to Plymouth express train. The troops had arrived at Plymouth Sounds and had entrained for Sling Camp. They had

been told that the first stop was Exeter Station, where food would be served from the rear carriage. Due to a line blockage, the train stopped at Bere Ferrers station instead. Unaware of the situation, and knowing that the train had stopped, the soldiers, instructed to collect the food, disembarked just as the express train sped through the station, killing ten soldiers. Their funerals were attended by a party of New Zealanders and garrison troops.

[185] The War Effort of New Zealand, edited by Lieutenant H.T.B. Drew, Whitcombe and Tombs Limited, 1923 page 252.

[186] NZR denoted New Zealand Rifles.

[187] Lieutenant Colonel (temporary Brigadier General) W.G. Braithwaite; DSO, Headquarters NZEF Main Body and Royal Welsh Fusiliers.

[188] The War Effort of New Zealand, edited by Lieutenant H.T.B. Drew, Whitcombe and Tombs Limited, 1923 page 256.

[189] The New Zealand Division 1916 - 1919: A Popular History based on Official Records, by Colonel H. Stewart, Whitcombe and Tombs Limited, 1921 page 527.

[190] Served with the Samoa Advance and 2nd N.Z. Rifle Brigade.

[191] General Fulton would command the Rifle Brigade in France until his death in the German Spring offensive in March 1918.

[192] The New Zealand Division 1916 - 1919: A Popular History based on Official Records, by Colonel. H. Stewart, Whitcombe and Tombs Limited, 1921 page 528

[193] At the start of the war a large military training area had been established there at Rugeley Camp. The area was officially termed "The Cannock Chase Reserve Centre" and it trained a Reserve Division composing mainly British youths as yet too young for the field.

[194] Corporal W. B. Wood of the 4th Battalion, Gordon Highlanders.

[195] The Australians had motorised ASC units, part of the AIF Main Body, in England from December 1914. These units had not disembarked in Egypt with the AIF due to the need for motorised transport in England and France. These troops were soon joined on 16th February, 1915 by the 9th Australian ASC Corps, commanded by Lieutenant Colonel Alfred Moon, AIF who was fondly remembered by the townspeople of Bournemouth for his speech at a recruiting concert in the Bournemouth Winter Garden. These ASC troops arrived in the middle of winter at Plymouth, with no-one expecting their arrival. The first two days were memorable, as they were spent on a cold and bleak railway station while signals were sent back and forth between military headquarters. Eventually they entrained for Romsey where they were billeted in civilian housing for the remainder of the winter months. At Romsey, both they and their vehicles were used to carry gravel for road building. In April they moved to Bulford, presumably sharing the camp there with the Canadians. They continued transporting gravel for the road construction on Salisbury Plain until June, 1915 when they were attached to the 17th Division and redesignated 17th Divisional Supply Column. They left for France on 9th July 1915 with their motor transports and served with the 17th Division at the Front[195] until rejoining the AIF upon its arrival in April 1916.

[196] The Bournemouth Daily Echo 7th June 1915.

[197] Empire Day was observed on 25th May.

[198] On 17th March 1917 Lance Corporal Henry M .T. T. Levinge, of the N.Z. Rifle Brigade, was killed in action. He was the son of Staff Surgeon Dr H.M. Levinge and reported as "a member of a family which had been fighting for the British flag since the days of the Crusades". It is supposed that this is the son of the same Dr Levinge who visited Christchurch.

[199] Sir Henry Page Croft, later 1st Baron Croft of Bournemouth was the MP for Christchurch 1910 to 1917 when the constituency was abolished. From 1918 the new constituencies were "Bournemouth" and "Christchurch and New Forest".

[200] The flag was still hoisted up until 1937 but this tradition has long since stopped and although town twinning has become more fashionable since 1975 the earlier tradition has been forgotten or ignored.

[201] Annabell - The Official History of the New Zealand Engineers During the Great War 1914 -1919 Evans, Cobb & Sharpe Ltd, Wanganui, New Zealand, page 228.

[202] Sydney Morning Herald 30th October 1916 article "Australians in Christchurch – One of the best spots in England". Sapper A.B. Whitehair writing to his friend at the newspaper.

[203] "Morning Post" report reproduced in The Christchurch Times 11th September, 1915

[204] Evening Leave granted 5pm until 10pm and on the Weekends 12:30 until 11pm.

[205] Bournemouth and the First World War – The Evergreen Valley 1914 to 1919 MA Edgington ALA – Bournemouth Local Studies Publication 1985.

[206] Diary of J Williamson MM Imperial War Museum P/433 page 15.

[207] Bournemouth Daily Echo July 27th, 1916 article titled "Military Sports at Christchurch".

[208] The 100 yard relay team from the NZ Medical Hospital at Brockenhurst comprised: Privates J.M. Pearson, Olphert, Evans, C.M. Gordon, R.P. London and Corporal L.C. Castleton.

[209] Attending: New Zealand Engineers: Lieutenants Newman and Corkhill ; Royal Engineers: Colonel Keen, Major Garton, Captain Simpson, Lieutenants Redstone, Reggatt, Joshine, Stone, Sealy, Grandage, Tapp and Beckton Australian Engineers Lieutenant Baldwin, Oliver, Lewis, Littler, Nolan, Christain, Chambers, Isaacs and Woodhouse

[210] Miss Sinton, Miss Martin, Miss MacDermott, Miss Loudon, Miss Brander, Miss Paul, Miss Ingram, Miss Campbell (married at 18 to Captain John Scobell Boissier), Miss Hardie, Miss Higgins, The Misses Richards, Miss Cornish, Miss Hamilton, Mrs Keen (CO's wife), Mrs Cooke, Mrs Yarborough, Mrs Garton, Mrs Locke.

[211] Diary of J Williamson MM Imperial War Museum P/433 page 48.

[212] Camps, Tramps and Trenches. Eric Miller A.H. and A.W. Reed, Wellington, New Zealand, page 111.

[213] He was the only son of Mr Tom Read, the chief forester on the Hinton Admiral Estate. He was married with two children and had a smallholding at Hill Farm, near Thorney Hill – on the outskirts of the Hinton Admiral Estate. He would later join the 15th Hampshire Yeomanry in France as a Company Sergeant Major, be awarded the Croix de Guerre in France and was killed during the German Spring Offensive of March 1918.

[214] As he had been the Regimental Colonel Commandant of the Royal Engineers, their band was given the honour of playing the "Death March" and the "Last Post" during the service.

215 Christchurch Times, 1st July 1916 an address by the Reverend Needham to local Christchurch Territorial Company.

216 The Christchurch Times, January 1916.

217 The Christchurch Times, 11th December 1915 – article entitled "Coast Precautions".

218 Bournemouth and the First World War – The Evergreen Valley 1914 to 1919 – MA Edgington ALA. Bournemouth Local Studies Publication 1985, page 27.

219 The prevailing belief was that the regulation only applied to "apartment houses" that always kept a register or unfurnished rooms. Unfortunately the Defence of the Realm Act specified anyone who takes in a visitor or lodger, for pecuniary reward, was obliged to fill in the required forms. The only exception is in the case of *bona fide* visitors, who pay nothing.

220 Sergeant Arthur Young was killed in action in Mesopotamia on 23rd/24th February 1917. He was 20 years old and had belonged to the Christchurch Territorial, before leaving with the 7th Hants to India in December 1914 and then Mesopotamia October 1916.

221 Private George Adey was killed in Mesopotamia 23rd/24th February 1917. He was 21 years old and had belonged to the Christchurch Territorial, before leaving with the 7th Hants to India in December 1914 and then Mesopotamia October 1916.

222 The Christchurch Times, 7th July 1917 article titled "Shocking Tragedy on the Line".

223 Colonel Napier quoted at Military Tribunal July 1917, The Christchurch Times.

224 *The Spectator*, 18th November 1916.

225 Christchurch Times 11th November 1916.

226 The Camouflaged Civilian – The letters of Alec Hutton 62576. The Great Adventure – edited by Jock Phillips, Nicholas Boyack and E.P. Malone. Allen and Unwin/Port Nicolas Press.

227 Unwilling Passenger by Arthur Osburn. London Faber and Faber Limited, page 226.

228 Andrew Macdonald "On My way to the Somme". Harper Collins Publishers 2005, page 52.

229 Armentières and the Somme, Cecil Malthus, page 102.

230 Thistle Dump was located at the corner of Turk Lane and Savoy Trench, while Green was located at the start of French Lane.

231 Grey River Argus, 24th March 1917 article entitled "Strenuous work under fire"

232 The Christchurch Times 14th October 1916.

233 JP Foynes "The Australians at Brightlingsea" published by the author 2002 ISBN 0952155532 page 13.

234 He was promoted to the rank of Major on 15th March 1917. He died in Wellington in 1949. His son was issued his Gallipoli Medallion in 1983.

235 Annabell - The Official History of the New Zealand Engineers During the Great War 1914 -1919 Evans, Cobb & Sharpe Ltd, Wanganui, New Zealand, page 230.

236 JP Foynes "The Australians at Brightlingsea" published by the author 2002 ISBN 0952155532 page 15.

237 J P Foynes "The Australians at Brightlingsea" published by the author 2002 ISBN 0952155532 page 32.

[238] J P Foynes "The Australians at Brightlingsea" published by the author 2002 ISBN 0952155532 page 18.

[239] J P Foynes "The Australians at Brightlingsea" published by the author 2002 ISBN 0952155532 page18.

[240] Christchurch Times, 23rd December 1916 article titled "Entertainment for ANZACS".

[241] On the Western Front a Field Company's strength was normally 10 officers and 220 NCOs and Other Ranks.

[242] Annabell - The Official History of the New Zealand Engineers During the Great War 1914 -1919 Evans, Cobb & Sharpe Ltd, Wanganui, New Zealand, page 100.

[243] Franz was born in Australia, was married and lived in Gisborne where he was a carpenter. On the Nominal Roll it was noted that he was of "alien extraction" in that he was German.

[244] Southern Command School of Instruction for Engineers.

[245] New Zealand Archives WA131/2 letter from CRE NZ Division to OC N.Z. Engineer Reserve Depot dated 6th November 1917.

[246] Imperial War Museum P/433 Sapper J Williamson MM diary extracts page 11 – his experience at Falmouth on the drill square with the Fusilier drill sergeant.

[247] Puggaree was the hatband colour designating which Regiment the wearer belonged to, for the Engineers it was Blue.

[248] Diary of Sapper J Williamson MM, Imperial War Museum P/433, page 49.

[249] The New Zealand Medical Service in the Great War 1914-1918 Lieutenant Colonel AD Carberry page 372.

[250] Imperial War Museum, London. Misc 221 Item 3180 Visit of Mr Reid Patterson –Actor – or listed as Anonymous Actor visiting the Western Front.

[251] Archives New Zealand WA131/2 letter dated 16th July 1917 from Major Keenan to Administrative Headquarters, NZEF, London.

[252] Archives New Zealand WA131/2 letter dated 5th July 1917 from CRE New Zealand Division to Headquarters, N.Z. Division.

[253] Archives New Zealand WA131/2 letter dated 16th July 1917 from Major Keenan to Administrative Headquarters, NZEF, London.

[254] Archives New Zealand WA131/2 letter dated 12th September 1917 from DAAG N.Z. Division to CRE, N.Z. Division.

[255] Archives New Zealand WA131/2 letter dated 10th September 1917 from CRE N.Z. Division to Headquarters, NZEF, London.

[256] Letters of Herbert James Tuck dated 17th January 1918. Imperial War Museum, London reference 11/36/1.

[257] General GS Richardson CB, CMG - General Officer Commanding the NZEF in the United Kingdom.

[258] Annabell – The Official History of the New Zealand Engineers During the Great War 1914-1919 Evans, Cobb & Sharpe Ltd, Wanganui, New Zealand, page 123.

[259] War Diary of the 1st Field Company.

[260] Imperial War Museum, London. Misc 221 Item 3180 Visit of Mr Reid Patterson –Actor – or listed as Anonymous Actor visiting the Western Front.

261 Annabell - The Official History of the New Zealand Engineers During the Great War 1914 -1919 Evans, Cobb & Sharpe Ltd, Wanganui, N.Z page 139.

262 War Diary of the 1st Field Company.

263 Camps, Tramps and Trenches, Eric Miller. A.H. and A.W. Reed, Wellington, New Zealand, October 1939, page 105.

264 Letter from Major Keenan to Administrative Headquarters NZEF, 8 Southampton Row, London dated 2nd August 1917 and CRE, N.Z Division, BEF, France dated 3rd August 1917.

265 Letter dated 7th September 1917 from Major Barclay, then OC NZE Reserve Depot Christchurch, Hampshire to CRE, N.Z. Division, BEF, France.

266 a rough bundle of brushwood used for strengthening an earthen structure, or making a path across uneven or wet terrain.

267 Christchurch Times, Saturday 3rd November 1917. Article titled "Unique Display by War Party".

268 Christchurch Times, Saturday3rd November 1917. Article titled "Unique Display by War Party".

269 The Christchurch Times, 23rd December 1916. Lecture on "Problems of the War and After " by the local MP Lieutenant Colonel Page-Croft.

270 Christchurch Times, January 1917 "The Farmer as a difficult individual".

271 http://www.1914-1918.net/women_orgs.htm.

272 Food prices have risen over 50-fold since the war years, so a five shilling meal in 1916 would possibly cost close to £20 in equivalent value in 2012.

273 The Christchurch Times 30th September 1916.

274 Imperial War Museum P/433 Sapper J Williamson MM diary extracts, page 11.

275 On 20th January 1917, the daily ration for each man was reduced for: cheese 3oz was reduced to 2oz; bread 1 ¼ lb to 1lb. In April, 1917 the daily jam ration was cut from 4oz to 3oz.

276 Letter from General G Richardson to Captain Bell dated 22nd January, 1917 Auckland War Memorial Museum MS 257.

277 Camps, Tramps and Trenches, Eric Miller. A.H. and A.W. Reed, Wellington, New Zealand, October 1939, page 153.

278 The New Zealand Division in France 1916-1919, Colonel H. Stewart, Whitcombe and Tombs Limited 1921, page 287.

279 Camps, Tramps and Trenches, Eric Miller. A.H. and A.W. Reed, Wellington, New Zealand, October 1939, page 152.

280 Diary of Captain ET Vachell, Imperial War Museum, 8th December 1917.

281 Annabell - The Official History of the New Zealand Engineers During the Great War 1914 -1919 Evans, Cobb & Sharpe Ltd, Wanganui, New Zealand, page.176.

282 Diary of Sapper J Williamson MM, Imperial War Museum P/433, page 46.

283 New Zealand War Committee Association.

284 Spring Offensive, Glyn Harper. HarperCollins Publishers 2003 ISBN 1 86950 481 X page 68.

285 Annabell - The Official History of the New Zealand Engineers During the Great War 1914 -1919 Evans, Cobb & Sharpe Ltd, Wanganui, New Zealand, page 183.

[286] War Diary of Headquarters N.Z Division Engineers for the month of April 1918.

[287] Extract from the War Diary of 2nd Field Company for the period 24th to 30th June, 1918 – Public Records Office, Kew Gardens, London.

[288] Unwilling Passenger, Arthur Osborn, London, Faber and Faber 1932, page 397.

[289] The remanding troops awaiting transport home and formed the 5th (Reserve) Battalion based at Stafford.

[290] The origin of the Freemasons in Brockenhurst is believed to have begun with the New Zealanders at No 1 Stationary Field Hospital, Brockenhurst. Colonel Barclay at the NZE Depot was a Freemason and read the Mason Rights at Major Jordon's funeral at Codford. Major Jordon was the second in command of the N.Z Command Depot Codford at the time of his death in an aeroplane accident.

[291] Annabell - The Official History of the New Zealand Engineers During the Great War 1914 -1919 Evans, Cobb & Sharpe Ltd, Wanganui, New Zealand, page 233.

[292] With Imperial currency, there were twelve pennies to a shilling and twenty shillings in one Pound. A New Zealand private soldier was paid five shillings a day, whereas a British private soldier receive one shilling a day.

[293] The Camouflaged Civilian – The letters of Alec Hutton 62576. The Great Adventure – edited by Jock Phillips, Nicholas Boyack and E.P. Malone. Allen and Unwin/Port Nicolas Press

[294] While You're Away – New Zealand Nurses at War 1899 – 1948. Anna Rodgers. Auckland University Press 2003 page 65.

[295] [295] While You're Away – New Zealand Nurses at War 1899 – 1948. Anna Rodgers. Auckland University Press 2003 page 64.

[296] [296] While You're Away – New Zealand Nurses at War 1899 – 1948. Anna Rodgers. Auckland University Press 2003 page 70.

[297] Diary of 4/129a Sapper TC Farrer CAB 45/251 The National Archives page 29.

[298] No 1 New Zealand Stationary Hospital.

[299] A Doctor's Story by Sir Fred Bowerbank, The Wingfield Press 1958, page 103.

[300] A Doctor's Story by Sir Fred Bowerbank, The Wingfield Press 1958, page 101.

[301] The War Effort of New Zealand – Lt HTB Drew- Whitcombe & Tombs Limited, 1923 page 114.

[302] While You're Away – New Zealand Nurses at War 1899 – 1948. Anna Rodgers. Auckland University Press 2003 page 82.

[303] While You're Away – New Zealand Nurses at War 1899 – 1948. Anna Rodgers. Auckland University Press 2003 page 82.

[304] Voluntary Aid Detachment. They were volunteers who undertook the non-medical work around the hospital.

[305] MS257 Transcript of Diary Major-General Sir George Richardson, Auckland War Memorial Library entry on 24th January 1916.

[306] N.Z. HOSPITAL Evening Post, Volume XC, Issue 72, 23 September 1915, page 4.

[307] 13/728 Corporal Thomas Phillips was a farmer from Cambridge near Hamilton and was serving with the Auckland Mounted Rifles on Gallipoli when he was wounded and evacuated to England.

[308] The War Effort of New Zealand, edited by Lieutenant H.T.B. Drew, Whitcombe and Tombs Limited 1923, page 118.

[309] New Zealand troops were grouped with Australians in the official British Army administration – recognizing no difference and possibly swayed by the ANZAC designation.

[310] Official History of New Zealand's Efforts in the Great War Vol II - France The New Zealand Division 1916-1919 Colonel H. Stewart C.M.G., D.S.O., M.C., Whitcombe & Tombs Ltd 1921, page 17.

[311] The New Zealand Medical Service in the Great War 1914 -1918, Lieutenant Colonel A. D. Carberry. Whitcombe and Tombs 1924, page 265.

[312] The New Zealand Medical Service in the Great War 1914 -1918, Lieutenant Colonel A. D. Carberry. Whitcombe and Tombs 1924, page 267.

[313] http://www.havering.gov.uk/index.cfm

[314] Plain Soldiering – N.D.G. James – The Hobnob Press page 159.

[315] Diary of Lance Corporal J Williamson IWM P/433 page 51.

[316] The New Zealand Medical Service in the Great War 1914 -1918, Lieutenant Colonel A. D. Carberry. Whitcombe and Tombs 1924, page 500.

[317] A Doctor's Story by Sir Fred Bowerbank, The Wingfield Press 1958, page 114.

[318] A Doctor's Story by Sir Fred Bowerbank, The Wingfield Press 1958, page 115.

[319] The New Zealand Genealogist. Vol 39 No312 ISSN 011-4012 page 242.

[320] The New Zealand Medical Service in the Great War 1914 -1918, Lieutenant Colonel A. D. Carberry. Whitcombe and Tombs 1924, page 500.

[321] HM Australian Transport Warilda initially brought Australian troops to the European theatre and later continued service as a hospital ship.

[322] While You're Away – New Zealand Nurses at War 1899 – 1948. Anna Rodgers. Auckland University Press 2003, page 148.

[323] While You're Away – New Zealand Nurses at War 1899 – 1948. Anna Rodgers. Auckland University Press 2003, page 149.

[324] The Camouflaged Civilian – The letters of Alec Hutton 62576. The Great Adventure – edited by Jock Phillips, Nicholas Boyack and E.P. Malone. Allen and Unwin/Port Nicolas Press, page 253.

[325] While You're Away – New Zealand Nurses at War 1899 – 1948. Anna Rodgers. Auckland University Press 2003, page 152.

[326] While You're Away – New Zealand Nurses at War 1899 – 1948. Anna Rodgers. Auckland University Press 2003, page 152.

[327] Christchurch Times, 25th December 1915 "Australian Soldier Run Over".

[328] Lady Malmesbury was appointed a Lady of Grace of the Order of St John of Jerusalem in August 1916, merited because of her work with wounded soldiers at Heron Court.

[329] The Balkan League comprised: Bulgaria, Greece, Montenegro and Serbia.

[330] The Central Powers were Germany, Austria-Hungary and the Ottoman Empire prior to Bulgaria joining.

[331] Official History of Australia in the War 1914 -1918 Vol II The story of ANZAC by C.E.W. Bean, page 774.

[332] The Battle of Loos (25th September – 19th October) and Battle of Champagne (25th September – 6th October). Heavy losses were sustained in both battles.

[333] 10th Irish Division from Sulva and French troops from Cape Helles.

[334] Official History of Australia in the War 1914 -1918 Vol II The story of ANZAC by C.E.W. Bean, page 777.

[335] Official History of Australia in the War 1914 -1918 Vol II The story of ANZAC by C.E.W. Bean, page 774.

[336] Official History of Australia in the War 1914 -1918 Vol II The story of ANZAC by C.E.W. Bean, page 779.

[337] MS257 Transcript of Diary Major General Sir George Richardson, Auckland War memorial Library entry dated 27th December, 1915.

[338] MS257 Transcript of Diary Major General Sir George Richardson, Auckland War Memorial Library, entry dated 27th December 1915.

[339] The French Army intended to stay in Salonika and help the Serbs, so in order to preserve the Entente Alliance, Britain agreed to do the same, thereby binding several British Divisions uselessly to Salonika for the duration of the war.

[340] Official History of Australia in the War 1914 -1918 Vol II The story of ANZAC by C.E.W. Bean, page 792.

[341] No1 New Zealand Stationary Hospital at Lembet Camp. Relived by Canada Field Hospital March 3 and proceeded to UK.

[342] Southend on Sea, England.

[343] Full title was New Zealand Military Advisor attached to the Dominions Section of the Imperial General Staff at the War office.

[344] Lieutenant Biles.

[345] MS257 Transcript of Diary Major-General Sir George Richardson, Auckland War memorial Library entry on 21st October, 1915.

[346] MS257 Transcript of Diary Major-General Sir George Richardson, Auckland War Memorial Library entry on 23rd December 1915. As a guide, the field allowance for a Brigadier General in the NZEF was six shillings a sixpence a day, so the room rate of £1 a day was three times that, so very expensive.